W9-CMS-006

Lineberger Memorial

Library

Lutheran Theological Southern Seminary    Columbia, S. C.

*The* NEW ENCYCLOPEDIA *of* SOUTHERN CULTURE

**VOLUME 11 : AGRICULTURE AND INDUSTRY**

Volumes to appear in

*The New Encyclopedia of Southern Culture*

are:

*Agriculture and Industry*   *Law and Politics*

*Art and Architecture*   *Literature*

*Education*   *Media*

*Environment*   *Music*

*Ethnicity*   *Myth, Manners, and Memory*

*Folk Art*   *Race*

*Folklife*   *Recreation*

*Foodways*   *Religion*

*Gender*   *Science and Medicine*

*Geography*   *Social Class*

*History*   *Urbanization*

*Language*   *Violence*

*The* NEW

ENCYCLOPEDIA *of* SOUTHERN CULTURE

CHARLES REAGAN WILSON  General Editor

JAMES G. THOMAS JR.  Managing Editor

ANN J. ABADIE  Associate Editor

VOLUME 11

# Agriculture
# and Industry

MELISSA WALKER  Agriculture Section Editor

JAMES C. COBB  Industry Section Editor

Sponsored by

THE CENTER FOR THE STUDY OF SOUTHERN CULTURE

at the University of Mississippi

THE UNIVERSITY OF NORTH CAROLINA PRESS

Chapel Hill

So Bikwl. ¹⁰/₀8   40.05

This book was published with the
assistance of the Anniversary Endowment Fund
of the University of North Carolina Press.

© 2008 The University of North Carolina Press
All rights reserved
Designed by Richard Hendel
Set in Minion types by Tseng Information Systems, Inc.
Manufactured in the United States of America
The paper in this book meets the guidelines for permanence and
durability of the Committee on Production Guidelines for Book
Longevity of the Council on Library Resources.
The University of North Carolina Press has been a member of the
Green Press Initiative since 2003.
Library of Congress Cataloging-in-Publication Data
Agriculture and industry / Melissa Walker, Agriculture section
editor ; James C. Cobb, Industry section editor.
p. 24 cm. — (The new encyclopedia of Southern culture ; v. 11)
"Sponsored by The Center for the Study of Southern Culture at the
University of Mississippi."
Includes bibliographical references and index.
ISBN 978-0-8078-3240-0 (alk. paper)
ISBN 978-0-8078-5909-4 (pbk.: alk. paper)
1. Agriculture—Southern States—History—Encyclopedias.
2. Agriculture—Economic aspects—Southern States—
Encyclopedias. 3. Industries—Southern States—Encyclopedias.
4. Southern States—Economic conditions—Encyclopedias.
I. Walker, Melissa. II. Cobb, James C. III. University of Mississippi.
Center for the Study of Southern Culture. IV. Series.
F209 .N47 2006 vol. 11
[HC107.A13]
975.003 s—dc22   2008700057
The *Encyclopedia of Southern Culture*, sponsored by the Center for
the Study of Southern Culture at the University of Mississippi, was
published by the University of North Carolina Press in 1989.
cloth   12 11 10 09 08   5 4 3 2 1
paper   12 11 10 09 08   5 4 3 2 1

*Tell about the South. What's it like there.*

*What do they do there. Why do they live there.*

*Why do they live at all.*

WILLIAM FAULKNER

Absalom, Absalom!

# CONTENTS

In 1989 years of planning and hard work came to fruition when the University of North Carolina Press joined the Center for the Study of Southern Culture at the University of Mississippi to publish the *Encyclopedia of Southern Culture*. While all those involved in writing, reviewing, editing, and producing the volume believed it would be received as a vital contribution to our understanding of the American South, no one could have anticipated fully the widespread acclaim it would receive from reviewers and other commentators. But the *Encyclopedia* was indeed celebrated, not only by scholars but also by popular audiences with a deep, abiding interest in the region. At a time when some people talked of the "vanishing South," the book helped remind a national audience that the region was alive and well, and it has continued to shape national perceptions of the South through the work of its many users—journalists, scholars, teachers, students, and general readers.

As the introduction to the *Encyclopedia* noted, its conceptualization and organization reflected a cultural approach to the South. It highlighted such issues as the core zones and margins of southern culture, the boundaries where "the South" overlapped with other cultures, the role of history in contemporary culture, and the centrality of regional consciousness, symbolism, and mythology. By 1989 scholars had moved beyond the idea of cultures as real, tangible entities, viewing them instead as abstractions. The *Encyclopedia*'s editors and contributors thus included a full range of social indicators, trait groupings, literary concepts, and historical evidence typically used in regional studies, carefully working to address the distinctive and characteristic traits that made the American South a particular place. The introduction to the *Encyclopedia* concluded that the fundamental uniqueness of southern culture was reflected in the volume's composite portrait of the South. We asked contributors to consider aspects that were unique to the region but also those that suggested its internal diversity. The volume was not a reference book of southern history, which explained something of the design of entries. There were fewer essays on colonial and antebellum history than on the postbellum and modern periods, befitting our conception of the volume as one trying not only to chart the cultural landscape of the South but also to illuminate the contemporary era.

When C. Vann Woodward reviewed the *Encyclopedia* in the *New York Review of Books*, he concluded his review by noting "the continued liveliness of interest in the South and its seeming inexhaustibility as a field of study." Research on the South, he wrote, furnishes "proof of the value of the *Encyclopedia* as a scholarly undertaking as well as suggesting future needs for revision or supplement to keep up with ongoing scholarship." The two decades since the publication of the *Encyclopedia of Southern Culture* have certainly suggested that Woodward was correct. The American South has undergone significant changes that make for a different context for the study of the region. The South has undergone social, economic, political, intellectual, and literary transformations, creating the need for a new edition of the *Encyclopedia* that will remain relevant to a changing region. Globalization has become a major issue, seen in the South through the appearance of Japanese automobile factories, Hispanic workers who have immigrated from Latin America or Cuba, and a new prominence for Asian and Middle Eastern religions that were hardly present in the 1980s South. The African American return migration to the South, which started in the 1970s, dramatically increased in the 1990s, as countless books simultaneously appeared asserting powerfully the claims of African Americans as formative influences on southern culture. Politically, southerners from both parties have played crucial leadership roles in national politics, and the Republican Party has dominated a near-solid South in national elections. Meanwhile, new forms of music, like hip-hop, have emerged with distinct southern expressions, and the term "dirty South" has taken on new musical meanings not thought of in 1989. New genres of writing by creative southerners, such as gay and lesbian literature and "white trash" writing, extend the southern literary tradition.

Meanwhile, as Woodward foresaw, scholars have continued their engagement with the history and culture of the South since the publication of the *Encyclopedia*, raising new scholarly issues and opening new areas of study. Historians have moved beyond their earlier preoccupation with social history to write new cultural history as well. They have used the categories of race, social class, and gender to illuminate the diversity of the South, rather than a unified "mind of the South." Previously underexplored areas within the field of southern historical studies, such as the colonial era, are now seen as formative periods of the region's character, with the South's positioning within a larger Atlantic world a productive new area of study. Cultural memory has become a major topic in the exploration of how the social construction of "the South" benefited some social groups and exploited others. Scholars in many disciplines have made the southern identity a major topic, and they have used a variety of methodologies to suggest what that identity has meant to different social groups. Literary critics have adapted cultural theories to the South and have raised the issue of postsouthern literature to a major category of concern as well as exploring the links between the literature of the American South and that of the Caribbean. Anthropologists have used different theoretical formulations from literary critics, providing models for their fieldwork in southern communities. In the past 30 years anthropologists have set increasing numbers of their ethnographic studies in the South, with many of them now exploring topics specifically linked to southern cultural issues. Scholars now place the Native American story, from prehistory to the contemporary era, as a central part of southern history. Comparative and interdisciplinary approaches to the South have encouraged scholars to look at such issues as the borders and boundaries of the South, specific places and spaces with distinct identities within the American South, and the global and transnational Souths, linking the American South with many formerly colonial societies around the world.

The first edition of the *Encyclopedia of Southern Culture* anticipated many of these approaches and indeed stimulated the growth of Southern Studies as a distinct interdisciplinary field. The Center for the Study of Southern Culture has worked for more than a quarter century to encourage research and teaching about the American South. Its academic programs have produced graduates who have gone on to write interdisciplinary studies of the South, while others have staffed the cultural institutions of the region and in turn encouraged those institutions to document and present the South's culture to broad public audiences. The center's conferences and publications have continued its long tradition of promoting understanding of the history, literature, and music of the South, with new initiatives focused on southern foodways, the future of the South, and the global Souths, expressing the center's mission to bring the best current scholarship to broad public audiences. Its documentary studies projects build oral and visual archives, and the New Directions in Southern Studies book series, published by the University of North Carolina Press, offers an important venue for innovative scholarship.

Since the *Encyclopedia of Southern Culture* appeared, the field of Southern Studies has dramatically developed, with an extensive network now of academic and research institutions whose projects focus specifically on the interdisciplinary study of the South. The Center for the Study of the American South at the University of North Carolina at Chapel Hill, led by Director Harry Watson and Associate Director and *Encyclopedia* coeditor William Ferris, publishes the lively journal *Southern Cultures* and is now at the organizational center of many other Southern Studies projects. The Institute for Southern Studies at the University of South Carolina, the Southern Intellectual History Circle, the Society for the Study of Southern Literature, the Southern Studies Forum of the European American Studies Association, Emory University's SouthernSpaces.org, and the South Atlantic Humanities Center (at the Virginia Foundation for the Humanities, the University of Virginia, and Virginia Polytechnic Institute and State University) express the recent expansion of interest in regional study.

Observers of the American South have had much to absorb, given the rapid pace of recent change. The institutional framework for studying the South is broader and deeper than ever, yet the relationship between the older verities of regional study and new realities remains unclear. Given the extent of changes in the American South and in Southern Studies since the publication of the *Encyclopedia of Southern Culture*, the need for a new edition of that work is clear. Therefore, the Center for the Study of Southern Culture has once again joined the University of North Carolina Press to produce *The New Encyclopedia of Southern Culture*. As readers of the original edition will quickly see, *The New Encyclopedia* follows many of the scholarly principles and editorial conventions established in the original, but with one key difference; rather than being published in a single hardback volume, *The New Encyclopedia* is presented in a series of shorter individual volumes that build on the 24 original subject categories used in the *Encyclopedia* and adapt them to new scholarly developments. Some earlier *Encyclopedia* categories have been reconceptualized in light of new academic interests. For example, the subject section originally titled "Women's Life" is reconceived as a new volume, *Gender*, and the original "Black Life" section is more broadly interpreted as a volume on race. These changes reflect new analytical concerns that place the study of women and blacks in broader cultural systems, reflecting the emergence of, among other topics, the study of male culture and of whiteness. Both volumes draw as well from the rich recent scholarship on women's life and black life. In addition, topics with some thematic coherence are combined in a volume, such as *Law and Politics* and *Agriculture and Industry*. One new topic, *Foodways*, is the basis of a separate volume, reflecting its new prominence in the interdisciplinary study of southern culture.

Numerous individual topical volumes together make up *The New Encyclopedia of Southern Culture* and extend the reach of the reference work to wider audiences. This approach should enhance the use of the *Encyclopedia* in academic courses and is intended to be convenient for readers with more focused interests within the larger context of southern culture. Readers will have handy access to one-volume, authoritative, and comprehensive scholarly treatments of the major areas of southern culture.

We have been fortunate that, in nearly all cases, subject consultants who offered crucial direction in shaping the topical sections for the original edition have agreed to join us in this new endeavor as volume editors. When new volume editors have been added, we have again looked for respected figures who can provide not only their own expertise but also strong networks of scholars to help develop relevant lists of topics and to serve as contributors in their areas. The reputations of all our volume editors as leading scholars in their areas encouraged the contributions of other scholars and added to *The New Encyclopedia*'s authority as a reference work.

*The New Encyclopedia of Southern Culture* builds on the strengths of articles in the original edition in several ways. For many existing articles, original authors agreed to update their contributions with new interpretations and theoretical perspectives, current statistics, new bibliographies, or simple factual developments that needed to be included. If the original contributor was unable to update an article, the editorial staff added new material or sent it to another scholar for assessment. In some cases, the general editor and volume editors selected a new contributor if an article seemed particularly dated and new work indicated the need for a fresh perspective. And importantly, where new developments have warranted treatment of topics not addressed in the original edition, volume editors have commissioned entirely new essays and articles that are published here for the first time.

The American South embodies a powerful historical and mythical presence, both a complex environmental and geographic landscape and a place of the imagination. Changes in the region's contemporary socioeconomic realities and new developments in scholarship have been incorporated in the conceptualization and approach of *The New Encyclopedia of Southern Culture*. Anthropologist Clifford Geertz has spoken of culture as context, and this encyclopedia looks at the American South as a complex place that has served as the context for cultural expression. This volume provides information and perspective on the diversity of cultures in a geographic and imaginative place with a long history and distinctive character.

The *Encyclopedia of Southern Culture* was produced through major grants from the Program for Research Tools and Reference Works of the National Endowment for the Humanities, the Ford Foundation, the Atlantic-Richfield Foundation, and the Mary Doyle Trust. We are grateful as well to the College of Liberal Arts at the University of Mississippi for support and to the individual donors to the Center for the Study of Southern Culture who have directly or indirectly supported work on *The New Encyclopedia of Southern Culture*. We thank the volume editors for their ideas in reimagining their subjects and the contributors of articles for their work in extending the usefulness of the book in new ways. We acknowledge the support and contributions of the faculty and staff at the Center for the Study of Southern Culture. Finally, we want especially to honor the work of William Ferris and Mary Hart on the *Encyclopedia of Southern Culture*. Bill, the founding director of the Center for the Study of Southern Culture, was coeditor, and his good work recruiting authors, editing text, selecting images, and publicizing the volume among a wide network of people was, of course, invaluable. Despite the many changes in the new encyclopedia, Bill's influence remains. Mary "Sue" Hart was also an invaluable member of the original encyclopedia team, bringing the careful and precise eye of the librarian, and an iconoclastic spirit, to our work.

The economy of a society provides the parameters for the development of its cultural life, and the history of the American South shows how its resources and role in the world economic system provided the context for the world-views and customs of its people. "Agriculture and Rural Life" and "Industry and Commerce" were separate sections of the *Encyclopedia of Southern Culture*, but the editors have combined them here to provide a connected survey of how southerners have made a living. The region's story was a global one from the beginning, as early settlers grew tobacco and sold it in Europe and participated in an international slave trade that provided the workforce that drove agricultural development through not only tobacco but also cotton, sugar, and other staple crops. Certain regions within the South, such as the Carolina Lowcountry, the Alabama Black Belt, and the Mississippi Delta, came to have such productivity that they gained special economic and political power and a certain cultural mystique of their own. Other places, off in the hill country and the piney woods, were not so productive, yet they nurtured a rural, working-class, yeoman culture that has dominated the South demographically and expressed a distinctive culture. Rural living, in any event, long provided a common vernacular of daily experience and the basis for a deeply entrenched folk culture that would lie behind much of the region's literary, musical, and artistic creativity.

Until recently, industrial and commercial life often appeared to take a backseat to agricultural development in the South, but the complex social and cultural realities of the region shaped their development in distinctive ways within the context of the United States. Cotton factors negotiated between planters and the world market, connecting seemingly isolated places to the broader world, as did railroads when they proliferated through the post–Civil War South. Textile mills exploded onto the economic landscape in that same era, exploiting the region's most popular crop. Planters and industrialists sometimes might be in conflict over economic policies, but they shared a common southern elite perspective in relentlessly pressing for lower wages of workers, who operated in an often exploitive world. Southern cities were intimately related to the industrial and commercial life and had their own versions of southern culture, which will be explored in greater depth in the *Urbanization* volume, to be published later.

Since the *Encyclopedia of Southern Culture* appeared in 1989, the southern economy has undergone dramatic changes. Cotton is no longer king, and the once dominant form of industrial life in the region, the textile mill, has headed overseas in search of the low-cost labor that once brought mills from New England to the South. The South has become a special place in the global economy, whether considering the role of such international companies as FedEx and CNN, the coming of Japanese and German auto factories, or the attractiveness of the region's recently booming economy to transnational populations. Indeed, the once defining poverty of the South has given way to a vital economy, although this prosperity has not enabled the region always to deal successfully with deeply rooted social problems that survive from an age of unjust racial and social-class relations or that have developed in the new economy that shows jarring extremes of wealth in the South as well as the nation. The prosperity and the social changes it has fostered raise fundamental questions about the new nature of "the South" in the contemporary world.

This volume of *The New Encyclopedia of Southern Culture* provides expanded coverage of the economy beyond the original *Encyclopedia*. We offer new entries on such key moments of economic life as agricultural innovation in the colonial period, the rural-urban migration in the early 20th century, the revolutionary changes that came out of the New Deal and World War II eras, and the recent globalization of the southern economy. The particular contributions of Native Americans and women are acknowledged more fully, while short entries provide extensive coverage of individual crops and industries. Whatever the topic, the editors have sought to balance the historical context of economic life in the South with contemporary developments, which is a goal of *The New Encyclopedia* series in general.

# Agriculture

The work of cultivating the soil, producing crops, and raising livestock has dominated the economy and shaped the culture of the South for more than 1,000 years. The region's natural environment—a temperate climate, abundant rainfall, and an array of rich soil types—lent itself to agriculture. The demands of farming in turn molded the region's culture, a culture that until recently undulated to the rhythms of the seasons rather than the regularity of the clock. Yet farming and rural life are characterized by uncertainty. Too much or too little rain, a hailstorm or a hurricane, insect pests and plant diseases can wipe out crops and lay a year's hard labor to waste. Farmers who produce for the market are vulnerable to competition from half a world away and fluctuations in prices shaped by forces well beyond their control. For most of human history in the American South, people have worked the land and struggled to cope with farming's unpredictability.

The South's agriculture has been as diverse as its landscapes. Though this essay tries to provide some sense of that diversity, it is only a brief overview. Inevitably, there will be omissions and oversimplifications. The rich scholarship listed at the end of this essay and the fine articles in this volume will guide the reader to a better understanding of the complexities of southern agriculture and the ways it shaped regional culture.

Long before Europeans arrived in the region, Native Americans cultivated the land. During the first millennium B.C., aboriginal peoples produced pumpkins, gourds, sunflowers, and other crops to supplement their hunting and fishing. By 1000 A.D. the Mississippian cultures across the South were growing large fields of beans, squash, and corn, which sustained a rapidly multiplying population. Using fire, men cleared patches of woodland and broke the soil for planting. Women planted, tended, and harvested the crops, activities that gave them considerable authority and power in tribal communities. Native American agricultural practice was well established by the time Europeans came.

The Spanish arrived in the early 16th century in search of gold and other mineral riches. Instead, they found woodlands punctuated with well-organized Native American villages surrounded by extensive fields. The Europeans brought diseases that cut large swaths through native populations, resulting in the obliteration of some communities and the abandonment of acres of rich agricultural land. In spite of the devastation of Indian communities, a rich cultural exchange took place between natives and new arrivals. Indians obtained new food crops such as sweet potatoes from the Europeans, and they shared their own harvests with the white-skinned newcomers.

Although the precious metals sought in North America failed to materialize in substantial quantities, Europeans nonetheless found lucrative sources of income. The Spanish and French, and later the English, traded furs with the Indian tribes. They also harvested timber and naval stores for European navies. Eventually, Europeans realized that the real treasure in southern North America would be found in following the lead of Native Americans. By the time the first English settlers in Virginia achieved a measure of economic and political stability in the early 17th century, Europeans had decided to cultivate crops for European markets.

Southern historians have spilled much ink debating whether colonial and antebellum-era southern agriculture was a precapitalist or capitalist enterprise. Such differences of opinion are rooted in varying definitions of capitalism. Whether capitalist or not, there is no doubt that the demands of European markets fueled the development of agriculture in the region. Virginians raised tobacco to satisfy European cravings. Carolinians produced cattle to feed slaves on Caribbean sugar plantations. European settlers flooded the New World in order to take advantage of opportunities created by the market. Whites eventually imported Africans in large numbers to provide the labor force that powered their market-driven agricultural production. As historian Peter Coclanis puts it, southern agriculture was always held in the "talons of the market."

European markets may have driven the development of southern agriculture, but colonial-era southern farmers did not simply import wholesale a European-style farming system to the New World. Neither the climate nor the labor force would allow for such a transplant. Instead, white southern farmers blended European practices with things they learned from Native American farmers and from Africans imported as slaves. Livestock production is one case in point. When chronic labor shortages in early Virginia and Carolina prevented colonial farmers from practicing the intensive herding common in Europe, colonials fenced their crops and allowed animals to range freely in unfenced woods. Mimicking Native American practice, they burned woodlands in the spring to enable forage to sprout. Colonists also used techniques learned from the Algonquian Indians of the Chesapeake region to grow tobacco. Similarly, historian Daniel C. Littlefield points out that the development of rice culture in South Carolina was a result of interaction between Europeans and Africans. Although white English settlers almost certainly initiated rice cultivation, slaves from the Windward Coast and Senegambia brought technical skills in rice cultivation to the Lowcountry, skills that they quickly adapted to the new environment. Like Native Americans, African slaves taught Carolina colonists new and more efficient means of clearing land.

As their willingness to learn and adapt methods from Native Americans and Africans suggests, colonial-era white southern agriculturists were innovators (although contemporary European critics rarely recognized that fact). Colonial farmers sought productivity gains through constant adaptation. As historian Joyce Chaplin has argued in her book *An Anxious Pursuit: Agricultural Innovation and Modernity in the Lower South, 1730–1815* (1993), the level of innovation among southern agriculturalists in the colonial period "reflects how white residents accepted modern theory about economic improvement and then manipulated information and resources to make the region yield more wealth." The result was an uneven but progressive accumulation of wealth in the Tidewater areas throughout the colonial period.

In the colonial South, access to water shaped both agricultural and social development. Water was the major means of transportation. Early agricultural settlement throughout the region was concentrated around navigable streams. Areas along waterways also held some of the richest and most easily tillable land. Because staple-crop producers—especially tobacco planters—needed vast tracts of land, neighbors were widely separated by their landholdings. Settlement was dispersed in the colonial South, leading to less frequent social interaction than might have been found in rural areas of the colonial North. Farmers closest to water transport produced food for local and distant markets as well as staple crops for international buyers. Farther away from rivers, livestock farmers grazed cattle and hogs on unfenced land, driving them to market in coastal areas several times a year. Large planters and small yeomen landowners alike gravitated to the waterways. A dearth of water transport routes slowed development of the piedmont regions until serious road-building projects were undertaken in the years just before and after American independence. Nonetheless, as Tidewater areas became more densely settled and land prices there rose, newcomers and yeomen were pushed to the frontiers of settlement. For many years, historians have argued that these frontier yeomen were subsistence farmers, and many did practice "safety first" agriculture, but recent scholarship indicates that most frontier yeomen simply moved to the frontiers to find access to new resources and new markets. Yeomen farmers devoted a large percentage of their time and resources to market production throughout the colonial and antebellum periods.

Tobacco was the first great southern staple crop. The Virginia planters who established great tobacco-growing plantations in the 17th century were not absentee landowners like Caribbean sugar barons. Instead, most personally directed the production of their tobacco crops. Tobacco is a demanding crop—one that requires 15 months of labor from planting to marketing—and planters took great pride in their levels of skill and judgment. Although tobacco had dominated the agricultural economy in Tidewater Virginia during the 17th century, overproduction and increased British import duties led to declining tobacco profits by the 1680s. In addition, tobacco exhausts the soil, forcing planters with finite acreage to switch to more sustainable crops. Virginia planters continued to grow tobacco well after independence, but they also began to diversify their production, raising more wheat and corn for England and its colonies. Tidewater planters also focused on developing a level of self-sufficiency on their plantations, establishing plantation workshops to manufacture cloth, shoes, and tools.

By the mid-17th century, two types of farm operations emerged in Virginia. At first, most farms were yeomen operations, worked by the landowner, his family members, and perhaps one or two hired or bonded workers. Some yeomen became small planters with more acres and more dependent workers, while others among the earliest arrivals were able to parlay fantastic tobacco profits into great landholding dynasties. Accumulating large tracts of land, these planters presided over plantations worked by dependent laborers. Planters came to dominate political life in the colony, a fact that often led to intense class conflict. Labor shortages plagued colonial-era southern planters. Although settlers experimented with enslaving Indians—with little success—in the early years, indentured servants from Europe provided the bulk of the colony's agricultural labor. The first Africans who arrived in Jamestown in 1619 had an ambiguous legal status, and some of the earliest Africans in Virginia eventually obtained their freedom and became landowning farmers. African workers were considerably more expensive than indentured servants until the mid-17th century, and the high death rate in the colony made these expensive workers a poor investment. As late as 1640, there were probably fewer than 150 Africans in Virginia. Nonetheless, by the mid-17th century courts and the House of Burgesses increasingly treated servitude among blacks as a lifelong hereditary condition. By 1680 Virginia colonists faced a shortage of indentured servants. In addition, newly freed indentured servants proved to be a discontented lot, as land shortages and falling tobacco prices made it difficult for them to establish themselves as independent landowners. After a class-based uprising against the colonial government in 1676, Virginia planters shied away from importing white indentured servants who would make demands for economic opportunity and political rights. Landowners preferred to invest in Africans who would never gain their freedom. By 1700 there were 10,000 African slaves in the colony.

Unlike their Virginia neighbors, early settlers of South Carolina did not immediately find an appropriate staple crop. They experimented with Mediterranean luxury crops like grapes, but Carolina winters proved too cold for large-scale grape production. Cattle provided a lucrative source of income for early Carolinians, who, by the turn of the 18th century, had also begun producing rice on a large scale. As in Virginia, Lowcountry planters faced constant labor shortages. They almost immediately turned to enslaved African laborers, importing workers from British plantations in the Caribbean.

As was the case with tobacco, rice production required large landholdings. Thus rural Carolina communities were also marked by a dispersed settlement pattern, but Lowcountry landowners were far more likely to be absentee planters than were their Virginia counterparts. Fearful of malaria, yellow fever, and other epidemic diseases prevalent in the swampy environment suitable for rice plantations, planters and their families often spent much of the year in Charlestown (modern-day Charleston, S.C.) or away from the colony, leaving the supervision of plantation labor in the hands of an overseer. Absentee ownership resulted in a unique form of slave management in the Lowcountry, one that would persist throughout the life of chattel slavery: the task system. The system allowed enslaved workers a measure of autonomy in setting their work pace. It also enabled planters to manage their operations with a minimum of supervision. Slaves working within the task system were assigned a particular task or set of tasks each day. Once that work was completed, the enslaved worker was free to pursue personal activities. Lowcountry planters also gave slaves access to their own garden plots, reasoning that if slaves produced food for themselves and their families, they would reduce the planter's costs in feeding his workers. Not only did planters require slaves to raise their own food, but they also often permitted them to exchange their surplus production for clothing, food, tools, or other goods. Again, the reasoning was that everything a slave was able to purchase was something the master did not have to provide. In addition to gardening and livestock raising, enslaved workers in the Lowcountry engaged in fishing and hunting to supplement their diets. Some were skilled carpenters or metalworkers, creating items for their own use and products for exchange or wages. These slaves accumulated tools and household property. The task system provided enslaved workers with an improved standard of living while also reducing masters' patriarchal authority.

In the mid-18th century, decreasing rice prices on the world market prompted

South Carolina planters to search for a new cash crop. Indigo, a plant that was the source of a beautiful blue dye, had been grown on a wide scale in the British West Indies until West Indian planters gradually abandoned the crop for sugar, giving South Carolinians opportunities to produce indigo as a means of diversifying their plantations. Indigo was a low-weight, high-value product. Thus it was cheap to ship and highly profitable to grow. Carolina planters did not abandon rice for indigo, however. Many continued to produce rice in their low-lying fields while devoting some upland property to indigo.

The Scots-Irish, German, and English settlers who populated the backcountry of Virginia, North Carolina, and South Carolina migrated to the region by way of Pennsylvania in search of a warmer climate and cheap land. These settlers focused at first on clearing land for food crops and grazing livestock for their own consumption and for sale in coastal markets. By the mid-18th century and after, when wagon roads began to link these frontier communities to fall-line towns, backcountry farmers turned more and more of their attention to the production of tobacco, hemp, wheat, and other cash crops. In the years after the American Revolution, backcountry settlers poured into Kentucky and Tennessee. Kentucky, in particular, attracted rapid settlement because of its access to the Ohio River.

Southerners developed a distinctly rural worldview that shaped their political ideas as well as their culture. Historian Timothy Breen has shown how a "tobacco mentality" developed among late colonial Virginia tobacco farmers. Their shared experience of tobacco cultivation—their pride in the judgment and skill required for successful tobacco cultivation—provided them with "a body of common rules and assumptions that helped bind them together." As tobacco planters sank further and further into debt in the middle years of the 18th century, this commonly held worldview evolved into an ideology about independence from tyranny of all kinds, be it British creditors or British lawmakers. Farmers all over the South extolled rural life as a simpler and superior one. Some people, most notably Thomas Jefferson, argued that farmers were the ideal citizens of the new Republic. In his famous 1781 writing (published in 1787) *Notes on the State of Virginia*, he argued, "Those who labour in the earth are the chosen people of God, if ever he had a chosen people, whose breasts he has made his peculiar deposit for substantial and genuine virtue." Unlike factory workers, who depended on others for their livelihood and thus were less able to make independent and virtuous political decisions, Jefferson said, "corruption of morals in the mass of cultivators is a phaenomenon of which no age nor nation has furnished an example." In August 1785 he wrote to John Jay, "Cultivators of the earth are the most valuable citizens. They are the most vigorous, the most independent, the most virtuous, and they are tied to their country and wedded to its liberty and interests by the most lasting bands." Agrarian ideology would permeate southern culture for decades to come.

Cotton, the crop that would become most identified with southern agriculture, arrived on the southern agricultural scene relatively late. Some planters in Georgia's Sea Islands began to produce long-staple (Sea Island) cotton in the 1780s. Soon, Sea Island cotton production spread to the adjacent Georgia coast and the Lowcountry of South Carolina. However, Sea Island cotton would not grow farther inland because it required 240 frost-free days to mature. The variety of short-staple cotton that could thrive in the uplands was too labor intensive to process profitably because its tufted seeds had to be removed from the fiber by hand. In the 1790s, the development of a mechanical cotton gin that effectively cleaned short-staple cotton and the invention of new and cheaper techniques for manufacturing cotton cloth led to a dramatic rise in southern cotton production. Migrants from the Carolinas and coastal Georgia soon were venturing in the piedmont regions of those states and further afield to Mississippi and Alabama, buying vast tracts of land from state and federal governments and from land speculators in order to establish new cotton plantations. Many of the migrants were younger sons of established planters or planters seeking to establish second plantations; others were yeomen farmers seeking to create their own plantation empires. These young planters took slaves with them. By this time, Virginia and Maryland were producing large numbers of surplus slaves. Slave owners there found a ready market among the ambitious planters in the "old Southwest," and a large internal slave trade developed. In Mississippi and Alabama, slaves cleared land, raised food crops and livestock to sustain themselves and their owners, and planted vast tracts of cotton. Between 1790 and 1815, cotton production in the United States increased some sixty-six-fold, from 3,135 bales per year to 208,986 bales.

Access to transportation was often a challenge in piedmont cotton-growing areas. Much of Mississippi and Alabama had access to good water transport, but in piedmont Georgia and a large section of Tennessee, supplies and crops had to be hauled overland. The advent of steamboats on western rivers in 1815 vastly improved transportation alternatives for farmers in the western regions of the South.

Cotton prices, while rising and falling, remained generally high throughout the antebellum period, sparking steady migration to the South's westward reaches and continuous expansion of cotton production. Some planters began to grow cotton in Louisiana and Texas. Planters in and around Natchez, Miss., pioneered cultivation of the rich alluvial soils in the Mississippi River flood plain. Their slaves built dikes to hold out annual delta floods and drainage systems to reclaim wetlands for cultivation.

Many areas of Tennessee, western North Carolina, and Kentucky proved too cold for short-staple cotton production. Corn, wheat, tobacco, and livestock continued to be major products in all three states. Kentuckians also grew hemp, and they transformed much of their grain into corn whiskey or wheat flour for eastern markets. By 1810 Kentucky and North Carolina were among the top whiskey-producing states in the nation.

States throughout the South had pockets of land unsuitable for large-scale staple-crop production. Historian Frank Owsley called these areas "the inner frontier." Yeomen gravitated to these inner frontiers, where land was relatively cheap. Yet few of these farmers were subsistence farmers; historian Bradley Bond has demonstrated that most engaged in high levels of market production, rarely raising enough for their own subsistence.

Agricultural development came to Florida more slowly than to its northern neighbors. Most of Florida's rivers did not have sufficient tidal flow to support rice cultivation. A few farmers grew long-staple cotton in northeast Florida, and with the development of roads in the 1830s, farmers in middle Florida began producing cotton. Livestock was the major agricultural product in most of Florida, and the state's piney woods were well-suited to unfenced grazing. Much of Florida's cattle production was sold in Cuba. The Spanish brought oranges to their missions in northern Florida as early as the 16th century, and subsequently Native Americans cultivated the citrus fruit. By the late 18th century, some commercial groves had appeared; botanist William Bartram reported both wild and commercial groves in the 1770s. Nonetheless, large-scale commercial production of citrus crops did not appear until the antebellum years, and most fruit and vegetable production did not take hold until the development of south Florida railroad lines in the late 19th and early 20th centuries.

The agricultural economy of southern Louisiana was dominated by sugar production. Migrants from the West Indies introduced sugarcane cultivation in the 1780s. Using West Indian techniques, they produced molasses and sugar, transporting crops to market on the state's extensive bayou network. Sugar proved enormously profitable, and those profits enabled the expansion of plantations, levee building, the clearing of large tracts of land, and the purchase of new machinery to process sugar more efficiently. Louisiana sugar planters used modern techniques of organizing labor, including assembly lines and clock-ordered management, to develop the South's most industrialized form of agriculture. They even attempted to coax more productivity from enslaved workers by offering them business-style incentives such as greater autonomy, better living conditions, and cash. Nonetheless, working conditions were terrible; in 1849 Louisiana had the highest death rate in the nation, largely because of the poor diet, malarial climate, and hard labor endured by slaves on sugar plantations.

In general, enslaved people had easier lives in the more settled plantation and farm country of the east than on the newer plantations farther west. Frontier living conditions in the developing regions led to poor living standards and intense labor demands throughout the year. Hard labor dominated the lives of most slaves. All over the South, enslaved men, women, and older children tended the fields. Many field tasks were gendered. For example, in some parts of the South, plowing was seen as skilled work and was assigned only to men, while women burned stubble from the fields and hoed. In other areas, men and women alike plowed, hoed, and harvested. Gender distinctions in the work of enslaved people were based on whether a job was considered to be skilled or unskilled labor; women were never assigned to skilled tasks, with the exception of tasks like cooking or nursing that were seen as women's work. On larger plantations, a few men worked as artisans, serving as blacksmiths, carpenters, and coopers. Most plantation buildings were constructed by slaves, many of whom were highly skilled craftsmen. Large plantations were more likely than small ones to boast house or domestic servants, slaves who devoted all their time and energy to caring for the master's household, family, and garden. Although being a house slave often carried considerable status and sometimes resulted in better living conditions, it also put enslaved people under much more intense supervision by whites. Small planters who owned five or fewer slaves were common, and on those properties, enslaved workers often worked side-by-side with the members of the master's family. Indeed, most southern planters owned fewer than 20 slaves, and those slave owners often supervised workers themselves rather than depending on overseers or drivers.

Regardless of white dominance and oppression, enslaved African Americans in rural areas built strong family and community lives, and they developed vibrant forms of self-expression. Enslaved households were based on a complex set of relationships in which men and women, the young and the old shared authority. African American men did not enjoy the same level of household dominance as white men. Nonetheless, slaves did form nuclear families. In spite of the fact that slave marriages did not enjoy legal protection and family members faced the persistent threat of being separated by sale, enslaved people married and had children. They also gathered informally with Africans Americans from nearby plantations for worship, weddings, funerals, and even work. In the upcountry, where few masters owned large numbers of slaves, landowners found it useful to pool the labor of their slaves at times of peak work. They organized corn huskings, log rollings (moving timber from newly cleared land), and other work parties. These gatherings gave African Americans time to socialize with friends from other plantations. Music was an important part of African American culture, with the African-influenced forms ranging from call-and-response field hollers to Negro spirituals and lively instrumental tunes favored by white masters. Enslaved people in rural areas were rarely allowed to form their own churches, for fear that they might use their worship hours to plot resistance if they were not supervised by whites. Instead, they usually attended church services with whites. Nonetheless, slaves often gathered informally (and sometimes secretly) for religious services led by their own self-taught preachers.

Living conditions for white yeomen farm families, even those who owned a slave or two, varied. Some were relatively prosperous, living in well-built and comfortable homes, while others dwelled in small, rudely appointed houses. Every member of the family was critical to the family economy. In all but the most prosperous yeomen families, women and children worked in the fields. Women and children also did most of the domestic labor: cooking, cleaning, sewing, and preserving food. As historian Stephanie McCurry has pointed out, white yeomen built their status on their control of dependent laborers, including family members, and they guarded this power jealously. The ideal of the white household head controlling his dependents in fact formed the basis for white political solidarity in the antebellum period. White men of all classes socialized in the context of political campaigns and elections. To some extent, Protestant churches formed a community center for whites, but yeomen women lived isolated lives with limited opportunities for interacting with others in the community. There were few publicly funded schools in the South in the antebellum period, so schools did not form community centers in the way that they later would.

A sharper gender division of labor marked life on plantations, but even there, white women were rarely idle. Most plantation women supervised the provisioning of the household and the slave quarters, directed the work of house slaves, and provided health care for white and black members of the community. Some women kept account books, and a few even ran plantations. Plantation women knew that their standard of living depended upon their enslaved laborers and that they shared with their slaves a dependence on male relatives, but such shared dependence did not necessarily breed understanding. Relationships between plantation mistresses and slaves varied from benign to downright brutal.

In some communities, planter families enjoyed a lively whirl of social activities that offered women (and men) an opportunity for frequent interaction with neighbors and friends, but in other areas, particularly the frontier regions, white planter women felt profoundly isolated, with little company except for children and slaves. Even in the most populated areas, women's social lives were circumscribed; plantation women did not cross boundaries into the neighborhood without the protection and sanction of their men.

Planter men enjoyed nearly complete dominance over all the members of their households, including wives, children, other relatives, and the enslaved. They also enjoyed a large measure of authority in the local community. A complex ideology of honor and paternalism shaped elite white men's identities.

Rural southerners looked upon charity as a private matter, and from the time of white settlement, the white communities of the South had always "looked after their own," whether their own were other whites or enslaved blacks. Southerners tended to scorn the idea of state-based aid to the poor, seeing it as a last resort for the lowest of the low. Community members who became ill or fell on hard times turned to their kin and neighbors for help, and even elite whites participated in a complex web of mutual aid networks. Women were the backbone of these informal support networks, building ties through visiting and an exchange of surplus farm products. Often mutual aid networks were the only source of cross-class (though not cross-racial) contacts between rural white women. Elites were more likely to dispense aid to those considered worthy of help, and such aid often served to buttress the superiority of elite whites, but the exchanges also helped poorer families survive misfortune.

Southern agriculturalists were sometimes derided as backward, particularly given their dependence on slave labor, but many of the South's farmers were progressive, reading agricultural journals and joining agricultural societies in search of better knowledge of farming. Reformers like Edmund Ruffin of Virginia, publisher of the *Farmer's Register*, urged his fellow farmers to practice crop rotation, to use guano, lime, and clover crops to replenish their soil, and to practice contour plowing in order to reduce soil erosion. As abolitionist criticism escalated, southern planters used their agricultural societies and publications to mount elaborate defenses of slavery. John Taylor of Carolina, a contemporary of Jefferson, shared the former president's belief that only a society dominated by farmers could preserve republican virtue, and he strenuously defended plantation slavery. He argued in *Arator*, his essay collection, that with proper management, slavery could benefit both slave and master. Virginia planter George Fitzhugh published many of his proslavery articles in *De Bow's Review*, a southern journal that promoted agricultural, commercial, and industrial progress in the region. As the 1850s wore on, secessionist viewpoints and proslavery arguments dominated southern agricultural journals, many of which ceased publication during the war years.

The Civil War devastated the southern countryside. By 1865 much of the South's physical and economic infrastructure lay in ruins. Land in Virginia, Tennessee, and portions of other states had been ravaged by battles. Many people had been displaced by the fighting, abandoning their farms. Other land-holdings had fallen into disrepair thanks to wartime poverty. Raiding troops on both sides had carried off livestock and tools and burned houses, barns, and corncribs. Most significant of all, the South's slaves had been emancipated, leaving landowners to grapple with the mammoth task of rebuilding without cash or an ample supply of forced labor. Restoring southern agriculture was a daunting task.

After the Civil War, variety continued to be a hallmark of the region's farming, and market forces remained the major factor in shaping the rural economy. In much of the South, particularly the upcountry areas not suitable for cotton cultivation, yeomen farmers and planters alike continued to produce tobacco, small grains, and livestock. Prairie rice was introduced on the Gulf Coast and in parts of the Arkansas Delta. Many Louisianans continued to raise sugarcane. In much of the South, however, cotton remained king. In the 1870s, southern cotton production recovered to prewar levels and then grew, even as prices fell. Most years, cotton was not particularly profitable, but southerners stubbornly persisted in staking their futures on the fluffy fiber.

Cotton remained labor intensive, and southern landowners struggled to find an adequate labor supply after the abolition of slavery. Many African Americans wanted to farm, and some acquired land in the postwar years, but most found it impossible to accumulate the cash for their own farms. Cash-strapped plantation owners found it difficult to pay wage laborers and also proved reluctant to allow workers the level of autonomy that came with wage work. Sharecropping emerged as a negotiated solution to the competing demands of landowners and landless freedpeople. The sharecropping system provided landowners with farm labor and the landless with access to land and hope for some measure of autonomy. Typically, a landowner provided the sharecropper and his family with land and housing in exchange for a share of the crop or occasionally a cash rent payment. The specific tenancy arrangements varied, depending on whether a sharecropper owned his own work stock and tools or whether he could afford to buy his own seed or pay cash rent.

Sharecropping re-created many of the most exploitative features of the ante-bellum plantation system, offering widely varying levels of autonomy. A share-

Sharecropper, Warren County, Miss., 1972
(William R. Ferris Collection, Southern Folklife
Collection, Wilson Library, University of North
Carolina at Chapel Hill)

cropper's entire family labored in the fields throughout the year. In the best situations, the family labored without close supervision from the landowner, but in the worst, the landlord or his hired foreman interfered in every aspect of the sharecropping family's work and lives, even prohibiting them from growing a garden or keeping livestock—both activities that would provide a landless family with some independence from landlord control. Since cash flowed only with the sale of the crop after harvest, farming families lived without income much of the year. In order to subsist until harvest time, sharecroppers depended on an advance of food, clothing, seed, and supplies from a merchant who was known as the "furnishing merchant." The furnishing merchant—often the landlord himself—held a lien against the future crop to secure the sharecropper's debt for subsistence supplies. At harvest time, the landowner took his share of the harvest while the furnishing merchant totaled the sharecropper's debt plus interest and subtracted it from the value of the remaining harvest. Anything that was left over constituted the sharecropper's profit for the family's labor that year. Much of the time, there was little left, and some years sharecroppers were unable to pay off what they owed, instead sinking further and further into debt.

Because landless farmers were dependent on the landlord for almost everything they needed to live, and because there were few other job opportunities in rural communities, elite white landowners exercised considerable control over the lives and fortunes of dependent blacks (and eventually an increasing number of whites). Avaricious landlords also used the furnishing system to gouge tenants with high interest rates and outrageous prices, and some landowners cheated tenants outright. As white supremacy reasserted itself in the last quarter of the 19th century, black tenants found themselves at a particular disadvantage. They were barred from legal recourse against unscrupulous landlords, and those who challenged the landlord's control could face arrest, eviction, or violence.

In the 1870s and 1880s, southern farmers faced a bleak future. Not only were cotton prices low, but prices for other farm commodities also fluctuated widely. The shift to an urban, industrial society drew yeomen farmers into a cash-based market economy that required the sale of crops and livestock and tied the value of farm products to ever more distant markets. Yeomen and planters alike lacked capital to invest in labor-saving equipment, supplementary fertilizers, and other improvements that would have increased their productivity. Transportation costs, especially via railroads, and access to credit were in the hands of distant businessmen who farmers believed were exploiting them.

Even as the region settled into a long period of decline after the Civil War, local-color writers began packaging an idealized rural South for northern and southern readers. These writers, some born in the North but most native-born southerners, portrayed the antebellum plantation South as a benign society of rural paternalism, colorful dialects, and even more colorful characters. Thomas Nelson Page's *In Old Virginia* (1887), Joel Chandler Harris's Uncle Remus stories (1880s), and Grace King's *Balcony Stories* (1983) promulgated this "moonlight and magnolias" version of southern history, a view that was popular with northern readers. Local-color writers also found the exotic among people in various subcultures of the rural South. Mary Noailles Murfree, writing under the pseudonym Charles Egbert Craddock, published *In the Tennessee Mountains* in 1884, popularizing the image of the isolated, somewhat backward, but noble mountaineer farmer. George Washington Cable and Kate Chopin introduced the nation to Louisiana Creole culture. Many local-color works were pastorals. Literary scholar Lucinda MacKethan notes that the pastoral is a genre that seeks "to resolve the tension between memories of a simpler past, associated with nature and rural society, and experience in a more complex present world." Given the national economic and social upheavals of the late 19th century, it is no wonder that southern local-color writers were popular both inside and outside the region.

Southern musical culture also flourished in the late 19th-century South. In the days before Victrolas and radios, itinerant musicians took minstrel shows to the thousands of small towns sprinkled throughout the rural South. Minstrelsy had its roots in the antebellum period but came into its own in the years after the Civil War. Minstrel shows included singing, dancing, and comic skits. Though the comic skits, at first performed by white people in black face, usually lampooned African American culture, minstrel shows also took rural African American musical and dance forms seriously, bringing them to audiences far beyond the plantation. All-black minstrel troupes were common by the 1870s, even though they found traveling the southern circuit difficult because of Jim Crow restrictions. The cultural forms rooted in the cotton fields and piney woods of the South would continue to evolve as each new generation added new techniques and themes and borrowed new things from other types of music and literature.

As the South's farm economy stagnated in the late 19th century, sharecropping spread. Many white yeoman landowners slipped into tenancy. A cycle of overproduction, volatile commodity prices, and indebtedness sucked many southern landowners, black and white, into farm tenancy and the crop-lien system. By 1900 about one-third of white farmers and three-quarters of black farmers in the South worked land they did not own. That year, per capita income in the South was half the national average, and much of that differential was due to the terrible conditions in the southern countryside.

Southern farmers organized to address the problems of expensive and scarce credit, exorbitant railroad rates, and exploitive marketing systems. Chapters of the Patrons of Husbandry, commonly known as the Grange, appeared throughout the South in the 1870s. The Grange advocated rural uplift and education and lobbied for government regulation of railroad rates and farm credit. Grangers organized cooperative stores to help farmers buy in bulk. Larger and more active than the Grange was the Southern Farmers' Alliance, founded in Texas in 1877. Alliance chapters and their companion organization, the Colored Farmers' Alliance, developed a farm organization that combined many of the social aspects of fraternal organizations with cooperative ventures and political activism. In addition to the issues raised by the Grange, the Alliance offered a critique of the agricultural marketing system. Seeking more control over the sale of their products, Alliance men organized marketing cooperatives to sell farm products. By 1892 the unresponsiveness of Democratic political officials in the South to Alliance demands led the organization to embrace the formation of a farmer-laborer party known as the People's Party or the Populists. In some states, this party achieved limited local success by allying itself with Republicans, but "fusion" politics faced a severe backlash from white supremacists and Democratic Party members. Facing repression and even violence at the local and state levels, and unable to marshal a broad national political base, the Populist Party faded in the 1890s, but many of its issues would later become goals of Progressive reformers. Nor did agrarian reform in the South disappear after the demise of Populism. Historian Connie Lester has shown how Progressive-era southern farmers continued their organizing and activism. Many organized more narrowly into commodity-based organizations such as cotton farmers, tobacco planters, and peanut growers. In Tennessee, many joined the Farmer's Union, an organization that allied itself with professional agrarian reformers within the state's Agriculture Bureau to advocate for state-supported agricultural education and aid to farmers.

Driven by market forces and new technology, southern agriculture began its long transition to modernity in the first decades of the 20th century. Historian Deborah Fitzgerald has argued that this period saw the emergence of an industrial ideal in agriculture. A new class of experts, including university professors, U.S. Department of Agriculture (USDA) employees, bankers, and agribusiness executives, urged farmers to apply new scientific knowledge of plant and animal science and industrial notions of specialization, mechanization, efficiency, and economies of scale to the farming enterprise. The loosely organized coalition of agrarian reformers who promoted the adoption of industrial farming methods grew out of the Country Life Movement. Building on the findings of President Theodore Roosevelt's 1907 Country Life Commission that reported that the backward nature of American agriculture, the financial struggles of farmers, and the isolation of rural communities were fueling youthful flight from the land, Country Life activists warned of an impending food shortage if the rural exodus continued. The solution, they maintained, was improved rural education and the adoption of the new agricultural machinery and techniques that were being developed in the nation's land-grant colleges and agricultural experiment stations to improve the standard of living among farm families.

The need for rural reform was especially obvious in the South, where most farmers remained mired in poverty and substandard living conditions. Yet southern farm families faced high barriers to adopting the new industrial agricultural model. Thanks to high levels of tenancy, the lingering economic effects of the Civil War, undercapitalized and undermechanized farms, the late 19th-century agricultural slump, and dependence upon particularly volatile agricultural commodities, most southern farmers had little capital to invest in modernizing their operations. As agriculture became increasingly "industrialized" throughout the nation, southern farmers were tied to supply, credit, and distribution networks geared to a commercial agriculture that they could not yet practice.

State and federal agencies joined with private foundations to help southern farmers modernize. The Rosenwald Fund (established by Sears, Roebuck executive Julius Rosenwald) and the Rockefeller family's General Education Board provided funds for rural schools and extension work among farm women and men. By 1914 when Congress passed the Smith-Lever Act, the USDA partnered with state and local governments to fund an extensive network of extension educators throughout the rural South. Agricultural extension agents taught landowning southern farmers modern farming methods, while home demonstration agents taught farm women improved gardening and food preservation practices, techniques for providing the family with a balanced diet year-round, and ways to inexpensively make fashionable clothing or home accessories. The primary goal of all these extension activities was to make the farm a more comfortable, attractive, and prosperous place to live. Handicapped by limited funding, the USDA's preference for aiding the prosperous landowners likely to be able to successfully adopt modern farming methods, and a segregated Extension Service, agents enjoyed limited success in helping the neediest southern farm families.

Southerners' disadvantage in the new industrial agricultural economy became apparent during the years from 1900 to 1914, a period so prosperous for most American farmers that it has been dubbed the "golden age of agriculture." During those years, national farm income more than doubled, and demand for farm products was high. Although some southern farmers did enjoy good years during the so-called golden age, most continued to struggle because of the high rate of tenancy and, for cotton farmers, the arrival of the crop-destroying boll weevil, which ate its way from Texas to Georgia between 1890 and 1920. During this period, tobacco farmers attempted to battle low commodity prices, cutthroat industry purchasing practices, and expensive production costs by organizing fertilizer and implement-buying cooperatives and entering into production-cutting agreements, but their efforts met limited success. Low prices made it difficult for rice farmers to purchase the expensive equipment and irrigation systems needed for efficient rice production. Even in the southern Appalachian highlands, where many yeomen landowners continued to combine subsistence farming with small-scale production for the market, market forces transformed farming and rural life. The independent yeoman culture of the mountaineers gradually eroded in the late 19th and early 20th centuries as timber and coal companies discovered the riches available in the southern Appalachians and lured local farmers to logging or mining jobs. Many eventually became dependent on off-farm wages. Some families sold their land or mineral rights to timber and mining companies who in turn wreaked enormous environmen-

Cotton scene on Popular Street, Macon, Ga., early 1900s (Ann Rayburn Paper Americana Collection, Archives and Special Collections, University of Mississippi Library, Oxford)

tal damage. Those who remained on the land found it increasingly difficult to make a living farming in the face of rising property taxes and higher expectations for an improved standard of living.

The First World War generated a brief period of optimism among many rural southerners. Demand for American farm products skyrocketed, and federal officials encouraged farmers to increase their production in order to feed war-torn Europe and the American army. Congress appropriated funds to hire additional extension agents for agricultural counties, and these agents fanned out over the South and the nation to promote industrial agriculture to new converts. Farm credit strictures were eased, enabling southern farmers to borrow large sums of cash for land, livestock, hybrid seed, chemical fertilizers, tractors, and implements.

At the same time, landless farmers led the first major wave of rural southerners to leave the land in search of better opportunities. Many draftees left the South for good. Northern labor recruiters flooded the region, offering workers free transportation north and the promise of good factory jobs. Between 1916 and 1921, as many as half a million blacks left the South, mostly sharecroppers fleeing the poverty and racial violence of the rural South for better opportunities in the industries of the North and West.

Optimism for better times on the farm proved to be short-lived. By mid-1920, as European farmers began to recover from the wartime disruptions, world demand for American farm products plummeted, followed by farm prices. Cotton prices dropped from 40 cents a pound in the spring of 1920 to 13.5 cents in December of the same year. Tobacco fell from 31.2 cents a pound to 17.3 cents in the same period. Prices recovered slightly after 1922, only to fall again after the onset of worldwide depression in 1929. As a result, rural southerners often marked the end of World War I as the beginning of the Depression. The economic downturn hit southern farmers, especially tenants, hard. Operating costs remained high even as commodity prices plunged. Credit that had been freely available during the war now dried up. Families were less self-sufficient and had higher standards of living than before the war, and they were often deeply in debt. While urban Americans were reveling in the consumer pleasures of the jazz age, radios, magazines, and Hollywood films reminded rural people of a glittering array of consumer products that they could not afford to buy and a lifestyle far beyond their reach. Thousands of southern families lost their farms to foreclosure in the 1920s, and tenancy grew still more. A disastrous flood on the Mississippi River in 1927 inundated more than 16 million acres, most of it farmland, and left tens of thousands of people homeless.

The onset of the Great Depression caused another plunge in commodity prices in the early 1930s. Cotton prices declined from 17 cents a pound in 1929 to 5 cents a pound by 1932, a far cry from the 1919 high of 41 cents. Using the slogan "Grow Less, Get More," President Herbert Hoover urged farmers to voluntarily cut production, but most did not comply, reasoning that unless most farmers reduced production, the few who did cut back would suffer disproportionately from reduced incomes.

To address the poverty and hardships of farmers, the federal government aggressively intervened during the Great Depression. President Franklin D. Roosevelt's New Deal reshaped the farmer's relationship to the U.S. government. In the end, most New Deal programs did little to help the poorest southern farmers remain on the land, but they did lay the groundwork for the profound transformation of southern agriculture, a transformation that aided large landowners at the expense of small owners and tenants.

The major New Deal agricultural program, the Agricultural Adjustment Act (AAA), provided cash payments to farmers who voluntarily agreed to reduce their output of certain over-produced commodities. Many landowners used this money to mechanize their farming operations, evicting sharecroppers who were no longer needed. Sharecroppers were shortchanged in other ways by New Deal programs. Although the law required that landowners share their AAA crop-reduction payments with sharecroppers in the same proportion as the sharecroppers shared the crop, landlords often failed to comply. Classified as farmers, government officials defined farm tenants as self-employed, and thus local relief officials declared most ineligible for work relief programs such as those sponsored by the Works Progress Administration.

Displaced sharecroppers tried to cope in a variety of ways. Some moved to towns and cities in search of jobs, though high urban unemployment and the cost of moving a family prohibited many from taking this approach. Other displaced landless southerners became migrant farmworkers, moving seasonally along the East Coast harvesting fruits and vegetables. Some sharecroppers pioneered interracial organizing in an attempt to pressure landowners to comply with federal law and the federal government to intervene on their behalf. The Alabama-based Share Croppers Union and Arkansas's Southern Tenant Farmers' Union protested massive evictions of tenant farmers by landowners in the wake of AAA crop-reduction programs and struck for higher agricultural wages. In spite of landless farmers' efforts, local, state, and federal authorities caved in to political pressure from powerful landowners and crushed the tenant unions. By the close of the Great Depression, farming was no longer a viable option for most landless southerners, and many landowners maintained an increasingly precarious hold on the land. At the same time, new federal minimum-wage policies made industrial jobs more attractive and integrated the southern labor force into the national market, a trend that lured people from the land.

The economic and natural disasters of the interwar years found expression in southern music and literature. As historian Pete Daniel points out, "Southern rural music—blues, country, gospel, work songs, and field hollers—evolved from the everyday trials, tribulations, and hopes of Southern farmers." Many southern whites in those bleak years listened to country radio broadcasts. Country music was the music of economically marginal rural whites, drawing from old British and American folk tunes, popular songs, and hymns. One of the first major country recording stars was Fiddlin' John Carson, whose biggest hits, including "Little Old Log Cabin" and "The Old Hen Cackled and the Rooster's Going to Crow," contained rural themes. Country performers in that era focused on hard times, singing about "eleven cent cotton and forty cent meat." Rural and urban southerners alike tuned in to the *Grand Ole Opry*, a Nashville-based radio show that went live in 1925, primarily as a vehicle to sell life insurance. Although the new radio show may have reflected the culture and sensibilities of the rural South, the *Opry*, despite its rustic veneer, was an agent of modernization in the countryside, providing listeners with a highly manipulated vision of rural life. By the 1930s, performers like Roy Rogers and

Gene Autry brought a western flavor to the southern themes of country music, broadening its appeal.

In the interwar period, country music was very much a white artistic form, while the Delta and Piedmont blues were decidedly an African American art form. Delta blues, born in the late 19th-century Mississippi Delta cotton fields, expressed a sense of alienation and rebellion in music that drew on spirituals, work songs, and field hollers for its 12-bar, 3-line, call-and-response style. Historian James C. Cobb has noted that the blues celebrated the very "antithesis of what Delta whites wanted their workers to be." African Americans gathered in rural juke joints on Saturday nights to play and listen to the blues. Many blues tunes extolled an alternative lifestyle of drinking, dancing, sex, and disregard for white notions of respectability. Delta blues' lesser-known cousin, the East Coast Piedmont blues, was born in the cities of the South's piedmont, where thousands of rural blacks settled in search of jobs in the early 20th century. In tobacco-processing centers such as Durham, N.C., and textile towns like Spartanburg, S.C., piedmont bluesmen incorporated an alternating thumb-bass pattern and a fingerpicking style into their guitar picking, distinguishing the style from its riverine relative. Blues singers also bemoaned poverty and natural disaster but added racism to the list of ills that plagued southern farmers. In "Dry Spell Blues," Son House sang that "the people down South soon will have no home / 'cause this dry spell has parched all their cotton and corn," and Charley Patton commemorated the 1927 Mississippi River flood's destruction of Delta farms in "High Water Everywhere." Bluesmen from Leadbelly to Bessie Smith and Pink Anderson lamented "these boll weevils / they will rob you of a home" in a tune aptly titled "Boll Weevil." In 1928 "Blind" Blake sang about the promise of a better life in northern cities in "Leaving for Better Times":

> I'm goin' to Detroit, get myself a good job
> Tried to stay around here with the starvation mob
> I'm goin' to get a job, up there in Mr. Ford's place
> Stop these eatless days from starin' me in the face.

Other blues singers focused on the pernicious effects of racism in the sharecropping system. In "Going Back to My Plow," Big Bill Broonzy noted that "Ought's a ought, figger's a figger / all for the white man, none for the nigger."

By the early years of the Depression, both blues and country singers began to incorporate political commentary into their depictions of country life. These songs often criticized the Hoover administration for ignoring the plight of the farmer and praised New Deal programs. For example, country singer Bob Miller noted that "the folks up in Washington are fat and full / while we've been starvin' on promises and bull!," and bluesman Jimmy Gordon sang "Lord, Mr. President, listen to what I'm going to say / you can take away all of the alphabet, but please don't take that PWA."

Southern literature, too, expressed the anxiety that rural southerners felt in coping with hard times and the pressures of modernization. A group of intellectuals known as the Southern Agrarians forcefully reiterated Jeffersonian agrarian ideals in 1930 when they published a controversial manifesto entitled *I'll Take My Stand: The South and the Agrarian Tradition*. The writers and philosophers who contributed to the volume extolled a countryside inhabited by a self-sufficient, paternalistic, and benevolent gentry class, and they warned that industrial capitalism and scientific agriculture were twin threats to both the soul of the rural South and the health of the nation. Theirs was an emphatic rejection of an urban industrial world. Several of the authors published other works with similar themes, including Allen Tate's novel, *The Fathers* (1938), and a number of Robert Penn Warren's short stories.

Other authors showed more ambivalence about the South's past as they explored rural hardship. In Ellen Glasgow's *Barren Ground* (1925), main character Dorinda manages to transform the worn-out Virginia farm she inherits into a fertile Eden, but the price is the loss of her soul and her womanly softness. William Faulkner's work dealt with the complex and crippling legacy of slavery on rural society in works such as *The Sound and the Fury* (1929) and *Absalom, Absalom!* (1936).

The literary portrayal of rural African Americans was rich and complex in the interwar period. White novelist Julia Mood Peterkin's *Scarlet Sister Mary* (1928) won the Pulitzer Prize for its nuanced depiction of rural African American culture on South Carolina Lowcountry plantations. Peterkin's characters, with their Gullah dialect, found dignity in their work on the farm and their rural community. Zora Neale Hurston's *Their Eyes Were Watching God* (1937) offered a portrayal of African American life in the all-black town of Eaton, Fla. Hurston did not ignore the ugliness of southern race relations, but she made African American characters and their relationships central to her story, not allowing whites to define them. Other African American writers were less positive about rural life, however. Richard Wright's collection *Uncle Tom's Children* (1938) exposed the harsh racial climate of the Jim Crow South. For example, in the novella "Big Boy Leaves Home," the title character becomes the target of a lynch mob after a confrontation with a white landowner's son, barely escaping with his life after watching his friend murdered.

A lighter side of southern rural life found expression on the *Lum and Abner* radio show. Launched in 1931 by Arkansas natives Chester "Chet" Lauck and

Findley Norris "Tuffy" Goff, *Lum and Abner* featured the inhabitants of the fictional rural community of Pine Ridge. At the country store run by the title characters, who also farmed and occasionally held local political office, farm people gathered and sought to resolve various dilemmas. Unlike many radio shows that featured rural characters, *Lum and Abner* were not backward hill-billies. The mountaineers of *Lum and Abner* were forward-looking, ambitious, smart, and largely successful in coping with hard times. Unlike the agrarians and others who rejected modernity, they found ways to reconcile the modern world with rural values of hard work and virtue.

World War II brought another wave of dramatic change to the southern countryside. Farmers again enjoyed high commodity prices because of war-time shortages, and as in World War I, federal officials urged them to increase their production levels as a matter of patriotic duty. New challenges arose, how-ever. The South's farm population declined by 22 percent during the war, as young people entered the military or took wartime jobs off the farm. Farm laborers and sharecroppers made up most of the population that left the south-ern countryside. The war transformed southern agriculture in profound ways. Out-migration sparked a farm-labor crisis, giving workers real bargaining power with landowners for the first time. Racial tensions intensified as African Americans challenged discrimination and whites worked to shore up the color line. During the war, ordinary southerners found that the federal government was an ever-increasing presence. In addition to the USDA, new agencies such as the Selective Service Administration, the Office of Price Administration, the War Manpower Commission, and the U.S. Employment Service intervened daily in the lives of ordinary people.

World War II sparked a revolution in agricultural productivity, one fueled by technological innovations that included the introduction of improved varieties of crops and animals (made possible largely by advances in genetics), mechani-zation, and the use of new chemicals to kill weeds and insect pests and to fer-tilize the land. The wartime labor shortage made mechanization and improved farming methods vital to landowners' survival. Southern farmers bought trac-tors and mechanical cotton pickers, used DDT to eliminate the boll weevil and other pests, and applied new herbicides to eliminate the need to weed crops by hand. In the 1950s and 1960s, many southern farmers diversified, giving up cotton for new strains of grains and livestock. The shift to new crops and to the mechanical cotton picker rendered most of the South's remaining sharecrop-pers obsolete, though many landowners still used day laborers on a seasonal basis. As a result, between 1940 and 1960, about half a million sharecroppers quit farming.

Government agricultural programs also contributed to the shift to large-scale commercial farming. A complex allotment system, a descendent of New Deal crop-reduction plans, assigned each landowner a specific number of acres for overproduced commodities like cotton, rice, and tobacco. The allotments quickly became assets in their own right that landowners bought and sold like commodities. To mitigate the price declines sparked by flooded commodities markets, the federal government frequently cut allotments. These cuts were distributed to local farmers by county-based agricultural boards dominated by large landowners. Small landowners often found their allotments too small to be profitable. Many responded by selling their farms and their remaining allotments to large landowners who could afford to offset allotment cuts by using more fertilizer, pesticides, and technology to increase their per-acre yields. By the 1960s a new capital-intensive form of agriculture had replaced the old labor-intensive system.

The social transformations accompanying the economic and structural transformations of the southern countryside reshaped daily life for most rural southerners. Thousands took off-farm jobs, learning to organize their lives around time clocks instead of the sun and the seasons. Many eventually moved to towns and cities, where they learned to cope with neighbors who lived within arm's reach. Farm people who had once depended on family and friends to help them cope with poverty, illness, and death learned to turn to social service agencies for assistance. Rural church congregations gradually diminished and sometimes disappeared as young people left rural communities. In the name of improving education, rural school districts consolidated schools. School and church had been the glue that bound many small rural communities, and without these institutions, community ties were undermined. Small southern towns dried up and died as the farmers who had once patronized small hardware, grocery, and feed stores left the land. National chain stores such as Wal-Mart drove locally owned retailers out of business, but they also provided rural people with access to the same types of consumer goods enjoyed all over the country. Large regional banks swallowed up local financial institutions, undermining the personal relationships with local bankers that farmers had once enjoyed and leaving them to depend upon distant bureaucrats to make decisions about operating loans and mortgages. Increasingly, farmers turned to government and quasigovernment agencies such as the Production Credit Association and the Farmers Home Administration for operating loans.

The postwar transformations of the rural South soon led to the emergence of a defiantly working-class culture that Pete Daniel has called "lowdown culture." Rural southerners and urban southerners with rural roots—black and white alike—embraced and celebrated a variety of cultural forms that were self-conscious rejections of middle-class pretensions. As Daniel puts it, "The working class wore their lowdown status with pride," rejecting elite notions of respectability. Among the working class, a rich cultural exchange between blacks and whites led to new developments on the musical front with innovations in blues and country music and the emergence of a new genre known as rock and roll. Memphis in the 1950s became the center of this musical vitality. Home to thousands of rural migrants who haunted its bars and clubs, the city became fertile ground for an emerging network of musicians. Legendary record producer Sam Phillips, black artists like Howlin' Wolf and Ike Turner, and white performers like Carl Perkins and Elvis Presley were all part of this cultural exchange.

Another cultural development in the postwar era was the emergence of stock car racing. Since Prohibition, some rural southerners had hauled illegal liquor from country stills into cities. These "trippers" became legendary in rural communities for their daring and skill in evading lawmen with their souped-up cars. By the 1940s, trippers were engaging in loosely organized racing. Postwar affluence and the "car culture" of the 1950s led to growing interest in stock car racing and the founding of a formal racing organization, the National Association for Stock Car Auto Racing (NASCAR). The popularity of NASCAR grew in the urban and rural South as a regular racing circuit was developed and race tracks were built.

The last third of the 20th century saw a continuation of the changes in the southern countryside as increasing numbers of small landowners sold out to bigger commercial farmers and took off-farm jobs. Farmers grew ever more dependent on federal agricultural programs, and many also became dependent on large agribusiness firms. A major structural change in the last half of the 20th century was the use of production contracts with farmers that gave the contractor control over many aspects of the farm operations, a practice pioneered by poultry processors. Other farmers turned to new crops, especially soybeans and peanuts. Late in the century, some farmers were carving out new niches in producing specialty foods for gourmet restaurants. Many farmers turned their operations into tourist attractions, mowing mazes in cornfields to appeal to families in search of a wholesome outing, establishing cut-your-own Christmas tree operations, and growing fruits and vegetables for local markets. Some truck farmers sold harvests at their own farm stands, while others engaged in community-supported agriculture, selling shares of the farm's harvest to local families.

Late in the 20th century, African American farmers waged yet another battle in their long war against discrimination. In 1997 a group of black farmers filed a class action suit against the USDA. The lawsuit eventually grew to include 26,000 families. They charged that the department had been engaged in a pattern of racial discrimination throughout the 20th century. Among other charges, plaintiffs accused the agency of systematically denying Farmers Home Administration loans to black farmers, unnecessarily delaying the processing of black farmers' loan applications, and holding African American loan applicants to higher financial standards than white farmers. They also accused the department of failing to investigate hundreds of complaints lodged by black farmers against it between 1983 and 1997. The case was settled in 2000 at an anticipated cost of $1 billion to the USDA, but payouts have been slow to come. Today, black farmers are again engaged in litigation with the USDA.

Most southern farm families who remained on the land at the end of the century enjoyed a higher standard of living than did their early 20th-century ancestors, but they usually did so because of off-farm income. As the first decade of the 21st century has progressed, many southern farmers have struggled to stay in business in the face of continued overproduction, steadily falling commodity prices, rising production costs and debt, foreign competition in some commodity production, and cuts in federal agricultural subsidies. Southern culture is changing, too. The imperatives of rural life no longer powerfully shape all aspects of southern culture, but elements of rural culture persist.

MELISSA WALKER
*Converse College*

Nancy D. Bercaw, *Gendered Freedoms: Race, Rights, and the Politics of the Household in the Delta, 1861–1875* (2003); Bradley G. Bond, *Political Culture in the Nineteenth-Century South: Mississippi, 1830–1900* (1995); T. H. Breen, *Tobacco Culture: The Mentality of the Great Tidewater Planters on the Eve of Revolution* (1985); Joyce E. Chaplin, *An Anxious Pursuit: Agricultural Innovation and Modernity in the Lower South, 1730–1815* (1993); Catherine Clinton, *The Plantation Mistress: Woman's World in the Old South* (1982); James C. Cobb, *Redefining Southern Culture: Mind and Identity in the Modern South* (1999); Peter A. Coclanis, *The Shadow of a Dream: Economic Life and Death in the South Carolina Low Country, 1670–1920* (1989); Pete Daniel, *Breaking the Land: The Transformation of Cotton, Tobacco, and Rice Cultures since 1880* (1980), *Lost Revolutions: The South in the 1950s* (2000), *Standing at the Crossroads: Southern Life in the Twentieth Century* (1986); Gilbert C. Fite, *Cotton Fields No More: Southern Agriculture, 1865–1980* (1984); Deborah Fitzgerald, *Every Farm a Factory: The Industrial Ideal in American Agriculture* (2003); Richard Follett, *The Sugar Masters: Planters and Slaves in Louisiana's Cane World, 1820–1860* (2005); Elizabeth Fox-Genovese, *Within the Plantation House-*

hold: Black and White Women of the Old South (1988); Paul W. Gates, *The Farmer's Age: Agriculture* (1960); Steven Hahn, *The Roots of Southern Populism: Yeomen Farmers and the Transformation of the Georgia Upcountry, 1850–1890* (1983); Randal L. Hall, *Lum and Abner: Rural America and the Golden Age of Radio* (2007); R. Douglas Hurt, ed., *African American Life in the Rural South, 1900–1950* (2003), *The Rural South since World War II* (1998); Jacqueline Jones, *Labor of Love, Labor of Sorrow: Black Women, Work, and the Family from Slavery to the Present* (1985); Lu Ann Jones, *Mama Learned Us to Work: Farm Women in the New South* (2002); Jack Temple Kirby, *Rural Worlds Lost: The American South, 1920–1960* (1987); Allan Kulikoff, *The Agrarian Origins of American Capitalism* (1992); Connie Lester, *Up from the Mudsills of Hell: The Farmers' Alliance, Populism, and Progressive Agriculture in Tennessee, 1870–1915* (2006); Daniel C. Littlefield, *Rice and Slaves: Ethnicity and the Slave Trade in Colonial South Carolina* (1981); Lucinda MacKethan, *Southern Spaces* (2005); Stephanie McCurry, *Masters of Small Worlds: Yeomen Households, Gender Relations, and the Political Culture of the Antebellum South Carolina Low Country* (1995); Robert Tracy McKenzie, *One South or Many? Plantation Belt and Upcountry in Civil War–Era Tennessee* (1994); John Solomon Otto, *The Southern Frontiers, 1607–1860: The Agricultural Evolution of the Colonial and Antebellum South* (1989); Ted Ownby, *American Dreams in Mississippi: Consumers, Poverty, and Culture, 1830–1998* (1999); Debra A. Reid, *Reaping a Greater Harvest: African Americans, the Extension Service, and Rural Reform in Jim Crow Texas* (2007); Paul Salstrom, *Appalachia's Path to Dependency: Rethinking a Region's Economic History, 1730–1940* (1994); Mark Schultz, *The Rural Face of White Supremacy* (2005); Rebecca Sharpless, *Fertile Ground, Narrow Choices: Women on Texas Cotton Farms, 1900–1940* (1999); Keith J. Volanto, *Texas, Cotton, and the New Deal* (2005); Melissa Walker, *All We Knew Was to Farm: Rural Women in the Upcountry South, 1919–1941* (2000), *Southern Farmers and Their Stories: Memory and Meaning in Oral History* (2006); Jeannie M. Whayne, *A New Plantation South: Land, Labor, and Federal Favor in Twentieth-Century Arkansas* (1996); Betty Wood, *Women's Work, Men's Work: The Informal Slave Economies of Lowcountry South Carolina* (1995); Gavin Wright, *Old South, New South: Revolutions in the Southern Economy since the Civil War* (1986).

## African American Landowners

Landownership gave African Americans a measure of economic security and greater independence from white control. Farm owners were their own bosses. They set their hours, controlled labor within their family, selected and marketed their own crops, and exerted a great deal of control over the education of their own children. Additionally, on their farms they were somewhat insulated from the humiliations of Jim Crow culture. Accordingly, from emancipation until the Great Migration, most black families sought landownership in order to fashion for themselves a meaningful freedom. After the federal government failed to supply Reconstruction-era blacks with the promised "40 acres and a mule," they made significant progress on their own despite widespread white hostility and prolonged agricultural depressions. By 1870 only 5 percent of all black families had achieved this goal; by 1910 a quarter had done so.

Some African Americans became free and began purchasing land soon after they first arrived in North America as slaves in the early 1600s. But as the transatlantic slave trade brought increasing numbers of Africans into bondage, whites passed new restrictive laws to maintain them in a dependent position. As a result, the number of black farm owners grew very slowly. By the 19th century, two subregional patterns had evolved. Before the Civil War, few African Americans obtained their freedom in the Deep South, but those who did frequently amassed property. While few in number, they constituted three-fourths of the South's affluent free people of color (those who owned more than $2,000 in property). They tended to be the descendants of whites, often receiving land and education through these family ties. They saw themselves as a separate "mulatto elite" and tended to identify with whites more than with blacks. This pattern was especially marked in Louisiana, where Spanish and French customs of interracial marriage and concubinage held sway.

Conversely, most free people of color lived in the Upper South, but few of these owned land before 1830. They had gained their freedom in a general wave of manumission that swept the region in the decades following the American Revolution. Most had not been related to their previous masters and did not derive long-term advantages from kinship ties with whites. Relatively few were literate or employed in skilled occupations. Those who did acquire land held only small parcels. Unlike African American landowners in the Deep South, those in the Upper South did not conceive of themselves as a separate "brown" society. Instead, they maintained social ties and intermarried with poorer blacks and slaves. Only 1 in 14 became slave owners, whereas fully a quarter of free people of color in the Deep South did so.

In the 1830s, regional patterns began to reverse. African American landowners in the Deep South lost ground, or at best merely held on as a group. At the same time, by their second generation after manumission, free people of color in the Upper South began to work their way into the skilled trades and professions and began to purchase land, matching the total property owned in the Deep South by 1860. When general emancipation came, they accelerated this trend. Although their holdings were usually modest in size, they made extraordinary progress.

African American farm ownership peaked between 1910 and 1920 at one-quarter of black farm families. This achievement was far from evenly distributed, as 44 percent of farmers in the Upper South came to own land, whereas only 19 percent did so in the Deep South. Generally, the sparser the African American population, the easier the path black farmers found to landownership. Even within subregions, much variation occurred. In Georgia, only 13 percent of black farmers owned their own land; in Alabama and Mississippi, 15 percent; in Louisiana, 19 percent; in South Carolina, 21 percent; in Arkansas, 23 percent; in Tennessee, 28 percent; in Texas, 30 percent; in North Carolina, 32 percent; in Florida, 50 percent; in Kentucky, 51 percent; in Maryland, 62 percent; and in Virginia, 67 percent.

Black farm owners have declined in number continuously from the 1920s to the present because of the same problems that have afflicted all small farmers, including boll weevil infestation and the lower prices and higher costs generated by an industrializing, globalizing economy. They have also been subject to the liabilities of racism, finding it particularly difficult to gain equitable aid from government agencies and banks. Additionally, since 1920 many young African Americans identified farming with the exploitation of slavery and sharecropping and have turned increasingly toward other occupations.

MARK SCHULTZ
*Lewis University*

W. E. B. DuBois, U.S. Department of Labor *Bulletin No. 35* (July 1901); Melvin Patrick Ely, *Israel on the Appomattox: A Southern Experiment in Black Freedom from the 1790s through the Civil War* (2005); Peggy G. Hargis and Mark R. Schultz, *Agricultural History* (Spring 1998); Leo McGee and Robert Boone, *The Black Rural Landowner: Endangered Species* (1979); Robert Tracy McKenzie, *Journal of Southern History* (February 1993); Gary B. Mills, *The Forgotten People: Cane River's Creoles of Color* (1977); Loren Schweninger, *Black Property Owners in the South, 1790–1915* (1990).

# Agribusiness

In the 1930 symposium *I'll Take My Stand*, Andrew Lytle criticized southerners who tried to "industrialize the farm; be progressive; drop old fashioned ways and adopt scientific methods." Conversion of farms into scientific, purely commercial endeavors "means the end of farming as a way of life." In the years since Lytle wrote these words, southern agriculture has been fundamentally restructured, leading to a decline in the number of southerners on the land and the increasing dominance of farming by fewer and fewer large operations. John H. Davis, a former assistant secretary of agriculture, coined the term "agribusiness" in 1955 to describe the vertical integration of agriculture through a company's control of the production, processing, and marketing of farm products. Agribusiness relies heavily on contract farming, whereby an agricultural business contracts with individual farmers for the delivery of produce at a set price. The company then processes the farm commodity and distributes it for sale. The term agribusiness gained a new visibility in the early 1970s, with the increasing dominance of American agriculture by corporations. The *Reader's Guide to Periodical Literature* did not use agribusiness as a category for indexing until 1971, when national attention was increasingly focused on it.

Southerners have engaged in agriculture as a commercial activity since the colonial era, when tobacco became North America's leading export. In the antebellum era, cotton was not only the centerpiece of the mythic romantic plantation but also a part of the world economy, as Confederates discovered with their failed policy of cotton diplomacy. For generations after 1865, however, southern farmers grew mostly cotton, corn, tobacco, and peanuts on small, relatively inefficient and nonproductive farms. Low income and widespread poverty characterized the system, which required labor-intensive cultivation. Once established, the system held on tenaciously. Markets, transportation, health and educational services, and credit were all inadequate to promote change, despite the efforts of reformers.

Beginning in the 1930s, and especially during and after World War II, the southern agricultural system underwent several fundamental changes. By the 1960s a revolution had been completed and millions of southerners had left farming. The mid-20th century transformation of southern agriculture led to the emergence of agribusiness in the contemporary South.

The federal government played a major role in the restructuring of southern agriculture. Farmers fighting the boll weevil welcomed federal government agents and supported Seaman A. Knapp's programs in the early 20th century to eradicate the insect. Knapp's demonstration farms, formalized as the Federal Extension Service in 1914, became a source of expertise for farmers inter-

Chicken "factory"—a major agribusiness enterprise (Gold Kist Corporation, Atlanta, Ga.)

ested in change. In the 1930s government policies reducing crop acreage in exchange for cash payments promoted a reduction in the surplus population of farm workers. Congressional farm policy over the years rewarded large growers rather than small operators and made increased capitalization and expansion more attractive. During the early 1960s, for example, government payments went to the top producers of major southern crops. In the Southeast, the top 20 percent of the cotton growers collected 61 percent of the payments. In Louisiana, 20 percent of the sugarcane growers received 72 percent of the subsidy payments, and 20 percent of the rice growers received 64 percent. In the three decades after World War II, direct government subsidies represented a major source of corporate farm income; in 1970 almost $5.2 billion was handed out.

The loss of labor during and after the 1930s also promoted critical agricultural change. By reducing farm acreage, the federal government had stimulated migration of displaced rural southerners to cities, and the need for servicemen and factory workers during World War II drew even more southerners away from agriculture. After the war, southerners continued to seek opportunities outside of the South. Almost a fifth of southerners left the region in the 1940s. More than 1 million blacks alone migrated in that decade. Southern agriculture had traditionally suffered from a labor surplus, according to economic historians, but between 1940 and 1960, the decline of the region's farm population was so drastic—almost 60 percent—that major changes in cultivation patterns occurred. Mechanization of farms also promoted labor decline and the growth of agribusiness. Machines were more efficient on large land acreages than small ones and reduced the need for human workers. With farm mechanization came the displacement of sharecroppers and tenants. Many sharecroppers were black, and the protests of the civil rights movement provided the last pretext for many landowners to dismiss, without any of the previous paternalistic concern, former tenants whose families in some cases had worked on the land for generations. The displaced tenants scattered, but some remained behind. By the 1970s wide gaps in income and lifestyle existed in southern rural areas between the prosperous agribusiness landowners and managers, on the one hand, and the unemployed or underemployed black poor on the other.

Mechanization laid the basis for agribusiness in the South in other ways as well. Although the first tractors appeared on farms during World War I, most farms in the South were too small or unprofitable for the machines. Southern farmers were comparatively slow to mechanize. In 1940 the value of machinery per Mississippi farm was $138, compared to $795 for farms in the Middle West. International Harvester developed a mechanical picker in the early 1940s, but fewer than 50 of them were produced during the war years. After the war, the machine, combined with the use of preemergent and postemergent herbicides, helped to change permanently southern farming, allowing farmers to cultivate and harvest the cotton crop with fewer and fewer workers. The tractor, in turn, enabled those who farmed many different crops to cultivate larger acreage in a less labor-intensive way. Tractors assisted southern farmers as they switched from cotton and corn to nonrow crops.

Southerners, in fact, increasingly turned from cotton to other farm commodities. By the 1960s much land that once grew cotton was woodland or pasture. By 1970 more than a third of crop acreage in Alabama, Florida, Mississippi, and Virginia was pasture, which promoted the raising of livestock. Cattle, hogs, and poultry assumed greater economic significance. Soybeans, though, were the clear beneficiary of the switch from cotton. Soybeans are extremely versatile in their uses and are not as labor intensive in cultivation as cotton. In 1940 southerners raised 7.6 million bales of cotton and 5.4 million bushels of soybeans, but by 1975 the figures were 3 million bales and 523 million bushels. The soybean through the 1970s was the centerpiece of southern agribusiness.

The emergence of large farm units made agribusiness possible in the South. The small plots cultivated by sharecroppers and tenants were anathema to centralized farming, but this had changed by the 1960s. In 1950 there were 2.1 million farms in the South, but by 1975 the number was only 720,000. The average farm size in these decades climbed from 93 to 216 acres. Sharecropper shacks symbolically vanished, and modern centralized operations appeared. Farm owners and part owners became typical agricultural figures. In the 1940s and 1950s, the percentage of land operated by full owners actually decreased. Many farmers now owned some land and rented additional acreage. Farm management became a crucial factor to success, and capitalization in equipment was more important for some farmers than the amount of land owned.

Geographer Merle Prunty Jr. has used the term "neoplantation" to describe an agricultural operation in which an owner or manager runs a farm using hired workers. It resembled an antebellum southern plantation in spatial arrangements but without the paternalism characteristic of that era. Large-scale farmers were the only ones who could profit from this scale of operation. The Delta and Pine Land Company plantation at Scott, Miss., embodied these changes. In the late 1930s, the plantation's 5,000 tenants raised 16,000 acres of cotton. By 1970 the plantation land area had expanded to 25,000 acres, but the workforce of laborers had declined to 500. Cotton grew on 7,000 acres of land, with the rest devoted to soybeans, corn, and grazing land for 3,000 head of cattle.

Changes in government farm policy, the mechanization of southern agriculture, the loss of farm labor, the diversification of farming, and the appearance of large farm units all were factors in nurturing agribusiness operations in the South. Vertical integration gradually appeared in new agricultural sectors after World War II, and demographic patterns in the South promoted this. Increasing urbanization and an accompanying mass market for prepared food brought the centralization of food production and distribution. Women were increasingly employed outside the home, and households needed new food services. Dairy and poultry producers, among others, found the delivery of their commodities to consumers concentrated in distant cities to be difficult without marketing assistance. Agribusiness offered a valuable economic service, and agribusiness companies often made large profits because of economies of scale from the new vertical integration. Critics charged, though, that individual family farmers—once celebrated by Thomas Jefferson as "God's chosen people"—had lost independence and management control, making them subservient to multimillion-dollar corporations.

In the 1970s, agribusiness became one of the major foundations for the economic prosperity of the Sunbelt. By the mid-1970s Florida was the nation's second-leading producer of fruits and vegetables, and Texas was number one in the size of cattle and sheep herds. Georgia led all states in the value of its poultry crop, and Arkansas was third; Georgia also topped the nation's agriculturalists in peanut production. In 1970 corporate farms were more pervasive in the South than anywhere in the nation except in the western states of California, Nevada, and Arizona. Corporations owned one-fifth of Florida's farm acreage, and 10 companies controlled 119,000 of Florida's 636,000 acres of citrus. Among the leading corporate producers, processors, and distributors in the South during the 1970s were the Coca-Cola Company, Southdown (a Houston sugar corporation), Tropicana (the Florida orange juice giant), Gold Kist (the Atlanta corporation dealing in poultry), and Southland (the Texas convenience-store operators). The Associated Milk Producers of Texas was a billion-dollar-a-year agribusiness firm. Energy-producing companies diversified into agribusiness in the early 1970s. Tenneco, for example, was a Houston-based natural gas company whose subsidiaries also produced crops and fertilizers and marketed and distributed agricultural products. Much of agribusiness wealth coming from exploitation of southern resources went out of the South, but, in any event, agribusiness was a key sector of Sunbelt prosperity.

Southern agribusiness operators faced increasing difficulties in the 1980s. Problems developed in the production of certain southern crops, and southerners suffered generally from the national farm crisis. As far back as the 1950s, farmers had faced a cost-price squeeze. In order to increase their efficiency, southern farmers used machinery, fertilizer, gasoline and diesel fuel, hybrid seed, and herbicides, and the costs of large-scale production meant that commodity prices had to keep up with costs. The increased exports of the late 1960s and early 1970s created the best of times. Southerners shared in the prosperity as national net farm income rose from $18 billion in 1972 to $33 billion in 1973. Optimistic farmers borrowed money to buy more land and more expensive equipment. Declining prices for crops in the mid-1970s and general discontent led to the formation of a protest group—the American Agriculture Movement—in the Great Plains states. Southern farmers who had once aspired to agribusiness success had joined the protest by October 1977. In November a nine-mile-long parade of tractors drove through President Jimmy Carter's hometown of Plains, Ga., to dramatize the cause. Difficulties grew worse during the 1980s as Ronald Reagan's administration cut back on federal government aid to farmers.

The last two decades have seen the concentration of agricultural production in fewer and larger corporate hands, resulting in the continued growth of agribusiness in the South. Hog farming, for example, traditionally a small-scale operation in the rural South, dramatically expanded in the 1990s. Hog farming in North Carolina is now a billion-dollar enterprise. Between 1988 and 1997, the state's hog population grew from 2.6 million to 8 million. A decline in the number of hog farmers in North Carolina accompanied the rise in the number of hogs during the same period. In 1986 some 15,000 farms with at least one hog operated in the state, but that number had fallen to 2,300 by 2006. Global markets are increasingly affecting agribusiness activities; the United States, for example, is the second-largest pork producer behind China and is one of the largest exporters. Finally, hog farming also represents the environmental concerns that came out of agribusiness operations, with hog waste from the increased number of hogs on farms becoming a health hazard by the late 1990s.

CHARLES REAGAN WILSON
*University of Mississippi*

William Adams, *Georgia Review* (Winter 1986), *Agricultural History* (January 1979); Pete Daniel, *Breaking the Land: The Transformation of Cotton, Tobacco, and Rice Cultures since 1880* (1985), *Standing at the Crossroads: Southern Life in the Twentieth Century* (1986); Gilbert C. Fite, *American Farmers: The New Minority* (1981), *Cotton Fields No More: Southern Agriculture, 1865–1980* (1984); Deborah Fitzgerald, *Every Farm a Factory: The Industrialized Ideal in American Agriculture* (2003); David R. Goldfield, *Promised Land: The South since 1945* (1987); Valerie Grim, *Agricultural History* (Spring 1995); Jack Temple Kirby, *Rural Worlds Lost: The American South, 1920–1960* (1987); Ingolf Vogeler, *The Myth of the Family Farm: Agribusiness Dominance of U.S. Agriculture* (1981).

## Agricultural Education

Generations of farmers learned traditional techniques associated with southern crops and stock at the sides of their elders. Yet, as science and technology fundamentally changed agricultural practices, and as farming transitioned from a lifestyle that most southerners engaged in to a business that fewer and fewer invested in, different interest groups took different approaches to championing agricultural education. The debate about whom agricultural education benefited and who should support it created deep divisions among southerners, pitted races and classes against each other, and galvanized philanthropists as well as local, state, and national politicians to either advocate or criticize public funding for agricultural education. The debate transcended sectional borders. Agricultural education even became part of informal foreign relations as well as foreign policy, with southerners of both races playing critical roles.

During the 18th and early 19th centuries, planters and progressive farmers educated themselves, gaining information about the merits of new implements, seeds, and cultivation techniques from British publications. For example, by 1760 Virginia planter George Washington implemented revolutionary new methods in crop cultivation, devised and widely publicized by Jethro Tull via his *Horse-Hoeing Husbandry*. Other planters and farmers accessed weather forecasts and other relevant information from almanacs, annual publications that came to be known as "farmers' almanacs." Two early examples were African American Benjamin Banneker's almanac that served Pennsylvania, Delaware, Maryland, and Virginia (1792–97) and immigrant John Gruber's *Neuer Hagerstauner Calender Stadt und Land* (*Hagers-Town Town and Country Almanack*; 1797–present) that focused on Maryland.

Printers believed that agriculturalists could benefit from periodicals that included articles and advertisements as well as running commentary among southern agriculturalists. John D. Legare began one of the earliest in the South, the *Southern Agriculturalist, Horticulturist, and Register of Rural Affairs*, in 1828. Other southern agricultural periodicals that appeared in print prior to the Civil War included *De Bow's Review*, launched by James D. B. De Bow of New Orleans, La., in 1846. He believed his journal would educate readers about scientific agriculture. Readers furthered the goal, and through letters to the editor they debated slave management, sugar refining, and cotton cultivation, among other topics. Farmers and planters often did not agree, so the copy reflected the dynamic nature of antebellum southern agriculture and the need for practical if informal education in methods and in market and business practices.

Slavery made agriculture an intensely political issue in the South, and publishers regularly used their serials as outlets for their political views. Sometimes the views of the editor did not reflect those of the intended readership. De Bow used his *Review* to argue for more commercial and industrial development to create a more independent South. This goal likely reduced elite planter support for his periodical, though it reflected an important aspect of Civil War–era southern nationalism and the role that practitioners played prior to the development of formalized agricultural education.

Some southern farm periodicals remained in production after the war, but new journals appeared as well. One of the most successful, Leonidas L. Polk's *Progressive Farmer*, began in North Carolina in 1886 with the goal of furthering "the industrial and educational interests of our people paramount to all other considerations of state." Polk and other members of the Grange believed that farmers had to educate themselves to make farming a profitable undertaking. Many Grangers sought reform of public education to make the curriculum more meaningful to farmers. Grangers educated themselves through Grange meetings and local, state, and national newspapers published by and for Grange members. Efforts to provide stable sources of information proved challenging, however, as Grangers bickered among themselves about which newspapers to endorse. Grangers also urged their legislators to take advantage of the national government's offer, via the Morrill Act of 1862, to support formal practical education in agriculture and mechanic arts.

The national government had committed itself to federal support of higher education in agriculture and mechanical arts on 2 July 1862, when President Abraham Lincoln signed the Morrill Act. The act outlined the policy of land-grant funding to "promote the liberal and practical education of the industrial classes in the several pursuits and professions in life." State legislators bore the responsibility of prescribing a system to educate its citizens in agriculture and mechanical arts "without excluding other scientific and classical studies, and including military tactics." The act made agricultural education a part of national war policy because the Morrill Act prohibited states in rebellion from realizing any benefits from the legislation. After readmission into the Union, many southern states accepted the land-grant funds, but they did not immediately invest in higher agricultural education. For example, Texas legislators accepted Morrill land-grant funds in 1871 but did not open the Agricultural and Mechanical College of Texas (now Texas A&M University) until 1876. North Carolinians began collecting Morrill funds in 1875 but did not charter North Carolina State University until 12 years later. The last of the ex-Confederate states to comply, South Carolina, did not officially establish its land-grant college, Clemson, until 1889.

During the decade of the 1880s, reformers' advocacy for improved agricultural education did not wane, even as economic conditions across the South worsened and support for the Grange declined. Polk continued to champion the merits of formal education to improve rural life through the *Progressive Farmer*. At the same time, farmers became more politically self-conscious as Farmers' Alliance membership grew across the South. By 1890 Polk served as president of the Southern Alliance, and the People's Party had emerged as an influential third party. Such politically motivated farmers helped ensure passage of important legislation related to agricultural research and education either directly through Populist influence or indirectly through Democrat and Republican efforts to disarm the Populist threat. The Hatch Act of 1887, sponsored by southerners William Hatch of Missouri and James Z. George of Mississippi, set aside national funding to help states establish agricultural experiment stations administered through the land-grant colleges, charging them with "acquiring and diffusing among the people of the United States useful and practical information on subjects connected with agriculture." In 1889 Alabamans used Hatch funding to establish secondary agricultural schools along with branch agricultural experiment stations in each congressional district in the state. By doing so, they improved rural secondary education and began a trend across the South.

In 1890 the U.S. Congress passed, and President Benjamin Harrison signed, the Second Morrill Act into law. The act stipulated that states should use proceeds from land grants to more completely endow and support colleges devoted to agricultural and mechanical arts. It also indicated that states could use a portion of the money to prepare instructors to teach elements of agriculture and the mechanic arts. The Second Morrill Act, however, also recognized southern segregation and did not penalize the land-grant colleges for segregating white and black students.

African Americans, increasingly isolated from influence in white politics as a result of white supremacy, found ways to secure authority over their own agricultural education. In 1876, the same year that Texas A&M University opened, Texas legislators voted to establish an agricultural and mechanical college for the benefit of colored youth. White Democrats in Texas, however, did not provide adequate funding for the college nor invest proportionately in its development as a land-grant institution. The Second Morrill Act provided additional funding but reinforced the model of racial segregation that the 1896 U.S. Supreme Court decision *Plessy v. Ferguson* made legal. The defeat of the Populist challenge in 1896 further reduced African American authority in the countryside, as white southern Democrats returned to power in southern politics. African Americans, however, remained committed to rural and agricultural education, and they remained visible members of southern communities and taxpayers to county government through the peak in African American landownership during the 1920s. These black farmers influenced local governments to allot meager funds to black educational goals, both formal and informal. They also secured private funding, either from among their race or from white, often northern, philanthropists. Not until the 1950s did a backlash against rural racism cause rural black parents to encourage their children to do anything other than pursue an agricultural education. Those who persisted often earned their education in northern and midwestern land-grant institutions, thus exacerbating the brain drain on southern agricultural education.

While African Americans and poor white farmers found their political voice muted during the 1890s, others realized their goals of furthering agricultural education. In 1893 Alfred C. True became director of the U.S. Department of Agriculture's Office of Experiment Stations, and he commissioned a study of how nature and agriculture were taught in country schools. In 1895 the American Association of Agricultural Colleges and Experiment Stations, an organi-

Conference of African American Smith-Hughes Teachers of Vocational Agriculture, September 1919, Prairie View A&M University, Prairie View, Tex. (Source: Papers of Jackson Davis, MSS 3072, Special Collections, University of Virginia Library)

zation composed of presidents of land-grant colleges and professors of agriculture, created a standing committee to document existing methods of teaching agriculture. By 1902 the committee reported that "agriculture has . . . been almost entirely neglected in the high school programmes [sic], and it is high time that the friends of agricultural education should make a systematic effort to have the claims of this fundamental industry acknowledged and satisfied in the curricula of the public schools." The obvious interest in forging a relationship between experiment stations and rural education and the success in Alabama caused southern states to invest in secondary schools in rural areas. Georgia did so in 1907, Virginia and Mississippi in 1908, and Arkansas in 1909. Farmers' Union members continued the calls for improved rural education into the 1910s, often helping forge connections between rural libraries, rural schools, and Boys' Corn Clubs and Girls' Domestic Science Clubs that demonstration agents had begun.

Not all southerners, however, advocated increased national influence over state agricultural education. Many southern states established departments of agriculture and farmers' institutes, and even state and regional fairs, during the late 19th and early 20th centuries in an effort to retain local and state control of agricultural education. National legislation in the form of the Hatch Act and the Second Morrill Act, however, provided funding that helped land-grant colleges become dominant providers of agricultural education.

Two additional pieces of national legislation, both written by southerners, helped consolidate public land-grant colleges' domination of agricultural education in the South. The Smith-Lever Act of 1914, championed by Hoke Smith of Georgia and Asbury Lever of South Carolina, helped diffuse "useful and practical information on subjects relating to agriculture and home economics, and to encourage application of the same." The legislation complied with the system of racial segregation enforced across the South, providing extension education through segregated schools and programs with lower levels of funding and staffing for African Americans. Finally, the National Vocational Education Act, also known as the Smith-Hughes Act of 1917, promoted education in agriculture and the trades and industries by providing funds to improve salaries and teacher preparation in agriculture and various vocational subjects, including home economics. Georgia representatives Hoke Smith and Dudley Hughes proposed this legislation.

After 1917, state and national government agencies cooperated to ensure that teachers of agriculture, home economics, and other vocational subjects at the secondary level met regularly with experts to discuss the latest subject matter and pedagogy. Leaders of each state's Extension Service or faculty at each state's land-grant institution provided leadership to further Smith-Hughes Act goals.

Organizations to support teachers as well as students began. The Future Farmers of Virginia provided a model for a national organization, the Future Farmers of America, which emerged out of the third annual meeting of the National Congress of Vocational Agricultural Students in 1927, but this special interest group was segregated. African American youth and teachers organized similar clubs, and state organizations existed across the South, such as the New Farmers of Virginia. The first sectional meeting of such clubs occurred at Virginia State University in 1927. By 1931 Dr. H. O. Sargent, the federal agent for agricultural education for African Americans, employed by the U.S. Office of Education, helped formalize a national organization, the New Farmers of America. It held its first meeting at Tuskegee Institute in 1935. In 1965 the New Farmers of America merged with the Future Farmers of America, and in 1988 the organization changed its name to the National Future Farmers of America Organization (NFFAO).

During the era of the Cold War, agricultural education took on new meaning beyond the South. The Point Four program emerged as an international relief effort undertaken by the U.S. Department of State. President Harry S. Truman introduced the idea as the fourth point in his inauguration address on 20 January 1949. He indicated that the United States must boldly provide technical assistance to poor people in "underdeveloped areas" who suffer because of "primitive and stagnant" economies. By doing so, experts in agricultural methods gained new educational outlets, and southern universities became involved in national defense efforts. Specifically, if Americans could improve the life for foreigners, those same foreigners might look more favorably on democracy rather than communism as a political philosophy. White as well as African American extension agents and vocational agriculture teachers served two-year stints as technical experts. African Americans often found themselves in places such as Liberia, where they tried to raise the nation's standard of living and develop its economic resources. White participants were often stationed in the Middle East or India.

The U.S. Department of Agriculture's Office of Foreign Agricultural Relations (OFAR), reconstituted from its foreign relations branch during the late 1930s, extended scientific agriculture and technical assistance to "friends from (and within) foreign lands." In 1949 the OFAR launched an effort to adapt the extension model of education in countries around the world. In the process, southern land-grant universities moved into the realm of foreign agricultural education, but competition among white and black land-grant institutions erupted over which schools worked in which places on which projects. Prairie View A&M University, Texas's traditionally black land-grant institution, worked through this program to rehabilitate the Booker T. Washington Industrial Institute in Kakata, Liberia, founded by James L. Sibley, a reformer who had also introduced the Jeanes system of teacher enrichment to Liberia. In addition to modernizing the institute's physical plant, technical assistants helped educate Liberians to assume faculty positions there. The undertaking generated increased support for agricultural education at Prairie View A&M, afforded an international work experience for selected staff, and provided an opportunity for African American extension agents and technical experts to apply their goals of racial uplift to the African continent.

In the early 21st century, as the numbers of farmers decline steadily, the interest in agricultural education remains steady, largely because of the expansion of interest in urban as well as rural employment in agribusiness. The NFFAO remains active in junior high and high schools, and the students involved include both genders and reflect the ethnic and racial population of the schools. Land-grant institutions remain the primary purveyors of both higher agricultural education and agricultural extension education. Topics covered in university curricula and through county and state extension offices appeal to a wide range of future agriculture teachers, organic farmers, market gardeners, stock and crop farmers, and agribusiness interests. This reflects the diversity of agriculture and farmers' approaches in a region known historically for cash-crop production and, today, for modern agribusiness and megafarming.

DEBRA A. REID
*Eastern Illinois University*

Debra A. Reid, *Reaping a Greater Harvest: African Americans, the Extension Service, and Rural Reform in Jim Crow Texas* (2007); Theodore Saloutos, *Farmer Movements in the South, 1865–1933* (1960); Elizabeth Sanders, *Roots of Reform: Farmers, Workers, and the American State, 1877–1917* (1999).

## Colonial Farming

Agriculture thoroughly dominated the economy of the southern mainland colonies of British America. More than 90 percent of the workforce labored in agriculture, with the majority of families living on farms. The practices of colonial farmers, especially those of the South, often earned the scorn of contemporary observers, portraying them as slovenly and wasteful farmers who abused the land, neglected their livestock, accepted low yields and small incomes, used primitive tools, and resisted innovation, preferring to follow traditional practices. Recent historians have challenged that view, claiming that the denigration of colonial agriculture was often based on inappropriate comparisons with European farmers, who faced much different conditions, and noting the impressive accomplishments of colonial farmers. Perhaps the most impressive of these accomplishments was the creation of what has been called a "mestizo" agriculture that brought together crops and farming techniques from Europe, Africa, and America to produce a new system of husbandry more productive than any of its sources.

One of the most striking characteristics of agriculture in the colonial South was its diversity. The plantation districts of the coastal South, where slaves, often working on units with as many as 100 laborers, produced rice, indigo, and tobacco for export to Europe, differed sharply from the southern backcountry, where small owner-operated family farms produced a diverse range of products for their own subsistence and small surpluses for export or sale in local markets.

Even the plantation South was far from homogenous, as different principal crops with differing labor and capital requirements led to sharply differing agricultural practices and contrasting social systems and cultures. In the Lower South (the coastal districts of Georgia and South Carolina), the major export crops were rice and indigo, plantations were large, planters were wealthy, and a majority of the population was enslaved. In the Upper South colonies of Maryland and Virginia around Chesapeake Bay, where tobacco was the main crop, plantations were smaller (indeed, much of the tobacco exported from the region was grown on family farms), planters were less rich, and the slave presence, while still large, was less overwhelming.

Another source of diversity in southern agriculture, and a topic much debated by historians, was the degree to which farmers produced surpluses for the market or concentrated on production for their own use, a distinction that tended to reinforce the plantation-farm dichotomy. Recently, historians have questioned this dichotomy, arguing that most agriculturalists ran composite operations, producing both for their own use and for the market.

Despite its diversity, southern colonial agriculture did share several common characteristics that bound it together and distinguished it from farming elsewhere in the Early Modern world. Perhaps most important was its relatively high productivity and the high incomes it generated for farm residents, especially in the 18th century, when real farm prices rose steadily as the terms of trade shifted in favor of agriculture. The high productivity and incomes generated by colonial agriculture had several sources, including the creativity of colonial farmers, evident in the mestizo systems they created; the abundance and fertility of the land; and the hard work of farm families, including farm wives, who often helped in the fields, did dairying, and kept gardens, all while performing all the indoor work usually associated with women. Because of the lucrative nature of colonial agriculture, the free population in the rural colonial South lived well by Early Modern standards, as is evident in their diet and material culture.

Although the uneven distribution of slaves contributed to the diversity of southern agriculture, it also helped bind it together. In the 17th century, when the slave population was relatively small and slave owning largely confined to wealthy, elite planters, slavery was primarily a source of diversity. In fact, the ownership of slaves was probably the most important difference between the agricultural elite (the gentry) and the majority of ordinary farmers. By the late 18th century, slavery's role had changed as a result of the vast expansion of the slave population, and slavery had become more of a unifying factor than a source of diversity. In the 1770s in the Upper South, roughly 75 percent of the households headed by white men contained slaves, a figure that approached 90 percent in the Lower South. The proportion of households with slaves was lower in the backcountry, but even there the share of households with slaves often approached 50 percent, while those who did not yet own slaves could, if they judged by the experience of their neighbors, expect to acquire one in the not-so-distant future. Thus, as the colonial period wore on, slavery became an increasingly common characteristic, one of the ways in which southern farming differed from agriculture in the rest of the world. Nowhere was the ownership of slaves so widespread as in the colonial South.

Two of the distinguishing aspects of southern agriculture—its high productivity and mestizo character—are especially evident in the plantation districts. The inventiveness and mestizo style of southern agriculturalists, which led to steady improvements in productivity and relatively large incomes, are evident in the price and production histories of rice and tobacco, the major plantation crops of the colonial era. Both crops exhibited an inverse relationship between price and production as prices tumbled and exports rose. Planters complained that the restrictions of English mercantilism caused the price decline, but their complaints obscure a more complex and interesting process in which planters improved production techniques, captured productivity gains, and passed the savings on to consumers in the form of lower prices. Lower prices drove the expansion of the industries by making rice and tobacco affordable to a growing share of the English population. In the Chesapeake tobacco industry, the productivity gains seem to have flowed from the gradual development of the "Chesapeake system of husbandry," a method of farming that blended European, African, and Native American farming techniques with methods worked out locally as farmers "learned by doing." Chesapeake planters created a highly productive system of agriculture, a labor-saving, long-fallow farming style with a 20-year field rotation using simple tools to grow tobacco and corn, while cattle and hogs were allowed to range freely in the still sparsely populated colonies.

Further south, in the coastal rice-growing districts, one finds a markedly different but equally innovative style of farming, this one blending African and European techniques to create a unique system of agriculture that provided the basis for the richest region in North America. Planters in the Lower South seem to have been especially experimental and innovative. "The culture of rice in South Carolina," David Ramsey noted in 1809, "was in a state of constant improvement," as planters developed new methods of irrigation, grew new varieties better suited to the local environment, and steadily improved the rice-cleaning process. This creativity reflected the mestizo character of Lowcountry agriculture and rested on the skills of slaves. Indeed, it has been argued that Africans introduced the technology of rice cultivation to the Lowcountry and that planters sought (and paid premium prices for) slaves from ethnic groups familiar with the crop. While the notion that the arrival of Africans is the key to understanding the rise of the rice industry seems insufficiently attentive to the role of European demand, Africans did bring important technical skills across the Atlantic, and the skills and knowledge of slaves were crucial to the success of the plantation colonies. This may have been particularly true with rice. The crop was grown in West Africa under a variety of conditions and by different techniques. Further, the Lowcountry task system placed major responsibilities for the organization of work in the hands of slaves while offering them incentives to work more efficiently.

As the history of rice suggests, the relationship between skills acquired in Africa and the work done by slaves in the Americas was important to the success of plantation agriculture. This issue has been most thoroughly developed in the rice industry, but it also has been studied in the case of livestock and tobacco. One hopes that as recognition of this fact spreads, references to newly arrived Africans as unskilled workers will disappear from the literature.

The inventive, mestizo character of southern agriculture that developed during the colonial period persisted into the 19th century. This is evident in the history of cotton, which would become the South's major 19th-century crop. While one cannot claim that the cotton boom was a clear example of the blending of agricultural techniques, aspects of the boom are understandable when we remember that it was the creation of farmers raised in a blended tradition in which it was common to borrow from and combine different styles to develop a technology appropriate to a new environment. The rise of both Sea Island and Upland cotton involved experimentation with varieties grown in different parts of the world in a search for one that would flourish in the particular environment of the Lower South. Once they found the appropriate variety, upland farmers applied to the new crop the methods they used to grow tobacco and grain. Thus, cotton was topped, suckered, and planted in hills, pre-Columbian style, and tobacco presses were used to create compact bales, while farmers pressured the legislature to adopt the inspection systems developed for tobacco to ensure the quality and reputation of the new crop. Eli Whitney's cotton gin is itself a good example of a blended, mestizo technology, as it combined an East India charka with English hackles. The success of the blended approach and the creativity of southern agriculture is evident in cotton's price and production history, which, in its early years, echoed that of rice and tobacco as improved productivity permitted planters to lower prices while improving quality, thus expanding the market for their crop.

RUSSELL R. MENARD
*University of Minnesota*

Judith A. Carney, *Black Rice: The African Origins of Rice Cultivation in the Americas* (2001); Lois Green Carr and Lorena S. Walsh, *Robert Cole's World: Agriculture and*

Society in Early Maryland (1991); Joyce E. Chaplin, *An Anxious Pursuit: Agricultural Innovation and Modernity in the Lower South, 1730–1815* (1993); Stanley L. Engerman and Robert E. Gallman, eds., *The Cambridge Economic History of the United States*, vol. 1, *The Colonial Era* (1996); Lewis C. Gray, *The History of Agriculture in the Southern United States to 1860* (1933); Cathy Matson, ed., *The Economy of Early America: Historical Perspectives and New Directions* (2006); John J. McCusker and Russell R. Menard, *The Economy of British America, 1607–1789* (1991).

## Consumption and Consumers

Consumption came to the rural South with the earliest Europeans. As colonists founded trading posts and settlements, they initiated a lively trade with Native Americans. In the 17th and 18th centuries, Indians exchanged beaver, otter, and fox furs and deerskins for a variety of manufactured tools, ammunition, clothing, household goods, and novelties offered by whites. As historian James Axtell has observed, consumption among Native Americans, like that of Europeans, grew out of new tastes and new aesthetic preferences as well as need. Native peoples quickly incorporated European trade goods into their daily lives. They found metal tools and weapons more durable and effective than those made of stone, bone, and wood. Iron pots lasted longer and often cooked more evenly than clay pots. Woven cloth was easier to fashion into clothing than deerskin, and it remained soft and pliable even when wet, meaning that it could be laundered. Alcohol and trinkets such as beads and mirrors may have been less beneficial, but they were in no less demand. Most of all, guns and gunpowder enabled the Indians to hunt ever larger quantities of game, which in turn allowed them to purchase still more trade goods.

European settlers, too, were consumers. By the early 18th century, many white colonists—particularly those of the prosperous middling economic ranks—eagerly acquired luxurious cloth and clothing, elegant furniture, fine china, silverware, and bedding. They used these items to improve the conditions of daily life and to entertain themselves, but also as conspicuous demonstrations of wealth and status.

Consumption could lead to debt, a perennial problem plaguing southern farmers. In colonial times, tobacco planters found that their tastes for manufactured goods, combined with low tobacco prices, often left them deeply indebted. They developed a collective consciousness of the way that debt threatened their autonomy, and historian T. H. Breen has shown how planters developed a critique of debt "slavery," which they blamed on ruthless British merchants and unfair imperial policies. Believing that the British government and its merchants were conspiring to render them dependent through debt, planters turned to the Revolutionary movement. Consumption not only led to calls for reform, but it also provided the revolutionary generation with a political tool. Rural southerners joined their brethren elsewhere in the nation in boycotting British goods—in withholding consumption—in order to bring pressure for political change.

After independence was assured, rural southerners continued to consume to whatever extent their economic position would allow. Access to consumer goods and attitudes about consumption varied by race, class, and even gender for the next 200 years. Wealthy planters of rice, cotton, sugar, and tobacco imported luxury goods such as pianos, carriages, and finely tailored clothing through the factors who marketed their crops. They also traveled to American and European cities for shopping sprees. They embraced consumption as a way to display wealth. By contrast, small farmers linked consumption with debt, and they sought to limit their purchases of manufactured goods. Unable to import goods or travel to distant cities to shop, they were limited to the items available in local general stores, and they often restricted their purchases to bare necessities. Yeomen farmers often characterized a taste for consumer goods as the product of weakness.

Even slaves participated in the antebellum consumer economy. Many slave owners encouraged slaves to earn small amounts of money by selling products from their own garden plots or doing skilled wage labor after they finished the day's work for the master. Slaves used their earnings to buy tobacco products, household goods, fashionable sewing notions, and even clothing from peddlers and general stores. Planters characterized slaves as wasteful consumers who threw away money purchasing gaudy luxury items, but they encouraged slaves to continue buying goods, both to reinforce the planters' own sense of superiority over foolish enslaved consumers and to make slaves more content with their lot.

The Civil War disrupted consumption patterns all over the South, and the rebuilding of the consumer economy took place in fits and starts. In the late 19th century, wealthy rural people continued to travel to the region's larger cities to acquire manufactured goods, but the average rural southerner shopped at general stores near home. By century's end, railroads had pushed into most corners of the South, bringing relatively easy access to consumer goods with them. Most rural railroad stops and many dusty crossroads were home to one or more country stores, where farm people came to buy canned goods, fresh fruit and vegetables, newspapers and magazines, farm machinery and tools, seeds, nails, candy, toys, tobacco products, shoes, cloth and clothing, and even luxuries like musical instruments. Most stores took farm-produced goods such as eggs and garden produce in exchange for these goods or extended credit until harvest time. Many country stores also served as furnishing merchants, advancing credit to sharecroppers in exchange for a crop lien. Croppers found that this credit came with a price, as many merchants charged exorbitant prices, imposed high interest rates, and attempted to control their purchases. Country-store merchants often accumulated large fortunes, and they wielded considerable power in rural communities.

Country stores were the province of white farm men, who saw them as sites for recreation. There, they played cards and checkers, told stories and off-color jokes, drank alcohol, and discussed politics. Women rarely felt comfortable in such rough environments and visited country stores only occasionally. As a result, men usually did the family shopping, presenting the storekeeper with a spoken or written list that the merchant gathered from shelves behind the counter. At this point, stores owners paid little attention to creating inviting displays of consumer goods. African Americans patronized country stores, but they were often treated disrespectfully and were ignored until all the white customers in the establishment had been accommodated. As a result of poor treatment and their fear of debt, African Americans limited their patronage of country stores.

Instead, African Americans and white women preferred to buy from itinerant peddlers, who brought goods directly to their doors. These merchants, often Jewish or Lebanese immigrants who later established retail establishments in the South's small towns, traveled by foot, horse, or mule and wagon throughout the countryside. They sold cloth and sewing notions, kitchen utensils, nails, mason jars, harnesses, candy, canned goods, staples such as coffee and salt, and other items. Like the owners of country stores, they accepted eggs, chickens, cured meat, home-canned vegetables, or other farm products as payment. Peddlers offered sharecroppers and African Americans alternatives to the country store, where purchases were carefully monitored, and they offered women the opportunity to shop in a comfortable environment.

The arrival of rural free delivery made mail order accessible to rural southerners by the early 20th century, and many eagerly embraced the autonomy and anonymity offered by this new retail outlet. South Carolinian Mamie Garvin Fields, an African American, wrote, "Some of them did think colored people oughtn't to have a certain nice thing, even if they had enough money to buy it. Our people used to send off for certain items." Sears, Roebuck and Co. and Montgomery Ward catalogs became ubiquitous in rural households.

By the 1920s and 1930s, several factors transformed consumption patterns in the rural South. Inspired in part by a desire to buy consumer goods and in part by better wages, many rural southerners sought cash incomes in the textile mills, lumber and mining camps, tobacco and furniture factories, and steel mills of the New South. At the same time, the automobile enabled rural southerners to travel greater distances for shopping. In the South's small towns, new types of retail establishments such as five-and-dime stores, department stores, and ready-to-wear clothing shops provided access to a wider variety of goods that were displayed in appealing ways. Grocery-store chains such as the Mississippi-based Jitney Jungle (founded in 1919) and Piggly Wiggly (founded in Memphis in 1916) offered shoppers a dazzling array of fresh and preserved foods. Unlike the South's general stores, grocery stores were self-service, allowing customers to make their own selections. These stores, while usually demanding that customers pay cash for goods, also did not attempt to control the purchases of sharecroppers. They also were spaces in which women felt comfortable. Finally, many of these stores implemented installment plans that enabled customers to acquire goods on credit but outside of the crop-lien system. Debt lost its power to create dependency for many rural southerners. The result of all these changes was an increasing southern fascination with consumption. For some, the preoccupation with buying things was a threat; for others, it was a source of liberation or a new identity; but either way, consumption rapidly became central to southern life and culture.

Rural consumers adapted new products for their own uses. For example, many farm families used their automobile motors to power milking machines and washers as well as cars. They purchased labor-saving household appliances and farm equipment that lightened the daily workload. Hot water heaters, gas and later electric stoves, water pumps, and lighting systems were particularly popular with rural consumers. One Tennessee farm woman told an interviewer, "The first thing I bought [that used electricity] was a stove, which I loved. I was ready to give up on that wood stove." Communication devices like the radio and telephone were also popular because they reduced rural isolation.

The prevalence of motor vehicles also created a new outlet for itinerant merchants. Rolling stores—trucks that carried goods from small-town stores to the countryside—appeared in the early decades of the 20th century. These rolling stores traveled regular weekly routes as peddlers had done, and they offered a wide variety of manufactured goods to rural housewives. Door-to-door salesmen also marketed their wares to farm households. Two well-known rolling stores were the W. T. Rawleigh Company of Illinois and the J. R. Watkins Company of Minnesota. Both carried spices and flavorings, salves, medicines, tonics, and toiletries. Itinerant merchants brought news of the outside world as well as manufactured goods to rural customers.

Change accelerated in the middle decades of the 20th century, bringing with it new patterns in southern consumption. During and after World War II, tens of thousands of southerners abandoned the risks of farming for the regular paychecks offered by off-farm jobs in the manufacturing and service sectors. Many of those who continued to cultivate the land turned to capital-intensive specialized farming, gradually reducing or even eliminating their production of food for home use. Farm wives continued to sew much of the family's wardrobe, but they also purchased ready-to-wear items. Increasingly, farm families became consumers instead of producers, a shift marked by the U.S. Department of Agriculture (USDA) in its 1965 *Yearbook of Agriculture*. The annual report was entitled *Consumers All*, and the cover featured a line drawing of a trim home, which could have come straight out of suburbia, and a family—presumably a farm family—indistinguishable from their urban counterparts. The volume featured articles by USDA experts providing farm families with advise on making wise consumer decisions.

Many African Americans came to see restrictions on their consumption as another way of denying them economic justice. Civil rights activists demanded access to jobs in retail stores, respectful treatment from clerks and store owners, and equal access to all services in stores and restaurants; in short, they defined consumption as one form of freedom, freedom to shop and to spend just as white people did. Activists used boycotts as one political tool for achieving these demands, and boycotts indeed damaged the economic health of many southern towns and cities. White merchants fought back by trying to outlaw boycotts, insisting on their freedom to employ whomever they pleased and to control the conditions under which they conducted business.

Meanwhile, rural depopulation in the 1950s, 1960s, and 1970s brought the decline of many small-town and country stores around the South. Instead people began to shop in K-Mart, Woolworth's, Jitney Jungle, and other chain stores that began to dot downtowns and the outskirts of cities and towns. Wal-Mart moved en masse into most areas of the rural South in the 1980s, providing access to a wide array of consumer goods at low prices. Wal-Mart and other so-called big box retailers are criticized for destroying small, locally owned businesses, which they often have, but the stores also provide rural consumers with easy access to low-cost goods. These stores have another appeal. As historian Ted Ownby puts it, "If general stores in the nineteenth century and plantation stores . . . [in] the twentieth century reinforced status differences simply through people's places in the process of shipping, stores such as Wal-Mart emphasize that all customers have the same experiences." They are democratic in their treatment of all customers, black and white, rich and poor, male and female.

At the beginning of the 21st century, most southerners do more consuming than producing. New technology continues to revolutionize the way rural consumers do their shopping. Internet shopping allows country people to enjoy a wide array of products from around the world. Antique and collectible shoppers in remote corners of the South patronize online auction sites such as eBay, enjoying the same access to goods as their urban counterparts. Today, southerners' access to consumer goods is limited only by the size of their bank accounts.

MELISSA WALKER
*Converse College*

Lewis E. Atherton, *The Southern Country Store, 1800–1860* (1949); James Axtell, *Natives and Newcomers: The Cultural Origins of North America* (2001); Edward L. Ayers, *Southern Crossing: A History of the American South, 1877–1906* (1995); T. H. Breen, *Tobacco Culture: The Mentality of the Great Tidewater Planters on the Eve of Revolution* (1985), *The Marketplace of Revolution: How Consumer Politics Shaped American Independence* (2004); Thomas D. Clark, *Pills, Petticoats, and Plows: The Southern Country Store* (1944); Lu Ann Jones, *Mama Learned Us to Work: Farm Women in the New South* (2002); Ronald R. Kline, *Consumers in the Country: Technology and Social Change in Rural America* (2000); Ted Ownby, *American Dreams in Mississippi: Consumers, Poverty, and Culture, 1830–1998* (1999); Betty Wood, *Women's Work, Men's Work: The Informal Slave Economies of Lowcountry Georgia* (1995).

## Country Stores

From 1865 to 1930, no institution influenced the South's economy, politics, and daily life of its people more than the country store. Hundreds, maybe thousands of these stores were scattered throughout the region.

The history of the southern country store begins with the merchant. He was initially an outsider who brought a cost-accounting mentality and objectivity believed to be somewhat foreign to the people among whom he settled. In the post–Civil War South, he created ways of exchanging goods and services with a minimum of cash, for in those times few people had much cash. The storekeeper had to connect with northern and western manufacturers in order to stock his store with goods. The connection ran from alleged Wall Street moneyed interests through the meat packers, fertilizer manufacturers, wholesale houses, and feed, grain, and cotton speculators down to the local country-store merchant.

Merchants always existed in the South, but their rise to power came after the Civil War. The storekeeper's fate was linked with that of both whites and blacks. Before the war, the slave's needs had been at least minimally met by his owner, the planter, and his labor was coerced, but after 1865 this system of control was ended. Freedom, however, did not bring financial security, and destitute blacks and many poor whites were forced to find food from any source and under any conditions. By means of "stomach discipline," through the medium of the commissary on the plantation and the store at the crossroads, it was possible to acquire an effective leverage over black and white labor. The commissary and the store were both political and economic institutions.

One aspect of the legal machinery by which the merchants operated was the strict application of lien laws enacted by state legislatures. The liens were crop liens or mortgages not only on land, as was generally true before the Civil War, but also on livestock and "all growing crops." But often the crops were not "growing"; liens might be placed on them even before they were planted. These laws originally were designed to give planters security for food and other supplies that they furnished their freed black tenants and sharecroppers, whom they were no longer required to support as slaves. But the laws were quickly used by merchants as well as planters. The lien system meant that the purchaser of a crop, usually cotton, was established at the beginning of the crop year, and often the purchaser came to be the local merchant.

In the post–Civil War period, credit was a critical problem throughout the South. Because only a few farmers could borrow money from a bank—if, indeed, there was a bank in the community—and because of the low value of land, the lien laws made it possible for a merchant to offer credit in small amounts to the hundreds of locals needing it. The system created an interdependence between the storekeeper and both the landed and landless black and white farmers and tenants of the area served by his store. The credit often took the form of coupon books, which were valid for trade only at his store, thus effectively restricting business competition. In addition to his monopoly over trade, the merchant charged interest on credit that sometimes ranged as high as 40 percent. On commissary accounts, planters often charged as much, if not more. Many merchants accumulated large fortunes, but there were great risks involved in merchandising at the crossroads. Merchants had financial obligations to their suppliers, and there were losses incident to weather, depression, crop failures, and overextended credit. When rumors spread that crops were not doing well, merchants often sent out inspectors or went out themselves to the farms to ascertain if their fears were warranted.

Country stores could be found throughout the United States, and their counterparts existed in other parts of the world. In the South, in addition to the "furnish" system incident to the lien laws, country stores played a central role in the social organization of most communities outside the mountain areas. They appear to have been the chief community organizer and builder, particularly in the old plantation and biracial areas, for a significant period of time after the Civil War.

Every village and town in any region requires some specific institution that attracts, in the words of sociologist Everett C. Hughes, "a configuration of other institutions about them so that they create a community of a certain kind." Population clusters from hamlets to cities have grown up around fortresses, castles, cathedrals, cabildos, and monasteries. A study of such central community institutions might well lead through the marketplace of the Greek city, the forum of republican Rome, the salons of Paris, the coffeehouses and alehouses of old London, the churches of New England, and the schools of the Midwest.

After the Civil War, a new series of population concentrations appeared in the South, necessitating new community organizations. Here and there, a county courthouse generated a town of lawyers and county officials around it. The southern county seems to have been almost as much a social as a governmental unit. Other communities sometimes emerged around a church, a trading post, an academy, or an inn. Despite the small concentrations of population, in predominantly rural areas a fair number of country stores had been scattered across the South before the war, serving largely white farmers, but their numbers dramatically increased after the war. Towns that grew up around country stores sometimes took the name of the local storekeeper.

In the postbellum South, three factors interacted to thrust the country store into a position of much greater strength and significance than it had held in the antebellum South. The first was sheer geographic isolation. Roads were unbelievably poor; traveling five miles from the crossroads over dirt roads that were almost impassable in bad weather was a problem for every farmer and sharecropper with his mule and wagon. Not until the coming of the Ford automobile did roads improve much, although they produced much discussion and complaint. High railroad freight rates added to the isolation. The second factor was the dominance of cotton in the economy. A botanical annual, cotton so occupied the lives and plans of those on the land that it became in effect an institutional perennial, the crop traditionally, easily, and unskillfully produced, transported, stored, and marketed. Under the circumstances, to have shifted from one crop to another would have required much more credit from money-lending sources than most farmers had access to. The third factor was the bi-racial structure of a society steadily moving from the racial controls of the ante-bellum South to the segregation of the postwar era. Whites and blacks came to live in two different but complementary social worlds. It was a situation ripe for trade and for new marketplaces to emerge.

Trade dictates a certain kind of relationship for those involved in it, and this had significance for the biracial agricultural South, especially in the decades following the Civil War. Local churches were divided racially as well as denominationally, and they were used, ordinarily, only one day in the week. Schools were racially segregated and used only seasonally and for limited times during the day and the week. Courthouses were few and far between, and none of these played an important communitywide integrating role. So the full force of the community's population could and did focus on the country store, which was open for business every day except Sunday throughout the year. Blacks and whites in the postbellum South more nearly approached equality in the store than anywhere else—certainly more than in other social institutions, where Jim Crow laws and customs effectively separated the races. Blacks patronized the white store along with whites and often were at liberty to try on hats, garments, and shoes as they fancied. A white customer might spend time bantering with blacks or with whites of a lower class than himself at the store, although he would never think of inviting such people to his home. There was an air of familiarity and tolerance at the store that was rarely matched elsewhere.

The country store also played an important role in meeting daily needs. The store stocked a bewildering variety of items, such as hats, corsets, gloves, blouses, stockings, and cheap perfumes for women; blue jeans, overalls, brogans, broad-brimmed hats, and "pridarita" (Pride of Readsville) smoking tobacco for the men; peppermint candy and crackers for the children; and rat cheese (ched-dar) for all. Axle grease, lard, kerosene, and other pungent-smelling items gave a characteristic odor to the place. When someone was born, was married, or died, the store provided the items needed for these rituals of life and death. The country store was no orderly department store; its goods were not likely to be very systematically arranged and displayed. Almost everything was to be found behind something else.

The country store flourished in the days before the coming of modern brick-store civilization and provided a characteristic feature of the southern land-scape. The store was often a barnlike, wood-frame structure to which additions were made as trade expanded. A wing or shed added on one side might be used for machinery, tools, and other heavy items, along with kerosene for home lamps. A wing added on the other side stored seed, fertilizers, stock feed, horse collars, trace chains, and general hardware. A second floor above the main floor was often added. Here among the coffins and caskets, the local Masons and Woodmen of the World met on designated evenings. These were rural male fraternities; modern urban service and luncheon clubs, such as Rotary and Kiwanis, had not yet been established. An office at the rear of the building could be added for desks, account books, and a big iron safe. To this inner sanctum, sharecroppers and tenants, as well as small landowning farmers, were admitted one at a time to go over accounts, to make or receive payments, or to arrange credit against next year's crop. The "drummer," or traveling salesman, representing a jobbing house in Baltimore, Cincinnati, or St. Louis, met the store owner at least once a year to take his order for wholesale supplies. The drummer was much more than a salesman; he was a visitor from another world, bringing exciting news and opinion from the outside and a fund of racy stories sure to go the rounds and to be repeated many times until he came again.

After the invention of the telephone, the store often was the only place in the community that had one. The big colorful catalogs of Montgomery Ward and Sears, Roebuck and Co., both of which were national country stores or country-store extensions of sorts, were put to considerable use through the medium of the store. Frequently, the merchant himself mailed or telephoned orders for his customers. The telephone made it possible as never before to get in touch with people in Chicago or any other place in the United States. More important for local people was the opportunity to make quick contact with the local doctor, if there was one, and relatives of a sick member of the family.

In the absence of a local doctor or a drugstore and druggist, who often served as a doctor or medical adviser, the country store reaped much profit from the sale of patent medicines. After food, probably the greatest demand by the rural population was for medicine. Prescriptions came by way of wall, fence, tree, or local newspaper advertising or from the satisfactory experience of neighbors and fellow church members. Historian Thomas D. Clark once noted that the manufacturer of Plantation Bitters claimed an annual sale throughout the South of $5 million worth of the product. Lydia Pinkham's Vegetable Compound for Women made, as Clark puts it, "advanced matronhood a positive joy" and also provided a means of getting one's picture along with a testimonial in a newspaper or an advertising leaflet.

The store operated as a general gathering place every day except Sunday (and sometimes even then if a church service was being held there) and in all seasons of the year. Weather and seasonal conditions nurtured two characteristic scenes played in the country store as theater. One was a summer scene. On

Interior of a Reganton, Miss., country store, 1973 (William R. Ferris Collection, Southern Folklife Collection, Wilson Library, University of North Carolina at Chapel Hill)

the unpaved sidewalk in front, men gathered on a hot day to loaf, whittle, play checkers, or pitch horseshoes and to comment on the attractions of passing women. In the winter scene, men and boys and sometimes a few women sat around the potbellied stove swapping yarns, arguing politics or religion, and recounting details of farming operations. There was a philosophy present in the assumptions underlying this talk, which now might be called a "cracker-barrel philosophy." The weighty matters under discussion required a sawdust-filled box for the benefit of tobacco chewers. It was a spitting society; everyone spat, even snuff-dipping women, if any were present.

The country store with its southern flavor is still to be found here and there in rural, isolated areas. Certain old-fashioned items of merchandise may still be found there, but now its line of merchandise tends toward the convenience store. A gasoline pump is likely to be found out front, helping attract business from passing motorists. Candy no longer comes in by the barrel; candy bars and vending machines are now common. Cash sales have increased, for banks have taken away the crop-lien credit business. Loafers still gather there, consuming quantities of bottled drinks. Between growing towns and cities has come the decline of other towns, so that many places, bypassed by the superhighways, are reverting to the level of villages, and villages to the level of hamlets. In these villages and hamlets, something like the old-time country store tends to hang on, and this accounts for, possibly more than any other single institution except the school, the persistence of such villages and hamlets. In altered form, the general store appears to have lasted longer as a pioneer institution in the South than in any other part of the United States.

EDGAR T. THOMPSON
*Duke University*

Lewis E. Atherton, *The Southern Country Store, 1800–1860* (1949); Jacqueline P. Bull, *Journal of Southern History* (February 1952); Gerald Carson, *The Old Country Store* (1954); Thomas D. Clark, *Journal of Southern History* (February 1946), *Pills, Petticoats, and Plows: The Southern Country Store* (1944); Grace Elizabeth Hale, *Making White-ness: The Culture of Segregation in the South, 1890–1940* (1998); J. Evetts Haley, *Charles Schreiner: General Merchandise* (1945); Lu Ann Jones, *Mama Learned Us to Work: Farm Women in the New South* (2002); Ted Ownby, *American Dreams in Missis-sippi: Consumers, Poverty, and Culture, 1830–1998* (1999); Arthur F. Raper, *Preface to Peasantry: The Tale of Two Black Belt Counties* (1936); Francis Butler Simkins, *North Carolina Historical Review* (April 1930); T. S. Stribling, *The Store* (1932); Harold D. Woodman, *King Cotton and His Retainers: Financing and Marketing the Cotton Crop of the South, 1800–1925* (1968).

## Crops

Southern culture and commerce have been shaped by a basic dependence upon agricultural production. Cotton, tobacco, corn, peanuts, pumpkins, squash, beans, Irish potatoes, sweet potatoes, chili peppers, and tomatoes are crops indigenous to the United States and were cultivated by Indians and later by colonists in the southern states. These crops continue to be major food and fiber crops. Wheat, rice, indigo, and sugarcane were introduced by Europeans and have become major commercial crops. Seed grain crops, such as soybeans and hybrid sorghums, today surpass all other crops in total acreage and were generally developed in the modern era from European and African stock. Major southern crops now in cultivation, ranked by acreage in production, are soybeans, cotton, rice, tobacco, and sugarcane. Soybean acreage in recent decades has exceeded acreage in cotton twofold. In 2004 the states of Alabama, Arkansas, Georgia, Louisiana, Mississippi, North Carolina, South Carolina, and Tennessee produced 571 million tons of soybeans.

During the colonial era, tobacco, rice, and indigo comprised the major commercial crops. However, throughout the colonial and antebellum periods, acreage in corn exceeded that of any other single crop. Most corn never reached the marketplace; instead, it provided sustenance for farm families and their animals.

Tobacco was the most valuable colonial crop. John Rolfe of the Virginia colony successfully cultivated and cured a West Indian variety of tobacco, which he first shipped to a British market in 1613. Exports from Virginia rose from 20,000 pounds in 1618 to over 500,000 in 1627. By the 1630s overproduction caused a slump in tobacco prices from luxury levels to those of a general commodity. The tobacco market subsequently became a mass market. Exports reached 18 million pounds by 1860. Tobacco farming has historically involved smaller acreages and more intensive labor than other crops. Today, southern farm income from tobacco regularly exceeds $1 billion per year.

Commercial rice production began in South Carolina in about 1694, with seed imported from Madagascar. First planted in tidal marshes, rice was soon cultivated along inland river marshes. Cultivation by flooding from ponds and then from tidal rivers employing an ingenious system of locks and dams facilitated rising production within a well-defined coastal region of the Carolinas and Georgia. Antebellum rice production involved large investments in land, mills, and slaves. The Civil War marked the end of a flourishing rice culture in the Carolinas, after which rice cultivation shifted to the Mississippi Delta and the prairies of southwest Louisiana and Texas.

Rice farming became mechanized in the coastal prairies of Texas and Louisiana, where reapers, combines, tractors, hydraulic pumps, rail transportation, cheap land, and improved plant varieties combined to virtually revolutionize the industry. In the 20th century, rice growing expanded in Arkansas and Mississippi and developed in Tennessee and California. The 3 million acres of rice in cultivation in 1980 generated approximately $1.3 billion in farm income. Rice ranked sixth in farm value among all U.S. crops. Although the nation's rice production accounts for only 2 percent of the world total, American rice comprises one-third of the total world trade in rice.

Indigo was introduced into the Carolinas from the West Indies by Eliza Lucas in about 1739. Parliament exempted indigo from import duties and offered a price subsidy that remained in effect until 1777. The American Revolution and the introduction of chemical dyes terminated this once profitable industry. Wheat production was commercially significant before the Civil War, with Virginia the leading wheat producer of the southern states. Wheat production and milling continued on a limited basis in most southern states into the 20th century. Texas remains in the early 21st century one of the leading wheat producers in the United States.

Cotton became commercially significant after the development of Eli Whitney's gin in 1793. One thousand pounds of cotton were shipped to England in 1789 and 4.5 million bales in 1861. Cotton became synonymous with slavery and the plantation system. The plantation survived the Civil War with the sharecropping and crop-lien systems. Acreage in cotton continued to climb into the 1920s. In 1926 production peaked, with 44.5 million acres in cotton producing 18 million bales. Declining prices, depression, war, government farm programs, and alternative employment opportunities resulted in the rapid demise of the Cotton Kingdom. By the 1970s, acreage in cotton had declined to about 10 million acres yielding approximately 10 million bales annually, and much of that production was in the irrigated lands of the Southwest, outside the traditional Cotton Belt. In 2005 Texas alone produced almost a third of the South's cotton.

Corn has been a pervasive crop in the South since frontier days. A large portion of the nation's total corn crop is still grown and consumed on southern farms and in local markets. Commercial production increased appreciably between 1970 and 1980, when U.S. corn production doubled. Kentucky, Georgia, and Texas led in acreage planted in 1980, with the value of the Texas crop being $402 million, the Kentucky crop $347 million, and the Georgia crop $188 million. More recently, the per-acre price of corn has surpassed that of cotton, resulting in some cotton producers devoting increased acreage to corn.

Despite rapid declines in farm population in the South since World War II, production of most crops has actually increased through the application of scientific farming techniques. Food crops, predominantly those indigenous to the region, continue to be widely produced and consumed, and the expansion of international markets has recently created new opportunities for farmers in the South. Agriculture and the agrarian heritage continue to play a dominant role in the economic and cultural development of the region.

HENRY C. DETHLOFF
*Texas A&M University*

Charles Aiken, *The Cotton Plantation South since the Civil War* (1998); Stuart Bruchey, *Cotton and the Growth of the American Economy* (1967); Pete Daniel, *Breaking the Land: The Transformation of Cotton, Tobacco, and Rice Culture since 1880* (1985); Gilbert C. Fite, *American Farmers: The New Minority* (1981); Deborah Fitzgerald, *Every Farm a Factory: The Industrial Ideal in American Agriculture* (2003);

Paul W. Gates, *The Farmer's Age: Agriculture, 1815–1860* (1960); Duncan C. Heyward, *Seed from Madagascar* (1937); Sam B. Hilliard, *Hog Meat and Hoecake: Food Supply in the Old South, 1840–1860* (1972); Joseph C. Robert, *The Story of Tobacco in America* (1949); John T. Schlebecker, *Whereby We Thrive: A History of American Farming, 1607–1972* (1975); Fred A. Shannon, *The Farmer's Last Frontier: Agriculture, 1860–1897* (1945); J. Carlyle Sitterson, *Sugar Country: The Cane Sugar Industry in the South, 1753–1950* (1953); James H. Street, *New Revolution in the Cotton Economy: Mechanization and Its Consequences* (1967).

## Diversification

The history of the American South has been inextricably bound to the agricultural development of the region. In spite of growing industrialization, especially since World War II, the land and the farmer have consistently remained among the most influential forces in the shaping of the southern economic, political, and cultural heritage. Almost as pervasive, too, has been the unceasing call for diversification of agricultural activities—a call whose limited success also reveals a significant characteristic of the southern farmer.

Prior to the Civil War, small, family-owned farms most often typified southern agriculture. These subsistence units were diversified and self-sufficient, producing corn, wheat, dairy products, fruits, sweet potatoes, and livestock. This diversification stemmed mainly from necessity, not from any consciously well-planned effort. Southern farmers toiled long hours to produce what they needed to survive, frequently growing small amounts of the already important cash crops—tobacco and cotton—to supplement their limited incomes. They were, however, generally unaware of (or ignored) calls by agrarian leaders to practice more progressive farming methods. Instead, through trial and error, they developed their own farming system—often employing backward methods—which soon became ingrained and handed down from generation to generation. This system proved difficult to change. Faced with both limited leisure and money, these modest landholders found their cultural opportunities restricted to a basic level, far different from those available to the planter class. They enjoyed quilting bees, corn huskings, family reunions, church events, and traditional folk music sometimes provided by a fiddler. These activities reflected their strong devotion to family, religion, and the land. They were proud, independent, and self-reliant but lacking in opportunities to learn about more progressive farming methods then being introduced in the 1840s elsewhere in the nation, especially in the North.

Tobacco plantations, with their accompanying slave labor, were self-sufficient in the 17th- and 18th-century South, and the large 19th-century to-bacco and cotton plantations primarily remained so. A growing emphasis upon producing more and more of the cash crops, however, proved a detriment to the land and to efforts for diversification. Both farsighted southern agrarian leaders and regional farm publications warned repeatedly of the dangers to the soil and to the overall development of the South in becoming dependent upon cash crops. Such prominent 19th-century agricultural spokesmen as Edmund Ruffin and John Taylor of Virginia, Dr. Martin W. Phillips of South Carolina, and George W. Jeffreys of North Carolina urged the growing of grain crops, the adoption of fertilizers, the raising of livestock, and other progressive meth-ods to stop the depletion of the southern soil. At the same time, the *Southern Cultivator* of Augusta, Ga., expressed the concern of many agrarian journals in contrasting the exhausted soil, inefficient methods of production, and gen-eral decay of southern farms to the more productive soils, higher land values, and diversification of northern farms. Southern agricultural fairs and societies reiterated that message. Some plantations, especially those in Maryland and Virginia, did move to wheat and cattle production, but only because tobacco could no longer be economically produced there. Plantation owners generally refused to adopt newer agrarian methods and thereby helped instill a resistance to change that was a portent of darker days for southern farming.

The Civil War and Reconstruction left most southern farmers, black and white, without the capital necessary for economic independence. To secure credit for equipment, food, seed, and other necessities, they pledged in advance to landowners and merchants part of the crops they helped produce. A crop-lien system evolved, with its accompanying tenant and sharecropping farmers, and dominated the South until the 1930s. It marked the nadir of southern agricul-ture. As decades passed, more and more farmers slipped into the sharecropper-tenant class, and destitution dogged their every step. Southern agrarian spokes-men pointed out the obvious: the agricultural system devastated the people and the region. But farmers could do little to change conditions. They lacked, most importantly, the capital to institute basic changes necessary to alleviate their oppression. Because of inadequate or nonexistent schools, illiteracy spread, and health conditions deteriorated as balanced diets became as rare as balanced agricultural practices. Stubborn farmers further exacerbated conditions by using backward methods handed down from previous generations. Sometimes they spoke out against their plight. Organizations and political parties, includ-ing the Farmers' Alliance and the Populists, advocated ideas such as agricul-tural cooperatives where farmers would control production and pricing. Lack-ing capital and effective leadership, farmers failed to effect changes.

The 20th century witnessed a continuation of these deplorable conditions. Many vigorous attempts to end sharecropping and tenant farming occurred: experiment stations set up by land-grant colleges introduced new farming methods; farm journals such as Clarence H. Poe's *Progressive Farmer* constantly stressed the benefits of diversified plant and animal production; Dr. Seaman A. Knapp did yeoman's work by going directly to poor farmers and demonstrating progressive, scientific methods; fairs, agricultural societies, and cooperative extension programs proposed new ways to confront old problems; and the U.S. Department of Agriculture blanketed the South with free literature and spokesmen urging diversification. But all of these efforts failed. Conditions remained strikingly similar to those of the 1880s, and southern farmers of the 1920s were the poorest group in the nation. Not surprisingly, their cultural pursuits reflected their meager circumstances and consisted of whatever they could create or imagine in their poor surroundings. Self-trained musicians provided accompaniment to homegrown songs that described the plight of the people, and the ever-present church and its strong message of eventual salvation provided solace against the bleak economic horizon. Ironically, the southern farmer's inability to change was paralleled by a strange but bountiful crop of writers. William Faulkner, Erskine Caldwell, Robert Penn Warren, Flannery O'Connor, Eudora Welty, and others graphically portrayed the farmers' destitution and in so doing established careers that led to international literary acclaim. A region that wore out both soil and soul was home to one of the greatest literary blossomings in America.

The Great Depression of the 1930s, along with World War II in the 1940s, ended the crippling economic system that had characterized southern farming since Reconstruction. The federal government, through New Deal enactments—especially the Agricultural Adjustment Act—accomplished crop reduction by paying landowning farmers to restrict their production. These federal payments provided the capital that had been so lacking for decades, and farmers began the slow, steady process of adopting many of the progressive, scientific measures proposed throughout the region's history. World War II and its aftermath witnessed millions of poor farmers leaving the region for better economic opportunities elsewhere in the nation. The events of the 1930s and 1940s effectively eliminated from southern agriculture the small, family farmer who for centuries had played an overwhelmingly important role in the region.

A true revolution became apparent in the region after 1945: farmers acquired larger tracts of land, tractor power replaced animal muscle, livestock production increased dramatically, new crops such as soybeans and peanuts grew where cotton once had grown, and scientific farming became accepted and necessary for survival in the new environment. Rising farm incomes provided a better way of life and decent housing; schools and health facilities now became available to southern farmers. Outside forces finally reshaped the southern farmer into the modern agricultural producer long yearned for by agrarian leaders. A decline in federal government price-support payments since the 1980s, fluctuating market prices, and the opening of new global markets resulted in continuing farm diversification in the South.

Diversification came to the South only after all internal attempts failed. This development helps underscore the South's reluctance to change and its tendency to continue with older, more conservative ways, even in the face of viable alternatives. For those farmers who survived the incredible decades of destitution to arrive at a new, better level of life, the most constant of all cultural heritages—the love of the land—still endured.

JOSEPH A. COTÉ
*University of Georgia Library*

Charles Aiken, *The Cotton Plantation South since the Civil War* (1998); Joyce E. Chaplain, *An Anxious Pursuit: Agricultural Innovation and Modernity in the Lower South, 1730–1815* (1993); Peter A. Coclanis, *The Shadow of a Dream: Economic Life and Death in the South Carolina Low Country, 1670–1920* (1989); Gilbert C. Fite, *Agricultural History* (January 1979), *Cotton Fields No More: Southern Agriculture, 1865–1980* (1984); Deborah Fitzgerald, *Every Farm a Factory: The Industrial Ideal in American Agriculture* (2003); Lewis C. Gray, *History of Agriculture in the Southern United States to 1860*, 2 vols. (1933); Clarence Hamilton Poe Papers, North Carolina Department of Archives and History, Raleigh; Gavin Wright, *The Political Economy of the Cotton South: Households, Markets, and Wealth in the Nineteenth Century* (1978).

## Farm Organizations, 19th-Century

In 1865, as southern soldiers returned to the fields they had abandoned to enlist in the Confederate and Union armies, they recognized the extensive rebuilding that would be necessary to restore their farms to previous productivity. Reconstruction of fences and outbuildings destroyed by armies in search of firewood and shelter, reclamation of fields gone to weeds after years of neglect, and restoration of herds and flocks confiscated to feed armies and haul military equipment were common tasks that greeted them. Needing capital and labor to rebuild and return southern agriculture to its antebellum profitability, farmers turned to the crop lien, as a substitute for cash, and tenancy/sharecropping to solve their immediate labor needs. Continued over decades, dependency on store credit tied to commodity production produced downward spiraling cycles of debt and one-crop agriculture that impoverished the South and pushed poor whites into tenancy on land they had previously owned. Black farmers became enmeshed in a sharecropping system that prevented advancement up the agricultural ladder to landholding status.

Focused on their own problems, southern farmers did not immediately comprehend that agriculture itself—the way people produced and marketed the fruits of the land—had been transformed by economic forces already apparent in the 1850s and public policy embraced during the Civil War. The antebellum market revolution foretold the transformation of capital, labor, and society that marked the Gilded Age and Progressive eras of American history. With the South removed from public debates and the legislative process, Congress acted to create the infrastructure that would facilitate the nation's transition to an industrial economy. The establishment of the national banking system met wartime needs, but, in the long run, promoted industrial capitalism and drew small producers into a cash nexus; the construction of a transcontinental railroad assisted the development of regional and national markets; the Homestead Act encouraged agricultural development on the Great Plains; and the establishment of a land-grant college system advanced agricultural and engineering research that facilitated capital-intensive scientific farming.

By the end of the century, farmers produced for overcrowded, highly competitive regional, national, and international markets. The decline of subsistence farming, which allowed producers to provide food and fiber for home consumption and market the surplus, disrupted the rural networks of friends and kin that sustained communities in hard times. In order to address the new demands and protect their interests in regional, national, and international markets, farmers joined a succession of agrarian organizations—the Patrons of Husbandry (the Grange), the Agricultural Wheel, and the Farmers' Alliance—that constituted a mass movement by the end of the century.

The three organizations were similar in a number of ways, and many farm activists transitioned through all the successive phases of the agrarian movement. All three drew upon existing networks of family, friends, and coreligionists as the foundation for local membership. All three adopted familiar organization and rituals that derived from extant fraternal organizations, particularly freemasonry. They eschewed divisive politics and advocated nonpartisan support for like-minded candidates of either party who were willing to advance the agricultural interests outlined in the organizations' "demands." All three promoted cooperativism as the most efficacious means of bypassing the monopolistic "middleman," reducing input costs, and improving farm prices. Finally, they advanced into new social relations by supporting active female membership and pursuing tenuous ties with black farmers. Although few blacks joined the Grange, both the Wheel and the Alliance created segregated parallel organizations for African American farmers.

Despite the common organizational threads, the Grange, the Wheel, and the Alliance were not mere copies of one another. Together their histories provide insight into the developing public debate over the role of the state in the emerging industrial economy. Each of the organizations engaged new constituencies, refined and expanded agrarian demands, and adopted methodologies of action different from the previous group.

Following a tour of the South in 1867, Oliver H. Kelly, a Minnesota farmer and reformer, worked with colleagues in the U.S. Department of Agriculture to found the Order of the Patrons of Husbandry. The first national organization of farmers, the Grange advocated rural uplift, railroad regulation, and cooperative purchasing and selling as mechanisms for addressing social and economic problems in the countryside. The Grange pioneered a number of initiatives that became characteristic of farm organizations generally, including female membership, the use of secret rituals, and nonpartisanship in the advancement of agricultural programs. Although the Grange appealed to mid-level commercial farmers eager to reduce costs and raise commodity prices, it suffered from the undue influence of members with nonfarm agendas, including local merchants, bankers, and politicians seeking the farm vote. When the Grange proved unable to resolve the debt problems that affected most farmers, membership declined after the late 1870s.

The Grange, however, influenced the southern countryside in education and railroad regulation and established the cooperative model that all other farm organizations employed. In their efforts to bring moral and educational uplift, Grangers promoted the construction of lending libraries and schools and encouraged members to read broadly and express their ideas in public forums and published essays. They valued agricultural education and actively supported the establishment of land-grant universities. In Mississippi, the Grange's Master Workman, Putnam Darden, was instrumental in the establishment of Mississippi A&M College (now Mississippi State University). Grangers believed that private enterprises such as railroads and telegraphs operated for the public good and were subject to greater public oversight than other enterprises. They pressured state legislatures to enact regulatory laws, create railroad commissions to oversee rates, and provide relief from what they perceived as monopolistic practices. Although poorly funded and short-lived, Granges established cooperative stores, warehouses, and cotton gins to control the costs associated with commercial farming. In 1876 state granges in Tennessee, Arkansas, Mississippi, and Louisiana underwrote the Southwestern Co-operative Association in Memphis, an effort to create a multistate distribution center that would be repeated by successive organizations. The influence of the southern Grange should not be underestimated, as local and state granges remained active in some areas until the end of the century and their organization provided a template for Agricultural Wheel and Farmers' Alliance rituals and agendas.

As the agricultural crisis deepened, farmers organized again in grassroots movements that developed national constituencies. Isaac McCracken founded the Agricultural Wheel in 1882 at a meeting of Prairie County, Ark., farmers. Depressed farm prices and mounting debt brought the disgruntled farmers together and shaped the organization's program for reform. Believing agriculture to be the "wheel" that moved the world's industrial economy, the founders adopted an ambitious list of demands that included currency reform through the free coinage of silver; abolition of the national banking system; regulation of railroad, telegraph, and telephone; restriction of the sale of public lands to American citizens; implementation of a federal income tax; and the popular election of U.S. senators.

The national Wheel built a hierarchy of local, county, and state organizations that spread through the Mississippi River valley. By 1887 the Wheel claimed 500,000 members in six states. African American farmers, under the supervision of white lecturers, organized the Colored Agricultural Wheel and advocated policies similar to its white counterpart. In 1889, after organizational meetings at Shreveport, La., and Meridian, Miss., the Agricultural Wheel merged with the Farmers' Alliance and established a loose confederation with southern labor to form the National Farmers' Alliance and Laborers' Union. The Colored Wheel never effected a similar merger with the Colored Alliance and had faded away by 1890.

The Farmers' Alliance first organized in Lampasas County, Tex., in 1877 and expanded into regional and national importance under the leadership of C. W. Macune. Like the Wheel, the Alliance adopted a platform of demands that addressed agricultural problems on several levels: farm costs and agricultural prices, banking and currency issues, transportation and communication, and access to policy making. Other similarities smoothed the merger of the two farm organizations: the limitation of membership to farmers, farm women, rural ministers, editors, and schoolteachers promoted a like-minded community of rural activists; a system of lecturers, rituals, and reform newspapers kept the membership on target; and mass meetings and social events elevated the dispirited and inspired a sense of participation in a larger cause.

Despite the similarities, the Farmers' Alliance was not the Grange or the

Agricultural Wheel, and the differences were important to the agrarian mass movement. Wheel membership included many farmers whose production more closely approximated that of subsistence farming. In contrast, the Alliance increasingly addressed the needs of mid-level commercial farmers, as evidenced by the evolving demands, the targets of mass activism, and the political focus of the organization. When voluntary cooperative purchasing and marketing efforts proved ineffective, the Alliance demanded a federal subtreasury system that would establish warehouses to store staple crops, provide low-interest loans on stored commodities, and rationalize the market through spaced sales. For subsistence farmers, the subtreasury represented a potential government incursion they were unwilling to support. The focus on commodity production was again apparent in the boycott against the "jute trust." Alliance cotton farmers put their complaints against industrial monopolists into action when they protested the rise in prices imposed by the American jute dealers, boycotted the sale of jute, and wrapped their cotton bales in alternative materials. As the Alliance formulated policy positions and engaged in public activism to protect the interests of agricultural producers, the organization became more political in its demands and actions, even as it claimed nonpartisanship.

Alliance leaders understood that implementation of the organization's ambitious plans required supportive legislation. Although they advocated nonpartisanship, Alliancemen positioned themselves to influence lawmakers and elect farmers to state and national assemblies. In the South, political power resided in the Democratic Party, and the Alliance initially acted through the party to effect change. Farmers mastered the political tactics used by their opponents to control mass political meetings and nominate their candidates for office. In races where they had no Alliance candidate, they demanded that office seekers measure up to the "Alliance Yardstick" in order to gain rural votes. By the early 1890s, Alliance insurgents represented a significant bloc in state legislatures, and several southern governors had Alliance connections or owed their election to the farm vote. Alliance leaders anticipated further gains in congressional elections and hoped to elevate men to the U.S. Senate. Alarmed Democrats mounted a counterattack with their own yardstick of democracy and race-baiting campaigns to drive a wedge between black and white farmers joined under the Alliance banner.

Against the backdrop of political turmoil, some Alliance members, encouraged by western miners, mounted a campaign for the creation of a third party. In the spring of 1891, they laid the groundwork for the People's Party, better known as the Populist Party. In the 1892 elections, Democrats forced Alliance members to choose between their economic interests and the party of their fathers.

Although many abandoned the insurgency, others opted to join the Populists, who hastily assembled candidates for office at every level. With the creation of the Populist Party, Alliance membership declined rapidly and the organization disappeared.

Although the Populist platform incorporated the Alliance demands, campaign rhetoric centered on the issue of free silver. The Populists mounted national campaigns for the presidency in 1892 and 1896, nominating James B. Weaver, a former Greenback Party candidate, in the first race and supporting William Jennings Bryan, the Democratic Party candidate, in the pivotal 1896 campaign. Populists supported Bryan, but they nominated Tom Watson, a Georgia attorney and newspaper publisher with no ties to earlier agrarian organizations, as their nominee for vice president. The defeat of the Populists in 1896 generally marks the historical end of the mass agrarian movements, although Populists in several states continued to mount campaigns through the end of the century. North Carolina Populists, under the leadership of Marion Butler, remained politically strong and won elective offices through fusion with the Republican Party.

In the early 20th century, as the result of speeches and actions by Watson and other politicians, Populism became associated with demagoguery in the public mind, and for many, farmers' movements were likewise tainted. However, the agrarian mass movement represented an important transitional moment in American political and social history. Farmers articulated the economic and political implications of the advent of industrial capitalism. Their demands for government regulation of public transportation and communication, their claims to public office, and their calls for improved education and reliable access to capital and credit were taken up by new voices in the 20th century. Echoes of the agrarian demands can be heard in farm legislation, regulatory policy, and constitutional law enacted during the administrations of Woodrow Wilson and Franklin D. Roosevelt.

CONNIE L. LESTER
*University of Central Florida*

Lawrence Goodwyn, *Democratic Promise: The Populist Moment in America* (1976); Steven Hahn, *The Roots of Southern Populism: Yeomen Farmers and the Transformation of the Georgia Upcountry, 1850–1890* (1983); Connie L. Lester, *Up from the Mudsills of Hell: The Farmers' Alliance, Populism, and Progressive Agriculture in Tennessee, 1870–1915* (2006); Robert C. McMath Jr., *Populist Vanguard: A History of the Southern Farmers' Alliance* (1975).

## Food and Markets, Women's Roles in

Just as food has shaped southern cultures, so has food played a central role in the female economy of the rural South. Women's production for market both complemented cash-crop agriculture and shielded farms and families against the vagaries of prices for staple commodities such as cotton and tobacco. Memoirs of rural life, oral histories with rural elders, farm periodicals, and reports of home-demonstration agents who worked for the Agricultural Extension Service reveal the intricacies and importance of women's commerce. Through their trade, women reduced indebtedness and reliance upon creditors, mitigated their own economic dependence upon men, and helped families to enjoy new consumer goods. They also found an outlet for entrepreneurial skills and talents.

In the early 20th century, southern farm women's production for market grew out of their production for home use. While the spread of cash crops in the South had undermined diversified agriculture, rural families still tried to meet as many of their own dietary needs as possible. Women cultivated gardens and preserved vegetables and fruits. They raised chickens for meat and eggs and kept a cow for milk and butter. A family's ability to achieve self-provisioning varied by class, race, and its ability to determine the crop mix. In the early 1920s, rural sociologists who surveyed a cross-section of North Carolina farmers found that both black and white landowners grew more of their own food than tenants and sharecroppers and that, in general, white families fared better than black families. Although many poor farm families suffered dietary deficiencies, many rural elders who remember the lean years of the 1920s and 1930s marveled that although cash was scarce they "didn't go hungry."

Through their marketing ingenuity, women turned a variety of goods into commodities for trade. Poorer women, in particular, gathered and sold what nature offered freely, foraging and selling berries that grew wild in the woods. For most farm women, poultry and dairy products formed the heart of their trade. A flock of chickens in the yard and a good milk cow or two provided a surplus for market as well as food for the family table. The fact that eggs and live chickens were available nearly year-round rather than seasonally enhanced their worth. Women stayed attuned to the market and calculated if eggs would be sold or eaten by their families. When income earning took priority, sales of goods deprived some families of food or left them provisions of inferior quality.

The products of women's labor entered channels of commerce in a number of ways, ranging from casual exchanges to formal, state-sponsored markets. Modest transactions occurred so routinely that they might be taken for granted. In eastern North Carolina, for example, women traded eggs house-to-house with men who peddled fish caught in the area's rivers. Storekeepers in country and town alike took butter, eggs, and live chickens in trade. Although the women might not have known it, they formed the first link in a supply chain, as rural storekeepers connected with scattered small producers and wholesale merchants located in cities. Itinerant merchants known as hucksters offered another marketing outlet. These traders traveled the South, paying cash for poultry and dairy products to the farm women who greeted them in their yards and for eggs that storekeepers had received from customers who brought them in for swapping. Women also controlled their own retail operations, thus sidestepping intermediaries as they sold butter, milk, eggs, and seasonal fruits and vegetables directly to individual customers.

One more mode of selling was state-sponsored cooperative markets. During the 1920s and 1930s, home demonstration agents who worked for the Agricultural Extension Service organized curb markets in county seats across the region. Responding to the downturn in the farm economy and women's desire to control their sales, curb markets expanded at the same time that prices for cotton and tobacco declined. Women praised these markets for helping them obtain good prices for their commodities. In a detailed study of the curb market in Augusta County, Va., Ann E. McCleary concluded that the retail outlet reflected "a blend of the modern idea of the farm woman as business-person intertwined with a traditional perspective of farm woman as producer."

Curb markets served didactic as well as economic purposes. Home demonstration agents seized the opportunity to teach lessons about the standardization of products and the self-presentation of the sellers themselves. Women who sold at the curb markets had to honor regulations that determined all aspects of sales, from the prices they charged to the appearance of their assigned stalls and how they pitched their products. In this regard, they joined a long tradition of public markets the world over that established rules to govern vendors and to protect consumers. Home agents coached marketing women on how to approach potential buyers with poise and decorum. While customers surveyed the displays of dressed poultry, eggs, cakes, vegetables, and fruits, sellers had to remain in their designated places and keep those spaces tidy. Market rules required women to wear washable white dresses whose uniform appearance suggested cleanliness and order.

In the era of Jim Crow, home demonstration markets practiced racial segregation. The bylaws that governed the market in at least one North Carolina county stated explicitly that only whites could sell under its auspices, and other markets followed the color line. Nonetheless, black home agents in the state acted as intermediaries between producers and buyers, encouraged club women to participate in city markets open to sellers of both races, and occasionally organized small curb markets of their own.

Many farm women enjoyed selling in a lively public venue where they mingled with friends and strangers, managed the transactions, and turned their private work into social labor. Sellers engaged in good-natured rivalries, and women reveled in the reputations their products and skills earned them. In addition, farm wives and mothers who could boast market earnings might influence how the family allocated its labor, and husbands and children who helped them set up and sell also witnessed the value of their labors firsthand.

The income-earning strategies that Victoria Williams Cunningham pursued in the 1920s and 1930s combined sales at a home demonstration curb market in South Carolina with sales to individual customers. At the market, her son Tom recalled years later, Cunningham sold milk, butter, and eggs all year and offered other goods as the seasons changed. In the spring, she supplied tender greens and tangy onions. In the summer, watermelons, cantaloupes, and garden vegetables filled her market table. In the fall and winter, she sold cured hams, sausage, and peanuts. Victoria Cunningham also maintained a route of customers in Darlington. The family had a telephone, and townsfolk called the farm about three miles away to place their orders. On their morning trips to school, Tom and his siblings delivered milk, eggs, and butter to town doorsteps. "My mother," he said, "knew exactly who got milk what day and how much."

During the bleakest years of the Great Depression, the income that farm women generated made a crucial difference for many families. Tom Cunningham could not estimate what proportion of the family economy his mother's earnings represented because he was a child during the heyday of her sales. He did know, however, that his mother "helped to keep body and soul together back during those Depression years, when there just wasn't any money. I know that she worked at it diligently and that my father worked at the farm and between the two of them, they kept the bills paid and we were fed well; we had adequate clothing even though sometimes we had patches on our elbows and knees. But we fared well. We got along real good. And I know it took both of them to do it." The Cunningham family was not alone.

Proceeds from women's trade often made a substantial difference in a family's budget. The cash and credit that women earned met mortgage payments and allowed any profits to be reinvested in the farm enterprise, underwrote home improvements, put extra food on the table, and bought school clothes for their children. Women's income sometimes provided the few small luxuries that rural children enjoyed, and in oral-history narratives southern elders often re-

member the ways in which women's earnings were spent with a loving precision unmatched in stories about men's income. In the early 1920s, when it came
time for Jessie Felknor to graduate from high school in east Tennessee, sales of
her mother's chickens paid for her class ring. Women used proceeds from the
"butter and egg trade" to underwrite education and invest in their children's
futures.

Farm women were crucial players in household and local economies, and
their goods entered regional and national economic channels. Women's earnings kept families afloat during hard times and helped them enjoy some of the
stock on store shelves during better times. Earnings might also shift the balance of power within farm families, giving women more influence over farm
decisions and a measure of autonomy. In hindsight, it is clear that commodities
like tobacco and cotton were the bricks of the southern farm economy, but the
products of women's labor were often the mortar that held it together.

LU ANN JONES
*University of South Florida*

Lu Ann Jones, *Mama Learned Us to Work: Farm Women in the New South* (2002), in
*Cornbread Nation 1: The Best of Southern Food Writing*, ed. John Egerton (2002); Ann
E. McCleary, in *Women, Family, and Faith: Rural Southern Women in the Twentieth
Century*, ed. Melissa Walker and Rebecca Sharpless (2006); Rebecca Sharpless, *Fertile
Ground, Narrow Choices: Women on Texas Cotton Farms, 1900–1940* (1999); Melissa
Walker, *All We Knew Was to Farm: Rural Women in the Upcountry South, 1919–1941*
(2000).

## Garden Patches

In addition to maintaining decorative formal gardens, southerners have a tradition of growing functional gardens that provide vegetables for their own tables.
They are called garden patches, garden plots, kitchen gardens, provision gardens,
or simply vegetable gardens. They have been locales for intercultural exchange
between the American Indian, European, and African ways of growing.

The first people of the Southeast to keep garden patches were the Indians.
As anthropologist Charles Hudson has noted, "In Creek towns, and probably
in Indian settlements throughout the Southeast, the women cultivated kitchen
gardens in addition to the large fields in the river bottoms, and these were
located in and around the town itself." From early times, then, the garden patch
was frequently associated with women and with essential provision of food for
the table. Corn, beans, and squash, the three principal agricultural crops, were
grown in such areas. Land for these garden patches would gradually become

exhausted, sometimes leading to the relocation of entire towns in the search for better land for essential garden areas.

To colonial European settlers, "gardening" meant not only working on well-planned, formal designs of trees, shrubbery, and flowers, but also the growing of food. The gentry imported plants and seeds from Europe and experimented with native plants. Robert Beverley notes that vegetable gardens were productive in Virginia, where the people had most of the "culinary plants" from England as well as indigenous ones. In North Carolina gardens, explains Julia Cherry Spruill, "were parsnips, carrots, turnips, beets, artichokes, radishes, several kinds of potatoes, leeks, onions, shallots, chives, and garlic." Salads included cabbage, savoy, lettuce, fennel, spinach, mint, rhubarb, sorrel, and purslane. Asparagus thrived under natural conditions, and celery, cucumbers, and squash were abundant.

An African American gardening tradition took root in the colonial Southeast as well. Yams, okra, tanniers, collards, benne, and other plants from West Africa all grew in the South on small "provision gardens," which slave owners sometimes encouraged and other times ignored. Some African plants and growing techniques entered Cherokee agriculture in the 17th century and were adapted by German immigrants in North Carolina and elsewhere and by English settlers. African plant stocks were frequently difficult to transplant, but southerners sometimes imported Caribbean plants or experimented with New World plant substitutes from the Indians.

The techniques of growing vegetables, as well as the plants grown, were another aspect of the African American tradition. A 19th-century planter on the Sea Islands off the coast of Georgia described a slave's garden as "a small patch where arrowroot, long collards, sugar cane, tanniers, ground nuts, beene, gourds, and watermelons grew in comingled luxuriance." The "comingled" look was the key, a form inherited from West Africa and still seen frequently in the American South. The mixture of plant types together, rather than separated out in orderly rows, seems to create an effective "garden climate," explaining the endurance of the form. By layering plants—planting two or three plants next to each other that grow to different heights—the insect population apparently can be reduced, weeds decreased through shading them out, and soil nutrients and water conserved.

The garden patch was a common part of life for blacks and whites on the antebellum southern plantation. The plantation mistress sometimes supervised work on garden plots and kept detailed records of her plantings. One 1834 diary reported that Eliza Mitchell was growing cabbage, strawberries, raspberries, snap beans, corn, cymblings, and sugar beets. Large plantations devoted acreage to the growing of such vegetables, which were used to feed the black workforce. Slave owners, according to most recent studies, let many slaves have garden patches. The bondsmen looked after their crops at the end of the workday, on Saturday afternoon, and on Sunday. Planters often gave slaves some weekend time to work on these and purchased fresh vegetables from their slaves as a way of providing incentive for their work, keeping up morale, and giving the workers extra money for occasional luxuries. If allowed, slaves would market their produce on Saturdays at crossroad stores or in towns. This trade was never as large in the South as in the Caribbean, but it was important. Most vegetables grown by slaves in their gardens were, however, for consumption by the families that grew them. The ability to control their garden patch and practice gardening skills promoted self-worth among the slaves. This was a family activity, and the family meal of homegrown and prepared vegetables became a simple but significant ritual reinforcing kinship.

Southern tenant farmers after the Civil War and into the 20th century found vegetable garden plots to be especially significant in their lives. Most of their time was devoted to raising cotton or other cash crops, for which they received minimal compensation. The garden plot was widespread among tenants and common among mill-town people whenever the land was available. Some landlords did not want tenants raising vegetables, believing that it took away from their cotton work, but most seem not to have discouraged it. James Agee in *Let Us Now Praise Famous Men* (1941) described an Alabama garden plot. He said it was close to the rear of the house, "about the shape and about two-thirds the size of a tennis court, and is caught within palings against the hunger and damage of animals." The palings were thin slats of pine, which were strung together with wire. Weeds stood outside these fence walls, while inside "the planting is concentrated to the utmost possible, in green and pink-veined wax and velvet butter beans, and in hairy buds of okra." Insects were a continual torment, with beetles and other pests a potential threat to vegetables at every step of the way.

As in earlier times, the fresh vegetables from the garden patch were an important part of the rural southerner's nutrition, especially for the tenants and sharecroppers. By the 1930s government investigations had identified problems with the southern diet, with its heavy reliance on starchy foods and supposed lack of fresh vegetable consumption. In 1936 Howard W. Odum pointed to statistics that showed the South was considerably above the national average, and also above every other region in the nation, in the amount of farm vegetables raised, suggesting changes in the dietary habits of the people of the region. He concluded that the statistics "indicate the relatively large dependence of the farm folk upon home produce." Novelist Richard Wright, in *Black Boy* (1945), recalled from his Mississippi and Arkansas childhood "the delight I caught in seeing long straight rows of red and green vegetables stretching away in the sun to the bright horizon."

In the modern South, the raising of vegetables, fruits, and other items in small garden plots is a continuing tradition. *New York Times* reporter Wayne King has noted that "one of the pleasures of gardening, particularly in the South, is reading the seed packets. Among radishes, as a mundane example, there are Crimson Giants, Red Princes, and Scarlet Globes. One can plant Southland's Louisiana Green Velvet Okra, Mississippi Sunshine Mammoth Edible All-Star Selection Blackeye Peas, Sweet Slice Burpless Hybrid Cucumbers, Dixie Hybrid Crookneck Squash, watermelons called Fat Boy or tomatoes called Big Boy." In addition to a diversity of plants to grow, there is progress on fighting the insects that always plagued the region. Individual gardeners go into their yards with spray tanks of insecticides strapped to their backs, wearing rain slickers, boots, and maybe even goggles, prepared to destroy threats to their summer salads.

Organic gardening has become fashionable in the region. One practitioner prefers to call it "biologically grown" food, because that phrase conveys the soil-building process and the holistic relationship between the plant and its environment. Organic farming generally is defined as farming that uses natural biological methods. It can be more difficult in the South than in the North because of the hotter climate, which dries up the organic matter in the soil. The long growing season and mild winters through much of the South mean more insect pests and weeds to fight, lessons learned by every generation and type of southern farmer sooner or later. Southern organic farmers fertilize with natural rock powder, seaweed, fish emulsion, compost, and manure. They plant legumes as crop covering, and they believe in crop rotation. Organic farming has become a business in parts of the South, but it is also important in terms of the suburban and city southerners who set aside land in their yard or on their small farms to raise vegetables.

The growth of interest in regional cooking among the middle class also has promoted the growing of vegetable patches. Southerners in the modern South, even those in cities, are not far removed in historical time from the rural farm South, and those southerners who continue to plant their garden patches and grow favorite southern vegetables are holding onto a long southern tradition that unites the people of the region.

CHARLES REAGAN WILSON
*University of Mississippi*

John B. Boles, *Black Southerners, 1619–1869* (1983); Catherine Clinton, *The Planta-tion Mistress: Woman's World in the Old South* (1982); Tom Hatley, *Southern Changes* (October–November 1984); Howard W. Odum, *Southern Regions of the United States* (1936); Julia Cherry Spruill, *Women's Life and Work in the Southern Colonies* (1938); Debby Wechsler, *Southern Exposure* (November–December 1983); Richard West-macott, *African American Gardens and Yards in the Rural South* (1992); Peter Wood, *Black Majority: Negroes in Colonial South Carolina from 1670 through the Stono Rebel-lion* (1974).

## Global Economy, Southern Agriculture in

Few students of southern history read Alfred O. Hero Jr.'s mammoth 1965 study *The Southerner and World Affairs* any more. Such neglect is unfortunate, be-cause there is still much of interest in this "heroic" study of southern opinions about and engagement with other parts of the world. Some of the author's find-ings might surprise today's readers, including the declaration with which he opens chapter 4 ("International Commerce and Related Issues"): "Until rela-tively recently the South was more closely tied to the world economy than was the industrialized North." Really? What about all that talk of southern isola-tion, seclusion, and sequestration? Until relatively recently, were not southern-ers part of a backward society and economy? And was not the economy of the region undeveloped or underdeveloped in comparison to other parts in the United States? These questions are complex, and, in order to answer them completely, one would need space for nuance and qualification. In broad terms, though, it seems fair to say that the South's historic trajectory, particularly its economic trajectory, cannot be understood unless it is embedded in the context of the wider world, if not the *entire* world.

Nowhere has the South's engagement with the world been more complete, historically, than in the field of agriculture. Shortly after the establishment of the first permanent European-sponsored colonies in the region, agricultural prod-ucts were being exported; but, more to the point, without imported (or with regard to Native Americans, exogenous) labor, capital, and knowledge, agri-culture itself in the southern colonies would have been well-nigh impossible. The entire colonial enterprise in the Americas was, of course, a manifestation of the outward thrust of the European economy, one key goal of which was the establishment, per mercantilist dogma—or, less insistently, beliefs or desires— of economic platforms conducive to the production and exportation of prod-ucts beneficial to both the European enterprisers involved and the European polities that sponsored them. Within a generation of settlement in Virginia (the first permanent English settlement on the mainland), settlers were exporting tobacco, and over the course of the colonial period, all of the southern colonies (with the partial exception of late-developing North Carolina) were exporting large quantities of agricultural commodities and forest products—rice, indigo, deerskins, and naval stores, in addition to tobacco—not only "home" to Britain but also to other British colonies and other parts of the Atlantic world.

Indeed, as a result of their export orientation (and the manner in which their exports were routed), the southern colonies came to be viewed by the British as exemplary mercantilist colonies, contributing much to the imperial bottom line. On the eve of the American Revolution, the combined value of commodity exports from the southern colonies—the vast majority of which exports consisted of agricultural commodities—comprised over 63 percent of the total value of commodity exports from the 13 colonies, even though the combined white and black population of the South constituted less than 47 percent of the population of the 13 colonies considered as a whole. All of this was before cotton was planted seriously in the South, much less added to the region's agricultural export mix.

As suggested above, the South's agricultural engagement with the wider world during the colonial period did not begin and end with its commodity exports, however important. Throughout the period, the region's agricultural labor force was comprised largely, indeed predominantly, of dependent workers of one sort or another drawn from other parts of the world, most notably Europe, the Caribbean, and West Africa. Over time, this workforce became increasingly dominated by African and African American slaves, who contributed not only their labor to southern agriculture but also their knowledge about cultivating certain crops—rice in particular. Southern agriculturalists, farmers and planters alike, benefited as well from inflows of capital from Europe, whether in the form of crop financing or credit for the acquisition of land, slaves, or agricultural inputs of one sort or another. And, certainly, other forms of "capital"— agricultural knowledge and technology—were transferred from Europe to the southern colonies as well.

Such transfers of intellectual capital also came from further afield. For example, the basic technology behind the cotton gin, which in the conventional narrative about the rise of the Cotton South is associated primarily with Eli Whitney and a few others, actually originated in China and India centuries before. Its spread was part of the worldwide diffusion of technology during the great era of globalization that the West refers to as the Early Modern period.

To invoke cotton is, of course, to usher the leading agricultural actor onto the southern stage. From its wee beginnings as a commercial crop in the South in the 1790s, cotton cultivation in the region spread rapidly, with production increasing, seemingly inexorably, throughout the ensuing century—indeed, into well into the 20th century. Much of the cotton produced was exported. Cotton ranked as the single most important U.S. export by far during the antebellum period, with the fleecy staple—along with two other "southern" crops, rice and tobacco—comprising fully 55 percent of the total value of U.S. exports over the entire period between 1815 and 1860. Although southern rice was rendered uncompetitive in international markets for decades after the Civil War—in fact, lower-cost rice from South and Southeast Asia was pushing southern rice out of the leading export markets in northern Europe well before 1861—cotton and tobacco from the South continued on as bellwether U.S. exports. These two commodities alone accounted for 30 percent of the total value of U.S. merchandise exports between 1861 and 1910, and 21.5 percent for the entire period between 1861 and 1940. If cotton production and exports from the western states began to become significant from the late 1920s on, *southern* cotton dominated the export market down through, and even after, World War II.

The history of the South and the fortunes of the inhabitants therein were linked closely, even inextricably, then, to export agriculture from the 17th century until the middle of the 20th century. Generally speaking, the social relations of agricultural production in the region were characterized throughout this lengthy period by vast asymmetries in rural wealth and power structures, with large proportions of poor, dependent laborers shouldering the burden. With social relations of this type, it is not surprising that the economic benefits arising from the region's agricultural exports—indeed, from the agricultural sector as a whole—were not widely shared. Furthermore, over time the relative importance in the region of a small number of staple crops, produced largely for export on large units of production (plantations, or "neoplantations") worked primarily by poor (and poorly equipped) dependent laborers, took its toll on both the region's overall economic performance and the material and social well-being of its inhabitants. Thus, we find the South lagging behind other sections of the United States according to most social and economic indicators throughout our nation's history, with the gap particularly wide between Appomattox and World War II. Only with, and in large part because of, the Great Depression did the South's retrograde rural economic and social structures begin to collapse, and only then did the region begin its real transformation into a modern economy.

This transformation, which was gradual and uneven, gained momentum in the late 1940s and 1950s. It was marked by several interrelated processes: drastic increases in mechanization in production and, particularly, harvesting; a significant rise in agricultural productivity; a massive decline in demand for year-round agricultural labor, and, as a concomitant, in the rural labor force; shifts at the margin toward a different mix of commercial-agricultural production (toward soybeans, poultry, hogs, fruits, truck, etc.); a sharp rise in rural manufacturing; and, over time, convergence upon national economic and social norms.

In light of such changes, it is not surprising that the South's agricultural sector, while still substantial, shrank in relative importance in the region's overall economy. In 1950, when only 7 percent of the U.S. workforce as a whole was employed in agriculture, almost a quarter of the South's workforce was still employed in this sector. By 1960, however, the percentage of the southern labor force working in agriculture had fallen to less than 10 percent, and this trend has continued unabated since that time. Today, about 2 percent of the South's workers make their living in agriculture. Over the past half century, agriculture's relative share of regional output has fallen dramatically as well.

Despite the relative decline of the southern agriculture sector over the past half century or so, this sector remains large in absolute terms, and the South remains an important exporter of farm products. In 2005, for example, Texas placed third among all states in the total value of agricultural exports, and in that same year southern states supplied the vast majority of the cotton, poultry, tobacco, peanuts, and cottonseed oil exported from the United States, a great deal of the rice and live animals and meats exported, and considerable proportions of exported fruits, tree nuts, feeds and fodder, and hides. If agriculture contributes far less in a relative sense to the region's economy than it once did, and if only a small proportion of southerners continue to make their living off of the land, the absolute value of southern agricultural exports remains high, and southern agriculture continues to contribute positively to the region's balance of trade.

Given the level of acrimony in the United States today regarding globalization, it might at first blush shock some that the inhabitants of the South—often viewed as preternaturally inward looking, conservative, and xenophobic—have traditionally been much more positive about free trade than have inhabitants in other parts of the United States. The powerful historical role of agriculture in the South and the region's long and deep integration in international markets render such feelings more understandable, however. Even in recent years, as the region has lost hundreds of thousands of manufacturing jobs—at least in part because of trade globalization—and as the region has been torn apart by issues relating to immigration (the globalization of labor), the South's inhabitants and the politicians who represent them continue to push and promote agricultural exports vigorously, including, ironically but revealingly, the expansion of agricultural exports of all sorts to Cuba, among other places.

PETER A. COCLANIS
*University of North Carolina at Chapel Hill*

Peter A. Coclanis, in *Globalization and the American South*, ed. James C. Cobb and William W. Stueck Jr. (2005); Pete Daniel, *Breaking the Land: The Transformation of Cotton, Tobacco, and Rice Cultures since 1880* (1985); Gilbert C. Fite, *Cotton Fields No More: Southern Agriculture, 1865–1980* (1984); Lewis C. Gray, *History of Agriculture in the Southern United States to 1860*, 2 vols. (1933); Gavin Wright, *Old South, New South: Revolutions in the Southern Economy since the Civil War* (1986).

## Good Roads Movement

The good roads movement in the South was at first primarily an attempt to convince farmers that road improvements would not be detrimental to their interests. Behind the campaign for better roads was the League of American Wheelmen, an organization of bicyclists that drew its membership almost exclusively from the Northeast. During the late 19th century, the league spent considerable time and money attempting to convince farmers in the South and elsewhere in the country that good roads would bring them greater economic and cultural rewards. The league also lobbied hard for a federal program aiding road building, and in 1893 Congress earmarked $10,000 as part of an agricultural appropriation bill establishing the Office of Roads Inquiry (ORI).

Limited funding and a need to gain grassroots support for a good roads movement mandated an investigative and educational role for the new federal agency. Campaigns to survey road conditions, win over opponents of road reforms, and demonstrate the proper techniques in road construction commenced. As part of this effort, the ORI launched an assault on the notoriously poor roads in the South. In cooperation with the national Good Roads Association and the Southern Railway, the ORI sponsored a Good Roads Train, which toured the states of Virginia, North Carolina, South Carolina, Georgia, Alabama, and Tennessee during the winter of 1901–2. At each of 18 stops, southerners listened to speakers explain the advantages of good roads and watched object-lesson demonstrations in proper road-construction methods. At the train's last stop in Charlottesville, Va., on 3 April 1902, Samuel Spencer, president of the Southern Railway, observed that the train had aroused enthusiasm for an improvement that he regarded as immensely important in the development of the South.

Eighteen local good roads associations were soon located in the six-state area. Members of these vanguard organizations and others that sprang up across the South during the first two decades of the 20th century translated the message of good roads into language that not only farmers but businessmen, educators, ministers, boosters, and politicians could understand. Their efforts were so extensive and unrelenting that historian Francis Butler Simkins considered the good roads movement in the South "the third god," along with industrial and educational projects, "in the Trinity of southern progress."

Southern state legislatures were slow, though, to appropriate money for road improvements. Prior to 1906, not one state in the South had started a state aid-for-roads program or established a highway department. Road improvements in the South were made by local good roads organizations, by county bond issues, or occasionally by states like North Carolina, which sponsored "Good Road Days," during which citizens actually labored to grade or resurface a stretch of road in their community. There was little understanding of the proper techniques necessary to ensure that improvements would last.

When the automobile arrived on the scene, southerners called attention to the poor road conditions in the South by employing reliability runs and interstate tours. In 1909, in conjunction with the Atlanta Automobile Show, the *Atlanta Journal* and the *New York Herald* sponsored a reliability run from Broadway in New York City to Atlanta's Peachtree Street. During the next two years, Charles J. Glidden directed two separate tours into the South. These contests received wide attention and gave rise to hundreds of similar efforts in every southern state.

By 1914, when 1,600 good roads delegates assembled in Atlanta at the fourth annual convention of the American Road Congress, it was evident that the question of good roads alone was no longer the single most important issue. Many southerners now envisioned good roads as a means of uniting North and South, bringing money and jobs into the South. The Capital Highway Association (1909), the Dixie Highway Association (1915), the Jackson Highway Association (1915), the Lee Highway Association (1918), the North and South Bee Line Highway Association (1917), and the Bankhead Highway Association (1920), among others, were all organized to promote the construction of new routes between the North and South.

In 1916 Congress passed the Federal Aid Road Act, which for the first time made funds available to southern states for road construction. Among its provisions, the new law required that all expenditures take place through state highway departments. By 1917 every southern state had a highway department, thus bringing state governments for the first time clearly into the good roads picture. The 1916 law, however, provided money for the construction of post roads only and had little impact on the overwhelming number of miles of ungraded, unpaved roads throughout the South. These tortuous roads hampered the mobility of thousands of soldiers stationed in camps in southern states during World War I, and good roads advocates were quick to point out the national defense benefits of further road improvements. Article after article appeared in the two most widely circulated promotional magazines of the good roads movement in the South, *Dixie Highway* (1915–20) and *Southern Good Roads* (1910–20). These publications urged Congress to address the problem with additional legislation and more money.

Following the war, Congress passed the Federal Aid Highway Act of 1921. A system of interstate and intercounty roads was designated to constitute the Federal Aid Highway Road System. The Dixie Highway, the Lee Highway, and the Atlantic Coastal Highway became part of this trunk-line system, but federal dollars had to be matched by states on a 50–50 basis, and southern state legislatures rarely appropriated enough money to get the South out of the mud and onto hard-surfaced highways. As late as the 1960s, roads in the South remained inferior to those in the North and Midwest. Nevertheless, the efforts of good roads advocates helped not only to increase the urban population of the South but also to end much of the sectional isolation that southerners had experienced throughout their history.

HOWARD PRESTON
*Spartanburg, South Carolina*

John Hollis Bankhead Sr. Papers, Alabama Department of Archives and History, Montgomery, Ala.; Cecil K. Brown, *The State Highway System of North Carolina: Its Evolution and Present Status* (1931); Dewey W. Grantham, *Southern Progressivism: The Reconciliation of Progress and Tradition* (1983); Philip P. Mason, *The League of American Wheelmen and the Good Roads Movement, 1880–1905* (1958); Josephine Anderson Pearson Papers, Tennessee State Archives, Nashville, Tenn.; Joseph H. Pratt, *South Atlantic Quarterly* (January 1910); Howard Preston, *Dirt Roads to Dixie: Accessibility and Modernization in the South, 1885–1935* (1991).

## Mechanization

During the antebellum period, the institution of slavery, the ignorance of many farmers, the lack of local markets where farmers could inspect and purchase implements, and the reluctance of plantation owners to invest in quality tools retarded the mechanization of southern agriculture. From the colonial period until the early 19th century, local artisans or plantation blacksmiths usually crafted the tools used in southern agriculture, and few implements were standardized. Technological change came slowly, and, prior to the Civil War, the sickle, cradle scythe, and shovel plow remained basic implements for cultivating and harvesting. By the late 1840s, however, more progressive farmers were beginning to use a variety of improved plows, harrows, and cultivators, many of which had been developed and manufactured in the North. By the mid-19th century, better farmers also used horse-powered threshing machines, corn shellers, feed mills, and fodder choppers. After the Civil War, an abundance of cheap labor, limited capital, inadequate credit institutions, and the large number of small farms limited technological change in the South. Southern farmers did not use the grain drill, corn planter, or reaper extensively until the late 19th century.

By the early 1880s, Louisiana and Texas farmers were applying midwestern wheat-growing technology to their rice lands. Although small fields and numerous drainage ditches slowed mechanization, grain binders enabled rice farmers to harvest 15 acres per day. In the late 1890s, some rice farmers experimented with steam traction engines for plowing and used elevators for loading rice into railroad cars and storage facilities.

Sugarcane growers replaced the plow with the disc cultivator during the 1890s and doubled the acreage one man could weed per day. The adoption of the disc cultivator was the most important technological change among sugarcane growers during the last half of the 19th century. By the turn of the 20th century, growers also were using slings, hooks, and derricks to lift the sugarcane onto wagons and railway cars. On the eve of World War I, cane-loading machines were in general use throughout the sugar region.

Further technological change lagged until the 1930s, when the Great Depression stimulated agricultural mechanization. At that time many landowners preferred to accept government payments from the Agricultural Adjustment Administration for taking land out of production rather than receive rent or cotton from tenants and sharecroppers. Frequently, that money was used to purchase tractors, milking machines, corn pickers, and grain combines. Bankrupt small farmers also sold their lands to larger, more prosperous farmers, and land consolidation enabled more efficient use of mechanized equipment. World War II stimulated mechanization because industrial jobs and the armed forces drew men and women away from agricultural work. Southern farmers who could afford to do so responded to resulting labor shortages by using more tractors, combines, peanut pickers, hay balers, and dairying equipment.

While southern farmers gradually made technological adjustments during the 1930s and early 1940s, agricultural engineers and tinkerers worked inde-

*Driver of a combine thrashing oats, Thomastown, La., 1940 (Marion Post Walcott, Library of Congress [LC-USF-34-53810D], Washington, D.C.)*

pendently or for farm-implement companies to solve the most perplexing technological problem in southern agriculture: mechanization of the cotton harvest. During the 1920s, Texas and Oklahoma farmers on the southern Plains began using sleds that stripped the cotton bolls from the plants, but mechanical pickers were not efficient until the International Harvester Company built the first practical spindle picker in 1941. Continued labor shortages after the end of World War II and technological improvements during the 1950s made the mechanical picker a commercial success. By the late 1960s, mechanical pickers harvested approximately 96 percent of the cotton crop. Because each two-row picker replaced approximately 80 workers, the machine displaced at least a million men and women in the harvest fields after the mid-1940s.

The development of the tractor hastened the mechanization of southern agriculture. Although only 1 percent of the farmers in the 11 cotton states owned tractors in 1920, the later small, general-purpose tractor produced after the mid-1920s was well suited for the southern farm. Great Plains farmers in Texas and Oklahoma adopted the tractor first, and southern farmers gradually turned to it as well. During World War II, Arkansas, Mississippi, Alabama, Georgia, and North and South Carolina farmers increased their supply of tractors by 100 percent. Until the end of World War II, however, the adoption of tractors and other mechanized equipment was a response to a declining labor supply rather than a cause of flight from the land. Even so, by 1945 less than 20 percent of the nation's 2 million tractors were located in the cotton states.

By the mid-20th century, the most mechanized southern farms were located on the Yazoo Delta or Basin, the coastal plain of Texas, and the southern Great

Plains in Texas and Oklahoma. In those areas, level terrain, large fields, and few obstructions made the farms ideal for the efficient application of mechanization. By the early 1970s, southern farmers began to use airplanes to dust their crops with pesticides, and the mechanical tobacco picker was practical in certain limited economic situations. Mechanical pickers also harvested citrus fruits, and eight-row planters seeded the cotton crop. By the late 1970s, tractors, combines, corn pickers or picker-shellers, pickup balers, and field forage harvesters were common implements on southern farms, and all major aspects of southern agriculture were mechanized.

Technological change has contributed to the decline of the southern farm population and agricultural workforce. Mechanization also has encouraged the consolidation of farms, stimulated a neoplantation movement, and enabled southern farmers to produce more food and fiber than ever before. By so doing, mechanization has helped improve the quality of southern farm life.

R. DOUGLAS HART
*State Historical Society of Missouri*
*Columbia, Missouri*

Gilbert C. Fite, *Agricultural History* (January 1950 and January 1980), *Cotton Fields No More: Southern Agriculture, 1865–1980* (1984); Neil Foley, *Journal of Southern History* (May 1996); Mildred Kelly Ginn, *Louisiana Historical Quarterly* (April 1940); Lewis C. Gray, *History of Agriculture in the Southern United States to 1860*, 2 vols. (1933); Valerie Grim, *Agricultural History* (Spring 1994); J. Carlyle Sitterson, *Sugar Country: The Cane Sugar Industry in the South, 1753–1950* (1953); James H. Street, *The New Revolution in the Cotton Economy* (1957); Bell Irvin Wiley, *Agricultural History* (April 1939); Nan Woodruff, *Journal of Southern History* (May 1994).

## Native American Agriculture

Despite stereotypes of Native Americans, southern Indians were farmers first for hundreds of years, organizing their economies and societies around agriculture. Native Americans first domesticated plants in the South early in the second millennium B.C. Woodland peoples supplemented their hunting by creating the Eastern Agricultural Complex around seed-bearing flowers and grasses. These first southern cultivars included sunflowers, sumpweed, knotweed, goosefoot, and ragweed, among others. By the first millennium B.C., southern farmers were also cultivating pumpkins and bottle gourds. Between A.D. 800 and 1000, they adopted more productive crops domesticated in Central America: varieties of flint corn, several kinds of beans, and new types of squash. Over the next 500 years, the Three Sisters (corn, beans, and squash) supported rapid population growth and the development of the Mississippian culture across much of the South. Agriculture provided the bulk of the native diet, and populous chiefdoms abandoned traditional gender roles that reserved farming for women. The large towns Hernando de Soto's expedition found in the early 16th century were surrounded by cornfields that stretched for miles along the riverbanks.

Mississippian farmers still used the stone axes and hoes of their woodland predecessors, however. This limited technology led them to ignore the stiff red clays under the South's upland forests. Instead, they cultivated land cleared from the hardwood forests and canebrakes that grew on the rich silts of the region's flood plains, especially the great bottoms along the Mississippi, Ohio, and other major rivers. Native men planted corn on natural levees, while women grew beans, squash, and other crops in large gardens surrounding their towns. Few large, docile mammals survived in the South after the Pleistocene extinctions, though, and therefore domesticated livestock played almost no role in Mississippian agriculture. Early European explorers found only a few dogs being bred and kept for meat. Mississippian hunters did work to manage game populations, continuing the old tradition of setting controlled fires in the surrounding forests to encourage new plant growth that would attract and increase populations of deer and turkey.

By the 1500s Mississippian agriculture and society were in decline across much of the South. Large-scale deforestation limited the silt river floods brought to the bottomlands. Continuous corn monocultures depleted soil nutrients, leading to land abandonment and population loss. European contact hastened the decay of farming in the South. Epidemic disease devastated native communities, and men abandoned the shrinking cornfields to hunt deerskins to trade for European goods. When English settlers first arrived in the South, local chiefdoms like Powhatan's Confederacy were still producing surpluses of corn, but populations were already declining. By the time explorers and settlers moved into the Deep South during the early 18th century, the large-scale farming of the Mississippian period had come to an end. Women had largely retaken control of native agriculture, planting corn and bean polycultures on smaller river-bottom fields. Exhausted soils were quickly abandoned to the encroaching forest, and towns moved more frequently.

Agriculture remained central to the society and worldview of the Indian peoples of the South, however. The major southern tribes continued to live in towns surrounded by communally owned cornfields. The Green Corn Ceremony, which marked the new year for most southern peoples, remained the most important festival in the region. Southern Indians were quick to adopt crops and farming implements from across the Atlantic, as well. Fig and peach trees planted by missionaries in Spanish Florida were soon being grown in orchards across the South. Native peoples also developed a taste for African crops like watermelon, black-eyed peas, and sweet potatoes. They traded for iron and steel hoes and axes to replace their stone-age technology. The Creek and Seminole, in particular, bred and often sold horses first introduced by the Spanish. As overhunting led to declining deer populations, southern tribes began adopting other European domestic livestock to supplement their subsistence, particularly chickens and hogs.

The American Revolution pushed the southern tribes to make farming their economic base once more. White ranchers and settlers poured into the western piedmont and over the Appalachians, encroaching on native hunting grounds. The deerskin trade declined during the last years of the 18th century, forcing native men to look for other sources of income. Those with credit and commercial contacts developed large herds of cattle and hogs, which they free ranged in the forests of the inland South and drove to markets in Mobile, Pensacola, and on the East Coast. At the same time, the federal government was putting pressure on the southern tribes to sell land to the United States. The new Republic's Indian policy was heavily influenced by Protestant missionaries, who linked conversion to Christianity with the adoption of Euro-American-style farming. U.S. officials hoped that if the southern Indians committed to agriculture and private property, they would assimilate into the white mainstream—or at least give up their hunting grounds to land-hungry settlers. Southern Indian agents like Return Jonathan Meigs and Benjamin Hawkins pushed the Cherokee, Creek, and other nations to abandon the hunt for settled farming and divide common fields into privately held family farms. Some, particularly native commercial leaders and many women farmers, responded positively to this "plan of civilization." In addition to livestock ranching, many joined their white neighbors in planting cotton.

Other southern Indians were less enthusiastic about the changes in gender roles, community relations, and economics that accompanied a turn toward commercial farming. Hawkins and other agents struggled to get their charges to abandon communal land holding or even to fence their fields. Native farmers were just as reluctant to trade hoes for plow cultivation. More importantly, many men were unable or unwilling to surrender their roles as hunters and warriors. Mounting intratribal tensions centered on the class and cultural divisions created by the new agricultural economy. Among the Cherokee and Creek, especially, men who raised cattle and cotton for sale to white merchants bought slaves, engrossed common land, and enriched themselves further. This farming elite monopolized access to merchant credit and federal annuities, and, as a result, dominated tribal government. In response, by the early 19th century, visionary nativists rejected Euro-American agriculture and called for a return to hunting and traditional gender roles. When the Red Stick faction revolted against the Creek National Council in 1811, they began by pointedly slaughtering the cattle and burning the farmsteads of wealthy Creek planters.

The defeat of the Creek and Seminole traditionalists during the wars of the 1810s cemented the power of commercial farmers among the southern Indians. In 1819 the federal government created a permanent appropriation to provide seed and farming implements through the Indian agents. White missionaries set up academies, such as the Brainerd School near Chattanooga, to teach agriculture to the children of the southern tribes. Ambitious native farmers joined the South's agricultural market and in many cases became wealthy planters. A large class of southern Indians was left behind, though, and continued to subsist on garden crops, small-scale hunting, and gathering.

This economic and social division was transferred to Oklahoma during the 1840s. Despite the seizures of property that accompanied Removal, leading native planters were able to rebuild their status in Indian Territory. The Five Civilized Tribes were more successful as farmers than native peoples on reservations elsewhere. Large planters quickly produced surpluses of corn that they sold to newcomers and to the U.S. military. Several native planters, particularly in the Choctaw and Chickasaw settlements along the Red River, acquired hundreds of slaves, planted large fields of cotton, and lived as southern gentlemen. Others, among the Creek and Cherokee in the northern part of the territory, grew enormous herds of beef cattle for sale. Poorer Indians were injured greatly by Removal, though. Taken away from their native lands, they lost the understanding of local ecology upon which their already marginal subsistence had been based. They quickly slipped down into poverty, relying on government handouts to survive.

This division among native farmers broke open during the Civil War. The wealthy slave owners who dominated the governments of the five southern tribes allied themselves with the Confederacy. Poorer natives tended to ally with the Union, and hundreds left Indian Territory for Kansas. Ultimately, both groups suffered enormously from the fighting. Requisitioning by Confederate troops, raids by Union forces, and guerilla battles between Indian factions combined to devastate farms in Indian Territory. Farms were abandoned, slaves escaped, and thousands of head of cattle were stolen by white and Indian rustlers. War and emancipation began the decline of the southern planter class among the removed tribes that was cemented by severalty in the late 19th century.

Some Native Americans resisted removal and remained in the Old South during the later 19th century, of course. In addition to reservation communities in Virginia, North Carolina, and south Florida, isolated settlements held out on marginal lands outside the Cotton Belt. In particular, many Choctaws took refuge in remote parts of Mississippi and Louisiana. Most of these communities practiced a subsistence agriculture largely indistinguishable from their poor white neighbors—cultivating corn and garden crops, ranging semiferal cattle and hogs in the surrounding forests, and hunting for meat and a small cash income from selling skins. By the early 20th century, these peoples' livelihoods depended increasingly on wage labor rather than farming—particularly in the lumber camps that dotted the southern forests.

LYNN A. NELSON
*Middle Tennessee State University*

Robbie Ethridge, *Creek Country: The Creek Indians and Their World* (2003); Charles Hudson, *The Southeastern Indians* (1976), *Knights of Spain, Warriors of the Sun: Hernando de Soto and the South's Ancient Chiefdoms* (1997); R. Douglas Hurt, *Indian Agriculture in America* (1996); Bonnie Lynn-Sherrow, *Red Earth: Race and Agriculture in the Oklahoma Territory* (2004); Theda Perdue, *Slavery and the Evolution of Cherokee Society, 1540–1866* (1979); Helen Rountree, *The Powhatan Indians of Virginia: Their Traditional Culture* (1992); Claudio Saunt, *A New Order of Things: Property, Power, and the Transformation of the Creek Indians, 1733–1816* (1999); Daniel Usner, *Indians, Settlers, and Slaves in a Frontier Exchange Economy: The Lower Mississippi Valley before 1783* (1992); Gregory Waselkov and Kathryn Holland Braund, eds., *William Bartram on the Southeastern Indians* (1995); Samuel Wells and Rosanna Tubby, eds., *After Removal: The Choctaw in Mississippi* (2004); Richard White, *The Roots of Dependency: Subsistence, Environment, and Social Change among the Choctaws, Pawnees, and Navajos* (1988); Murray Wickett, *Contested Territory: Whites, Native Americans, and African Americans in Oklahoma, 1865–1907* (2000); William Woods, "Population Nucleation, Intensive Agriculture, and Environmental Degradation: The Cahokia Example," *Agriculture and Human Values* (2004).

## New Deal and Southern Agriculture

The Great Depression exposed and exacerbated two glaring problems in early 20th-century southern agriculture: low prices caused by overproduction of farm commodities and chronic rural poverty. During the 1930s, Franklin Roosevelt's New Deal administration tackled both of these important issues, but with mixed results.

Overproduction difficulties plagued American farmers, especially southern cotton and tobacco producers, for a decade prior to the Depression. Though many proposals emerged during the 1920s to address the problem, none had been implemented. During the 1932 campaign, Roosevelt made aid to the nation's farmers an important part of his New Deal platform. He endorsed the "voluntary domestic allotment plan" promoted by M. L. Wilson, a Montana State College agricultural economics professor, who called for voluntary crop reduction by growers in exchange for government payments (subsidized by a tax on processors).

On 16 March 1933 Roosevelt sent to Congress an agricultural bill based on the allotment plan. After two months of debate, Roosevelt finally signed the Agricultural Adjustment Act into law on 12 May. Cooperating producers of seven major commodities, including cotton and tobacco, would receive payments. The programs were to be overseen by a new agency within the U.S. Department of Agriculture: the Agricultural Adjustment Administration (AAA).

Late passage of the farm bill meant that a special problem resulted for the AAA's Cotton Division because producers across the South had already planted their crops. Secretary of Agriculture Henry A. Wallace decided to pay growers in exchange for destruction of up to a third of their crops. The "plow-up campaign," as it came to be known, was a massive endeavor that needed quick implementation before the crops matured. The AAA utilized agents of the Agricultural Extension Service and appointed farmer committees (often members of the large landholding elite) to educate producers about the plan, sign them up, oversee crop destruction, and deliver $161 million to 1 million producers for the destruction of 10.5 million acres. Producers benefited financially and psychologically from the doubling of cotton prices to 10 cents per pound as a result of these efforts, plus price-support loans provided by the Commodity Credit Corporation to those who agreed to hold their crops off the market temporarily.

A plow-up was not needed for tobacco producers in 1933. Instead, the AAA oversaw a marketing agreement reached between growers and manufacturers: domestic buyers agreed to purchase at least as much tobacco as in 1932 at a minimum average price of 17 cents per pound, while 95 percent of producers agreed to reduce their planted acreage in 1934. By the end of 1933, most growers enjoyed two and a half times the amount for their crops as they received in 1932.

Important changes occurred to the AAA's programs in 1934. Congress added peanuts and sugarcane as enumerated commodities eligible for benefits (citrus fruits, strawberries, and watermelons, among other smaller commodities, would be added later in the decade). In addition, the AAA's second year saw a demand by many cooperating cotton and tobacco producers to make crop reduction mandatory. The reason for this plea was that noncooperators tended to benefit more from the programs than the cooperators (because the amount that noncooperators received from the price increase on a full crop outweighed the additional income that cooperators received from their crops plus the government checks for their reduced acreage). Grassroots pressure resulted in passage of two new production-control laws, the Bankhead Cotton Control Act and the Kerr-Smith Tobacco Control Act, both of which made compliance with the AAA's cotton and tobacco programs virtually mandatory. Each law specified that, if two-thirds of the growers agreed in an annual referendum, the AAA would assign production quotas for the next season. A producer could theoretically raise more than his assigned quota, but no profit would be seen from the excess amount due to heavy taxation. By the end of 1935, New Deal policies resulted in raising cotton prices to a healthy 12 cents per pound and tobacco to a robust 20 cents per pound.

A massive upheaval for the AAA took place in January 1936, however, when the Supreme Court ruled not only against the constitutionality of the processor taxes used to finance the AAA programs but also the AAA's production-control contracts with growers. As critics excoriated the high court's ruling, Roosevelt worked with Congress to find a quick expedient. After repealing the Bankhead and Kerr-Smith Acts to avoid useless litigation, Congress passed the Soil Conservation and Domestic Allotment Act (SCDAA). Under this law, signed by Roosevelt on 29 February 1936, the government would continue to make payments to farmers (from the federal treasury rather than from processor taxes) but ostensibly for soil-conservation practices rather than solely for production control. Growers would receive checks for "diverting" acreage formerly used to raise such soil-depleting crops as cotton and tobacco to soil-building crops such as grasses and legumes, and for implementing approved soil-conservation practices.

The SCDAA proved to be an inadequate production-control measure. Drought conditions kept agricultural production low in 1936, especially for tobacco, but the return of good weather in 1937 coupled with no restrictions on planting led to a bumper tobacco crop of 866 million pounds and a record cotton yield of almost 19 million bales. Tobacco prices held steady at 23 cents per pound because of a low carryover from the previous year, but cotton prices plummeted to 8.4 cents per pound until Roosevelt agreed to offer price-support measures guaranteeing growers 12 cents per pound if they pledged to participate in a new production-control program being devised by the government.

On 16 February 1938 Congress passed the Agricultural Adjustment Act of 1938. This law was the culmination of efforts undertaken by Secretary Wallace over the previous two years to create a long-term price-support scheme for American farmers based on a combination of the administration's previous efforts: acreage restrictions, production quotas, conservation payments, and price-support loans. This system would be the basis of the federal government's agricultural programs in the post–World War II years. By this time, Roosevelt did not have to worry about potential legal challenges—a much friendlier Supreme Court presided than was the case during his first term.

Concurrent with the Roosevelt administration's price-adjustment policies were efforts to provide relief to desperate rural Americans. The first New Deal agency to address southern rural poverty was the Federal Emergency Relief Administration (FERA), created on 12 May 1933—the same day that the AAA was established. Led by Harry Hopkins, the FERA sought to provide immediate relief to the nation's needy. Working with his staff, Hopkins improvised a series of programs for rural Americans designed to promote self-support among destitute farm families. Organizationally, the FERA provided the money, set general policies, and provided oversight to state relief agencies that implemented its programs.

The main FERA programs involved "rural rehabilitation" efforts: providing supervised credit for farmers working good land; creation of suburban communities for displaced industrial workers to enable them to survive through a combination of part-time industrial work and subsistence farming; and re-settlement projects, whereby the government planned to purchase submarginal land from farmers in order to relocate the farmers to more productive land. Yet another early New Deal effort to attack rural poverty—the subsistence homesteads program—was based outside of the FERA. Placed within its own division of the Department of the Interior, the Division of Subsistence Homesteads was responsible for distributing loans to help displaced industrial workers purchase subsistence farms. Relatively few, however, were able to get assistance because of inadequate funding, and these programs did very little to alleviate the overall problem of rural poverty in the South or elsewhere in the country.

On 30 April 1935 Roosevelt issued an executive order that consolidated the FERA programs, the subsistence homesteads program, and other rural poverty-based projects from other agencies under the new Resettlement Administration (RA) to be headed by Rexford Tugwell. The RA struggled to help clients despite low appropriations and strong conservative criticism. Over the next two years, the RA retired over 9 million acres of submarginal land while relocating its owners. The agency also constructed and maintained sanitary camps for migrant workers. Southern farmers made up over half of the RA's half-million rehabilitation clients who received loans and other assistance to increase their chances of remaining on their land. Sixty-one resettlement communities were also maintained by the RA in the South. Nevertheless, like the FERA programs before it, these efforts were only able to aid a fraction of those in need.

Upset by personal criticism, inadequate funding, and declining influence in the Roosevelt administration, Tugwell resigned in late 1936 and was replaced by Will Alexander, who was destined to head the last manifestation of the RA: the Farm Security Administration (FSA). Following Roosevelt's signing of the Bankhead-Jones Act on 22 July 1937, the FSA was created as the agency empowered to continue the RA's work while appearing to address the specific concerns of southern tenant farmers and sharecroppers highlighted in a report issued by the President's Commission on Farm Tenancy. FSA funds provided by Congress for its most publicized function—making loans to tenants wishing to purchase farms—were paltry. In its first two years, the FSA received 146,000 applications but could only offer 6,180 loans nationwide. Seventy percent of this total went to southern tenants, but only to those deemed the least risk. The most desperate who applied were simply passed over.

New Deal policies began the process of permanently altering southern agriculture while providing positive benefits for a majority of the region's farm owners. Efforts to boost farm income were moderately successful. Though farm income was only 58 percent of pre-Depression levels, prices were higher and most owners were able to hold onto their land. Though tobacco culture would remain relatively static until the 1950s, southern cotton culture was greatly impacted by the New Deal. Government policies led to increasingly mechanized cotton production on less acreage, resulting in reduced need for large numbers of nontenured operators, especially tenants and croppers. Massive evictions were under way across the South by the late 1930s. Thus, the AAA added greatly to the plight of many southern agricultural producers on the lower rung of the agricultural ladder who lack political support to counter these trends. Though some programs were established for the poorest farmers, Congress kept this aid to a slow trickle, ensuring that a vast majority would receive little aid. The Great Depression, and the New Deal's response to it, accelerated trends of land consolidation, mechanization, and labor displacement that would be solidified by the mid-20th century.

KEITH J. VOLANTO
*Collin College*

Anthony J. Badger, *Prosperity Road: The New Deal, Tobacco, and North Carolina* (1980); Sidney Baldwin, *Poverty and Politics: The Rise and Fall of the Farm Security Administration* (1968); Roger Biles, *The South and the New Deal* (1994); Pete Daniel,

*Breaking the Land: The Transformation of Cotton, Tobacco, and Rice Cultures since 1880* (1985); Keith J. Volanto, *Texas, Cotton, and the New Deal* (2005).

## New Deal–Era Farmer Organizations

Problems faced by poor farmers in Alabama and Arkansas in the 1930s resulted in the founding of two separate and distinct organizations. Although the tenants and sharecroppers they represented faced similar problems, important differences between Alabama's Share Croppers Union (SCU) and Arkansas's Southern Tenant Farmers Union (STFU) ultimately prevented the two organizations from forming an alliance. First, the SCU was affiliated with the Communist Party while the STFU's orientation was toward the Socialists. A second important difference between the two organizations involved their racial makeup. The SCU was, for most of its existence, a black-only union, while the STFU was avowedly interracial. Both endured harassment and violence at the hands of white authorities, but the SCU's racial configuration made it an especially vulnerable target. Given the political and economic impotency of African Americans in Alabama's Black Belt, authorities were able to wage a bloody campaign against farmers who allied with the SCU. Arkansas's STFU members faced violence, too, but their interracial membership complicated the efforts of local authorities to exercise the same level of intimidation faced by the SCU in Alabama. Neither organization succeeded in achieving their goals, suggesting that their different origins and the racial characteristics of their members mattered less than the larger historical forces arrayed against poor farmers of both races.

In late 1930 two African American farmers, brothers Tommy and Ralph Gray, generated interest in forming a union among black farmers in Tallapoosa County, Ala., convincing many of them to write the Communist Party's *Southern Worker*. The party had been organizing black workers in nearby Birmingham, and many of their members had rural roots, so officials were receptive to the overture from the Gray brothers. Responding to a direct request from the Grays early in 1931, the Communist Party sent Mack Coad to organize the Colored Farmers and Workers Union (CFWU) in Tallapoosa County. The situation there for black sharecroppers had worsened considerably that spring, in part because the crisis of the agricultural depression had been exacerbated by a serious drought and prompted planters to withhold advances. But some planters were motivated, as Robin D. G. Kelley suggests, by "the calculated effort to generate labor for the newly built Russell Saw Mill." Without cash or food advances, black farmers would be forced to accept employment at the mill. By July

1931 the union was 800 strong and had expanded its agenda beyond the original demand that advances be continued, an agenda that included a minimum wage of a dollar a day, a three-hour midday rest for all laborers, and a nine-month school year for black children. Planters, aided by local law enforcement officials, responded almost immediately. Sharecroppers near Camp Hill were the first to feel the wrath of white authorities when a posse raided a union meeting and assaulted those in attendance. They then attacked Tommy Gray and his family. Several union members were subsequently harassed, beaten, or arrested on trumped-up charges. This violent repression seriously eroded the membership base of the CFWU, and in August 1931 the remaining 55 members reorganized as the SCU. As the SCU grew in late 1931 and early 1932, it attracted the attention of one of its most famous members: Ned Cobb, known as Nate Shaw in Ted Rosengarden's *All God's Dangers* (1974). Cobb, unfortunately, became one of the victims of a violent confrontation in late 1932 near Reeltown, a confrontation originating over a landlord's decision to repossess property belonging to a union member. Wounded in an exchange of gunfire, Cobb was later convicted, along with five others, of assault with a deadly weapon and sentenced to 12 years in prison.

The SCU endured these challenges and adapted to a changing landscape as New Deal programs were implemented in 1934. The Agricultural Adjustment Administration (AAA) provided planters with the opportunity to receive subsidies in exchange for removing up to 30 percent of their acreage from production of certain commodity crops. Many planters refused to share crop subsidy payments with their tenants and sharecroppers and, to add insult to injury, because the crop-reduction program reduced labor needs, many sharecroppers and tenants were evicted. The SCU began orienting its demands toward those grievances and subsequently sponsored strikes of cotton choppers and cotton pickers.

Even as the SCU began shifting its demands to address problems arising out of the implementation of the AAA, farmers in Poinsett County, Ark., formed the Southern Tenant Farmers Union in July 1934 in order to protest against similar practices there. Under the auspices of two homegrown socialists, Henry Clay East and Harry L. Mitchell, a small group of black and white farmers met in a schoolhouse on the Norcross plantation, and there they made a momentous decision. When the issue of their racial makeup came up, one Isaac Shaw, who had lived through the infamous Elaine, Ark., race massacre of 1919, rose to his feet and argued for an interracial union on the grounds that planters had long been adept at pitting white and black tenants and sharecroppers against each other. Burt Williams, a white tenant farmer, whose own father had been a Ku Klux Klan member, joined Shaw in supporting an interracial union. Arguing that their grievances were identical and that planters would only "divide and conquer" if they organized segregated chapters, they demonstrated a keen awareness of planter tendencies to manipulate racist fears.

The STFU, like the SCU, faced a violent response from local authorities, but they persisted in their organizing efforts. The STFU recorded no fewer than 23 separate acts of violence perpetrated against members of the STFU in four northeastern Arkansas counties. Instead of responding in kind, the union followed a cleverly designed policy to inhibit the ability of planters to use racism to divide their organization. When a black organizer was arrested in late 1934, union officials hired C. T. Carpenter, an attorney from Marked Tree, Ark., to represent the man, preacher C. H. Smith. Although some in the STFU wanted to storm the courthouse on the day Smith came up for trial, Carpenter suggested that only white members of the union accompany him to the courthouse. Smith was released into Carpenter's custody and walked out of the courthouse flanked by more than a dozen white members. In mid-1935, when white members holding a meeting in Marked Tree received word that an organizing meeting of the black sharecroppers in nearby Gilmore had been broken up by plantation thugs, they loaded only white members onto the back of a truck and headed for Gilmore, leaving their black members behind. In doing so, they were turning on its head the planter strategy of using racism to keep white and black sharecroppers from recognizing their common interests. However, planters were sometimes successful in playing into the racist fears of black and white sharecroppers. When planters in Cross County evicted only black tenants and sharecroppers, it did not encourage their white counterparts to form an alliance with them and start an STFU chapter. One prominent black member of the union in Marked Tree, E. B. "Britt" McKinney, came to regard the white leadership of the union as "new masters," even though he was then serving as the vice president. He was expelled from the union because of his outspoken criticisms and attempted to form a separate all-black union.

Meanwhile, both the SCU and the STFU sponsored cotton pickers' strikes, with some success, in 1936 and 1937, and the two groups flirted with an alliance. It appears that the SCU was more serious about allying with the STFU than the other way around. Mitchell, clearly the leader of the latter, had serious reservations about the Communist Party. He permitted an alliance with Commonwealth College near Mena, Ark., only to split with the group after prominent communists outlined a more radical agenda than he was comfortable with. He also orchestrated an ill-fated alliance with the Congress of Industrial Organizations (CIO), but when that union insisted that STFU members send their dues directly to the CIO office, Mitchell and others withdrew from the merger, taking most of the STFU membership with them. Although he was himself forced by the threat of violence to leave the Arkansas Delta and relocate to Memphis, Tenn., he maintained the union office in Arkansas for several years.

Despite these setbacks, the STFU enjoyed some success in its efforts to attract attention to the situation facing sharecroppers and tenants. Mitchell, an articulate and forceful representative of the union, traveled to Washington, D.C., in mid-1935 and spoke to U.S. Department of Agriculture officials. Although a small group of liberals within the department were sympathetic, they were overruled and later purged; but Mitchell also gave interviews to the press, and the publicity resulted in an investigation that forced some concessions on the part of AAA officials. Planters would not be allowed to engage in wholesale evictions and would have to share crop subsidy payments with certain classes of tenants. By the time this took place, however, many tenants and sharecroppers had already been evicted, and planters, ever in control on the local level, regained mastery over the administration of the AAA programs.

Although it is clear that neither the SCU nor the STFU achieved their goals and succeeded in coming to the aid of destitute tenants and sharecroppers, they had exposed the injustices operating on plantations in the South and the complicity of federal officials. In retrospect, these organizations were fighting a corrupt system that was itself in the midst of a profound transformation, a transformation that would have no place for the landless laborers who flocked to the two unions. New Deal programs funneled cash into the hands of planters, allowing them to begin a transition from labor-intensive to capital-intensive agriculture. World War II accelerated this transition and contributed to a wholesale abandonment of the rural South by those seeking better opportunities in the war industries. The transformation of the plantation system accelerated in the postwar era, and by 1960 the category "sharecropper" was dropped from the U.S. Census of Agriculture, a testament to the disappearance of the landless laborers who had struggled so valiantly against oppression in the 1930s.

JEANNIE M. WHAYNE
*University of Arkansas*

David Eugene Conrad, *The Forgotten Farmers: The Story of Sharecroppers in the New Deal* (1965); Pete Daniel, *Breaking the Land: The Transformation of Cotton, Tobacco, and Rice Cultures since 1880* (1985); Anthony Dunbar, *Against the Grain: Southern Radicals and Prophets, 1929–1959* (1981); Donald H. Grubbs, *Cry from the Cotton: The Southern Tenant Farmers' Union and the New Deal* (1974); Robin D. G. Kelley,

*Hammer and Hoe: Alabama Communists during the Great Depression* (1991); Paul E. Mertz, *New Deal Policy and Southern Rural Poverty* (1978); Jeannie M. Whayne, *A New Plantation South: Land, Labor, and Federal Favor in Twentieth-Century Arkansas* (1996).

## Part-Time Farming

Many southern farmers are part-time farmers. Defined as those who earn more than half their income from off-farm sources, part-time farmers devote most of their time to a job away from the farm while spending weekends and evening hours engaged in some subsistence and market-oriented farming activities.

The shift to part-time farming in the South first began among the residents of southern Appalachia late in the 19th century. As lumber and mining companies moved into the mountains, farmers were lured into wage labor that they called "public work" to distinguish it from work on the privately owned farm. Appalachian farmers often began off-farm work on a seasonal basis in the winter months, using jobs to earn cash that was used to pay taxes or improve the family's living standards through the purchase of consumer goods, livestock, and farm equipment. Over time, rising land values pushed up property taxes, forcing mountain farmers to work off the farm for longer and longer periods of time each year in order to retain their hold on the family land. These men maintained farm operations with the assistance of wives and older children. By 1930 fully 58 percent of southern Appalachian farmers earned most of their income from off-farm jobs.

The trend toward part-time farming that began in the southern mountains soon spread to other parts of the South. By the mid-20th century, a variety of forces combined to transform agriculture in the lowland, piedmont, and Black Belt areas of the South. Mechanization, shifts in federal farm policy, and structural changes in the agricultural economy led to the displacement of sharecroppers and an increase in large-scale commercial farming. Small landowners found it increasingly difficult to make a living through full-time farming, especially as agricultural and industrial development led to steadily rising property taxes. In the same period, many manufacturing facilities were established in the South's rural areas, creating new opportunities for off-farm employment. Small landowners often took off-farm jobs and carried on with their farming activities after hours. The production of tobacco, row crops, beef cattle, and hogs proved particularly well-suited to part-time farming.

While some have turned to off-farm employment as a means of saving the farm, one 1980s study in rural Georgia found that a majority of part-time farmers consciously rejected full-time farming early in life. They engaged in part-time farming because they enjoyed the farming lifestyle but also wanted the more secure income levels provided by an off-farm job. Future trends in part-time farming are not clear. The number of part-time farmers in the southern states actually fell from 57 percent in the 1997 Census of Agriculture to 47 percent in 2002. Whether this is a temporary decline or a long-term trend remains to be seen.

MELISSA WALKER
*Converse College*

Peggy F. Barlett, *Rural Sociology* (Fall 1986); Ronald D. Eller, *Miners, Millhands, and Mountaineers: Industrialization in the Appalachian South* (1982); John M. O'Sullivan, *Rural South: Preparing for the Challenges of the 21st Century* (June 2000); U.S. Department of Agriculture, *Census of Agriculture* (1997 and 2002), *Economic and Social Conditions of the Southern Appalachians* (1935).

## Plantations

During the 16th and 17th centuries, Englishmen established plantations, also called colonies, in Ireland, Virginia, Bermuda, Plymouth, Massachusetts Bay, Jamaica, and elsewhere. During the 17th century, however, the term "plantation" gradually came to mean an extensive agricultural enterprise where proprietors or managers directed large labor forces in the production of export crops. Thereafter, plantations remained colonial only in the important sense of their economic relationship to faraway markets.

Plantations of this sort developed first in North America on the Virginia peninsula between the James and York Rivers, the first tobacco kingdom, and then spread throughout Tidewater Virginia and Maryland. As white indentured labor gave way to black slavery in the final decades of the 17th century, plantations in the Chesapeake Bay region came to resemble those that Europeans had earlier founded in the Caribbean and northeastern Brazil. South Carolina was from the 1670s a plantation society concentrating on rice and indigo production. Georgia followed suit during the middle of the next century. The plantations of the Carolina-Georgia Lowcountry fostered the greatest personal fortunes in the North American colonies at the time of the Revolution, and Virginia planters numbered disproportionately among the ranks of the founders of the Republic. George Washington, Patrick Henry, Richard Henry Lee, Thomas Jefferson, James Madison, and George Mason were all planters.

The westward surge of plantations began early. Thomas Jefferson grew tobacco in Virginia's piedmont before the Revolution. The culture of upland (short-staple) cotton, however, was the incentive for expansion both of plantations and black slavery. Eli Whitney's famous gin, invented in 1793, was rapidly duplicated and deployed. Both old and newly made planters pressed into Cherokee and other Indian lands. Andrew Jackson planted cotton and grew wealthy as a pioneer in the Nashville basin. Huge plantations and fortunes were created early in the Mississippi Delta hinterlands and near Natchez. A mature Cotton Kingdom did not appear, however, until the fierce Creek and Seminole were subdued and moved (with the Cherokee and other tribes) farther west. This agricultural empire stretched in a great crescent from south central Virginia, southwesterly around the Appalachians through the central Carolinas, piedmont Georgia, the Black Belt of south central Alabama and central Mississippi, up and down the wetlands of the lower Mississippi, and westward into eastern Texas. The latter area comprised a cotton frontier during the 1850s. There were also tobacco (and tobacco-cotton) plantations in Virginia and North Carolina, hemp plantations in central Kentucky, rice and Sea Island (long-staple) cotton plantations in the Carolina-Georgia lowlands, and enormous sugar estates in southeastern Louisiana. In addition to these great export staples, plantations produced, both for consumption and sale, corn, Irish and sweet potatoes, peanuts, and legumes.

Geographers and historians have characterized the plantation as a frontier institution, a flung-out settlement form tied to and dependent upon "metropolitan" capital, industry, and markets. Metropolises for antebellum planters were the textile manufacturing and financial centers of New England, Britain, and Europe. Agents, or factors, arranged sales and shipment of crops and purchases of both durable and luxury consumer goods for planters, their families, and slaves. Frontier estates were sometimes imposing examples of foreign sophistication. The interior walls of Andrew Jackson's Hermitage, for instance, were covered with French wallpaper, and guests drank from expensive, imported crystal. Some riverside mansions in Mississippi and Louisiana were furnished even more lavishly. Most plantation headquarters were more modestly appointed, however. The typical frontier "big house" probably evolved from a simple open-hallway log or board home, which gradually acquired a second story, a prefabricated portico, and columns, all crudely resembling the neoclassical style.

During the three decades before the Civil War, a planter was defined by the number of slaves owned—20 or more being a significant threshold—rather than by acres of land possessed or pounds of crops grown and shipped. Labor directly affected the amount of land that might be worked and crops that might be grown. Agriculturists believed that 20 or more slaves enabled farmers to achieve certain economies of scale on good, extensive acreage. By this measure, there were not many planters or plantations in the Old South. Of 8,039,000 whites living in 15 slave states in 1850, only 384,884 owned any slaves at all. Of these, 46,274 possessed 20 or more. Only about 2,500 had 30 or more, and only a handful of "great planters" owned 100 or more slaves. Wade Hampton III, the greatest of all planters and a Confederate general, held about 3,000 blacks in bondage on plantations in South Carolina and Mississippi.

Historians are agreed that, despite their relatively small numbers, planters largely directed antebellum economic, political, and social life. About half of all slaves worked on plantations, and their products dominated southern exports and conferred power upon planters. States adopted the federal ratio method of counting three-fifths of slave populations in determining representation in legislatures, and taxes on slaves were generally low. It is no wonder that the status of planter was the region's beau ideal and that the yeomanry and professional men alike aspired to own plantations.

The Civil War destroyed slavery but not plantations. Ownership of large entailments persisted. Various historians estimate that about half of all plantations were still held by the same families 15 years after Appomattox. The most dramatic changes wrought by emancipation were in the tenure of labor and the occupancy pattern on plantations. Sharecropping replaced legal bondage in much of the South, and sharecroppers, who were former slaves during early postbellum decades, lived in cabins on subdivided tenant farms instead of in centrally grouped quarters. What geographers term the "fragmented plantation" was born. Sharecroppers, especially blacks, submitted to nearly as much supervision from owners and overseers as during slave times. Sharecroppers had no rights to crops under their care, and, despite technical and legal differences, their situation resembled that of hired laborers. In districts where whites predominated, fragmented plantations were often worked by white tenants who occupied the higher statuses of share tenant or cash renter and who tolerated less supervision by planters and their agents. From the 1880s until about 1935, however, thousands of white farm owners and tenants fell into the status of sharecropper, while many blacks fled the countryside. By the 1930s most sharecroppers were white.

Fragmented plantations gradually and painfully came to an end between 1935 and 1955. The boll weevil ruined many cotton plantations, particularly in the older regions where the land, owners, and tenants alike were poorer than elsewhere. Laborers fled, and scattered tenant houses were vacated. New Deal crop reduction and subsidy programs for cotton and tobacco had dramatic results: planters evicted thousands of tenants and then began to invest in labor-saving machinery. As mechanical cotton harvesters, herbicides, and pesticides became available during the 1940s, the reconsolidation of plantations gathered momentum. Sharecroppers became hired workers and then were unemployed, as machines and chemicals performed their wonders. Millions fled the countryside in this new American enclosure movement. Bulldozers finally demolished tenant cabins to clear ever-larger fields.

What emerged from this radical transformation was the neoplantation. Superficially it resembled the antebellum model: the owner-manager's power over labor and equipment was centralized once more, and workers (now but a handful on each plantation) once more lived in centrally grouped housing. Neoplantations are more capital-intensive and less labor-intensive than were earlier ones. On the modern plantation, there is little reason or opportunity for the paternalism that characterized antebellum plantations and subsequent sharecropper estates. Present agricultural approaches are altogether different. By 1955 the West (especially California and Arizona) had established ascendancy in cotton production, while much of the old plantation South was abandoning the crop. Cotton still grows in the lower Mississippi Delta districts and in Texas, but typical neoplantations are more likely sown with soybeans, grain, sorghum, peanuts, and increased amounts of corn. During the 1960s, innovative planters in Mississippi's Delta counties also adopted rice culture from neighboring Louisiana and Arkansas's Grand Prairie and later developed catfish ponds. Many neoplantations produce beef cattle, others are huge dairy operations, and some specialize in pecans. A few dozen former fragmented cotton and corn plantations with poor, sandy soil—many of them in southern Georgia and northwestern Florida—have evolved into hunting preserves that also contain timber.

Most neoplantations differ little from large farms in Iowa or California ranches—except, of course, where peculiarly southern crops such as sugar are grown. The term "plantation" remains applicable because neoplantations are concentrated in the historical plantation region and because use of the word persists.

JACK TEMPLE KIRBY
*Miami University of Ohio*

P. P. Courtenay, *Plantation Agriculture* (1980); Francis Pendleton Gaines, *The Southern Plantation: A Study in the Development and the Accuracy of a Tradition* (1925); Lewis C. Gray, *History of Agriculture in the Southern United States to 1860*, 2 vols.

(1933); Merle C. Prunty Jr., *Geographical Review* (October 1955); Arthur F. Raper, *Preface to Peasantry: A Tale of Two Black Belt Counties* (1936); Edgar T. Thompson, ed., *The Plantation: An International Bibliography* (1983).

## Rural Life

Just as a truly solid South has never existed in an overall regional sense, there has never been a hard and fast pattern of rural life across the region. Much of the developing South, and especially that part designated the "Old Southwest," spawned and nurtured an arrested form of frontier American culture that reflected the particular environmental influences to which people were exposed. Southerners were not the only Americans set adrift in such a large mass of virgin land; none, however, implanted this experience more indelibly in their folkways and modes of rural life. The availability of a seemingly inexhaustible amount of reasonably fertile land, a wide variety of trees, generous rainfall and water resources, and a benign climate supplied the natural ingredients for the development of a distinctive culture. Rural southerners, as much by individual choice as by circumstance, made dual responses to the land. Some came as land-greedy plantation masters, but more remained yeoman subsistence farmers. Both created an isolated regional folk culture that sustained almost two centuries of social continuity, but with definite intrasectional variations.

Southern geographical isolation was a central influence in sustaining one of the most pronounced broad-patterned cultural lags in American history. This powerful and pervasive influence shaped folkways by blending old human forms and customs with necessary adaptations mandated in the new country. Though the southern way of rural life for individual families and communities appeared simple and uncomplicated, in fact the regional pattern was highly complex.

FOLK CULTURE. From the beginnings of English settlement to the present, the modes of rural southern life have been compared and measured against those of older, more mature civilizations, nearly all of which were industrially and technologically oriented. Internally, the southern rural way of life included social classes with subtle boundaries, but common to all of them was a taste for regional foods, the prevalence of folk customs, the importance of blood relationships, and a sense of Old World origins. Much of the so-called aristocratic or patrician planter class rose from the common yeoman folk masses and brought up with them many of their tastes and manners. Only after the Civil War and the rise of cities, industries, and diversified commercialization did class distinctions become more sharply defined and divisive.

Nurse with newborn baby and mother, Kentucky, early 1900s
(Photographic Archives, University of Louisville [Kentucky])

Perhaps it was a tragic lapse in southern history that the rich regional folk culture was denied sufficient time to mature intellectually and economically before its progress was rudely disrupted by war. Few if any of the regional decision makers of the antebellum South truly comprehended, though, the dynamics of their emerging folk society. In large areas of the developing South in 1860, much of the population had only begun to make transitions from the primitive log-cabin frontier stage to a more mature and intensified social and economic pattern of life. In some areas, an inordinately long interval prevailed between stages. The stifling barriers of the great landed hinterland had barely been breached with roads, stream channels and crossings, and railroads. The rural population remained almost wholly dependent upon the small yeoman subsistence farm as its main source of livelihood.

Rich natural resources remained only partially explored and exploited. The necessary human talents and skills had not been developed, nor were there facilities to bring the resources into profitable production. Two primary resources, the great forest belt and the coal and iron seams, had begun to make miniscule contributions to the economic and cultural advancement of the earlier rural South. Of greater significance was the lag in institutional developments. Rural southerners lacked the necessary vision and entrepreneurial leadership to generate ample institutional support to bring into fruitful production the rich natural bounties of the land. Paradoxically, the rural southern population lived frugal, if not impoverished, lives in many places atop some of the richest resources in America. The agrarian population generated insufficient capital to do more than organize and sustain struggling institutions. It developed no important universities, supported no notable libraries, and sustained only a limited number of banks.

The earlier emigrants who pursued with frenetic passion and expectation the public-land frontier in the Lower South moved almost entirely within a virtually impregnable folk culture. They clung tenaciously to blood relationships. These people were of predominantly Anglo- and Afro-American origins. Yeoman farmer and planter alike transported in their cultural baggage a defined set of folkways and ancient traditions. For instance, a Mississippi countryman would not have felt awkwardly out of place among country folk of rural hinterland Virginia. He would have readily recognized family names and those of country churches and their denominations, the limited nature of rural schools, common tastes in foods, modes of entertainment and sports, and, most of all, the general social customs. Most likely his people had relatives who remained behind in the Great Migration. This was even more true in those other wellsprings of southern population, the Carolinas and Georgia.

RELIGION, WOMEN, FAMILY, COMMUNITY. No social force had greater or more diverse impact on the rural southern way of life than religion. The Protestant church, whatever denominational label it bore, was a durable institutional bedrock. Within a loosely defined theological context, rural southern Protestants were exposed to a strong folk mix of biblical fundamentalism, Sabbatarianism, emotional conversion experiences, and periodic spiritual rejuvenation. The great wave of unbridled emotional revivalism that occurred in Virginia, the Carolinas, and Kentucky in the mid-18th century and the early part of the 19th spread throughout the rural South. No recurring social event in the lives of most southern countrymen became more fixed institutionally than the annual revivals and camp meetings. The sustained spiritual results of these gatherings are hard to measure beyond the general observations that they no doubt served mightily to keep the church and denominational torches aflame. Conversions, backslidings, and spiritual rebirths were frequent and fervent.

The social influence of the annual revivals was more discernible. They were recurrent punctuations between the growing and harvesting seasons, when either the bounteous grace of nature was visible or the will of God was evident in crop failure. Both were occasions for earnest supplication. In some vague historical manner, the annual southern country revival meetings almost seemed to be a link with Old World pagan harvest festivals; the sometimes unrestrained emotional atmosphere even offered a trace of the ancient Grecian seasonal rites of the Eleusinian Mysteries.

Although the ways of rural southern life had a sharply masculine tone, the role of women in regional history has been vital. Homemaking alone involved a multiplicity of onerous tasks for most of two centuries. Not only did the country woman perform all the functions of mother, nurse, family counselor, and spiritual leader, she also was spinner and weaver, knitter, seamstress, quilter, fruit and vegetable preserver, butcher, and supplemental field hand. She busied herself in soap making, tending livestock, and looking after the garden and orchard. Without doubt, as many women and children worked in the rural South from 1820 to 1920 as in any other section of the United States. As late as 1930, the South had the largest number of women, white and black, engaged in agricultural work of any region in the nation.

In addition to her numerous labors, the country woman kept track of kinships and relatives and remembered ancient folk rhymes, ballads, party games, and the ingredients and applications of folk remedies. She was the main preserver of the Sabbath, leant a softness of tone to the raw frontier, and in a humble way encouraged certain social refinements. However much rural southern women appeared in the background in abstract historical documentation, they provided the solid warping of the social fabric of the rural South in all its ages.

Although the rural southern family was of a strongly patriarchal nature, where the grandfather and father assumed predominant roles in most matters, the mother supplied the human adhesive that held the family together. Generally, rural families were close-knit and numerous. In the newer areas of the region, emigrants moved and settled down as family units, and one still finds southern communities where common family names predominate. Historically, the more isolated neighborhoods were the most cohesive because of family ties, especially so in the highland South.

Rural southern families were unified, but members became widely dispersed as they followed the moving frontier westward. Literally hundreds of families in time had members living all across the western part of the country. Travelers repeatedly commented upon the restlessness and constant movement of people in search of new and cheaper lands. Americans are now diligently searching for their blood roots in older settled areas, and southern genealogists, in particular, have produced sizable collections of books, family trees, and guides in tracing an astonishing dispersal of people of common ancestral roots. Throughout the South, countless small or private cemeteries dot the landscape, serving as mute repositories of personal historical information that rival the records of county clerks, the census schedules, and collections of family papers. Regardless of the social and economic fortunes of the deceased, in historical perspective they become a vital link in the human history of this age.

Local neighborhoods are just as important an influence in unifying yet dividing the rural South. Modernizing influences such as improved transportation, the introduction of specialized skills and services, the availability of scientific medical care, new types of merchandising, and the rise of urban centers all worked to make the rural southern community a place of both warmhearted, generous neighborliness and bitter personal strife.

No more appealing nostalgic chapters can be found in the history of the rural South than those describing neighborly common workings such as logrollings, the harvesting and processing of field crops, and the assisting of neighbors fallen victim to misfortune. Of an even more human nature was communal aid in births, in sickness, and in death and disaster. Whatever country neighbors lacked in skill and sophistication, they made up for in human concern for the welfare of neighbors in need.

Conversely, rural southern neighborhood rifts could be violent, senseless, and irreconcilable, with the old bitterness sometimes lingering on for generations. Few or no southern communities escaped fusses and violent incidents. Columns of southern country weekly newspapers and court dockets are filled with accounts of squabbles ranging from disputes over land boundaries and religious beliefs to straying livestock, women, dogs, and politics. The rural southern temper could become overheated with suddenness, and rural memories of injuries were long and brooding.

In a pleasanter vein, rural southerners of all ages generated and passed on an impressive body of folklore. Indian-like, they handed down by word of mouth customs, traditions, superstitions, and wild yarns. In a region subjected to serious educational and cultural lags, the spoken word was of historical importance, and the folktale of local origin was well adapted to giving a living sense of time and place. In the passing decades it became rich grist to the writers who created a more durable published form of literature. This rural frontier heritage has been important in the development of a regional literature.

RURAL INSTITUTIONS. The southern rural way of life sustained several institutions common to all parts of the South: the local county seat, the country church, the one-room country school, the general store, the weekly newspaper, and the fourth-class post office. The county seat with its court days was at once a center of justice after a fashion and of public administration, a market town, a local gathering place, and a limited professional center. For vast numbers of rural southerners, the county seat was the nearest they ever came to visiting an urban community. Country churches were as varied in forms and rituals as they were numerous. Scarcely any community was without at least one church. The southern landscape from the Potomac to the Trinity was dotted with Calvaries, Bethels, Enons, Shilohs, Mt. Sinais, Hebrons, Lebanons, Mount Pleasants, Rocky Hills, Shady Groves, and Campgrounds. These were as much social centers as spiritual founts. Possibly more communicants took home from church information about crop prospects, cotton and tobacco prices, coon dogs, squirrel hunting, and local news than impressions of what the preachers had said in their interminable sermons on the subject of eternal damnation.

No rural southern institution gathered about itself a warmer aura of human nostalgia than the general or country store. Seated at crossroads all across the South, the stores were combination merchandising and farmer markets, sources of credit, medicine, and simple bits of luxury, news centers, resorts for sage advice, and eternal places for gossiping and yarn spinning. Southern crops planted and grown in words around country-store stoves and on their porches far surpassed those actually planted in neighboring fields and ultimately listed in the tables of decennial censuses. Had these "store crops" ever reached maturity, the South would have made a fabulous showing against the rest of the nation.

In a region largely without access to banks, the general or furnishing store was a life-sustaining source of credit for the maintenance of an informal type of cash flow. Without this, much of the rural southern agricultural system would have been even more seriously handicapped. In large measure, general stores in hundreds of isolated rural southern communities shaped the life of their customers and served as a cardinal link between southern countrymen and the outside world of capital, industry, and contemporary technological and material advances. Stove-side and porch forums were places where every subject of interest to an agrarian society was discussed and southern humankind's most complex problems were settled with authoritative certainty.

If older southerners have recalled with a certain romantic nostalgia the country store with its heterogeneous mixture of merchandise, smells, and excitement, they have even more fondly recalled one-room country schools and angelic or martinet teachers. For many parts of the South, the primitive schoolroom tucked away in an obscure corner was the only real intellectual gesture people made in a raw country environment. Emphasis on the "three R's" prepared rural youth to function in a plain and unsophisticated society where technical and industrial challenges were absent. Commercial intercourse in most communities seldom was more demanding than simply understanding merchants' accounts at settling-up time at the end of crop seasons. If an individual became literate enough to read the Scriptures, then he or she had achieved one of the main objectives of an education. There was doubtless reward enough in a countryman's signing his name to a land deed, an application for a marriage license, a mortgage, or any other formal document filed permanently in a county clerk's office. He could also form a vague and partisan political opinion from reading the local country weekly newspaper.

Wherever a new county seat was located, an editor-printer appeared to claim the honor of publishing an official organ. The modest four-page southern weekly was essentially a bulletin of legal notices, the voice of the Democratic county officials, and a broadside for the advertising of worthless proprietary medicines. Nevertheless, the modest news and editorial columns reflected the turnings and workings of the rural southern mind and, almost universally, the partisan and prejudiced opinions of the editors. News columns, especially those called "locals," while astonishingly puerile, reflected the folkways and the sterility of life in rural communities where little of interest happened except birthing and dying. With an authority backed by printer's ink, editors commented on all subjects, upheld public morals, lectured readers on their decorum or lack of it, and discussed politics, religion, and the weather with the certainty that there was only one side to every question. Many of them crusaded effectively for or against public issues. They preached diversification of field crops without being able to suggest solutions to credit, transportation, and marketing dilemmas.

LITERARY IMAGES. Country weekly papers portrayed rural southerners in their changing moods and in varying social and economic conditions, and they also welcomed them into the world with birth notices and ushered them out of it with eloquent obituaries. Historically, they preserved the countryman's personality and image as raw material for more formal writers. As southern backwoods emigrants pushed deeper inland, they evolved into a new genre of backwoodsmen. Often far removed from the seasoning influences of refining institutions, they regressed culturally. Early regional authors found the country greenhorns captivating subjects for their essays and books. Such natives as Augustus Baldwin Longstreet, William Tappan Thompson, John Jones Hooper, Joseph Glover Baldwin, and George Washington Harris gave immortality to an assortment of southern backcountry types. While these authors distorted descriptions of their fictional characters, they conveyed a strong realistic sense of an important segment of southern life. At the time these genre authors were writing and publishing their books, the country newspapers ran space-filler stories of a kindred nature, partly under the guise of semihumorous news items. Foreign and domestic travelers in the antebellum South left accounts of their experiences, many of which were as distorted as the writings of the professed regional humorists.

The rural southerner and his way of life with its crises and triumphs survived the Civil War and Reconstruction as a literary theme. In the writings of George Washington Cable, James Lane Allen, Mary Noailles Murfree, Ellen Glasgow, and Joel Chandler Harris, the southerner appeared in many guises, ranging from sophisticated plantation gentry to lowly field hands living close to the footstool of nature and the land. Whatever his role, he exhibited color out of proportion to his condition. Whether it be mountain feudist, sharecropping peasant, tobacco-stained constituent of political demagogues, narrow-minded communicant of a rural evangelical church, or just plain yeoman subsistence farmer, the southerner personified a rural region of the nation floundering against diversity and change, almost always being confronted by the uncertainties of time and fortune.

A later generation of southern writers peopled their books with similar countrymen. William Faulkner gave evidence in his writings that he was conversant with the earlier chroniclers of the backwoods. So did Thomas Wolfe, Erskine Caldwell, Thomas Stribling, and Elizabeth Maddox Roberts. Eudora Welty's characters are rural Mississippians who have direct blood relationship with the pioneers who moved from the Carolinas to settle that state.

In the field of nonfiction, state and local libraries bulge with personal memoirs and regional histories that collectively detail a major portion of the southern rural experience. In a more formal manner, Benjamin B. Kendrick and Alex M. Arnett, *The South Looks at Its Past* (1935); Rupert B. Vance, *The Human Geography of the South: A Study in Regional Resources and Human Adequacy* (1932); W. T. Couch, ed., *Culture in the South* (1949); Herman C. Nixon, *Possum Trot: Rural Community, South* (1941); and Howard W. Odum, *Southern Regions of the United States* (1936) are largely books about rural southerners. Even the U.S. Census reports reveal eloquently the unfolding fortunes of the rural South and its people over almost two centuries.

The tempo of life in earlier years was set by recurring crop seasons, plantings, workings, and harvestings, each separated from the other by intervals suggesting a chronic state of laziness and idleness. The agrarian life in its natural rhythms allowed time for neighborliness and the exercise of a distinctive form of rural civility in both social and business intercourse. Even the drawling speech of the rural southerner in some measure reflected the impact of time and the land, the homogeneity of human origins, the cultural lags, racial mixture, geographical isolation, and stubborn resistance to change. These, however, in time were subjected to the inevitable revisions born of lowering old barriers.

CHANGE AND CONTINUITY SINCE 1920. The folkways of life in the rural South underwent marked changes in the decade following 1920. Already the boll weevil invasion had shaped the future for one segment of regional agriculture. The rise of towns and industries, the acute depression at the outset of that decade, the impact of consolidated schools and of higher education, the coming of new systems of merchandising, and then the later Great Depression and the New Deal with its various rural problem-solving agencies—all revised, if they did not destroy, the old patterns and customs of southern rural life. Added to these were the scientific breakthroughs in wood-using industries, the spread of modern highway systems, the creation of the Tennessee Valley Authority, the introduction of the Rural Electrification Administration, and the enormous impact of mechanized farming. Within two decades, these forces practically erased the bolder outlines of the traditional approaches and patterns of rural life.

For more than a century, the course of rural life in the South was unplanned. After 1920 most of the old rural institutions were caught in the web of failure. The system of sharecropping and tenant farming that had flourished from 1865 to 1920 was on the brink of utter collapse. No longer could the South survive this waste of human energy and soils. Both white and black tenants deserted the farm by hundreds of thousands, driven away by biting poverty. In fact, one of the most dramatic social and economic changes that occurred in the rural South in this century was the almost complete departure from the land by black farmers.

In reality, the cherished dream of a self-sufficient rural America never materialized at any period in southern history. Neither did Henry W. Grady's eloquent oratorical fantasy of a contented agrarian southern population living off the land ever come even remotely near realization. As late as 1930, Howard W. Odum could ask the rhetorical question about the human condition of the rural South: "Are not its white people still more than 90 per cent of the earlier stock? Are they not of Protestant faith, Sabbath observing, family loving and patriarchal, of religious intensity, quarreling with the government, individualists taking their politics, their honors, and their drinking hard? Their attitudes toward work and play, toward women and property, toward children and their

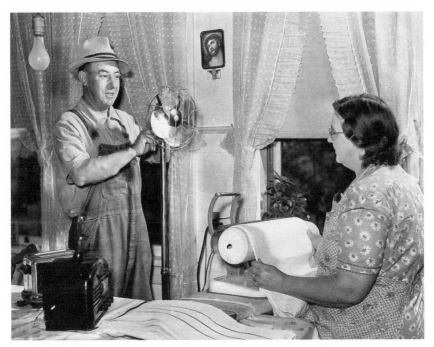

By the 1940s, electricity brought fans, radios, and other conveniences to rural southerners, such as this couple in Knox County, Tenn. (Arthur Rothstein, Library of Congress [LC-USW-3-4061-D], Washington, D.C.)

work, toward the dominant leaders are still much the same as was the early vintage. Both Southeast and Southwest are still frontier folk; the Southeast, parts of which are the oldest of the United States culture, reflecting a sort of arrested frontier pattern of life." This, he thought, still formed a baseline for recovering in the South what might have been.

Southern folk stubbornly held onto cherished standards of conservative Protestant beliefs and personal relationships even in the face of urban modernity. The linkage with frontier political concepts was not broken. Though severely strained, the once viable spirit of obliging neighborliness survived in isolated rural islands in more tentative forms. Change has come most completely, though, in the loss of neighborhood-centering institutions, especially with standardization of the schools at all levels. The crusaders of the late 19th and early 20th centuries who declared war on the lethargic rural ways of life were more successful than they knew. The consolidation of schools practically obliterated neighborhood boundaries by removing core centers, and what this revolution in education failed to accomplish the good roads crusade finished.

By the end of the 20th century and the beginning of the 21st, the social, cultural, and statistical patterns of the rural South had only fading resemblances to the past. Thousands of old and cherished country homesteads had been smashed to earth to make way for pastures and woodlands. Beloved old churches once serving thriving congregations stood vacant, with most of their strict Sabbatarian communicants lying in nearby neglected cemeteries. Sites of the famous campgrounds long before had fallen victim to the pines, and few people could point out the places where country schools, stores, and fourth-class post offices stood. Even villages and towns succumbed to the ravages of time and progress, forgotten except as names on the pages of local histories.

Nonetheless, southerners strive for continuity. Incessantly searching, blacks and whites on the trail of ancestors have turned genealogy into an important southern industry. Weed-grown and abandoned graveyards, like earlier regional Indian mounds, have become rich informational sources linking present descendants with the past. Four identifiable human-interest areas survive from the earlier southern rural way of life: a love of sports, a taste for regional foods and cooking, an all but inerasable streak of religious fundamentalism, and the love of a good folksy yarn.

There lingers on in the southern psyche a yearning to escape into some simplistic air-conditioned and cellophane-wrapped Jeffersonian Valhalla, located conveniently near a modern shopping mall, not too far from a football stadium, with free access to a good color television set to relieve the mind of serious concern with social and cultural lags and deficient showings in economic statistical tables. Large areas of the old rural South have fallen victim either to urban sprawl, super highway rights-of-way, airports, or industrial sites. Each year 200,000 more acres of land are gobbled up in this way. The old southern rural pattern of life has been broken beyond hope of restitution.

THOMAS D. CLARK
*Lexington, Kentucky*

John D. Boles, *The Great Revival, 1787–1805: The Origins of the Southern Evangelical Mind* (1972); Joyce E. Chaplain, *An Anxious Pursuit: Agricultural Innovation and Modernity in the Lower South, 1730–1815* (1993); Thomas D. Clark, *Pills, Petticoats, and Plows: The Southern Country Store* (1944), *The Southern Country Editor* (1948), ed., *Travels in the Confederate States* (1948), *Travels in the New South*, 2 vols. (1962), *Travels in the Old South*, 3 vols. (1959); Peter A. Coclanis, *The Shadow of a Dream: Economic Life and Death in the South Carolina Low Country, 1670–1920* (1989); W. T. Couch, *These Are Our Lives* (1939); Pete Daniel, *Standing at the Crossroads: Southern Life in the Twentieth Century* (1986); James D. B. De Bow, *Statistical View of the United States, Embracing Its Territory, Population—White, Free, Colored and Slave—*

Moral and Social Condition (1854); J. Wayne Flynt, Dixie's Forgotten People: The South's Poor Whites (1979, 2004); Margaret J. Hagood, Mothers of the South: Portraiture of the White Tenant Farm Woman (1939); Randall L. Hall, Lum and Abner: Rural America and the Golden Age of Radio (2007); Arthur Palmer Hudson, Humor in the Old Deep South (1939), Folklore Keeps the Past Alive (1961); R. Douglas Hurt, ed., African American Life in the Rural South since World War II (1998); Jack Temple Kirby, Rural Worlds Lost: The American South, 1920–1960 (1986); Herman C. Nixon, Possum Trot: Rural Community, South (1941); Howard W. Odum, Folk, Region, and Society: Selected Papers of Howard W. Odum, ed. Katherine Jocker, Guy B. Johnson, George L. Simpson, and Rupert B. Vance (1964), Southern Regions of the United States (1936), The Way of the South (1947); Lu Ann Jones, Mama Learned Us to Work: Farm Women in the New South (2002); Frederick Law Olmsted, A Journey in the Back Country (1860); Frank L. Owsley, Plain Folk of the Old South (1949); Ben Robinson, Red Hills and Cotton: An Upcountry Memory (1942); Theodore Rosengarten, All God's Dangers: The Life of Nate Shaw (1975); Louis D. Rubin Jr., Writers of the Modern South: The Faraway Country (1966); Mark Schultz, The Rural Face of White Supremacy (2005); Melissa Walker, All We Knew Was to Farm: Rural Women in the Upcountry South, 1919–1941 (2000).

## Rural-Urban Migration

Sustained migration by rural southerners to urban places within the region began in the 1880s. From that point onward, rural southerners in growing numbers have chosen to leave the region's countryside, migrating to cities in the South as well as those in the North and West. While some southern cities, such as New Orleans, have long attracted large numbers of foreign-born immigrants, most southern cities depended upon a steady influx of native-born rural migrants to support their population growth until only very recent times. The 9 percent of the South's population residing in urban areas in 1880 grew steadily to 32 percent in 1930 and to 67 percent in 1980. The decisions of millions of rural southerners to leave agriculture and embark upon life in city and town drove the process of southern urbanization and helped transform the South from a predominantly rural and agricultural region to an urban and industrial one.

From the 1880s to the 1930s, southerners migrated to the region's cities primarily to bolster the economic prospects of the rural household. The contours of southern agriculture, with its high rates of tenancy, flawed credit and marketing institutions, low productivity, and low incomes gave rural southerners strong incentive to migrate to cities in search of higher earnings. Young men seeking to acquire the means to establish themselves as farmers in their own households were especially likely to migrate, alternating stints as rural wage workers as loggers or sawmill workers, with temporary forays into cities as factory or construction workers before returning to commence farming and begin a family. Generally, rural black men were more likely than their white counterparts to leave the rural South but less likely to migrate to a city within the region. Blacks, if they did migrate to a southern city, usually moved on, in stepwise fashion, to an urban place in the North or West. Overall, black males were less likely to migrate to southern cities than whites and instead chose destinations outside the region.

After 1910 rural southern women migrated to the region's cities in increasing numbers, finding employment as office workers, sales clerks, factory operatives, and domestic servants. Changes in urban labor markets demanded larger numbers of female clerical and office workers. At the same time, incremental improvements in rural education meant that rural southern women had the opportunity to attain the basic educational skills necessary for clerical work. Migration held different meanings for women than for men. While male migrants tended to view urban migration as a temporary expedient that would allow them to earn the means to return to the countryside and start a family, women saw in urban life a chance to escape the constraints of a rural social and economic order that limited their life choices to that of farmer's wife. Urban migration and employment offered these women a limited degree of independence and income that was difficult to achieve in the countryside. These benefits largely accrued to white women. Black urban women found their employment options limited to a narrow range of domestic and service occupations, and consequently, they were less likely than white women to migrate to southern cities.

Southern cities developed an array of educational and charitable institutions to address the needs of rural migrants and integrate them into urban life. Settlement houses such as the Methodist Church's Wesley Houses (1903), for whites, and Bethlehem Centers (1913), for blacks, catered to the needs of a largely migrant urban poor. The Young Men's and Young Women's Christian Associations established subsidized dormitories for young workers as well as employment agencies and worker-training programs to integrate migrants into the urban labor market. Private commercial colleges, which appeared in all leading southern cities by the 1910s, offered training to migrants, especially women, in the rudiments of office work.

Depression and war transformed rural-urban mobility patterns in the South, hastening both the pace of out-migration from agriculture and in-migration to cities. New Deal agricultural policies set in motion a series of events that would lead to the eventual collapse of sharecropping as the principal means of organizing southern agriculture. Commodity price supports and acreage restrictions initiated in the 1930s and wartime labor shortages during World War II provided incentives for landowners to shift from sharecropping to wage labor and begin the process of mechanizing production. The widespread adoption of mechanical cotton harvesters in the 1950s removed the "harvest bottleneck" that had been the last prop supporting sharecropping.

World War II initiated a period of industrial expansion in the South that provided a powerful magnet for rural people just as agriculture's labor needs plummeted. The rural exodus after World War II dwarfed the movement in the first half of the century. No longer was migration to the city a seasonal or temporary phenomenon intended to bolster the rural household; rural people were leaving agriculture permanently to work in the region's burgeoning factories. Those parts of the rural South most heavily invested in plantation agriculture faced especially dramatic population loss. The Alabama Black Belt and the Mississippi Delta—two of the most important cotton growing regions in the South—saw especially heavy exodus of former sharecroppers as planters mechanized production or shifted land to other, less labor-intensive uses, such as livestock or forestry. Technological improvements and consolidation in flue-cured tobacco production led to heavy out-migration from tobacco-belt counties in the southeastern states in the 1960s and 1970s.

The rural South benefited from regional economic development trends in the second half of the 20th century. Interstate highways and the expansion of the electric power grid in rural regions meant that industry could locate closer to ready sources of labor in the southern countryside. By the late 1970s, the pace of rural out-migration began to level off, as rural industrialization absorbed some of the labor that was leaving agriculture and as the region began to receive in-migration. In 1930, 67 percent of employed heads of households in the rural South worked in agriculture; by 1960 that figure had fallen to 28 percent. In 1990 only 7 percent of rural heads of households worked in agriculture. The rural South had been transformed into a manufacturing and services region.

The rural South in the 1980s and 1990s faced divergent population trends. Rural areas that had access to desirable natural features or urban areas and their amenities, or which possessed a strong local employment base, were able to reverse the outflow of population and experience in-migration and population growth. Growth was concentrated in rural areas near the region's dynamic cities or clustered along tourist-related coastal and mountain regions. Access to employment in metropolitan regions allowed people in these rural areas to remain in the countryside.

Rural areas more remote from urban areas with a history of plantation agriculture continue to be characterized by high levels of poverty and unemployment. These rural regions continue to send migrants to the region's cities in search of work. Promoting economic growth in this portion of the rural South stands as the region's greatest development challenge.

LOUIS M. KYRIAKOUDES
*University of Southern Mississippi*

John B. Cromartie, *Rural America* (February 2001); Louis M. Kyriakoudes, *Social Origins of the Urban South: Race, Gender, and Migration in Nashville and Middle Tennessee, 1890–1930* (2003).

## Sharecropping and Tenancy

Since the post–Civil War years, the plantation landlord and the tenant farmer have been among the most prominent figures in the nation's perception of the South. They have been graphic symbols of the region's ruralism, poverty, and cultural backwardness, and they have exemplified the paternalism, exploitation, and social-class dimensions of southern agriculture. Until the mid-20th century, these images undoubtedly reflected the reality of several million southerners whose lives were blighted by crop-lien tenancy.

Tenancy was a response to the disorganization and poverty of southern agriculture following the Civil War, becoming widely established by about 1880. Former slaves and landless whites needed access to land and compensation as laborers, but landlords lacked money for wages. To organize production, landowners allowed these workers to farm plots of 20 to 40 acres on a crop-sharing basis. They also undertook the support of their tenants during the crop season by extending credit for food and living necessities, secured by liens on their portions of the crop. Often this credit was arranged through rural store owners, or furnish merchants, who were also general suppliers of feed, fertilizer, and implements. Planter-landlords with many tenants, however, frequently furnished them directly, through plantation commissaries. This crop-sharing and lien-financing system was necessitated by the South's dearth of farm-production credit. It reflected the limitations of agricultural technology; this system sustained the large force of unskilled labor that was needed as long as cotton and tobacco remained unmechanized.

Relatively few of the South's landless farmers were independent cash renters;

Sharecropper family at home in Alabama, 1935
(Walker Evans, Library of Congress [LC-USF-342-8147-A], Washington, D.C.)

most were share tenants and sharecroppers. The latter two levels of tenancy were defined by the farmers' contributions to production and their need for subsistence credit, as well as by how closely they were supervised by landlords. Share tenants often owned mules or equipment and might be able to supply some seed or fertilizer. Their furnishing needs varied, as did their supervision. Accordingly, their portions of the crop could be as much as two-thirds or three-fourths—less, of course, advances and interest. Sharecroppers, on the other hand, usually possessed no work stock or tools and contributed only labor. Dependent on lien credit for nearly all living necessities and working under much supervision, they ordinarily received no more than half the crop, from which "furnishing" and interest were deducted.

In the chronically depressed southern agriculture of the late 19th century and the early 20th century, tenancy increased steadily as many farmers lost their land. It reached its peak in 1930, when the census counted 228,598 cash renters, 772,573 sharecroppers, and 795,527 other tenants (mostly share tenants) in 13 southern and border states. Tenancy was the dominant pattern in staple-crop production. In 1937 the President's Committee on Farm Tenancy estimated that tenants and croppers were 65 percent of all farmers in the Cotton Belt and 48 percent in tobacco regions. Approximately two-thirds of southern tenants

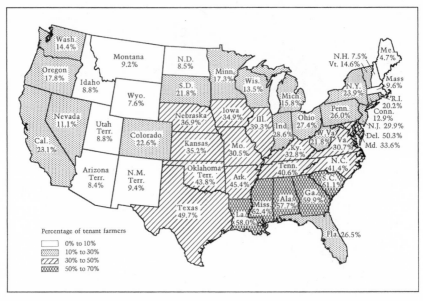

Farm Tenancy, 1890

Source: George B. Tindall, America: A Narrative History, 2d ed., vol. 2 (1988).

were white, although among croppers, the lowest tenure group, the number of whites and blacks was about equal. Share tenants, croppers, and their families easily comprised nearly half the 1930 southern farm population of 15.5 million.

Southern tenancy was the context for a culture of rural poverty. Tenants and croppers received some of the lowest incomes in America, rarely clearing more than a few hundred dollars per year. Their more common experience, especially in years of low crop prices, was to receive no net income at all because their shares of crops could not cover high-interest furnishing debts. These scant earnings kept rural southerners living at the bottom of the national scale. Cotton and tobacco tenants lived in the fields they worked in pine-board cabins that lacked window glass, screens, electricity, plumbing, and even wells and privies. Thousands of families were without common household furnishings, stoves, mattresses, or adequate clothing and shoes. The poorest croppers subsisted on a furnish-store diet that relied heavily on salt pork, flour, and meal. Owning no cows or poultry and tending no gardens, they seldom consumed milk, eggs, or fresh vegetables. Malnutrition compounded wretched living conditions to make chronic illness a major feature of rural life, as malaria, pellagra, and hookworm infection stunted the development of children, shortened lives, and lowered the economic productivity of the poor.

Crop-lien tenancy was both exploitive and paternalistic. One of the familiar figures of southern rural lore was the tightfisted landlord who kept all accounts, charged exorbitant interest on advances, and took over his tenants' cotton for debts. As part of the local power structure, planters were in a position to make whatever settlements they wished, without challenge from illiterate tenants. Perhaps the greatest tragedy of this system was that exploitation was built into it. A landlord, hard-pressed by mortgage and tax obligations, production costs, and low crop prices, often could not profit without cutting as deeply as possible into his tenants' shares. Moreover, as planters extended credit, they also supervised tenants' farming, leaving the least skilled, especially, with little opportunity to develop competence and self-direction. Tenancy thus bred dependency among the poor.

Tenants had little security on the land. They worked under year-to-year verbal agreements that left landlords free to dispense with their services at settling time. With a great surplus of unskilled labor at hand, planters usually felt little need to hold dissatisfied or unwanted tenants. Most landless farmers were highly mobile, moving as often as every year or two. This transience was socially and economically wasteful; it deprived tenants of any role in their communities and reinforced illiteracy by preventing regular schooling of their children. It destroyed incentives to maintain farm property and contributed greatly to soil erosion.

The southern public's perception of tenancy conformed to traditional American views of poverty, which have been highly judgmental toward the poor. Rural poverty was so pervasive as to be the expected condition of landless farmers. Moreover, tenants and croppers were often seen as unworthy and shiftless people who had neither the ability nor the desire for self-improvement. Yet, at the same time, the assumption frequently expressed in the 1930s was that any ambitious, industrious farmer could work his way up an agricultural ladder, progressing from sharecropping to securer levels of tenancy and then to small landownership. These persistent views were a major impediment to efforts to reduce rural poverty.

The Great Depression focused national attention on southern tenancy. Ironically, this public notice came as the system was beginning to break down. As hard times intensified, many landlords cut their own expenses by abandoning crop sharing, discontinuing furnishing, and converting to wage labor. This trend grew during the New Deal. Under the Agricultural Adjustment Administration (AAA), acreage-reduction contracts decreased labor needs, and, in effect, encouraged landlords to dispense with tenants to avoid sharing government payments with them. This impact of the AAA was brought forcefully to public attention after 1935 by the protests of the Southern Tenant Farmers'

Union. Tenancy continued as a national issue as the New Deal attempted to alleviate rural poverty through federal relief, the Bankhead-Jones Farm Tenant Act of 1937, and the Farm Security Administration.

Sharecropping declined significantly in the 1930s, and in the following decades southern agriculture underwent massive changes that swept away crop-lien tenancy. Mechanization was the most revolutionary development. From the 1930s onward, the number of tractors on southern farms increased dramatically, and after World War II the cotton picker came into general use. Landlords employed wage workers to meet their more limited labor needs and discarded outmoded crop-sharing arrangements. Crop and livestock diversification and chemical weed control made farming still less labor intensive. This transformation of southern agriculture was accompanied by a great exodus of the rural poor from the land and, in many cases, from the region.

PAUL E. MERTZ
*University of Wisconsin–Stevens Point*

James C. Cobb, *The Most Southern Place on Earth: The Mississippi Delta and the Roots of Regional Identity* (1992); David E. Conrad, *The Forgotten Farmers: The Story of Sharecroppers in the New Deal* (1965); Pete Daniel, *Breaking the Land: The Transformation of Cotton, Tobacco, and Rice Cultures since 1880* (1985); Gilbert C. Fite, *Cotton Fields No More: Southern Agriculture, 1865–1980* (1984); Charles S. Johnson, Edwin R. Embree, and Will W. Alexander, *The Collapse of Cotton Tenancy: A Summary of Field Studies and Statistical Surveys* (1935); Paul E. Mertz, *New Deal Policy and Southern Rural Poverty* (1978); Arthur F. Raper, *Preface to Peasantry: A Tale of Two Black Belt Counties* (1936); U.S. National Resources Committee, *Farm Tenancy: Report of the President's Committee* (1937); Rupert B. Vance, *Human Factors in Cotton Culture: A Study in the Social Geography of the American South* (1929); Jeannie M. Whayne, *A New Plantation South: Land, Labor, and Federal Favor in Twentieth-Century Arkansas* (1996); Thomas Jackson Woofter Jr., *Landlord and Tenant on the Cotton Plantation* (1936).

## Soil and Soil Conservation

Soils are natural bodies, the result of unique interactions of soil-forming factors. Once soils were thought of as merely the residuum from rocks. Parent material is indeed an important factor in soil formation, or soil genesis, because it is the source of many elements needed for plant growth. As parent material is exposed at the earth's surface, it is altered by processes that can be related to climate, topography, living organisms, and the amount of time the material remains near the surface before being dissolved, eroded, or buried. Soil properties have always placed limitations on food production. With limited ability to transport plant nutrients or food, indigenous people focused on the relationship of soil to plant growth for both native vegetation and domesticated plants.

Soils of the South are regionally diverse. Over small areas such as on a farm, soil differences can be significant for agricultural uses or for location of a house. Regional generalizations about soils are useful for considering the interaction of soil with southern history. For example, plants require carbon, oxygen, and nitrogen, which are available in the atmosphere. Hydrogen is acquired from the uptake of water. Atmospheric nitrogen needs to be converted to reactive nitrogen, which the plant can utilize. Under natural conditions, this conversion is accomplished by lightning, the work of microorganisms, or legumes. Plants also need phosphorus and three elements known as the "bases"—calcium, potassium, and magnesium—in rather large quantities. In addition, plants need small quantities of at least seven other elements that can come only from soil minerals. Food grains, because of their rapid growth and seed production, require much more rapid uptake of these elements than native vegetation. When used for human food, these elements are removed from the site. Replenishment from weathering of minerals is too slow for food crops but usually fast enough to support slow-growing natural vegetation. The distribution of essential elements among soils is so uneven that some soils can produce low levels of agronomic crops and sustain the export of nutrients for a very long time (consider the long-term experiments at the University of Illinois and Rothamstead Experiment Station). Phosphate- and calcium-poor mineral material such as the granite present in many piedmont and coastal plain soils would produce only a few crops before failing to make available sufficient quantities for rapid food-crop growth. In the era before commercial fertilizer, the content of calcium, magnesium, and available phosphorus in the soil therefore defined the prime agricultural areas of the South.

Two soil-forming factors, age and climate, are frequently overemphasized in discussing southern soils. Soils developed in granitic rock of the piedmont and the coastal sediments—formed from their geologic erosion—are among the most infertile in the continental United States. Although humid conditions leach and acidify soils, not all of the soils in the South are poor in these essential elements. Base-rich igneous rock, as well as sedimentary sources such as limestone and calcareous materials, developed soils that are notably more fertile than soils formed from the granite and granite-derived sediments of the coastal plain.

Native Americans as well as European colonists found the alluvial soils along rivers, not the interfluves, to be the preferred setting for agriculture. The recurrent overflows deposited valuable plant nutrients—phosphorous, potassium, and calcium as well as nitrogen bound up in the organic matters. The most fertile alluvial soils were along the Mississippi River, where Native Americans of the Mississippian culture developed a highly effective economic and agricultural system, often located on alluvial terraces. The system spread to other small river systems. Town Creek Indian Mound, a historical site in North Carolina, is one such example. In the base-poor piedmont section of Virginia, North Carolina, South Carolina, and Georgia, fertile, base-rich soils are scattered in a north-south pattern formed in mafic rock, high in fero-magnesium minerals. Naturalists find remnants of native prairies there. Indians would have likely found these areas to be good hunting grounds. Further, Native Americans established a transportation route along the patterns of base-rich soils. European migrants later used the route to travel south, calling it the Great Wagon Road. Hernando de Soto found Native Americans growing corn in Florida, not on the coastal flatwoods but along the central ridge, where phosphatic sands provide nutrients. Undoubtedly, the early explorers and traders learned by the actions of the Native Americans where the best lands were.

Native Americans—and Europeans after they arrived—coped with low-fertility, acidic soils by felling and burning trees and brush. Burning made available in the upper-soil surface various nutrients that had been taken up by the deep-rooted trees and stored in the trunks and limbs. While Native Americans did plant some crops, their use of fire to create more productive hunting grounds eventually created the open, parklike landscape that early travelers often observed. The export of nutrients in agricultural crops quickly removed the nitrogen, phosphorus, potassium, calcium, and magnesium, elements that the deep-rooted trees had taken up and stored in trunks and limbs over several decades. These elements were released in plant-available form as trees were burned or rapidly decomposed in cultivated fields. Then the system needed to be repeated. It required that natural, slow-growing vegetation be allowed to grow for several years before enough nutrients were contained in their biomass to fertilize a food crop when the biomass was cut and burned. Before commercial fertilizers were available, most crops were grown in widely spaced, cleanly tilled rows that, combined with intense rainfall and rolling terrain, led to erosion. Unlike many northern and midwestern soils, most southern soils could not sustain continuous crop production and therefore prompted migration to the West. The disparity between the potentials of the southern and midwestern soils to support continuous cultivation and a dense rural population was ap-

Severely eroded land, part of 160 acres that only 35 years earlier had been planted with cotton, near Carrollton, Miss., 1950 (USDA—Soil Conservation Service [SCS-INF-164 Rev. 9-75])

parent in the numbers of rural youth available to fight in the Civil War. In 1860, Alabama, Georgia, and Mississippi supported an average of 17.3 rural residents per square mile, while Ohio, Indiana, Illinois had an average of 37.5 rural residents per square mile.

Other soils of the South were better favored, at least agriculturally. Soils developed in limestone beds are often higher in the bases. In many cases, they will include more phosphorous, derived from the skeletal remains of organisms. Limestone-derived soils are found in the Shenandoah Valley, the Ridge and Valley Province of the Appalachians, the Kentucky bluegrass country, and the Nashville basin. Some of these high-base soils may be shallow to bedrock, but they are valuable for pasture grasses and domesticated grasses such as corn, wheat, and other grains. The appellation "Breadbasket of the Confederacy" aptly fit the Shenandoah Valley. Soils of the Shenandoah made possible a style of agricultural often associated with conservation, sustainability, and good husbandry. But the soil properties have to provide the opportunity, and not all soils of the South provided the possibility of this type agriculture. Many Germanic, Swiss, and English migrants to this area came from base-rich soils of Europe that permitted continuous cultivation with proper care. Soil properties had created much of the agricultural methods and preference that the Europeans brought to the New World.

The primary horse-breeding areas of the South developed in soils with copious quantities of both calcium and phosphorus for large-boned animals. The primary areas were the Virginia horse country based around Loudon County, the Kentucky bluegrass, the Nashville basin, and later the area of phosphatic sands on the Florida ridge.

Other base-rich southern soils played a larger role in southern agriculture—especially the plantation economy. The Black Belt of Alabama and Mississippi and the blackland prairie of Texas developed along the shoreline of an ancient inland sea. The soils are rich in the bases derived from the skeletal remains of organisms. The Black Belt developed into Alabama's primary cotton and cattle area. On the blackland prairie of Texas, farmers produced cotton for decades on the bases and nitrogen accumulated in organic soils. Farmers in these areas were not as dependent on commercial fertilizers as their neighbors on the base-poor lands. The clays in these two groups of soils are similar to the soils of the Mississippi Delta. Clays developed in calcareous materials often have more layers than the clays developed in the granites of the piedmont. Such clays have a great capacity to hold both bases and water. The capacity to swell and then shrink, dependent upon wetness, gives soils their reputation for cracking. The soils of the Mississippi Delta were greatly influenced by the glacial materials from the upper Midwest that were transported by the Mississippi River. They too were base-rich and noted for their productivity. Western Tennessee and the east banks of the Mississippi and Yazoo Rivers are capped by wind-deposited loess, primarily silt-sized particles. The cotton culture around Natchez predated the westward migration of cotton. The base-rich loess hills supported the plantation economy, but loess is highly erodible. Erosion eventually proved the undoing of this once prosperous region.

Reformers tried to adjust southern agriculture to its environment. One of them, Edmund Ruffin, promoted marl ostensibly to correct the acidity problem of southern soils, but it had other advantages not always recognized. Marl, deposited in an aquatic environment, included phosphorus. Also, in a low-base environment, the application of calcium carbonate made more of the bases and phosphorus available to the plant. Raising the pH level enhances microorganisms, which take up bases. As the microorganisms die off, they release bases and phosphorous that the plant takes up. However, the low content of bases and phosphorus in the soil minerals ultimately limited the efficacy of marl. Southerners of a later era learned to apply lime along with other elements necessary for plant growth.

Commercial fertilizers eventually became of immense importance to southern agriculture and its economy. One could argue that developments in technology and sciences related to plant growth benefited the South as much as or more than the base-rich areas of the Midwest—though both came to rely on commercial fertilizers, which in turn permitted denser rural populations. The image of a southern landscape, especially the piedmont, dominated by small cotton farms is more a creation of the fertilizer era than of natural soil qualities. Among Americans, southerners led the way in importing guano, ostensibly for the nitrogen supply, but the guano included other nutrients as well. In the late 19th century, southerners imported Chilean nitrates and mined southern deposits of phosphorus. The Haber-Bosch process of fixing nitrogen, developed in Germany around World War I, provided nitrogen at an affordable price. The availability of fertilizers increased the value of the coastal-plain soils in the farmer's eyes since the nitrogen, potassium, phosphorus, and lime could now be supplied economically. Also, these soils had better tillage properties for mechanized farming than did many piedmont and Black Belt soils. With a supply of plant nutrients, southern farmers could now take advantage of other geographical and climatic advantages by raising crops that required a longer or earlier growing season.

Since European settlement, erosion has been a problem in the South. Native Americans had developed a sustainable system in the prefertilizer era: fire recycled nutrients to provide game habitat and allowed for a very limited amount of cropland. The region had the highest intensity and duration of rainfall in the continental United States. Climate, combined with an affinity for cleanly tilled, widely spaced rows on sloping hillsides, unleashed erosion. Subsequent loss of topsoil (the growing medium) was to be lamented. But many southern topsoils, and especially the subsoils, were not loaded with nutrients, as the historical literature too often assumes. Topsoil "richness" was limited to the nutrient content of rotting vegetation and/or the ash that could be obtained from burning the biomass that took several years to grow. The amount of nutrients exported in food crops quickly removed the nutrients (the phosphorus content of 150 bushels of corn grain is approximately equal to the amount of phosphorus in a 20-year-old stand of pine trees). Many historians had adopted the shibboleth that modern technology and farming methods cause more erosion than small, animal-powered farming methods of the past. The exact opposite is true, however. Farmers no longer plant steep hillsides, once accessible with mules or horses. Herbicides and tractor-powered conservation tillage permits one to keep the ground clothed continuously in growing plants or crop residues. Fertilizers make possible more pasture and small grain, conditions that retard erosion. Most importantly, fertilizer and plant breeding produce quick-growing, closely spaced plants that form a canopy rapidly. The denser crops permit less erosion than the sparse plant populations of old.

DOUGLAS HELMS
*Natural Resources Conservation Service*
*Washington, D.C.*

Stanley W. Buol, ed., *Soils of the Southern States and Puerto Rico*, Southern Cooperative Series Bulletin No. 174 (1973); Douglas Helms, *Agricultural History* (Fall 2000); Daniel D. Richter Jr. and Daniel Markewitz, *Understanding Soil Change: Soil Sustainability over Millennia, Centuries, and Decades* (2001).

## Sustainable Agriculture

The question of agricultural sustainability is as old as agriculture itself. It has been estimated that of the 80 billion humans who have ever lived, only about 10 percent have depended on agriculture for survival. Humans were very successful as hunter-gatherers, but this system probably only supported a population of about 4 million people (compared to today's 6.5 billion). Agriculture most likely evolved in response to the inability of ecosystems to support expanding hunter-gatherer populations. Ever since the transition to agriculture beginning about 10,000 years ago, the question of sustainability has been of utmost importance to the human condition.

The natural fertility of most southern soils is quite low. Native Americans practiced agriculture in river bottoms, where soil fertility was constantly replenished by seasonal flooding. In other areas, slash-and-burn agriculture was practiced by Native Americans and later at an accelerating rate by colonists. Forests were cut and burned, followed by a few years of crop production, then the land was abandoned and the process repeated on an uncut block of forest. This system can be maintained at moderate-to-low productivity levels as long as sufficient time (25–50 years) is allowed between successive cropping periods. The system breaks down quickly when increasing population pressure shortens the cropping cycle. In Europe, land degradation and declining productivity stimulated interest in a systematic, scientific approach to agriculture, including the use of crop rotations, application of manure, and, later, soil-conservation measures such as contour plowing and planting and strip-cropping. These ideas were gradually adopted in the "new world."

Many American farmers used some sustainable practices until the 20th century, though they also engaged in other types of soil use. After World War II, American farmers were encouraged to expand their operations as agriculture industrialized through increased mechanization and inputs such as synthetic pesticides and fertilizers. Many farmers turned away from sustainable practices, but others resisted industrial agriculture.

Immediately after the war, Robert Rodale in eastern Pennsylvania, concerned about the kinds of chemicals being used and their impact on human health, began what was to become the Rodale Institute. Its influence spread south, and ideas about "organic" and healthy agriculture began to take hold.

The birth of the environmental movement in the 1960s led to questions about the wisdom of industrial-style farming. The publication of *Silent Spring* in 1962 by Rachel Carson is associated with the beginning of the modern environmental movement. She was disturbed by the wide-scale use of synthetic, chemical pesticides, and she challenged the practices of agricultural scientists and the government. Carson's work spawned environmental activism, and many nongovernmental organizations (NGOs) were formed that later joined forces with organic farmers and others highly critical of the industrialized system of agriculture prevalent in the latter half of the 20th century. This was the beginning of the modern sustainable-agriculture movement. A basic premise of sustainable agriculture is that farms are collections of interrelated biological processes that function as a system in a social context, not merely a series of industrial processes guided by "bottom-line" economics. The idea of sustainability was buoyed by the 1987 United Nations "Brundtland" Commission report, "Our Common Future," which introduced the concept of sustainable development as "development that meets the needs of the present without compromising the ability of future generations to meet their own needs."

The 1960s saw the rise of social and political activism as a result of the civil rights movement. It was not a far step from civil rights for African Americans to careful reflection on the issues of tenancy and sharecropping for all southern farm families. VISTA (Volunteers in Service to America) volunteers worked with farmers to invent new holistic independent farming systems. *Mother Earth News* and the "back to the land" people brought all the inventiveness epitomized in the *Whole Earth Catalogue* to the question of viable rural lifestyles.

During the 1970s and 1980s, U.S. agriculture was in crisis. Crop prices fell under competitive market conditions and political pressures. More than 200,000 farms went bankrupt, rural communities lost viability, and land values decreased. As a result, much attention began to be placed on reducing the costs of production and the negative environmental consequences of farming. Conservation issues, the value of forests, and water quality began to be counted in the equation as negative effects of industrial agricultural were seen from the "dead zone" in the Gulf of Mexico to the degradation of the Chesapeake Bay.

During the 1980s, a coalition of organic farmers, NGOs, and environmentalist organizations pushed Congress and the U.S. Department of Agriculture to establish funding for research and education programs for alternative agriculture systems. The result was the establishment of the Low Input Sustainable Agriculture Program (LISA). In 1989 the National Research Council published *Alternative Agriculture*, a landmark study that focused the attention of the scientific community on the role of alternative methods in modern production agriculture.

In the 1990 Farm Bill (officially the Food, Agriculture, Conservation, and Trade Act of 1990), Congress defined sustainable agriculture as "an integrated system of plant and animal production practices having a site-specific application that will, over the long term" satisfy human food and fiber needs; enhance environmental quality and the natural resource base upon which the agricultural economy depends; make the most efficient use of nonrenewable resources and on-farm resources and integrate, where appropriate, natural biological cycles and controls into farming; sustain the economic viability of farm operations; and enhance the quality of life for farmers and society as a whole. The 1990 Farm Bill also transformed LISA to SARE (Sustainable Agriculture Research and Education). By 1992 the LISA and SARE programs had been recognized for creating new alliances among farmers, nongovernmental organizations, university scientists, agribusiness, and government, resulting in the emergence of a new vision for U.S. agriculture. The SARE program is managed in partnership with regional land-grant universities and includes collaborations with farmers, NGOs, and other state and local agencies.

In the southern region a key collaboration involves SARE and Southern Sustainable Agriculture Working Group—commonly known as the "Southern SAWG." Founded in 1991, the Southern SAWG is the region's nonprofit leader in advocating for a sustainable food and farming system. Programs and activities are focused on helping family farms that promote community-based food systems in the southern United States. The Southern SAWG promotes collaborations among farmers, community organizations, and consumers with the goal of positively changing policies that impact farm communities. An important trend in the South has been the shift from independent to contract production. This trend happened first in poultry production and more recently with swine and tobacco. The sustainability of vertical integration and contract production is questioned by many who see this structure as leaving farmers with little or no control of the terms of production. This trend is seen as part of the globalization of the food system, in which wealth and power are concentrated in the hands of a few major corporations and the gap between farmer and consumer grows ever larger.

Sustainable agriculture is much more than a simple collection of practices. Its application is site specific; there is no set formula of practices or procedures that constitute a sustainable-agriculture system for all locations. Some of the practices or technologies that are associated with sustainable agriculture include controlled rotational grazing management, biological control methods, conservation tillage practices, long-term crop rotations, integration of crops and animals, and free-range or pastured poultry.

There is much current interest in the southern region in connecting farmers and consumers by direct marketing strategies. These include local farmer's markets, community-supported agriculture, small-farmer cooperatives, direct sales to institutions, and others. Southern pride in its heritage and culture has fostered strong interest in local food. It has its own indigenous "slow food" movement emerging from the Chapel Hill, N.C., area and now taken up in Mississippi and elsewhere. Consumers see the importance of issues relating to local food systems for many reasons. There is a growing belief by those associated with the movement that the current centralized food system is vulnerable and unsustainable in light of fossil-fuel shortages and the potential impact of global climate change. It follows that the question of the sustainability of our food system is one that should be of constant interest to us—at least three times each day.

J. PAUL MUELLER
*North Carolina State University*

JOHN M. O'SULLIVAN
*North Carolina A&T State University*

Wendell Berry, *The Unsettling of America: Culture and Agriculture* (1996); Pete Daniel, *Lost Revolutions: The South in the 1950s* (2000); Linda Flowers, *Throwed Away: Failures of Progress in Eastern North Carolina* (1990); J. L. Hatfield and D. L. Karlen, eds., *Sustainable Agriculture Systems* (1994); R. Douglas Hurt, *American Agriculture: A Brief History* (1994); R. B. Lee and I. DeVore, eds., *Man the Hunter* (1968); Moreton Neal, *Remembering Bill Neal: Favorite Recipes from a Life in Cooking* (2004); Neill Schaller, *Agriculture, Ecosystems, and Environment*, vol. 46 (1993).

## Women and Agriculture

Since the beginning of recorded history, women in the South have played a significant role in agriculture. The native women of the Southeast grew the crops that, along with intensive gathering and the men's hunting, sustained their families. Early in the 17th century, observers from the Jamestown colony reported Powhatan women working in groups to cultivate small fields of corn and beans, which they relocated every three years. Further south, Creek women cultivated communal cornfields and kept family-sized vegetable patches.

The Cherokee maintained a fairly rigid division of labor wherein men helped clear fields, planted, and hunted. Women cultivated the food crops, mostly large quantities of corn and beans along with peas, squash, and potatoes. Elderly women watched for predators. After the Cherokee acquired livestock in the 18th century, women had to exert diligence to keep animals such as wolves and mountain lions from the unfenced fields. Agriculture was a significant part of Cherokee women's social and sexual identity, with commemorations such as the Green Corn Ceremony connecting corn to the community and women to rebirth and reconciliation. After Europeans came to Georgia, the Cherokee added peach orchards, hogs, and sweet potatoes and began to sell their products to the new arrivals. When Americans began to exert power over the Cherokee, they transferred responsibility for farming to men, stripping women of much of the source of their power and social standing.

Beginning in the early 17th century, women from Africa came to the South. As slaves, they grew rice and tobacco and later sugarcane and cotton for the world markets. By the 19th century, more than 90 percent of slave women in rural areas worked in the fields, and in some places the majority of field workers were women. Women's work varied by crop and location. In some places, overseers or owners made work assignments by ability, not sex, and they expected women to perform the same tasks in the same quantity as men. At other times, work was divided by sex, and men and women might have worked in segregated gangs. The cash crops of the slave South depended on the labor of women. Despite their long hours in the fields, some slave women also gardened for their own families, raising peas, beans, onions, cabbages, turnips, melons, and pumpkins to augment their meager rations.

In the antebellum South, the wives of yeomen worked outside, gardening, milking, and caring for chickens. They provided for their families and participated in the cash economy only rarely. The poorer their families, the more likely the women were to do fieldwork. Slave-owning women were least likely to work outside, but as families moved from the Atlantic seaboard westward, at least some wealthy women found themselves slaughtering hogs and performing other outside chores.

After emancipation, many black women remained with their former owners, with the Freedmen's Bureau aiding landowners in forcing freed slaves to sign labor contracts. Many labored much as they had before the Civil War, even continuing to work in gangs: plowing, cutting wheat, splitting cordwood, planting potatoes and rice, and, of course, performing every step involved with cotton and tobacco cultivation, which dominated the postbellum agricultural economy. Rather than being under the employ of one farmer for an extended period of time, some freed women hired out to do specific agricultural chores. Although whites interpreted such behavior as indolence, black women chose to work on schedules dictated by the growing season, working particularly at times of heaviest labor (planting, cultivating, and harvesting).

With a shortage of cash and an abundance of workers, southern landowners turned to the crop-lien system to finance their farm enterprises. The failure of the government to reapportion acreage ensured that most former slaves would remain landless, and the insecurity of the southern economy forced poor white farmers into dependence. As more southern farmers, both black and white, became sharecroppers or tenant farmers, they moved away from subsistence farming to growing staple crops. Poor white women began to spend less time on domestic production and more in the fields. The decline in food crops made feeding their families more and more difficult. The forced reliance of their men on the landowners for everything from coffee to doctors' services affected the power structure in many farm families. Most workers received a family wage in which they were paid as a unit rather than as individuals. Men usually controlled the family wage and women had few funds to call their own.

Protests over the abuses of the crop-lien system began shortly after the close of the Civil War, and women cared deeply about the Grange, Southern Farmers' Alliance, Populist Party, and other cooperative movements. Reforms that focused on women included increasing their production of food products. By World War I the Cooperative Extension Service of the U.S. Department of Agriculture was sending female home-demonstration agents to work with farm women on such critical topics as canning and other types of food preservation. Women who grew enough food to feed their families saved precious cash for other purposes. As transportation improved, those who grew more than their families could eat and lived near an urban area could market their eggs, butter, vegetables, and dressed poultry to urban women. Selling farm-raised goods brought much-needed money into perpetually cash-poor farm families.

The economic depression that gripped southern agriculture in the 1920s and 1930s hurt farm families, and women worked harder than ever for little return. Mechanization pushed sharecroppers and tenant farmers off the land as owners could farm more land with fewer hands. Farm wives became town wives with dramatically altered situations, although many continued keeping chickens, gardens, and even cows at their town homes. For those who stayed on the farm, New Deal reforms such as the Rural Electrification Administration and crop subsidies eased difficult living situations. World War II brought high commodity prices and opportunities for off-farm employment for women.

After the end of World War II, farm families changed dramatically. Many people who had moved to town for wartime jobs elected to remain in urbanized areas. Those who continued to live in rural areas could commute into town for a waged job and return to the farm at night. Expensive equipment required farmers to "get big" or get out, and many left agriculture. The relatively small number of women who remained on the farms changed their work significantly. Some took an increasing role in bookkeeping and other farm management tasks. Many accepted off-farm employment, the proceeds of which subsidized the farming operation. Other women began performing more of the farm work as men took off-farm employment and as technology began to substitute for physical labor. Farming remained challenging, however, and women actively participated in the farm protest movements of the 1980s. By the early 21st century, the number of women farming on their own was rising. Women have increasingly moved into niche and specialty farming, such as organic vegetable production, and specialty livestock production, such as goats, llamas, and alpacas. They continue to be an integral part of agriculture in the South, their roles changing as farming itself changes.

REBECCA SHARPLESS
*Texas Christian University*

Joan E. Cashin, *A Family Venture: Men and Women on the Southern Frontier* (1991); Laura F. Edwards, *Scarlett Doesn't Live Here Anymore: Southern Women in the Civil War Era* (2000); Margaret Jarman Hagood, *Mothers of the South: Portraiture of the White Tenant Farm Woman* (1939); Lu Ann Jones, *Mama Learned Us to Work: Farm Women in the New South* (2002); Stephanie McCurry, *Masters of Small Worlds: Yeoman Households, Gender Relations, and the Political Culture of the Antebellum South Carolina Low Country* (1995); Theda Perdue, *Cherokee Women: Gender and Culture Change, 1700–1835* (1998); Rebecca Sharpless, *Fertile Ground, Narrow Choices: Women on Texas Cotton Farms, 1900–1940* (1999); Melissa Walker, *All We Knew Was to Farm: Rural Women in the Upcountry South, 1919–1941* (2000); Melissa Walker and Rebecca Sharpless, eds., *Work, Family, and Faith: Rural Southern Women in the Twentieth Century* (2006); Marli F. Weiner, *Mistresses and Slaves: Plantation Women in South Carolina, 1830–80* (1998); Betty Wood, *Women's Work, Men's Work: The Informal Slave Economies of Lowcountry Georgia* (1995).

## Agricultural Cooperatives

Small farmers have always confronted the problem of diffusion. Functioning as atomized units, they find economic difficulty on either end of market transactions. As producers, they cannot control the price of their crops by matching supply to demand; as consumers, they cannot create economies of scale to lower the prices of their supplies. To overcome this problem, American farmers have at times sought to combine their resources to improve their prices or lower their costs. While there have been notable successes, the record of agricultural cooperatives has proven generally dismal nationwide. The depressing history of the South's agricultural cooperatives proves the point. While there have been some successes, especially in recent years, the long history of agricultural cooperation in the South has been one marked by repeated failures. The failures have not been for lack of trying; instead, they are the result of a deeply entrenched economic, political, and social order resistant to the demands of small farmers.

The reorganization and expansion of southern staple agricultural markets that placed family-operated farms at the center of production in the late 19th century provided the setting for the first calls for cooperation. As more farm families came to rely on staple crops like cotton and tobacco for their livelihoods, the effects of the cyclical booms and busts of global commodity markets took a great toll on the rural people of the South. And as prices fell, calls for creating cooperatives increased. In the early 1870s, as prices fell as a result of the panic of 1873, a product of the Minnesota prairie called the Patrons of Husbandry (or, more commonly, the Grange) provided the first vehicle for southern farmers interested in cooperation. Inspired by Thomas Jefferson's faith in the yeomanry and informed by the labor theory of value, Grangers not only pressed for cooperation but also sought to rein in railroads and other "middlemen" that made their living from the sweat of farmers' brows. The Grange appealed to landowning farmers, however, and therefore had only limited success in a region where tenancy and tight credit were the hallmarks of rural life.

The Grange did inspire a series of homegrown cooperative movements. In the 1880s numerous cooperatively minded groups sprouted out of the local soil. Among them were the Farmers' Union (Louisiana), the Agricultural Wheel (Arkansas), and the Farmers' Alliance (Texas). The Alliance proved the most durable and popular, as farmers from Texas to Virginia rushed to join in the late 1880s. Unlike the Grange, the Alliance appealed to all southern farmers, including African Americans, who were called to join the segregated Colored Farmers' Alliance. Local chapters across the South created a shadow economy of cooperative stores and warehouses designed to allow members to bypass the credit merchants and middlemen they blamed for their condition. This made the Alliance powerful enemies who turned their energies to undercutting support for the group. The Alliance's decline, however, had as much to do with race as economics. The Alliance's openness to both black and white farmers became a liability as Democrats beat back the biracial challenge of the Populists in the 1896 elections. As white southerners flocked back to the Democratic Party, they largely abandoned their support for the Alliance, itself the backbone of support for the Populists in the South.

Calls to form cooperatives did not end, however, with the disappearance of the Alliance. Local organizations dedicated to the cooperative marketing of specific crops continued to pop up throughout the South, although few had much success. Others again attempted to organize the entire South but within the limits of Jim Crow segregation. In 1905, for example, organizers in Texas picked up the banner of the Farmers' Union and reconstituted it as an all-white organization. Given the large amount of the region's crops grown and marketed by black farmers, the group's failure is not surprising.

In the 1910s the campaign for agricultural cooperatives gained some support from the federal government. Interested in improving the conditions of the nation's rural folk, Congress created the Agricultural Extension Service in 1914 and soon put it to work helping farmers to organize themselves. Their work initially focused on truck crops and largely left the South's staple crops untouched. Besides, high prices for cotton and tobacco during World War I quieted talk of cooperative marketing. The postwar bust, however, loosened tongues, and talk of cooperation again filled the air. The loudest voice was that of Aaron Sapiro, a California lawyer

who had helped organize many of that state's growers into powerful cooperatives like the Sun-Maid raisin growers. Sapiro sought to organize southern farmers, black and white, along the same lines by creating cartel-like organizations that would control the majority of the crops reaching the market and thus give farmers greater power in dictating prices. Attempts to organize cotton growers failed, but among the flue-cured tobacco growers of the Carolinas and Virginia, Sapiro had some success. As with the Alliance, however, these cooperatives engendered animosity from the South's economic elite and ultimately faded from view. While the economic despair of the early 1930s again generated calls for cooperation and further government support under the auspices of the Federal Farm Board, few farmers were willing to join.

With the creation of New Deal farm programs for the South's staple crops in the 1930s, the demand for agricultural cooperatives faded. Federal cotton, tobacco, sugar, and rice programs seemingly solved the farmers' traditional problems of overproduction and low prices by limiting acreage and providing guaranteed minimum prices. While the programs met some resistance, most southern farmers embraced them wholeheartedly. Managed by local committees elected by growers, the programs answered cooperative agriculture's traditional call for democratic participation without upsetting local customs or subverting the South's economic and social elite. Cooperation had been co-opted.

The goals of agricultural cooperatives—equity and democracy—remain rhetorically powerful in the rural South. But the power of agricultural cooperatives remains weak. As of 2003, there were only 713 agricultural cooperatives in the South (30 percent of the national total); 513 of these were for the purchasing of supplies, not the selling of crops. This relative weakness is not an accident of history, but a result of it.

EVAN P. BENNETT
*Florida International University*

Nathaniel C. Browder, *The Tri-State Tobacco Growers Association, 1922–1925: The Co-Op That Failed* (1940, 1983); Lawrence Goodwyn, *Democratic Promise: The Populist Movement in America* (1976); James L. McCorkle Jr., *Agricultural History* (Winter 1998); Robert C. McMath Jr., *Populist Vanguard: A History of the Southern Farmers' Alliance* (1975); Stanley B. Parsons, Karen Toombs Parsons, Walter Killilae, and Beverly Borgers, *Journal of American History* (March 1983); Jeannie M. Whayne, *Agricultural History* (Summer 1998); Victoria Saker Woeste, *The Farmer's Benevolent Trust: Law and Agricultural Cooperation in Industrial America, 1865–1945* (1998).

## Agricultural Societies, Antebellum

Agricultural societies played a critical role in shaping the contours of antebellum rural America. Through societies, farmers created a collective structure with enough clout to give voice to advocates of "systematic," or scientific, farming. Societies sponsored agricultural addresses by prominent community leaders and held fairs to celebrate agrarian life. Though generally articulated as a utilitarian movement by historians, agricultural leaders aimed at a broader mission of social improvement, all the while preserving the nation's agrarian tradition.

The tenuous nature of antebellum agricultural societies makes it hard to establish firm numbers. The last figure compiled before the Civil War by the U.S. Commissioner of Patents reported the existence of 912 organizations. While groups of the early national era were organized from the top down, most antebellum agricultural societies were true local phenomena, reform cells dedicated to the overall principle of agricultural improvement but accounting for regional differences and farmers' suspicion of gentlemen, or book, farming. These agricultural societies faced a number of issues and problems. The severe downturn in farm prices experienced shortly after the War of 1812 exerted pressure on many farmers to seek new methods to restore agriculture's profitability. Soil infertility and erosion had lowered yields and exacerbated westward migration. Merchant and commercial classes were on the rise. Agrarians believed their success in gaining congressional tariffs on foreign manufactured goods came at the farmers' expense. In addition, social collapse seemed to be creeping ever closer, evident by poverty, gang violence, prostitution, and riots in the cities, and by cock fighting, gouging, and other blood sports in the rural areas. Motivated by a reform ideology that paralleled other causes but was steeped in a new land ethic, antebellum agricultural societies assumed the role of rural lyceums, debating causes and solutions to a variety of national ills.

Agricultural societies expanded their

reach by utilizing the 40-plus agricultural journals published in the antebellum era. The journals printed meeting notices, personal letters from farmers both north and south of the Mason-Dixon Line, and hundreds of agricultural addresses that provided agrarians their *raison d'etre*. At a time when "rural" still defined America, the journals reveled in the lives of the people who, at work or at rest, in political and social spheres, organized their world around the cycles of life on the farm. The majority of these journals rarely survived past five years, but some mainstays, such as the *American Farmer*, based in Baltimore and edited by John Skinner, and the Virginian Edmund Ruffin's *Farmer's Register*, had lengthy runs and significant influence. Such journals helped agricultural societies cross-fertilize new methods for farming and promote rural unity. However, the journals may have aided in further exacerbating sectionalism by highlighting regional disparities in practices and ideas. Northern reformers, frustrated by the lack of change in southern practices, grew increasingly demonstrative in their complaints to their southern brethren. By the late 1840s, southern agrarians saw value in progressive agriculture only if it preserved or strengthened slavery. As a reflection of the growing distance of southern farmers from their northern brethren, the leaders of the Southern Central Agricultural Association of Georgia in 1853 organized the Agricultural Association of the Slaveholding States in order to foster unity and increase the "wealth, power and dignity" of its members.

Another division that agricultural societies had to fight against was that between city and country. Here they found that annual agricultural fairs helped to span the divide. Fairs prominently placed the best of the agrarian life on display to the larger community, serving as a reminder to rural inhabitants of the bounties of their calling and, to visitors, of agriculture's fundamental importance to the nation. In the more populated northern regions, fairs were held in the major cities or villages of the county. Southern agricultural societies, with their distance to major entrepôts being considerably farther, initially held their fairs at members' farms. As they grew in popularity, farmers hoped the fairs' communal reverie would lead to a revival of the national agrarian spirit.

While antebellum agricultural societies sparked successful changes in certain farming practices, they were largely ineffectual in sustaining agrarianism. They could not stop the draw of the West, nor federal partiality for manufacturers. The planter-based economy that dominated southern society agendas limited the scope of reform to elite farmers, and they were suspicious of any federal support for improvements. The rural unity agricultural societies sought to engender was a chimera. The distinct individualism that farming bred, when combined with the growing sectionalism, proved insurmountable. With the coming of war, the golden age of agricultural societies was over.

JOHN C. SAVAGIAN
*Alverno College*

Steven G. Collins, *Agricultural History* (Winter 2001); Albert L. Demaree, *The American Agricultural Press, 1819–1860* (1941); Drew Gilpin Faust, *Journal of Southern History* (November 1979); Paul W. Gates, *The Farmer's Age: Agriculture, 1815–1860* (1960); Lewis C. Gray, *History of Agriculture in the Southern United States to 1860* (1941); James Henretta, *William and Mary Quarterly* (January 1978); Fred Kniffen, *Annals of the Association of American Geographers* (December 1949); Donald Marti, *Agricultural History* (January 1980); Wayne C. Neely, *The Agricultural Fair* (1935); Sarah T. Phillips, *Agricultural History* (Autumn 2000); Samuel Reznick, *American Historical Review* (1933); Margaret W. Rossiter, in *The Pursuit of Knowledge in the Early American Republic: American Scientific and Learned Societies from Colonial Times to the Civil War*, ed. Alexandra Oleson and Sanborn C. Brown (1976); Charles Sellers, *The Market Revolution: Jacksonian America, 1815–1846* (1991).

## Apples

Southerners who grew up on a farm before World War II remember the farm orchard with its big apple trees, as well as the bewildering number of apple varieties—Red June, Limbertwig, Horse Apple, Transparent, Early Harvest, Blacktwig, Yates, Magnum Bonum, Kinnaird's Choice, and on and on. From the farm, orchard apples were picked fresh from June until November and then stored in cellars or pits during the winter. They were eaten stewed, baked, fried, and in pies. They were made into jelly, preserves, and apple butter. Apple juice was made into cider and vinegar (and brandy!). Apple slices were dried in the sun or preserved with sulfur

fumes. All of this southern lore has been virtually forgotten, as is the astonishing fact that southerners developed over 2,000 unique apple varieties.

English settlers brought apple seeds to the South in the early 1600s, and for the next 200 years most apple orchards started with trees grown from free, durable, and portable seeds. Each apple seed is genetically unique and will produce a unique tree and fruit. Seedling apple trees usually bear ordinary or inferior fruit most suitable for cider (consumed in huge quantities in the colonial period), but some seedling trees have fruit suitable for cooking and fresh eating.

During the colonial period, southerners transplanted the occasional root sprouts from good apple trees to replace inferior trees in the orchards and to swap for root sprouts from neighbors. Two hundred years of this process resulted in each farming community developing its own good apple varieties.

By the early 1800s, most of the South had lost its frontier flavor, money was more available, and a middle class had developed. This sparked the rise of small nurseries selling grafted fruit trees to replace hit-and-miss seedling trees. Grafting, a nonsexual means of reproducing fruit trees, allows hundreds of exact progeny to be produced each year from a single fruit tree. Southern nurseries grafted the local trees prized in nearby communities, thus perpetuating the good apples developed during 200 years of seedling orchards. Typically, a southern nursery would list from 100 to 300 different apple varieties in its catalog or flyer, an enormous number by

*Small boy with an apple in his mouth, holding a basket containing apples (Photographer unknown, Library of Congress [LC-USZ62-55135], Washington, D.C.)*

Appalachians to north Georgia and Alabama. The Ozarks area of Arkansas also was a site of major apple production. These commercial orchards prospered through World War I, but most went bust when the price of apples dropped precipitously after 1920. American commercial apple production moved increasingly to eastern Washington, which now grows over half of the apples in the United States. The leading southern states are Virginia and North Carolina, which, together, annually produce about 5 percent of U.S. commercial apples.

Railroads were essential for commercial orcharding, but they were the death knell for most farm orchards. Towns and cities grew up along railroads, and the lure of steady wages and city life eroded agrarian life in the South. Subsistence farming died out, and with it went the need to grow fruit for family use. Apples, shipped cheaply from as far away as New York, Michigan, or Washington, could be bought year-round in southern towns and cities.

As farm orchards died out, so too did the southern nurseries serving them. Of the 2,000 or so named southern apple varieties grown in the 1800s and early 1900s, only about 500 are still extant. Most of the surviving old apple varieties are being preserved in the Southern Heritage Apple Orchard, part of Horne Creek Living Historical Farm near Winston-Salem, N.C. Three or four small nurseries still sell "antique" or "heirloom" southern apple varieties.

LEE CALHOUN
*Pittsboro, N.C.*

modern standards. Nurseries, large and small, used traveling salesmen ("tree peddlers") to sell their nursery stock.

These apple varieties were for farm orchards because apples were an important food for southern rural families. A farm orchard might have up to 40 large apple trees of 10 or more varieties for cooking, fresh eating, winter storage, drying, or cider. Surplus apples were sold from the back of a wagon in nearby towns. Commercial orcharding in the South had to wait for the construction of railroads into the southern Appalachians in the 1870s and 1880s to move apples quickly and cheaply to distant markets.

From about 1890 to 1920, high prices for apples led to a boom in commercial orcharding in the South from Maryland and Virginia down the spine of the

Creighton Lee Calhoun Jr., *Old Southern Apples* (1995).

## Aquaculture

Aquaculture is often simply referred to as "fish farming," but it is really a form of agriculture that involves the cultivation of a variety of aquatic animals and plants. Although aquaculture was not practiced in the United States until the mid-19th century, its origin dates back 4,000 years to ancient China. Aquaculture has developed into a billion-dollar industry in the United States and has been one of the fastest-growing agricultural enterprises over the last decade. This is in part due to an increase in per capita consumption of seafood, increased health consciousness, and a decline in natural stocks because of overexploitation. The top 10 aquaculture-producing states are (values in parentheses represent production in millions of dollars): Mississippi (250), Arkansas (110), Alabama (103), Louisiana (101), Washington (93), California (70), Florida (57), Virginia (41), Idaho (38), and Texas (35).

Recreational fishing provided the stimulus for aquaculture in the southern United States in the late 1950s and early 1960s because of the increasing demand for baitfish. This expanded into the culture of fish such as largemouth bass, crappie, and sunfish for stocking into farm ponds and reservoirs. By natural progression, the culture of food fish soon followed. This was initially concentrated in Arkansas, where the buffalo fish, a regional food fish, was the fish of choice. However, because of the limited market appeal of buffalo fish, another regional favorite, channel catfish, began to be cultured as well. Because of its more desirable characteristics as a food fish and wider market appeal, catfish production increased rapidly, with about 10,000 acres in production in Arkansas by the mid-1960s. Catfish were also cultured in other southern states, including Alabama, which was instrumental in developing early pond culture techniques for catfish and other fish.

Catfish culture started in Mississippi in the late 1950s, but not until about 1965 did the industry begin to develop as a commercial entity. By 1980 the industry was vertically integrated and expanding rapidly. In 2006 there were about 150,000 acres of catfish producing 550 to 565 million pounds annually, primarily in Mississippi, Alabama, Arkansas, and Louisiana. Mississippi is the leading producer of catfish, with about 60 percent of total production.

Most of the catfish produced in Mississippi and Arkansas is in the Mississippi Delta, where favorable physical resources exist for pond culture. Although physical resources were important, socioeconomic factors played a major role in the development of the catfish industry. The socioeconomic system that existed in the Delta provided a large pool of unskilled labor that had little choice but to work in agriculture. These factors—coupled with the fact that a downturn in traditional row crops such as cotton and soybeans made capital available for new enterprises—provided incentive to develop the catfish industry. Another important factor contributing to the development of the industry was the farmers. They were truly pioneers who were willing to take the risks associated with aquaculture. Without their spirit and hard work, the industry would not have developed as it has.

Catfish is by far the largest aquaculture product in the United States, but there are a number of other aquatic species cultured in the southern states. Other major aquaculture crops include crawfish in Louisiana, ornamental fish in Florida, and baitfish in Arkansas. Several other aquatic species are cultured in the southern United States, including saltwater shrimp, freshwater shrimp (prawns), tilapia, hybrid striped bass, oysters, clams, alligators, and various plants.

Although the United States is the second-largest market for seafood, Americans are not major consumers of seafood products on a per capita basis (16.6 pounds) compared to Japan (120 pounds) and other countries where fish is the primary source of animal protein. Americans typically eat meat. For example, in 2004 the per capita consumption of beef, chicken, and pork was 67.6, 80.5, and 52 pounds, respectively. There was a 9.2 percent increase in per capita consumption of seafood from 2000 to 2004 in the United States. Since seafood is highly nutritious, seafood consumption in the United States will probably continue to increase gradually.

Presently, only a relatively small portion of seafood consumed is from aquaculture, but that will increase because the demand for seafood continues to grow and natural stocks continue to decline. Aquaculture will by necessity grow to meet market demands, and the bulk of that growth will likely be in the southern states.

EDWIN H. ROBINSON
*Mississippi State University*

John A. Hargreaves and Craig S. Tucker, in *Biology and Culture of Channel Catfish*, ed. Craig S. Tucker and John A. Hargreaves (2004); David J. Harvey, *Fish Farming News*, vol. 13, issue 5 (2006); Robert R. Stickney, *Aquaculture in the United States: A Historical Survey* (1996), ed., *Encyclopedia of Aquaculture* (2000).

## Boll Weevil

The cotton boll weevil, *Anthonomus grandis* (Boheman), migrated from Mexico across the Rio Grande River near Brownsville, Tex., in 1892. The weevil's annual fall dispersal carried it to Louisiana in 1903, to Mississippi in 1907, and to the far reaches of the Cotton Belt in the early 1920s.

By depositing eggs in the cotton square, the boll weevil prevented development of the locks of fiber. Farmers relied on the cultural method—a series of adjustments in growing practices—to reduce the weevil's damage. As farmers adopted parts of this system, especially planting earlier with early maturing varieties, the production figures inched upward, but recovery was usually short of preweevil levels.

During the initial infestation, many communities exclusively dependent on cotton underwent boll weevil panics or depressions similar to other economic depressions. When landlords decided not to plant during the coming year, black and white tenants often migrated in advance of the weevil—to the west,

Farm boy with a sack full of boll weevils that he has picked off of cotton plants, Macon County, Ga., 1937 (Dorothea Lange, Library of Congress [LC-USF34-017872-E], Washington, D.C.)

north, and east. The weevil, along with industrial opportunities available during World War I, spurred movement to northern cities, as did the severe infestations of Georgia and South Carolina in the early 1920s. The insect, meanwhile, entered southern folklore, as Huddie "Leadbelly" Ledbetter popularized the well-known "Boll Weevil" song, and the town of Enterprise, Ala., in 1919 erected the Boll Weevil Monument to honor the pest that dramatically affected southern life.

Several factors favorable to growing cotton under weevil conditions—drier climate, colder winters, and fertile land—accelerated shifts in cotton production to west Texas, the northern part of the Cotton Belt, and the Yazoo Delta in Mississippi. Natural and human factors kept some areas out of cotton pro-

duction long after the weevil's arrival. In Alabama's Black Belt, clay-ridden soils prevented early crops. Absentee owners of the old Natchez District no longer wished to risk a cotton crop. The weevil compounded problems of soil erosion and depleted soils in the piedmont plantation belt of Georgia. The finest of America's cottons, Sea Island, was eliminated.

The agriculturalists who had long summoned the southern farmer to diversify welcomed the weevil as a blessing in disguise. For most farmers, the blessing was indeed well disguised. Basic farm crops such as corn and other grains increased, but they supplied little income. The lack of a good marketing system and unfamiliarity with growing, grading, and packing methods beset productive truck farmers. Southerners tried to create markets for peanut oil and sweet potatoes, with little success. Local markets were insufficient for the many who tried dairy farming.

Some boll weevil–induced agricultural developments endured. Farmers of southwest Georgia and southeast Alabama substituted peanuts for cotton. Local plants processed the peanut-fed hogs. Southern farmers converted cotton fields to pasture and upgraded cattle herds, especially in Alabama's Black Belt.

Insecticides, beginning with calcium arsenate in 1919 and followed by a new generation of synthetic ones after World War II, provided some relief. But this increased investment in the crop, along with fertilizers and machinery, brought a shift from extensive planting under the tenant system to planting cotton on the better lands under attentive management.

Cotton continued as an important crop, but the boll weevil destroyed faith in it as a certain source of income and revealed the dangers of reliance on a single crop. Southern farmers and businessmen, mindful that the persistent weevil could strike repeatedly, became more receptive to new crops and industries. Although the boll weevil had some beneficial long-term effects, such present-day interpretations should not overshadow the human plight it caused the tenants and small-farm owners at the bottom of the agricultural ladder.

DOUGLAS HELMS
*Natural Resources*
*Conservation Service*
*Washington, D.C.*

Douglas Helms, "Just Lookin' for a Home: The Cotton Boll Weevil and the South" (Ph.D. dissertation, Florida State University, 1977); Walter D. Hunter and Warren E. Hinds, *Mexican Cotton-Boll Weevil*, Bureau of Entomology Bulletin No. 114, S. Doc. 305, 62nd Congress, 2d sess., 1912; Arthur F. Raper, *Preface to Peasantry: A Tale of Two Black Belt Counties* (1936).

## Cattle

By the early 21st century, the cattle industry was generating billions of dollars for the southern economy. But the modern cattle industry and 21st-century cattle bear little resemblance to the herding practices and animals of southerners' agricultural forebears.

Cattle are not indigenous to the Western Hemisphere and were first introduced to the North American continent by Spanish explorers and colonists in the 16th century. By the late 1500s, Spanish missionaries in Florida had introduced Indians to cattle raising and to Spanish ranching techniques that had been adapted to the American environment by settlers in the West Indies. A century later, Anglo colonists in the Carolina backcountry developed an extensive cattle business that also utilized Old World herding traditions modified by experiences in Barbados. By the middle of the 18th century, this burgeoning cattle culture had spread throughout the Indian nations of the Southeast, while Spanish-influenced cattle herding also took root in northern Mexico and south Texas. These various regional and cultural varieties of cattle herding would eventually coalesce in Louisiana and Texas to create the style of ranching and the cowboy culture most associated in the popular imagination with the latter state.

While cattle ranching in the different southern regions traced its cultural lineage back to a variety of sources—British, Spanish, even African—by the early 19th century there had developed a recognizably American (and largely southern) style of livestock raising. At the center of this ranching system was the open range. In the colonial era, European colonists had adapted to the New World's seemingly inexhaustible supply of land and sparse population by developing an agricultural system anchored by fence laws, which allowed livestock to roam free—subsisting off of native grasses, cane, forest mast, and anything else they could consume—and required farmers to build fences to protect their growing crops. Under this system, livestock owners marked or branded their animals during periodic roundups and sold selected animals to drovers who seasonally drove herds of cattle and hogs to markets in coastal and river towns. Even in areas heavily devoted to the cultivation of such staple crops as cotton and tobacco, the open-range system reigned supreme in the South until after the Civil War. On large plantations, some slaves carried out the specialized tasks of looking after livestock and building fences; this early African American participation in the southern cattle industry would continue among black cowboys in the Southwest after the war.

The cow was a valuable, multipurpose animal for farmers in the pre–Civil War South. In addition to their marketability, cattle provided meat for the table, labor for the fields, and milk and the dairy products made from it, as well as byproducts such as leather and tallow. Before the 20th century, the vast majority of cattle in the South were of an undetermined breed, backcountry descendants of a variety of European cattle brought to American shores in the colonial era and after. Referred to as native, scrub, or "cracker" cattle, these animals remained of comparatively low value and small size, though generations of life in the often harsh environment of the southern open range rendered them resilient and resistant to disease.

Some large planters and other wealthy hobby breeders began importing purebred British cattle (Devon, Shorthorn, etc.) into the South during the antebellum era, the earliest step in a century-long "progressive" process that would remake southern cattle raising after the midwestern style developed in the 19th century. In addition to the introduction of purebred animals, other characteristics of this midwestern system included fenced pastures and winter feeding (both of which became mandatory as the spread of stock laws gradually closed the open range in the postwar era), the sowing of specialty pasture grasses and hay crops, and the founding of various breeders' and cattlemen's associations. All these characteristics were eventually adopted by cattle raisers in the South, though the process was not uniform and played out over several generations and amidst struggles rooted in the region's racial, geographic, and socioeconomic divisions.

Although the beef cattle industry had been growing before the Great Depression, New Deal–era programs, carried out by Extension Service personnel in the decades after 1933, resulted in the conversion of millions of acres in the South from row crops to pastures and hayfields and to the importation of hundreds of thousands of Hereford, Angus, and other purebred beef cattle. By the 1950s beef cattle grazed in fields formerly planted to cotton, corn, and other crops. Ideally suited to the modern part-time farmer, beef cattle raising was by far the most common agricultural activity in the South and in the country by the 21st century, and the more than $14 billion generated by the industry in the former slave states surpassed the value of any other commodity.

BROOKS BLEVINS
*Lyon College*

Brooks Blevins, *Cattle in the Cotton Fields: A History of Cattle Raising in Alabama* (1998); John D. W. Guice, "Cattle Raisers of the Old Southwest: A Reinterpretation," *Western Historical Quarterly* (April 1977); Terry G. Jordan, *North American Cattle-Ranching Frontiers: Origins, Diffusion, and Differentiation* (1993), *Trails to Texas: Southern Roots of Western Cattle Ranching* (1981); Forrest McDonald and Grady McWhiney, *Journal of Southern History* (May 1975).

## Christmas Tree Farming

Farmers produce Christmas trees in every state in the South. A range of native and exotic conifer species grown as Christmas trees on plantations include pines, spruces, firs, cedars, and cypresses. Throughout the South, small "choose & cut" farms enable local customers to select a tree from the field or purchase precut Christmas trees, greenery, or other gift items from a farm store. These farms often diversify into other value-added enterprises that bring the public onto the farm in a paying capacity. These activities, encompassed by the concept of agritourism, include pumpkins, pick-your-own berry crops, nature trails, farm tours, lodging, special events, and even harvest festivals.

In the higher elevations of the southern Appalachians, a large wholesale market has developed around the production of native Fraser fir Christmas trees. Fraser fir has soft, dark-green foliage that holds up well as a cut tree. North Carolina is the second-largest producer of Christmas trees in the United States, behind Oregon. Virginia ranks eighth in the nation.

This southern wholesale market began in the 1940s with the harvest of mature Fraser fir trees from the native stands on Roan Mountain along the North Carolina–Tennessee border. Forty-foot trees were cut down. Only their tops were shipped to Christmas tree retail lots. By the early 1950s, the harvesters were learning to grow Christmas trees more cheaply on farms at 3,500 feet, where the climate was more predictable, instead of at 5,000 feet. They pulled wild seedlings from stands on Roan Mountain to plant in their fields. The first plantation-grown Fraser fir were sold in the 1950s. Tree quality improved through the 1960s as farmers learned optimum practices. The first of 10 Fraser firs was sent to the White House in Washington, D.C., in 1971 upon winning the National Christmas Tree Association tree contest. After this recognition, the industry grew rapidly through the 1990s to become a major agricultural commodity in the southern Appalachians.

Most Christmas trees are grown from seed or rooted cuttings. It can take up to five years to produce a seedling that is large enough to be planted in a field. Most seedlings are grown in raised beds or containers and then transplanted into other raised beds at wider spacing. Many farmers buy field-ready transplants from nurseries, but others grow seedlings or transplants for their own use or to sell as an additional enterprise.

Christmas trees are an intensive crop to grow. It can take 4 to 10 years in the field to produce a six-foot Christmas tree, depending on the species grown. The pines, cedars, and cypresses grow faster than firs and spruces, which have only a single flush of growth each year. All Christmas trees are pruned to increase branch density and to maintain a conical shape. Christmas tree fields are irrigated if needed, fertilized, limed, managed for weeds and ground cover, scouted for pests, treated for insects and diseases as they occur, inventoried, and tagged for market. During harvest, trees are cut, hauled, baled, moved again, stored, and finally loaded. By one estimate, a mature Christmas tree has been visited or handled over 150 times before it leaves the farm.

Most Christmas tree farms are small, part-time, family-run businesses. However, farms of all sizes rely on migrant labor during the growing season and harvest. In North Carolina and Virginia, wholesale Christmas tree farms collectively employ and house several thousand workers during peak seasons.

A number of issues face the Christmas tree industry. Soil-borne diseases threaten long-term sustainability of production. Pressures from urban and resort development compete for farmland. An aging farmer population translates into lost production as farms are sold. Competition from artificial tree sales and shifting demand as fewer families display any tree have eroded traditional markets over the last decade.

Yet, Christmas comes every year, and new generations of children are being taught the tradition of displaying a Christmas tree. More families than ever are visiting a Christmas tree farm despite the decline in national retail sales of trees. Christmas trees continue to provide income to farm families and contribute to a unique agricultural way of life.

JEFF OWEN
*North Carolina State University*

National Christmas Tree Association, *Real Tree Agricultural Census* (2005); Jill R. Sidebottom, *Crop Profile for Christmas Trees in North Carolina Mountains*, Cooperative Extension Service, North Carolina State University (May 2003); USDA, *Census of Agriculture* (2002).

## Citrus

Citrus frequently appears in the iconography of Florida: a ripe, juicy orange; groves of fruit-laden trees extending to the horizon; the child reaching for a healthy snack from a backyard tree— images of a nature that is merged seamlessly with commerce and domestic life. This commingling reflects nearly perfectly the complex interplay of climate, geography, economics, and culture that frame the history of citrus. The modern orange, lemon, and lime are all products of centuries of human tinkering for markets, exemplars of "second nature," and yet they are marketed as exemplars of a pure and healthy nature and employed in the marketing of other commodities, including the "commodity" of a naturally healthy South.

The long-standing association of citrus and the semitropical South suggests an ancient heritage and natural affinity, but citrus only arrived in the Western Hemisphere as part of the "Columbian Exchange," cultivated in Spanish settlements, its seeds rapidly dispersed and taking root in wild groves over the southern countryside or tended by Native Americans. Sustained commercial citriculture in continental North America began in the 18th century, as British planters expanded beyond their Barbados base. Observing that the Carolina Sea Islands lay at around the same latitude as Morocco and Valencia, and failing to account for climatic differences between western and eastern continental shores and the Gulf Stream's mediating effects on western Europe's climate, the British planters expected citrus to thrive in the Carolinas (an example of the "latitude fallacy"). Ironically, a century-long respite from hard freezes seemed to confirm their expectations, and citrus production flourished in English groves in Charleston, S.C., and, after 1763, northern Florida. Following the United States' annexation of Florida, citriculture expanded rapidly along navigable rivers to the Atlantic and Gulf coasts, driving demand for young trees beyond what nurseries and wild groves could supply. This demand was met with an important technological advance, a commercial technique for budding sweet China oranges onto the stumps of hardy wild oranges. "Topworking" produced bearing trees in only three years, and the South's first citrus boom was under way. By the early 1830s, citrus was eastern Florida's leading agricultural product, with annual citrus exports exceeding 2 million oranges from St. Augustine alone.

An era of more frequent cold snaps, initiated with a punishing freeze in 1835, drove most growers from South Carolina and Georgia. The center of commercial citrus production held around St. Augustine and along the St. Johns River until after the Civil War, when railroads began reaching deep into the Ridge, a high region running along the center of the peninsula. In addition to these more southerly areas, groves appeared all along the Gulf Coast from Pensacola to Texas, as growers experimented with new cold-resistant varieties such as the Satsuma. Still, the dictates of climate, and the economic incentives of Florida's land promoters and railroads, continued to move the center of citrus production southward. An exceptionally harsh cold snap in 1894–95 knocked many north Florida citrus counties off the market for a decade, while southern counties recovered and even exceeded production within four years. Similarly, every cold snap tested the resolve of north Gulf Coast growers, and by the 1930s citrus production in the South was all but limited to peninsular Florida and the southernmost county of Texas. By 2000 the center of citrus production had shifted south of Sarasota and toward the center of the state (and away from increasingly valuable residential land on the coasts).

Moving groves to less frost-prone areas was only one means to enhance productivity. Growers employed an arsenal of technologies to increase yields, from pesticides and fertilizers to systems to enhance frost protection and methods to accelerate or delay postharvest ripening. Between 1890 and 1992, Florida's citrus growers increased fivefold the number of acres under cultivation; but yields increased over 43 times, with each bearing tree producing between two and three times as many oranges.

But increased productivity did not

Unloading a grapefruit truck at a juice plant in Weslaco, Tex., 1942 (Arthur Rothstein, Library of Congress [LC-USF33-003648-M4], Washington, D.C.)

as determined by samples analyzed by chemists.

It is ironic, then, that citrus, genetically engineered over the thousands of years since it was first domesticated and enmeshed fundamentally in market-driven scientific agriculture, remains such an attractive symbol of nature's bounty, especially in Florida. Millions of southerners live with citrus in their immediate environs. They experience the seasonal cycles of a productive citrus tree; many walk into their own yard and pick a perfect sun-ripened orange; few reflect on their fruit tree's status as an exemplar of "second nature." Fewer still reflect on the symbiotic relationship between the citrus industry and the successful promotion of their state as a tourist destination, a place to raise a family, start a business, or retire. Florida's most successful promoters traded in claims of healthy climate, clear water, and a bountiful nature, exemplified by the iconic image of an orange tree heavy with fruit.

CHRISTIAN WARREN
*New York Academy of Medicine*

John A. Attaway, *A History of Florida Citrus Freezes* (1997); T. Frederick Davis, *Florida Historical Quarterly* (April 1937); Steven Stoll, *The Fruits of Natural Advantage: Making the Industrial Countryside in California* (1998); Christian Warren, in *Paradise Lost? The Environmental History of Florida*, ed. Jack E. Davis and Raymond Arsenault (2005); Jerry Wood Weeks, "Florida Gold: The Emergence of the Florida Citrus Industry, 1865–1895" (Ph.D. dissertation, University of North Carolina at Chapel Hill, 1977).

stop market volatility; it could in fact aggravate the cost of seasonal fluctuations. Consequently, the single most significant technological change in citrus production in the 20th century was the advent of frozen concentrated orange juice in the late 1940s. The ability to store processed citrus for years smoothed seasonal differences, helped growers regulate prices, and assured consumers a reliable, consistent-tasting (if not authentic-tasting) beverage. But frozen concentrate takes citrus yet another step farther from nature. Instead of marketing boxes of oranges, selected and priced by color, size, and quality, growers sell on the basis of the quantity of fruit sugars in each truckload of citrus brought to the juice plant,

## Communal Farms

Scholarly attention has focused on the large, successful, and well-known communal farms of the Northeast—including those of the Shakers, the Harmony Society, and Oneida. There have been, however, a number of significant communities in the South. The Shakers established Pleasant Hill and South Union in Kentucky in the early 1800s. Nashoba, an interracial Tennessee commune, was founded east of Memphis on the Wolf River in 1825 by Frances Wright, a reformer from Scotland. The name for the community derived from the Indian word for "wolf." The experiment lasted until 1828 and was intended as a model society for slaves, whom Wright and her followers purchased and prepared for freedom, and for whites, who lived in cooperative arrangement based on the ideas of reformer Robert Dale Owen. Wright left Nashoba in 1828 for Owen's New Harmony commune in Indiana, and the Tennessee settlement was gradually phased out. Another notable 19th-century communal farm was founded by Cyrus R. Teed at Estero, Fla. Its basis was the philosophy of Koreshanity, which claimed to explain the astronomical and religious principles of the universe, and it lasted from about 1900 to 1917.

Clarence Jordon, a Georgia Baptist preacher, conceived the idea for Koinonia Farms, a Christian community that began operations near Americus, Ga., in 1942. The name for the farm came from the Greek word for "fellowship" or "communism," and the intent of its founders was for the community to share its worldly goods. It was to be a religious and material inspiration to the surrounding impoverished rural areas of south Georgia.

The farm experimented with new scientific techniques for raising poultry and livestock and taught them to other farmers. It later successfully grew grapes, pecans, and peanuts, providing an adequate income for the group. Despite its economic success, Koinonia Farms became controversial in the 1950s and 1960s because of the vocal support of its members for racial equality and pacifism. Physical violence and an economic boycott from nearby whites challenged its survival, but it outlasted these threats. The community, which in the early 1980s included about 50 people living at Koinonia, launched a program to then provide low-cost housing to Georgia's rural poor. Koinonia remains an active, faith-based organization with numerous ministries promoting social justice.

In the late 1960s and early 1970s, a new wave of community building began. These communal experiments grew out of the counterculture. Many of these latter-day communards were veterans of the civil rights movement, Vietnam War protests, and campus-reform struggles. Of the modern communes in the South, two are especially noteworthy.

The first of these is called Twin Oaks, a commune near Louisa, Va. Inspired by B. F. Skinner's novel *Walden Two* (1948), Twin Oaks was started by eight people committed to the principles of behaviorist psychology. In June 1967 they moved onto a 123-acre farm that was purchased from a retired tobacco farmer. Farming supplied food for the group, and their income was supplemented by the sale of handwoven hammocks. Although many other communes have not worked, Twin Oaks became a thriving enterprise in large part because of firm rules on work and cooperation. By 1983 the community had grown to include some 80 members. As of 2007, it remained dedicated to such ideals as ecology, egalitarianism, and nonviolence and had a diverse population whose members typically stayed at Twin Oaks for seven years.

Another intriguing escape from the mainstream of American life is The Farm in Summertown, Tenn., about 80 miles southwest of Nashville. In 1970 Stephen Gaskin led a group of San Francisco hippies from California to this 1,750-acre farm. Like Twin Oaks, The Farm is based on a mixture of idealism and practicality. The Farm has a number of businesses—including a book-publishing company, a mail-order food store, and a citizens band radio repair operation. The Farm has its own international relief organization, called PLENTY, which is recognized by the United Nations. The Farm is organized along the lines of a religious group, following the teachings of Gaskin, which are based on a combination of Judeo-Christian ethics and Eastern mysticism. By 1983, The Farm had 950 members in Summertown and later grew to 1,600 members, making it easily the largest working commune in America. In the 1990s the farm renewed its focus in en-

couraging social change through exemplary projects, launching the Ecovillage Training Center using such new technologies as solar energy and biofuels.

In the future, the South may continue to attract more social experiments like communes because of the benign agricultural climate, the relatively low price of land, and the increasingly tolerant attitude of southerners toward alternative lifestyles.

ANGUS K. GILLESPIE
*Rutgers University*

Rupert Fike, ed., *Voices from the Farm: Adventures in Community Living* (1998); Stephen Gaskin, *Monday Night Class* (1974); Rosabeth Moss Kanter, *Commitment and Community: Communes and Utopias in Sociological Perspective* (1972); Kathleen Kinkade, *A Walden Two Experiment: The First Five Years of Twin Oaks Community* (1973), *Is It Utopia Yet? An Insider's View of Twin Oaks Community in Its Twenty-Sixth Year* (1994).

## Corn

Corn has over 500 industrial uses, most of which are little known. For nearly three centuries, maize, or Indian corn, had scores of everyday uses in the South, far more than all other crops combined. The area devoted to corn production in the South in 1920 was 46 million acres, the high point in acreage. That represented 44.6 percent of the nation's total. As food, it was basic to survival. Southerners, like other rural Americans, ate it as roasting ears, popcorn, hominy grits, cornbread, dodgers, hoecake, johnny cake, pone, mush, fritters, spoon bread, pudding, porridge, parched corn, fish-frying batter, hoppin' John (with peas), succotash (with beans), cornstarch, and, in the Southwest, tamales, tortillas, atole, and posole. They consumed it with meats and sweets and washed it down with corn liquor. This staple grain was on the southern table in some form at practically every meal.

The horses, mules, and oxen that helped to produce crops ate their share of corn, as did the hogs and poultry so vital to southern diets. As animal feed, corn topped all other crops by a wide margin. It was fed green in growing season and as dried grain, fodder, and silage during other months.

Southerners also employed corn for nonfood purposes that all but stagger the imagination. They used cobs for pipes, torches, corn shellers, tool handlers, jug stoppers, fishing corks, back scratchers, litter, hair curlers, missiles (for the popular corncob fights), salt and pepper shakers (hollowed), knothole plugs, and, above all, kindling. Other Americans certainly used corn products in the same ways, but probably not to the same extent for so long a time as southerners did.

Corn, cornmeal, and whiskey served as money to pay millers, weavers, preachers, and taxes, and whiskey was a universal home medicine. Ears of corn were used as darning eggs and as ornaments. Grains served as jewelry and as popcorn Christmas tree strings and were used in games such as bingo and hully gully.

Not to be outdone by the grains they yielded, husks (shucks) had a wide range of uses. They became dolls, dust-ers, writing paper, weaving material for chair backs, padding for pillows and mattresses, packing for fruits, vegetables, and fragiles, and wrapping for sausages, tamales, ash cakes, and cigarettes. Even silks were useful. Settlers smoked them as tobacco, formed them as hair for dolls, and steeped them to make medicines. Stalks and leaves were adapted for use as scarecrows, bamboo-like fences, thatching, and for erosion stoppage. Fodder became insulation inside and outside cabins, and fodder stacks and shocks occasionally served as shelter for families at night and during bad weather, or as places for drunks to sleep off their corn-liquor overdose.

Corn was, without serious rival, the universal plant of the South. Little wonder that southerners fashioned around it a culture of language, literature, poetry, music, art, and humor.

NICHOLAS P. HARDEMAN
*California State University*

Nicholas P. Hardeman, *Shucks, Shoes, and Hominy Blocks: Corn as a Way of Life in Pioneer America* (1981); Sam B. Hilliard, *Hog Meat and Hoecake: Food Supply in the Old South, 1840–1860* (1972); Paul Weatherwax, *Indian Corn in Old America* (1954).

## Cotton Culture

In the last decade of the 18th century, cotton cultivation swept up small farmers, slaves, and planters into a way of life that came to epitomize the antebellum South. Fueled by rising demand and improvements in ginning technology, cotton cultivation began its migration southwestward across the South. The Civil War ended slavery, and, after a struggle over tenure and control

Children picking cotton at an unidentified location, early 20th century
(Georgia Department of Archives and History, Atlanta)

of the crop, a sharecropping and crop-lien system emerged that lasted three quarters of a century. The new labor arrangements absorbed not only former slaves but also increasing numbers of white farmers who lost their land.

Between World War I and the Great Depression, cotton production shifted dramatically to the West. Depression and federal acreage-control policies marked the beginning of a new era, as planters relied upon dependable government payments and tractors to produce more cotton on less acreage. Defense industries during World War II pulled laborers from the rural South and raised expectations of those left behind. At the same time, International Harvester developed a successful mechanical cotton picker on the Hopson Plantation near Clarksdale, Miss.

Over the next two decades, the mechanical picker and synthetic chemicals such as DDT, parathion, and 2,4-D replaced millions of farm laborers. New cultivation practices, especially irrigation, suited western growing areas, so cotton continued to migrate to the West. In 1860 approximately two-thirds of all American cotton was produced east of the Mississippi River, but a century later this area was producing only a third of the national total. Before mechanization, cotton farmers began their work in the spring, breaking the land, running rows, and planting. After the plants emerged, constant chopping and cultivation continued until lay-by time in midsummer. In the autumn when the bolls opened, workers picked the seed cotton, and then it was ginned and baled for sale. While some seeds were put aside for planting, the bulk was crushed for oil, cattle feed, and other products. The cottonseed industry emerged as an important southern enterprise.

Under slavery, the plantation owner

or white overseer supervised the cultivation of the crop, and a black driver served as the field foreman. Some plantations operated a task system that allowed slaves to complete a set amount of work each day, and others used a gang system that required all slaves to work together. After emancipation, sharecroppers made contracts during the Christmas season, sometimes received an advance in wages from the landlord, and arranged for credit. At settlement time, their share of the crop went primarily to pay back furnishing merchants, who charged exorbitant interest rates. Some sharecroppers drifted into peonage, a form of debt-bondage that bound them to the land. Still, most croppers moved often, usually within the same community. Most lived in primitive and unsanitary shacks, and few benefited from education, health care, or adequate nutrition. It was out of this culture that the blues, country music, and gospel music emerged.

In the last decade of the 19th century, the Mexican cotton boll weevil crossed the Rio Grande River and began eating its way northeastward through the Cotton Belt. All attempts to halt its march failed, but the Federal Extension Service emerged from the effort to educate farmers on how to cope with its devastation. While instructing farmers on better methods of cultivation, extension agents encouraged them to purchase implements, fertilizer, and consumer products. Ultimately, nearly every county in the nation boasted agents, and this network, tied to the American Farm Bureau Federation, became a powerful political force. The Extension Service was well situated to take advantage of New Deal programs and push for mechanization and chemicals.

In the early years of the New Deal, the Agricultural Adjustment Administration (AAA) hoped to raise commodity prices by cutting production. It drastically reduced acreage, and, despite AAA contracts that forbade displacement of tenants, planters forced sharecroppers off the land. As small owners and sharecroppers attempted to cope with acreage reduction, federal money fueled the drive toward mechanization by larger farmers. Before complete mechanization occurred after World War II, landowners utilized wage laborers to perform the seasonal chopping and picking chores. Many former sharecroppers survived by securing relief from government programs, and large numbers of ex-farmers fled to northern and western cities in search of work and survival.

After 1945, with the perfection of the mechanical picker and effective herbicides, there was little need for large numbers of farm workers in the cotton area. Cotton farmers in the older growing areas were unable to take advantage of mechanization as well as those in the West and turned to other crops. The changes set in motion by the New Deal and by mechanization exacted a tremendous human cost and became, in some respects, a mechanical and chemical enclosure movement that forced farmers off the land into cities. By 1970 practically all cotton was machine harvested, and herbicides kept the fields clean of weeds. The cotton culture that had epitomized the slave and post–Civil War South continued its migration to the West, leaving behind diversified farms on enlarged units. Texas is the leading cotton-producing state in the nation, producing 8.886 million bales of cotton in 2005–6, more than half of the total production in the United States. The term "cotton South" became almost solely historical in its meaning.

PETE DANIEL
*Smithsonian Institution*
*Washington, D.C.*

James C. Cobb, *The Most Southern Place on Earth: The Mississippi Delta and the Roots of Southern Identity* (1992); David E. Conrad, *The Forgotten Farmers: The Story of Share-croppers in the New Deal* (1965); Pete Daniel, *Breaking the Land: The Transformation of Cotton, Tobacco, and Rice Cultures since 1880* (1985); Gilbert C. Fite, *Agricultural History* (January 1980); Eugene D. Genovese, *Roll, Jordan, Roll: The World the Slaves Made* (1974); Donald H. Grubbs, *Cry from the Cotton: The Southern Tenant Farmers' Union and the New Deal* (1971); Jack Temple Kirby, *Rural Worlds Lost: The American South, 1920–1960* (1987); Henry I. Richards, *Cotton and the Agricultural Adjustment Admin-istration* (1936); James H. Street, *The New Revolution in the Cotton Economy* (1957); Harold D. Woodman, *New South—New Law: The Legal Foundations of Credit and Labor Relations in the Postbellum Agricul-tural South* (1995); Lynette Boney Wrenn, *Cinderella of the New South: A History of the Cottonseed Industry, 1855–1955* (1995).

## Dairy Industry

Production of milk and dairy products in the early South was not significantly different from that in the North. Considerable divergence appeared in the 19th century, though, because of slower urban growth in the South. While the old dairy belt emerged in the North to supply milk for commercially manufac-tured dairy products in a national mar-ket and fluid milk to large cities, south-erners haphazardly supplied their towns with fluid milk, made their own butter, and at times bought canned milk and cheese produced in the North.

The dairy picture in the South changed surprisingly little from the 19th century until about World War II. Dur-ing that era, many small farmers across the region kept and milked a few often mixed-breed cows, separated the milk, fed the skim to the hogs, made their own butter, and sold the surplus cream in town or shipped it on the railroad to market. Along with the sale of a few eggs, it allowed them a small but steady cash flow. By the 1930s an increasing number of small cheese-manufacturing plants had appeared in the South, and better roads brought motor-truck car-riers to pick up whole Grade B milk from many small unspecialized pro-ducers. Near the towns, dairy specialists milked cows, bottled fluid milk, and sold it to town residents. At the same time, dairymen near larger cities were selling fluid milk to processors who pasteurized it and sold it on the local market.

From World War II onward, the growth of highways and urban centers in the South transformed dairy pro-duction, processing, and marketing. The small Grade B, or manufacturing, milk producer swiftly disappeared, and dairy farming in the South became more specialized than in any place other than California and the far West. By the 1960s the average cow population of Texas dairy farms was roughly twice that of Wisconsin, a state whose total dairy production dwarfed that of any other state in the Union. During the 1970s efforts toward market rationalization and integration, carried on by large merged milk-producer cooperatives, increasingly blurred distinctions between dairy farming in the South and the rest of the nation.

E. DALE ODOM
*North Texas State University*

Lewis C. Gray, *History of Agriculture in the Southern United States to 1860*, 2 vols. (1933); Thomas R. Pirtle, *History of the Dairy Industry* (1926); John T. Schlebecker, *History of American Dairying* (1967); Andrew Schmitz, William G. Boggess, and Ken Tefertiller, *American Journal of Agricultural Economy* (December 1995).

## Farm Security Administration

During the Great Depression, the New Deal administration wrestled with the problem of massive and chronic rural poverty. Between 1935 and 1946, the Farm Security Administration (FSA) was the federal agency that worked to uplift some of America's poorest people.

The FSA began as the Resettlement Administration (RA), created by President Franklin D. Roosevelt's executive order in May 1935. The RA consolidated federal programs for classifying rural land, retiring submarginal farms, and resettling their residents. Also transferred to the RA were rural subsistence homesteads for surplus industrial workers, pilot suburban housing projects, and several cooperative farm communities started with federal relief funds. But the largest responsibility assigned to the new agency was the rural rehabilitation work of the Federal Emergency Relief Administration (FERA). Faced with the urgent needs of destitute farmers, especially southern tenants and sharecroppers, the FERA had attempted to keep them on the land with a combination of production and living credit and close supervision of their farming. Acquiring this rapidly growing program made the RA an antipoverty agency.

The RA's responsibilities expanded in July 1937, when Congress passed the Bankhead-Jones Farm Tenancy Act providing a modest lending program to help tenants buy farms. President Roosevelt assigned this new work to the RA, which was renamed the Farm Security Administration.

Even though the FSA never reached a majority of the poor and often bypassed the most impoverished, its programs gave substantial aid to many farmers during its peak years of 1937–42. The largest program was always rural rehabilitation. The FSA's 1941 report, for example, indicated loans or grants (typically a few hundred dollars per case) being received by more than 600,000 southern families. County FSA supervisors helped clients write farm- and home-management plans and gave technical advice. At its best, this supervision improved the farming skills, self-direction, nutrition, and health of the poor. Among other programs that the FSA promoted for low-income farmers were cooperatives for marketing produce and purchasing supplies, joint ownership of breeding livestock or machinery, farm-improvement loans, prepaid health-care plans, and debt-adjustment loans. However, farm-purchase lending under the Bankhead-Jones Act was so poorly funded that the FSA could serve only a few thousand borrowers per year, making little impact on tenancy.

Under southern administrators Will W. Alexander (1936–40) and Calvin B. Baldwin (1940–43), the FSA attempted a comprehensive attack on rural poverty, but its efforts were short-lived. Congress slashed the FSA's funds during World War II and disbanded it in 1946. A few of the FSA's credit functions survive in a successor agency, the Farmers' Home Administration.

PAUL E. MERTZ
*University of Wisconsin at Stevens Point*

Sidney Baldwin, *Poverty and Politics: The Rise and Decline of the Farm Security Administration* (1968); Paul E. Mertz, *New Deal Policy and Southern Rural Poverty* (1978); Brenda J. Taylor, in *The New Deal and Beyond: Social Welfare in the South since 1930*, ed. Elna Green (2003).

## Fence/Stock Laws

An abundance of land and a comparative scarcity of people in the colonial South influenced the development of an extensive style of agriculture. A key feature of this agriculture was open- or free-range livestock raising. Under this system, colonies (later states) and localities passed fence laws, which permitted livestock owners to allow their animals to range freely over the countryside and required farmers to erect fences to protect their crops. Fence laws and the open range held sway in the South until after the Civil War.

In the late antebellum era, the slow but steady importation of expensive purebred cattle (and to a lesser extent hogs) by some planters and patrician hobby ranchers and the expenses associated with fencing in expanding acreages of cropland led to early clamorings for the passage of stock laws—mandates requiring livestock owners to keep their animals in fenced enclosures. Dissatisfaction with the open-range system picked up steam after the Civil War, as planters and other farmers faced the prospect of repairing and rebuilding war-ravaged fences without the aid of slave labor, as southern agriculture became more land intensive, and, later, as the tenets of agricultural progressivism infiltrated the region in conjunction with the New South creed.

Beginning in the latter half of the 1860s, large swaths of the more intensively cultivated sections of the South were converted to closed-range territory, reflecting both racial and class prejudices on the part of stock-law proponents. These stock-law districts were created by a variety of means, such as bills passed by state legislatures and proclamations by county revenue boards or court commissioners. Most state legislatures eventually enacted local-option legislation that granted county officials the authority to conduct district elections and in some cases the power to close the range based on landowner petitions and in lieu of elections. One such bill, an act passed in the Georgia general assembly in 1872, precipitated two decades of contentious local-option struggles and, according to historian Steven Hahn, reflected fundamental class conflict while contributing to the rise of agrarian protest.

Hahn's examination of the stock-law controversy in his seminal book *The Roots of Southern Populism* remains the most widely recognized study of the southern range question, but it has also contributed to a one-state focus that has tended to distort the saga of the closing of the range in the region. Most in-depth studies of the stock-law controversy have focused on Georgia and its rather early experience with stock-law battles. (Mississippi's legislature passed a similar local-option law 20 years after Georgia, for example, and Alabama did so only in 1903.) In many, if not most, areas of the South—and certainly in the less-cultivated regions such as Appalachia and the Piney Woods—the starkest local-option contests took place in the early 20th century and reflected the same socioeconomic and cultural tensions found in other Progressive Era debates. Even if the stock-law controversy contributed little if anything to the rise of late 19th-century populism in much of the South, 20th-century range conflicts continued to reflect deep divisions within the southern populace. Hahn attributes these divisions to the struggles between haves and have-nots in an emerging capitalistic society. Other scholars have modified Hahn's materialistic interpretation or have re-cast the divide on some other axis: rural vs. urban, isolation from vs. exposure to market forces and progressivism, those who expected to benefit from stock laws vs. those who did not.

Regardless of underlying theory, the opposing sides tended to share characteristics over the years and across the region. Championing stock laws were "progressive" agriculturists (usually planters and larger farmers), railroad companies (who annually faced thousands of dollars in restitution payments for killed or injured animals in open-range districts), coal and timber companies, townspeople, and state-sanctioned messengers for progressivism such as land-grant university personnel and representatives of the U.S. Department of Agriculture. Opposing the closing of the range were those least likely to benefit from the stock law: small and landless farmers and larger landowners with marginal land and significant livestock holdings.

The story of the demise of the open range in the South presents a typically diverse picture. Whereas fertile regions dominated by large planters, such as the Alabama Black Belt, were largely off-limits to open-range herders by 1880, the open-range tradition survived well into the 20th century in much of the South in locations as diverse as the Neches Valley of Texas, where laws closed the open range in the 1950s, and the Blue Ridge region of Virginia, where fence laws remained on the books in a couple of remote counties in the early 21st century.

BROOKS BLEVINS
*Lyon College*

Brooks Blevins, *Cattle in the Cotton Fields: A History of Cattle Raising in Alabama* (1998); Steven Hahn, *The Roots of Southern Populism: Yeoman Farmers and the Transformation of the Georgia Upcountry, 1850–*

*1890* (1983); Shawn Everett Kantor, *Politics and Property Rights: The Closing of the Open Range in the Postbellum South* (1998); J. Crawford King, *Journal of Southern History* (February 1982); Thad Sitton, *Backwoodsmen: Stockmen and Hunters along a Big Thicket River Valley* (1995).

## Fertilizer

In the 1840s and 1850s, an agricultural reform movement occurred in the South as planters and farmers sought some means of restoring their worn-out fields. Farm journals of the period recommended increased use of lime and manures. At the same time, superphosphate and Peruvian guano were introduced as commercial fertilizers. By 1860 their use had spread from Maryland and Virginia into the Carolinas and Georgia.

Billboard advertising fertilizer, Laurinburg, N.C., 1938 (Marion Post Walcott, Library of Congress [LC-USF-51099E], Washington, D.C.)

After the Civil War, the problems of exhausted land and quick returns on cotton and tobacco crops combined to greatly accelerate the use of fertilizers. To meet this demand, the fertilizer industry began to move southward. In 1868 development of the South Carolina phosphate deposits began, and Charleston soon became an important fertilizer center. In the 20th century, phosphate mines were developed in Florida and North Carolina, and they now produce a significant amount of the worlds' phosphate requirements.

Fertilizer was in most demand for use on cotton, and a mixed product (in 200-pound bags) containing the three principal plant nutrients (nitrogen, phosphorus, and potassium) was popular with southern farmers. Many farmers commonly prepared their own mixtures by combining superphosphate and kainit (a potash salt) with cottonseed meal. The general use of fertilizers had several effects on southern culture. The Cotton and Tobacco Belts were extended into areas where their cultivation was previously unprofitable. The old compost heap was abandoned, and farmers tended to limit cultivation to old upland fields. Commercial fertilizers stimulated intensive farming, particularly in trucking areas, and assured higher yields per acre. Finally, the use of commercial fertilizers was responsible for bringing mechanized farming to the South.

During the 1880s the South benefited from the Morrill Act of 1862, which provided for state colleges of agriculture, and later from the Hatch Act (1887), which provided for agricultural experiment stations. Between 1933 and 1990, the Tennessee Valley Authority (TVA) operated the National Fertilizer Research Center (NFDC). This center had fertilizer research facilities at Muscle Shoals, Ala., that were used to develop new and improved fertilizer products and processes. The center also had agriculture and fertilizer research programs in all states of the nation. These programs were conducted in cooperation with the agriculture universities and the industries of each state. This center has been disbanded, and the facility is now the Environmental Research Center, which has as its objective to solve some of the nation's environmental problems. About 60 percent of fertilizers produced in the United States today are made with technology developed by the TVA. Some of the type of research formerly conducted by the TVA is now conducted by the International Fertilizer Development Center, which is located adjacent to the NFDC.

The South continues to supply much of the phosphate and some of the sulfur and ammonia used in fertilizer production in the country. Vast changes have occurred in the industry during the last 50 years. Consumption of fertilizer, particularly outside the South, has increased greatly. Concentrated fertilizers have replaced low-analysis materials. Mixtures of solid materials (Bulk Blends) and liquid type fertilizers have replaced essentially all of the bagged fertilizer. Mechanical handling and custom application is now common. In 2001 southerners used about 15 million tons of commercial fertilizer (28 percent of national consumption).

In the early part of the 21st century, most of the potash used in the southern states is imported from Canada. A significant amount of the nitrogen (urea and ammonia) is imported from those states and foreign countries that have large amounts of natural gas. This is be-cause the main ingredient of these types of fertilizers is natural gas. Most of the phosphate materials are from Florida and North Carolina. Mechanization of farming has resulted in consolidation of the traditional family farm into larger farms. The amount of labor per unit of crop production has decreased significantly. At the same time, there has been consolation of the fertilizer industry to a few large producers. These changes have helped keep the cost of food and fiber to a reasonable level and have encouraged the export of agricultural goods.

FRANK P. ACHORN
*Killen, Alabama*

RICHARD C. SHERIDAN
*Tennessee Valley Authority (Retired)*

Association of American Control Officials, *Commercial Fertilizer* (2001); Richard C. Sheridan, *Agricultural History* (January 1979); Rosser H. Taylor, *North Carolina Historical Quarterly* (July–October 1953).

## Forage Crops

Forage refers to animal food of plant origin, particularly that providing feed for domestic animals. It may include pasturage, browse, hay, silage, green chop, and crop residues. Forages are the mainstay of grassland agriculture, that is, agriculture based on grasses, legumes, and other fodder or soil-building crops. Grassland farming with forage crops has many environmental benefits, including improving soil and water quality and reducing soil erosion and soil nutrient losses. In addition, forage-crop production requires far less pesticide and fossil fuel energy input compared with row crops.

TABLE 1. *Some Common Forages of the Southern Region.*

## Grasses

| Perennials | | Annuals | |
|---|---|---|---|
| Warm-Season | Cool-Season | Warm-Season | Cool-Season |
| Bahiagrass | Kentucky bluegrass | Corn | Barley |
| Bermudagrass | Orchard grass | Crabgrass | Oats |
| Big bluestem | Reed canarygrass | Millet, browntop | Rye, cereal |
| Carpetgrass | Rescuegrass | Millet, foxtail | Ryegrass, annual |
| Dallisgrass | Tall fescue | Millet, pearl | Triticale |
| Eastern gamagrass | Timothy | Sorghum, forage | Wheat |
| Indiangrass | | Sorghum, grain | |
| Johnsongrass | | Sorghum-sudan hybrids | |
| Switchgrass | | Sudangrass | |

## Legumes

| | | | |
|---|---|---|---|
| Kudzu | Alfalfa | Alyce clover | Clover, arrowleaf |
| Perennial peanut | Alsike clover | Cowpea | Clover, ball |
| Sericea lespedeza | Birdsfoot trefoil | Lespedeza, Korean | Clover, berseem |
| | Red clover | Lespedeza, Kobe | Clover, bur |
| | White (Ladino) clover | Soybean | Clover, button |
| | | Velvetbean | Clover, crimson |
| | | | Clover, subterranean |
| | | | Vetch, hairy |
| Native species | | | Winter pea |

In pre-Columbian times, the southeastern United States was mostly covered by dense forest. Nevertheless, reports from the first explorers of the region tell of fire-maintained savannahs and canebrake river bottoms, some as large as 25 miles wide and more than 100 miles long. With few exceptions, southern forages in common use today are intentional or inadvertent imports from Europe, Africa, and Asia (Table 1). Excluding the Mississippi Delta and the Black Belt soils of Alabama and Mississippi, the majority of soils of the region are inherently acid and infertile. Historically, the South has been a row-crop region. In comparison to the country as a whole, the South has about 12 percent of the farmland and roughly 25 percent of the farms. These figures imply that farm size in the South is generally smaller (200 acres) than the national average (526 acres). About 41 percent of the farms have pasture and 53 percent have cattle.

The South possesses a wide range of climates, ranging from temperate in the Appalachian Mountains, where cool-season perennial forages (bluegrass and tall fescue) predominate, to subtropical along the Gulf Coast, where warm-season perennials (Bermuda and Bahia grasses) are most prevalent (see Table 1). Where soils and climate permit, a combination of cool- and warm-season forages is desirable. This climate provides for an extended season of production that can support grazing livestock during much or most of the year.

Agricultural statistics tell little about the importance of grassland farming and forage crops. Most forages are not widely marketed because they are consumed on the farms where they are produced. Nevertheless, the value of forages, based on their contribution to human food of animal origin, probably exceeds that of any other crop. The food-producing system represented by forage crops and ruminant animals (cattle, sheep, and goats) is of vast importance to the region's agricultural economy. The percent of nutrients from forages consumed by various classes of ruminants range from 30 percent to more than 80 percent, the highest being by beef cows. The basis for the forage-ruminant system is that, because of their multichambered stomachs and the bacteria that live there, ruminant animals can digest high cellulose-containing forage plants. Animals with a single-chambered stomach, such as pigs, poultry, and humans, must rely heavily on concentrate feeds such as cereal grains, fruits, and selected vegetables.

An essential element in understanding the contribution of forages to food production and agricultural stewardship is that forages can be grown on land unfit for row-crop production because it is too steep, too rocky, too sandy, too shallow, or too wet. This marginal land can contribute to food production without the destruction of our soil resource base only through the forage-ruminant system.

Forages are also grown on good land in rotation with row crops. As a rotational crop, forages play an important role in reducing soil erosion, conserving water, and providing an optimal economic return. The use of forages on steep land and in rotation with other crops is fundamental to agricultural sustainability. In the *Grass Yearbook of Agriculture* (1948), P. V. Cardon declared, "Around grass, farmers can organize general crop production so as to promote efficient practices that lead to permanency in agriculture." He was using the word "grass" in a broad context that included legumes. Gerald Mc-Carthy, in *North Carolina Agricultural Experiment Station Bulletin* 73 (1890), acknowledged, "Ever since agriculture became an improved art, grass and clover have been regarded as the foundation of all enduring, prosperous farming." Without doubt, forages have a key role to play in the sustainability of our agricultural resource base.

J. PAUL MUELLER
*North Carolina State University*

D. M. Ball, C. S. Hoveland, G. D. Lace-field, *Southern Forages* (2007); Robert F. Barnes, C. Jerry Nelson, Michael Collins, and Kenneth J. Moore, eds., *Forages: An Introduction to Grassland Agriculture* (2003); A. J. Franzluebbers, *Integrated Crop-Livestock Systems in the Southeastern USA* (2007); Jack R. Harlan, *Theory and Dynamics of Grassland Agriculture* (1956).

## Garvey Movement

The Universal Negro Improvement Association (UNIA) was a worldwide organization that flourished in many areas of the rural South in the early 1920s. People who joined the UNIA and others who supported its goals became part of what is now called the Garvey Movement. Incorporated in Harlem in 1918 by a Jamaican named Marcus Garvey, the UNIA established over 400 divisions in the former Confederate states. The UNIA gained popularity through an internationally distributed weekly newspaper called the *Negro World*. Its fundamental mission was to promote the economic, social, and political independence of people who identified themselves racially as Negroes and as descendants of African people. Although dozens of large local divisions of the UNIA were organized in urban areas, especially outside of the South, there were also hundreds of small divisions in rural southern counties. Notable concentrations of UNIA divisions occurred in southern Georgia, the Mississippi Delta, the Arkansas Delta, and the sugar parishes of southeastern Louisiana. Although isolated from the metropolitan divisions of the UNIA, which held open mass meetings, conducted color-

ful parades, and drilled publicly in the UNIA's African Legion uniforms, rural southern divisions stayed connected to the UNIA program and philosophy through weekly meetings held in country churches, through study of the UNIA Constitution and the Negro Bill of Rights, and through Garvey's editorials and addresses in the *Negro World*.

The UNIA program had as its primary, long-term goal the creation of a black-ruled nation in Africa, which Garvey referred to as "the Motherland of all Negroes." This nation would provide a vanguard against oppression for all blacks in the diaspora. This nation would have to be economically strong, politically independent, and armed and equipped to defend itself. To the deeply religious rural, southern Garveyites, so-called African Redemption involved more than reclaiming the continent from white imperialist nations. It also meant continuing the spiritual redemption begun by missionaries to Africa from the black Baptist and African Methodist Episcopal churches. A local and immediate goal of the UNIA was for individuals to defend and protect themselves and their communities. White-controlled law enforcement was notoriously ineffective in the rural South, and special issues of UNIA concern were the lynching and rape of black people that ordinarily went unpunished.

UNIA division organizers in the rural South were typically married, middle-aged, landless farmers. Some were cotton sharecroppers, some raised sugarcane, and many were tenants on North Carolina tobacco farms. Most were literate and had literate children in their households who attended school. UNIA wives tended to be "keeping house" rather than laboring as domestics or farmers for white people. Most were identified by the census enumerators as "Negro" rather than "Mulatto." Many lived in black-majority communities, and almost all were native-born southerners (rather than West Indians, as were many Garvey supporters in urban areas). A number of important UNIA organizers were preachers, and many organizational meetings were held in churches at three o'clock on Sunday afternoons. Although men were prominent in the leadership of the movement, rural women played particularly significant roles in organizing divisions and promoting the tenets of Garveyism: independence, education, separation from whites, and stronger black communities.

MARY G. ROLINSON
*Georgia State University*

Mary G. Rolinson, *Grassroots Garveyism: The Universal Negro Improvement Association in the Rural South, 1920–1927* (2007); Robert A. Hill, ed., *Universal Negro Improvement Association and Marcus Garvey Papers*, vols. 1–7 (1983–1990); Tony Martin, *Race First: The Ideological and Organizational Struggles of Marcus Garvey and the Universal Negro Improvement Association* (1976); *Negro World* (1920–33).

## Hog Production

Swine were the primary nonhuman companions of Europeans exploring eastern North America. The animals adapted well to the climate and landscape of the coast and interior. Would-be colonists made conscious efforts to "seed" potential outposts with swine to provide sustenance for themselves and future settlers. The success of this strategy is evidenced through a variety of colonial commentaries. In his *History of Virginia* (1705), Robert Beverley observed, "Hogs swarm like Vermine upon the Earth and are often accounted as such." According to William Byrd's *History of the Dividing Line between Virginia and North Carolina* (1728), "The only Business [in North Carolina] is raising Hogs, which is manag'd with the least trouble, and affords the Diet they are most fond of. The Truth of it is the Inhabitants of N Carolina devour so much Swine's flesh, that it fills them full of gross Humours." In some ways, Byrd's observations suggest more about his disdain for backcountry-subsistence culture than his understanding of the realities of hog production in the region. What he failed to realize was that rural folk throughout the southern colonies used pork for more than mere subsistence.

Cross-cultural trade in pork throughout Florida had been a mainstay early in the 1600s. The Apalachee tribe produced hogs in large numbers in response to the demand for meat in Spanish missions. Trade had grown so immense that colonial officials pressed for the establishment of customs officers to regulate the exchanges. Early settlers to South Carolina also purchased pork from neighboring Native Americans. Markets in Virginia and the West Indies made hog production one of the chief exports of colonial North Carolina.

Nearly all southerners raised swine, regardless of landholdings. The goal for most was a balance between subsistence

*Farmer in his Sunday best, feeding his pigs, Benton, Miss., 1975 (William R. Ferris Collection, Southern Folklife Collection, Wilson Library, University of North Carolina at Chapel Hill)*

and market production. In certain areas of the South, however, by the late antebellum period hogs had more economic value than local cotton crops. The persistence of the open range in the region offered land-hungry yeomen the opportunity to enter the market economy through ownership of large numbers of swine. Farmers on small landholdings would have the option to unload surplus meat to plantation owners and townspeople. The strength of long-distance trading networks organized by the Southeast's numerous livestock drovers also broadened the possibilities of lucrative commercial hog ventures. The ravages of the Civil War did not allow growth in swine to last. From 1860 to 1880, hog populations declined

dramatically throughout the South. Yet, even as traditional patterns of livestock husbandry waned, outside interest in developing pork-as-business emerged.

Experts, building off the momentum of federal funding for agricultural extension through the Smith-Lever Act of 1914, touted the benefits of a balanced agricultural economy through commercial hog production. The challenge, however, was twofold: convincing farmers to turn away from familiar patterns of producing cash crops and helping those who were interested apply methods of midwestern corn-hog agriculture in which they had relied on the less labor-intensive benefits of the open range. Ultimately, economic depression thwarted the push to encourage commercial hog production in the region. Farm families and agricultural experts throughout the 1920s and 1930s turned to hogs as the path to safety-first agriculture.

Swine populations in the South did not see steady growth until the 1960s and a dramatic increase until the 1980s. Wendell Murphy of Rose Hill, N.C., represents the change in southern hog production, making his mark in the business rather by accident. In 1969 a cholera outbreak forced him to shut down his operation, but Murphy was unwilling to wait out a federal quarantine to start anew. He began to contract with producers, providing them a stable price per animal while he took the risks of selling on the open marketplace. The poultry industry had first applied this method of contract farming to its growing production in the South during the 1940s. Murphy adapted the concept and was equally successful. In 1997 *Forbes* magazine referred to Murphy as "the Ray Kroc of Pigsties."

The other revolution in hog production brought about through Murphy's influence has been total-confinement operations. Traditional hog farming had been done almost exclusively outside, on wet and dry lots and pastures. Even with the potential for expansion, swine farmers in the South lagged behind the Midwest in product quantity and quality. Moving operations completely inside allowed for closer management. Feeding and watering became automated processes. Waste filtered through floor slats to holding lagoons adjacent to barns. The advantages were numer-

ous, according to advocates of these methods. Labor costs fell, investments were not wasted on fencing and fence repair, and overall sanitation improved. Total confinement required less land and labor to produce more hogs. This method catapulted North Carolina into direct competition with the Midwest.

Along with the growth, however, problems have emerged. Small-time hog farmers have struggled to remain in business, unable to keep up with the economies of scale inherent in confinement operations. Added to these economic realities are pressing concerns over the ecological ramifications of large-scale hog production—foul odors and vast wastes. In the wake of two 1995 swine waste-lagoon breaks in North Carolina that released millions of gallons of feces and urine onto area landscapes, local residents, scientists, and legislators questioned the near unchecked growth of the industry. In 1999 state legislators in North Carolina passed a moratorium on new and expanded hog farms—yet, in the most recent agricultural census, North Carolina remains second only to Iowa in total hog production.

MICHAEL D. THOMPSON
*Pfeiffer University*

Sam Bowers Hilliard, *Hog Meat and Hoecake: Food Supply in the Old South, 1840–1860* (1972); Jack Temple Kirby, *Mockingbird Song: Ecological Landscapes of the South* (2006), *Poquosin: A Study of Rural Landscape and Society* (1995); Forrest McDonald and Grady McWhiney, *Journal of Southern History* (May 1975); Michael D. Thompson, *Agricultural History* (Spring 2000).

## Home Extension Services

The U.S. Department of Agriculture (USDA) developed Home Extension Services to disseminate information to the farming community. Home extension has its roots in the Progressive Era and the country life movement. Theodore Roosevelt authorized the Country Life Commission to investigate rural life. The report paid special attention to farm women and, finding they were overworked and lacked modern technologies, recommended improving their conditions. In order to improve agricultural scientific study, Congress had passed the Morrill Acts of 1862 and 1890 that established land-grant colleges. Agricultural reformers eager to spread helpful information to farmers published bulletins and spoke at farmers' institutes, conferences, and agricultural fairs. Still, a minority of farmers gained access to new scientific knowledge. Eventually, reformers realized they had to take the information directly to the farmer.

Seaman A. Knapp, a professor at what is now Iowa State University, was instrumental in developing the concept of demonstration work. Knapp helped draft the first experimental station bill that was the precursor to the Hatch Act of 1877. This act appropriated federal funding for experimental stations to gather and disseminate practical scientific knowledge to farmers. In 1903 the Mexican boll weevil threatened Texas cotton production. Using five demonstration farms in Texas and Louisiana, Knapp was able to convince farmers that using good farming practices of crop rotation, deeper plowing, fertilizers, and improved seed selection could prevent crop destruction. When farmers saw that these improved techniques worked, they immediately implemented them and the cotton crops were saved. Impressed by Knapp's success, the USDA earmarked $40,000 to expand demonstration programs, creating the Cooperative Demonstration Work of the USDA.

Knapp saw the advantages of expanding demonstration work for women, boys, and girls. In the early 1910s, agriculture agents organized girls into Tomato Clubs, boys into Corn Clubs, and women into Canning Clubs. The benign names of these organizations belie the lofty and transforming goals of the reformers, who wanted to educate the rural population and lift them out of poverty through scientific farming, efficiency, mechanization, and improved profits. Later, the organizations were renamed home demonstration and 4-H clubs.

In 1914 Congress passed the Smith-Lever Act that provided federal money to land-grant universities to establish and administer Extension Services. The universities trained agents in the latest agricultural scientific knowledge, who would then educate the rural population through demonstrations and USDA publications. The agents would be assigned to counties with the expectation that local governments would pay up to 50 percent of their salaries. The Rockefeller General Education Board also provided substantial funding. County agents reported to district agents, who in turn reported to state directors, who were usually responsible to the dean of the agricultural state college. Smith-Lever shared the goals of the country life movement of rural uplift and efficiency and wanted to improve living conditions for rural women. Importantly, Smith-Lever dictated policies based on a gendered division of labor—men as farmers growing crops, women as homemakers taking care of domestic needs. This dichotomy did not reflect the reality of farm life.

Tuskegee Institute pioneered demonstration work for African Americans, but this work developed slower because many county governments refused to fund demonstration programs for blacks. Authority over black extension work was centered in three black colleges: Tuskegee, Hampton Institute, and, briefly, Prairie View State Normal and Industrial College in Texas. Programs directed at black southerners had contradictory goals. In the segregated South, the Extension Service wanted to improve conditions for blacks without their developing greater independence. Throughout the first decades of extension work for blacks, the programs were underfunded and agents were overworked with much larger districts than their white counterparts.

Today, the Extension Service works with local governments and community leaders to improve rural life with a broad range of educational programs in agriculture, community resource development, nutrition, family issues, lawn and garden programs, and youth development. Membership in Home Demonstration clubs has declined as women left the farm and worked outside the home. However, 4-H is still an important aspect of rural life, and it has adapted and changed to stay vital.

MINOA D. UFFELMAN
*Austin Peay State University*

Laurie Winn Carlson, *William J. Spillman and the Birth of Agricultural Economics* (2005); Mary S. Hoffschwelle, *Rebuilding the Rural Community: Reformers, Schools, and Homes in Tennessee, 1900–1930* (1998); Jeannie Whayne, in *American Life in the Rural South*, ed. R. Douglas Hurt (2003).

## Horses and Mules

Horses and mules once dominated the southern agricultural landscape. Before tractors replaced them, horses, mules, and, to a limited extent, oxen pulled plows, cultivators, and wagons across the American South. Horses were common in the South throughout the region's draft animal era, but mules filled a central and unique place in southern agriculture and culture. Beginning in the early 19th century, in agricultural journals such as the *Southern Planter*, southerners debated the merits of each type of draft animal. Planters were the first to adopt mules because they perceived mules as hardier than horses. Thus, mules fit well into an agricultural system that provided little incentive for slaves to care for draft animals. In addition, as the hybrid cross between a jackass and a mare, mules were innovative in the context of a slave-based agriculture, but they also buttressed the slave system. On the eve of the Civil War, mules were an increasingly important component of plantation agriculture, even though mules were not produced to any great extent in the region and they cost more than horses.

Linked to slavery before the Civil War, mules became almost universally employed on southern farms in the late 19th and early 20th centuries. In 1930, for example, mules outnumbered horses nearly two to one in the South as a whole. In the Deep South, the discrepancy was even more pronounced. The 1930 agricultural census reported just over 37,000 horses and 353,633 mules. Because mules were so widely employed during the first half of the 20th century, the majority of southerners, black and white, had some contact with the animals. "Forty acres and a mule" became the unfulfilled hope of millions of African Americans who understood that land and a way to work it were the keys to economic freedom. New Deal photographers cemented the relationship of the South and mules in Americans' minds, especially the relationship of mules, monoculture, and sharecropping. Images of thin mules, eroded fields, and run-down cabins tied mules to the perception of the South as a backward, even benighted region. Innovative in 1850, by 1950 mules symbolized the negative features of southern agriculture and life. Farm horses and mules quickly disappeared from the South in the decade following World War II as several technologies—tractors, cotton pickers, herbicides, pesticides, and improved varieties of cotton—converged to allow full mechanization of cotton production. In addition, World War II

catalyzed a massive demographic shift that saw southern farms and plantations emptied of thousands upon thousands of laborers.

Because cotton and tobacco farmers did not produce mules on a significant scale, a vibrant mule trade developed between the Deep South and mule-producing states such as Kentucky, Tennessee, Missouri, and Texas. Millions of mules, through the efforts of horse and mule traders, made their way by foot or rail to southern farms. Many midwestern farmers bred their large draft mares to jacks and sold the mule produced by that union to mule traders. Consequently, when midwestern agriculture mechanized in the 1920s, the Deep South was faced with the challenge of setting up mule-breeding programs to supply its needs. Significant progress occurred in this vein during the late 1930s and early 1940s under the auspices of U.S. Department of Agriculture funding and county agents, but mechanization eliminated the need for draft animals, so mule-breeding programs ended. The mules and horses that were no longer needed often were processed as food for pets.

While mules connoted sharecropping and low status, horses often carried an aura of higher status. Overseers and planters generally rode horses, not mules. Slaves and then both black and white sharecroppers first and foremost used mules to earn a livelihood, but horses and mules were so important to farm families that they played a key role in southern life, literature, and culture. Because of their unique nature and role in the South, mules were especially important in literature and music. Numerous songs and stories exist that feature mules in some way, from Zora Neale Hurston's works to many of William Faulkner's novels. By the early 1960s, horses and mules were no longer a significant aspect of southern agrarian life.

GEORGE B. ELLENBERG
*University of West Florida*

George B. Ellenberg, *From Mule South to Tractor South: Mules, Machines, and the Transformation of the Cotton South* (2007); William Ferris, *Mule Trader: Ray Lum's Tales of Horses, Mules, and Men* (1998); Jack Temple Kirby, *Rural Worlds Lost: The American South, 1920–1960* (1987); Robert Byron Lamb, *The Mule Is Southern Agriculture* (1963).

## Insects and Insecticides

The topic of insects and insect control in the southern United States necessarily centers on the cotton boll weevil. This quarter-inch-sized beetle had previously lived in relative obscurity in its native Mexico and Central America. After crossing the border into Brownsville, Tex., around 1892, however, the boll weevil exploded in population because of the abundance of cotton crops. Either flying or hitching rides on cotton bales, the pest reached Louisiana in 1903, Mississippi in 1907, and Georgia in 1916. To an extent unprecedented in American history, the boll weevil crippled agricultural production, reducing yields by as much as 90 percent in some regions. Southerners, thoroughly hooked on cotton, did not know what had hit them.

The effort to control the boll weevil became a national obsession and, as such, a litmus test for insect-control tactics in general. The solutions that farmers and entomologists devised would eventually have a pivotal impact on the way American farmers approached the challenge of insect control nationally. Through a confluence of events, the boll weevil played a direct role in the nation's early 20th-century transition to chemical insecticides, synthetic products that would later prove to have serious health and environmental hazards. In this respect, the boll weevil is correctly understood to be one of the most important insects to have entered not only the American South but also the United States as a whole.

For all its impact on 20th-century insect-control tactics, the boll weevil is best understood in the context of what came before it. Massive insect attacks on southern staple crops were common occurrences throughout the southern United States, and they began within a decade of Anglo-American settlement. During the colonial era, southern planters cleared forests along the East Coast to plant single crops designated primarily for exportation. The replacement of Native American subsistence agriculture with Euro-American commercial agriculture caused ecological disruptions that fostered infestations by native and imported insects. When southern farmers in the early 19th century cleared land to plant large plots of cotton, they were following the same blueprint that was written a century earlier by their pioneering ancestors. They were, in short, well aware that destructive insects were a fact of agricultural life, especially when human beings transformed the environment as extensively as they did to plant commercial crops in a monocultural fashion.

Staple crops dominated southern agriculture throughout the colonial period. Tobacco, which fueled the economy of Virginia and much of North Carolina before the American Revolution, repeatedly succumbed to destructive insects. Green worms, cut worms, the tobacco flea beetle, and horn worms in particular worried farmers much in the way the weather did. The scientific knowledge needed to combat these insects was spotty at best, and, in many cases, the planter had no idea what he was encountering. In other cases, however, as with the four-inch-long horn worm, the culprit was as unmistakable as it was ineradicable. When the tobacco market began to fluctuate after 1740, many planters in the Upper South turned to wheat. Again, though, planted as extensively as it was, wheat readily fell to the ravages of insect pests. Most notable was the Hessian fly (first appearing on Long Island in 1778), which joined several wheat-eating weevils and grubs to destroy eastern crops. Planters in South Carolina found their rice crops under siege by, as rice farmer John Drayton explained, "attacks from a small bug, equally injurious to [rice] as the Hessian fly is to wheat." Native Americans, who had once planted a beans-maize-squash complex for local consumption, never encouraged these insect pests in the way that Anglo planters did. Insect pests were responding to the expanded scale and scope of com-

mercial agriculture, a connection that settlers were quick to appreciate, especially as they turned land over to cotton in the early 19th century.

Rather than modify production, southern farmers chose to expand and deal with the adverse consequences as they came. By the 19th century, southern planters had devised a variety of methods to battle insect pests. As late as 1860, formal science offered farmers little help in managing insect enemies. Southern farmers, as a result, did as their cohorts throughout the nation did: they spread information by word of mouth and through agricultural newspapers. This information was entirely personal, based on direct observation and experience with trial-and-error methods rather than subtle conceptions of biological principles. One agricultural writer lent insight into this approach when he explained, "Many intelligent farmers look with distrust on all recommendations issuing from any other source other than that of practical experience." In the pages of such publications as the *Southern Cultivator* and *Southern Planter*, farmers detailed catalogs of control methods, including cultural, biological, and chemical tactics. Never intending to eliminate insect pests, planters spoke of controlling or managing them through the most effective combination of strategies appropriate for specific crops and conditions.

"The farmer's life," according to a *Southern Cultivator* writer, was "a never ending conflict with insects." Nevertheless, southern planters did not deem the situation hopeless. Cultural methods that farmers advocated included planting "lure crops" to attract injurious insects away from commercial crops, sowing late and harvesting early to avoid insect outbreaks, diversifying crops (however modestly) to minimize insect populations, and using physical barriers (such as ditches and tar patches) to block the inevitable march of insects. Biological methods primarily involved birds. Farmers encouraged the tactic of surrounding their crops with bird houses and releasing chickens into pastures to eat grubs burrowed in cow dung. More sophisticated biological control methods involved planting lure crops that attracted an insect's enemies into the infested staple crop. Removal of pests by hand was both the simplest and probably the most common method of avoiding damage. Farmers spent considerable time weeding and pruning crops to reduce opportunities for infestation. Chemicals tended to make southern farmers nervous, exposing them to what one writer called "pseudoscientific professors whose aim it is to take advantage of the willingness of farmers to believe that the revelations of science may be made directly available to them." Nonetheless, they experimented with nicotine dust, hellebore, sulfur powder, and pyrethrum—all natural insecticides—in combination with cultural and biological tactics. Well into the middle of the 19th century, southern planters pursued pest management through ad hoc methods forged in a decentralized context.

As the United States began to professionalize, urbanize, and industrialize, the reliance on personal observation and homegrown solutions yielded to the allure of expertise. The bureaucratic consolidation of pest-control strategies into the hands of formally educated experts was the most notable change to affect the quest for pest control in the 19th century. One reason for this concentration of expertise was the rapid westernization of commercial agriculture. In many respects a replication of the environmental transformations that drove the southern staple economy, western expansion led to insect outbreaks unprecedented in their intensity. Chinch bugs demolished corn and wheat, Rocky Mountain locusts descended upon the Great Plains, the potato beetle wiped out root crops nationally, and the San Jose scale destroyed fruit trees from California to New York State. By the 1870s several states, including North Carolina and Tennessee, initiated agriculture experiment stations to investigate these insect outbreaks (and others), while the federal government established a Division of Entomology to further assist farmers struggling to save their crops from imported insect pests. These governmentally supported institutions provided a natural focal point for insect experts to meet, refine techniques, enhance their status, and publish a wide range of agricultural reports.

Professional changes complemented bureaucratic ones. Most notably, the field of "economic entomology"—the branch of entomology interested in agricultural pests per se—began to mature into a powerful discipline. Economic entomologists effectively worked with farmers to analyze traditional provincial pest-control tactics in the context of insect life cycles and insect-plant interaction. It would seem logical to link the demise of the American farmer's power over insect control to the arrival of economic entomology. However, until the 1890s, entomologists and farmers worked harmoniously under the auspices of state and federal governments to refine cultural, biological, and chemical techniques through basic biological and ecological principles. Without alienating farmers, economic entomologists—many of whom began by working farms—successfully updated homegrown insect-control solutions with basic scientific concepts.

And then came the boll weevil. If bureaucratic and professional developments did not immediately undermine the traditional decentralized approach to insect control, the boll weevil did. In light of the midcentury outbreaks that plagued western agriculture, the boll weevil initially struck most entomologists and farmers as yet another invasive insect that had to be controlled through a variety of methods. Accordingly, the Bureau of Entomology's powerful chief, Leland O. Howard, sent entomologist Tyler Townsend to the Texas-Mexico border to investigate the situation with local planters. Townsend, after testing several methods, returned with a strong plea for cultural control. The most efficient way to handle this pest, he explained, was to burn fields, allow hogs to forage, rotate crops, and—most controversially—create "no cotton" zones. Howard embraced these recommendations wholeheartedly, and he even convinced the Texas governor to enact the plan. Farmers, however, drew the line at being told what to do

by legislators. Overwhelmed by protests, the Texas legislature dropped the issue, refusing to regulate cotton crops. Texas would be left to its own devices, as would other southern states. Indeed, no southern state was able to marshal the political will to pass regulatory laws regarding "no cotton" zones, and, as a result, the boll weevil was, as the Texas state entomologist concluded in 1901, "to be met and mastered by the planters themselves." The weevil problem, despite considerable federal and state appropriations for continued research, proved far beyond their control. By 1922 the boll weevil had covered more than 60,000 square miles of the Cotton Belt.

Failing to diversify, southern planters sowed the seeds of their own dependence on insecticides. The political inability to promote cultural control fueled the triumph of chemical insecticides not only for the boll weevil, but also for insect pests in general. Timing and context were everything. The inability of entomologists and farmers to successfully apply cultural methods cut against the grain of a new Progressive Era ideology that demanded quick results from experts who addressed public problems unilaterally. L. O. Howard, in the words of one historian, found himself with "egg on his face" over the boll weevil's unopposed advance into the 20th century. As a status-conscious bureaucrat mindful of his record, he needed measurable outcomes, and this political imperative drove Howard to put the Bureau of Entomology's substantial weight behind chemical control as the favored solution to the nation's insect problems. World War I placed even greater emphasis on immediate re-sults—whether it was for insecticides to protect troops or their food supplies—that favored chemical solutions prom-ising short-term positive impact. Given the meteoric rise of chemical manufac-turing companies, as well as laws such as the Insecticide Act of 1910 (intended to keep bogus elixirs off the market), it becomes clear how broader precondi-tions fostered what proved to be a rapid chemical transition.

In 1916 an employee of the Bureau of Entomology discovered that covering cotton with arsenical dust for the dura-tion of the growing season killed adult weevils. Planters responded eagerly and with desperation to these hope-ful results. By 1919 they were dusting crops with 3 million pounds of calcium arsenate a year; by 1920 the figure had spiked to 10 million pounds; and by the late twenties it was around 60 to 70 million pounds. While calcium arsenate had its advantages, its disadvantages were palpable. The chemical killed neighboring crops (such as legumes), destroyed the natural enemies of the cotton aphid (thus encouraging a new cotton pest), and often burned cotton plants when its powder was not prop-erly refined. Whatever health dangers the chemical posed were obscured by political logrolling and corporate influ-ence peddling that ensured that proper tests were not undertaken. Despite these drawbacks, cotton farmers pursued the calcium arsenate option with a glass-half-full optimism. A 1945 report put out by the Smithsonian Institution captured this attitude when, after listing the many problems with calcium arse-nate, it conceded that "the proper use of calcium arsenate for weevil control often means the difference between a profit and a loss in cotton production." Insofar as an improvement was needed, it had to be one that was "more toxic" and could "kill boll weevils by contact." In other words, there was no going back to the multifaceted farmer-inspired solutions of the past. A Rubicon of sorts had been crossed.

Although hardly perfect, the fed-erally backed approach to boll weevil eradication with inorganic insecticides provided a model for the nation as a whole to follow. Whether it was scale insects in the West, corn borers on the Great Plains, or the gypsy moth in the East, farmers and entomologists (as well as municipal, state, and federal govern-ments) reflexively turned to chemical insecticides to battle insect depreda-tions. By 1929 insecticide manufactur-ers such as DuPont and Hercules were producing over $23 million worth of insecticides annually. By 1934 American farmers were saturating crops with 90 million pounds of arsenicals, 73 million pounds of sulfur, 10 million gallons of kerosene, 21 million pounds of naph-thalene and paradichlorobenzene, and 2 million pounds of rotenone. These farmers were more than prepared to incorporate DDT and related organic insecticides when they hit the mar-ket with rave reviews in 1945. By 1966 cotton farmers alone were consuming 73 percent of the nation's DDT supply. "Chemical warfare on insects has be-come an accepted part of our yearly life," remarked a City College biology professor. "It will never be outlawed."

The professor was correct, although he could not have predicted the power of Rachel Carson's *Silent Spring* (1962) to dampen agricultural enthusiasm for organic insecticides and inspire concrete federal restrictions on chemicals that Carson exposed as lethal to the ecosystem and the humans who populated it. Public outrage, legislative restrictions, and widespread evidence of insect resistance to organic insecticides led to a mild resurgence of creative experimentation not unlike the kind that prevailed in the 19th century. On this point the boll weevil, again, serves as a representative example. With the ban on DDT in 1972, researchers worked to pioneer a system of integrated pest management that relied on viral pesticides, pheromones, and "crop ecosystem simulation models" in a quest for total eradication of the cotton pest. These efforts soon yielded to the insecticide malathion. This insecticide, however, kills not only boll weevils but also the natural enemies of the beet armyworm, another cotton pest, leading to its proliferation as the boll weevil declines. From another angle, advocates of biological control, which Carson strongly favored, have countered the malathion option with the introduction to cotton fields of *Catolaccus grandis*, a parasite that eats weevil larvae. And so, as in the 19th century, a number of options are on the table.

But if history is any guide, malathion, or some more toxic version of it, will remain the most popular option. Today, after all, there are over 10,000 chemical insecticides registered with the Environmental Protection Agency.

Cultural and biological options, *Catolaccus grandis* notwithstanding, pale by comparison. Agriculture in the American South has played a critical role in confirming the advice that one insecticide advocate gave in the 1920s: "Let us spray." There is little in the history of insecticide use in the South to suggest a reversal of this problematic philosophy.

JAMES E. MCWILLIAMS
*Texas State University*

Thomas R. Dunlap, DDT: *Scientists, Citizens, and Public Policy* (1981); L. O. Howard, "Progress in Economic Entomology in the United States," *Yearbook for the Department of Agriculture for 1899* (1899); Edmund Paul Russell, "War on Insects: Warfare, Insecticides, and Environmental Change in the United States, 1870–1945 (Volumes 1 and 2)" (Ph.D. dissertation, University of Michigan, 1993); Richard C. Sawyer, *To Make a Spotless Orange: Biological Control in California* (1996); James Whorton, *Before Silent Spring: Pesticides and Public Health in Pre-DDT America* (1974).

## Knapp, Seaman A.

(1833–1911) AGRICULTURAL REFORMER.

Seaman Asahel Knapp brought many experiences to his goal of improving southern agriculture. As editor, college president, essayist, teacher, and organizer, he acquired the skills necessary to secure acceptance of his most important idea: the Farmers' Cooperative Demonstration Work program.

Reared in Essex County, N.Y., Knapp graduated from Union College. Acting upon a physician's advice to seek outdoor activities, he moved to Iowa in 1866 and began a lifelong study of agriculture. As professor and president of Iowa State College (now University), he urged farmers to adopt scientific farming practices. Knapp also edited the *Western Stock Journal and Farmer*, emphasizing the use of better livestock and the diversification of crops. In 1885 he became head of the North American Lumber and Timber Company and moved to Louisiana. For the next decade, he convinced farmers that rice could be grown by using modern agricultural practices. In 1898 Knapp joined the U.S. Department of Agriculture, which sent him to Japan, where he discovered a rice strain more suitable to America's mechanized demands.

Panic struck Texas cotton farmers in 1903 as the boll weevil devastated wide areas. Knapp's effort to combat this insect gained for him a national reputation and set into motion an agricultural program that promised hope for the South. Backed by financial guarantees from local citizens to compensate for any losses, Knapp persuaded farmers to try methods on their own lands that few had been willing previously to employ. They began using crop rotation, deeper plowing, better livestock, diversification, improved seed selection, and fertilizers. Initially, 7,000 to 8,000 farmers joined the program. The results were impressive. Cotton yields increased 50 to 100 percent over farms using older methods. The boll weevil remained, but Knapp's ideas offset losses from the insect and the Farmers' Cooperative Demonstration Work program was born. Impressed by Knapp's success, the U.S. Department of Agriculture and later the General Education Board provided funds to spread the program throughout the region. The General Education Board's commitment stemmed from its belief that as the economic status of rural taxpayers increased, better schools would result. Farmers' Cooperative Demonstration projects also contained educational programs including boys' and girls' farm groups—the forerunners of the 4-H clubs.

By the time of Knapp's death in 1911, the Farmers' Cooperative Demonstration Work program was firmly established in the South. A fitting tribute to Knapp's efforts occurred in 1914 with the passage of the Smith-Lever Act, which incorporated the Farmers' Cooperative Demonstration Work ideas into national law.

JOSEPH A. COTÉ
*University of Georgia Library*

Rodney Cline, *The Life and Work of Seaman A. Knapp* (1936).

## Migrant Labor

Migrant labor in the South entered the public consciousness abruptly on Thanksgiving Day 1960 with the airing of the CBS documentary *Harvest of Shame*. Walter Cronkite exposed the stark living and working conditions of southern black families forced to migrate up and down the East Coast following the low-paying, short-term jobs to be found in fruit and vegetable agriculture. But the story behind that exposé began a hundred years before, in the racially based postemancipation agricultural labor system that developed in the South following the Civil War.

In the Reconstruction South, the dispersed pattern of individual tenancies that became known as sharecropping secured the family-based, semiautonomous work system preferred by former slaves, but sharecroppers remained landless and economically dependent on plantation owners. For survival, sharecroppers often combined tenancy with seasonal wage labor in increasingly concentrated and extensive farming operations. By the late 19th century, for example, Louisiana sugar plantations came to depend on the migration of cotton sharecroppers whose own harvests were completed in time to help with the cane harvest.

With the turn of the 20th century, coincident developments in agriculture reinforced the growing system of migrant labor. As the boll weevil began to severely reduce cotton productivity in the South, large areas of mid-Atlantic agriculture began a transition from production of staple crops like wheat, no longer competitive with large-scale western production, to fruits and vegetables, or truck crops, for consumption by growing urban populations. These new types of agriculture offered bursts of seasonal employment, particularly during the harvest, first for local immigrant populations in need of income to supplement industrial employment, but soon also for underemployed farmworkers from the South facing ruin from poor cotton crops.

Migration for seasonal farmwork expanded with the agricultural depression of the 1920s. Around the same time, commercial agriculture in Florida expanded rapidly with the draining of large areas of the Everglades. Dis-

placed cotton sharecroppers migrated to winter-season farm-labor jobs in south Florida and from there joined a year-round migration up and down the East Coast as far north as New England. The migration grew as the Depression deepened in the 1930s, fed by widespread evictions of sharecropping families—the collateral result of New Deal policies to end the surpluses causing low prices.

While some displaced sharecroppers migrated west as depicted in John Steinbeck's *The Grapes of Wrath* (1939), others joined the ongoing migration to the citrus and truck farms of Florida and into the East Coast migrant stream. Both black and white farmworkers joined this stream, but along the East Coast, unlike in the West, white migrants primarily found work in packing sheds, which offered higher wages and some legal protections. Black migrants predominantly were hired for fieldwork, receiving the lowest wages and no labor protections.

Although the safeguards for sharecroppers within the New Deal agricultural programs remained unenforced, the federal government did create a program to assist displaced tenants migrating in search of seasonal farmwork. The Farm Security Administration (FSA) within the U.S. Department of Agriculture operated farm-labor camps that provided migratory farm labor with a safe and sanitary home base as well as a range of social services, including health care, child care, and educational opportunities. Camps were segregated in the Jim Crow South, but they provided similar conditions and opportunities. However, as workers began to find employment in industry following the outbreak of World War II, growers feared labor shortages, signaled by rising wages, and pressed Congress to alter the FSA labor-camp program into a labor-supply program, facilitating delivery of workers where needed rather than expanding worker autonomy.

Congress further responded to grower demands for assistance in securing seasonal workers with a wartime foreign labor-importation program, popularly known as the bracero program. In the West, Mexican workers predominated, while in the East, Caribbean workers made up most of the imported farm workforce. Domestic farmworkers found themselves removed from the FSA labor camps and frequently without work that increasingly went to imported labor. Some found jobs in northern cities and war industries, but others simply faced greater uncertainty and unemployment.

Apart from the few who had benefited from the FSA migratory labor camps, most migrant farmworkers experienced marginal living and working conditions. As documented periodically beginning in the 1930s by local and national journalists, workers on the whole lacked sanitary facilities, safe equipment, and protection from agricultural chemicals in the fields, and they faced housing with little or no running water, inadequate toilets and window screening, and filthy bedding. Both private and governmental efforts on behalf of migrants gained momentum in the 1960s, bringing regulation of field conditions, transportation, and housing as well as access to health care, education, and other social services, including legal aid.

Farmworkers have always expressed their discontent with wages and conditions by withholding their labor when they could, often simply by moving on. But while the United Farm Workers was gaining national attention for job actions in California in the 1960s and 1970s, farm labor organizing in the South lagged behind. Although the Southern Tenant Farmers' Union had achieved a few successes in the 1930s, effective organizing did not reach the South until the 1990s, when the Farm Labor Organizing Committee and other more local organizations brought models that were pioneered in the West and Midwest to areas in North Carolina and Florida.

The World War II labor-importation program continued until 1964 and was followed by a more limited labor-importation program authorized by U.S. immigration law that continues to operate today. Black farmworkers in the South have gradually been replaced by progressive waves of guest workers and refugee and immigrant workers from Central and South America and the Caribbean. Since the 1970s, these groups have been joined by Mexican farmworkers who have migrated from Texas into Florida and other southern farm-labor markets. Most of these groups are now part of transnational migration cycles that incorporate months and sometimes years of work in the United States with periodic and sometimes permanent return to a home community in another country. This transformation has changed the face of southern agriculture in a way that would make it unrecognizable to southern planters of even 50 years ago.

ANNE B. W. EFFLAND
*Independent Scholar*

David Griffith and Ed Kissam, *Working Poor: Farmworkers in the United States* (1995); Cindy Hahamovitch, *The Fruits of Their Labor: Atlantic Coast Farmworkers and the Making of Migrant Poverty, 1870–1945* (1997); Jacqueline Jones, *The Dispossessed: America's Underclasses from the Civil War to the Present* (1992); Joseph P. Reidy, *Agricultural History* (Spring 1998); Charles D. Thompson Jr. and Melinda F. Wiggins, *The Human Cost of Food: Farmworkers' Lives, Labor, and Advocacy* (2002).

## Peaches

Elberta, Georgia Belle, Blake, Redglobe, Jefferson, Dixired, and Winblo; O'Henry, Cresthaven, Harvester, and Fireprince. All of these names are recognized and held in wide esteem by many southerners. They are a few of the varieties of the South's most celebrated fruit, the *Prunus persica*, or the peach.

The fruit, long synonymous with summer in the South, was first cultivated in China over 4,000 years ago and later traveled to Persia (where Europeans initially thought it had originated) and, prior to the first century, to southern Europe. Spanish trees were brought to the Americas in the 1500s. The plant adapted well and multiplied wildly. Southern tribes of Native Americans were cultivating the plant and preserving the fruit by drying by the time of European settlement in the region.

Peach trees were so common in the region that early botanists and settlers thought the plant to be indigenous to the continent.

During the colonial era and early statehood, peaches were widely cultivated in the South on a small scale. The fruit was principally used in the making of peach wines and brandies and in the feeding of hogs.

The first sizable southern orchards were established in the 1850s. William Gregg had planted some 8,000 peach trees on his farm, Kalmia, in South Carolina and shipped peaches to northern markets before the Civil War. In 1857, P. J. A. Berckmans established the Fruitlands Nursery near Augusta, Ga., and, by flatboat and steamship, shipped the first Georgia peaches to New York in 1858. Dr. Berckmans founded the Georgia Horticultural Society in 1876 and was a national leader in research studies of the plant. (Much later his nursery would be transformed into the Augusta National golf course.)

In the 1870s Samuel Rumph of Marshallville, Ga., discovered a variety acclaimed as "the perfect peach." He named it after his wife, Elberta, and remarked at the time that he hoped that it would "travel well." It did. Although the Elberta is no longer commercially grown in substantial amounts, for generations it was by far the most popular variety for southern growers. For decades, Elbertas were marketed as *the* peach of the South. With improved rail transportation and the propagation of the Elberta and other varieties, growers began shipping to the northern markets in earnest. Peaches became a commodity, and Georgia, the "Peach State," led the industry for generations.

Partially in answer to the coming of the boll weevil to the region in 1917 and volatile cotton prices, farmers in the Carolinas began greatly expanding peach production in the 1920s. In South Carolina, production increased fivefold in the state from 1924 to 1941. In 1946 the state surpassed Georgia for the first time in production, and in 1948 South Carolina outproduced California to lead all states. Spartanburg County, in the piedmont, alone had over 3 million peach trees in 1951. North Carolina also began producing sizable quantities of peaches in the 1920s and, for a time, was second only to Georgia in peach production. The tiny town of Candor was the self-proclaimed "Peach Capital of the World" (one of several towns in the South so proclaimed).

Texas, Arkansas, Alabama, and Virginia are the leading peach producers among the rest of the southern states. Production in Texas is increasing, and growers there receive some of the highest prices for their fruit, on average, in the region. Most of the peaches grown in these and the other southern states are locally marketed.

The peach industry has always been labor-intensive, especially in the field. Trees each have to be pruned, thinned, and harvested individually by hand. In the past, hundreds of packing houses—some run cooperatively, some by brokers, and some by individual growers—employed thousands of seasonal workers during harvest to sort, package,

and load the peaches. Modern packing houses have become much more efficient than the scores of wooden, tin-roofed "peach sheds" that they have largely replaced. They are bigger (and much fewer in number) than their predecessors. Today, customized software and specialized equipment is used to pack peaches much faster and with less labor and fewer errors than just ten years ago.

With a few exceptions, most of the southern farmers who first grew peaches as a cash crop did so as an extension of the traditional home orchard on a relatively small scale while continuing to tend other crops. As the industry grew, more farmers planted more trees, and many of them made peaches their principal, if not exclusive, crop. As an example, out of a total of more than 1,400 commercial orchards in South Carolina in 1950, more than 1,000 had fewer than 50 acres of trees, representing 45 percent of the total number of trees.

Recent trends show a much higher concentration of production with the biggest growers. In South Carolina, by 1996 the number of commercial growers had declined to 153. Of these, 94 were smaller growers with fewer than 50 acres in trees, less than 14 percent of the state's total. The 33 largest growers—those with more than 100 acres—tended over 1.6 million trees, more than 80 percent of the state total.

South Carolina and Georgia are the exceptions among the southern states. Most of the other states' growers have smaller orchards and grow almost exclusively for local markets. Virginia's last packing house closed in the mid-1980s. Alabama, with about 110 relatively small-acreage growers, now produces about 20 million pounds of peaches annually, picking almost all of the crop in eight-quart "market baskets."

State universities and U.S. Department of Agriculture facilities have largely replaced the private state and national pomological and horticultural organizations as the primary researchers for peach cultivation. New scientific developments affect all aspects of the peach industry, from breeding and rootstock development to nutrition, pest control, cultivar evaluation, and other horticulture practices, as well as packaging and marketing.

One thing that the researchers have not been able to affect is the weather. Untimely hail, severe drought, or prolonged rainfall all can mean a short crop for a farmer. And nothing is more disastrous than a prolonged or severe drop in temperature at the wrong time in the spring. A southern grower noted in his diary in 1865, "The peach crop is sometimes lost by yearly frosts, and having no other means of subsistence, it would be precarious for a dependence." Some crop reduction results from frost damage every year in the South. More rarely, a severe cold wave of Canadian air will arrive in the South at a critical time to wipe out the region's entire peach crop.

Georgia produced over half a billion pounds of peaches in the 1920s, when the state had an all-time high of 16 million peach trees in cultivation. South Carolina peaked in the 1950s and had a crop of 480 million pounds as recently as 1984. Although still a significant industry, peach production in both states has declined over the last two decades, with Georgia averaging 120 million pounds in 1999–2001 and South Carolina 135 million pounds over the same period. The two states are the second- and third-largest state producers of peaches in the country. Each has about 10 times more peach trees than North Carolina, the next-largest peach producer in the South.

While the South's commercial peach industry has declined and there are fewer trees in the region, the peach is still firmly rooted in the South. Barring late freezes, hailstorms, or other natural calamities, southerners can annually look forward to enjoying fresh, southern peaches each summer. Whether buying out of a pickup truck beside the road, stopping in at a farmer's market or roadside stand, or, if fortunate, filling a peach basket with perfect fruit that you yourself have selected and picked in an orchard, southerners can still enjoy the arrival of each peach crop. No matter how it is eaten, the peach is a part of summer that all southerners can savor.

MIKE CORBIN
*Spartanburg, South Carolina*

American Pomological Society, *History of Fruit Growing and Handling in United States of America and Canada, 1860–1972* (1976); Mark Catesby, *Natural History of Carolina, Florida, and the Bahama Islands* (1771); Mike Corbin, *Family Trees: The Peach Culture of the Piedmont* (1998); Lewis Cecil Gray, *History of Agriculture in the Southern United States to 1860* (1932); S.C.

Agricultural Statistics Service, *South Carolina Fruit Tree Survey 1996* (1997); T. L. Senn and J. Sam Taylor, *The Commercial Peach Industry in South Carolina*, Bulletin 393 (June 1951).

## Peanuts

Peanuts, pinders, groundpeas, and goobers are names applied to a nutritious food that has been a part of southern culture since colonial times. Groundpea is most descriptive, as the plant is a legume and belongs to the pea family, botanically known as *Arachis hypogaea*. Peanuts were known in South America around 2,800 years ago. Spanish explorers carried them to Spain in the 16th century, and traders carried them to Africa. Peanuts possibly arrived in the South on slave-trading vessels, which carried them as food for slaves. The Congo name for peanuts, *nguba*, became "goober" in the South.

Originally produced by slaves and free blacks for local use and sale, peanuts were exported from South Carolina soon after the Revolution. In the antebellum period, they were grown locally in most southern states, but Wilmington, N.C., was the principal commercial market from 1830 to 1860. Nicholas N. Nixon of New Hanover County was the largest producer and promoter of the scientific cultivation of peanuts. Lack of commercial development in other southern areas was due both to competition from cotton and the tedious hand labor required in peanut production.

The Civil War created a national market for peanuts. Soldiers of both armies fighting in Virginia found locally grown peanuts a portable, nourishing food, confirmed by the famed Civil War song "Goober Peas." Soldiers who returned home wrote to Virginia for more peanuts, and the commercial industry was born. Between 1865 and 1868, production tripled each year, and the 1869 crop was estimated at over 600,000 bushels. From 1868 to 1900, Norfolk was the peanut capital of the United States, and it was succeeded after 1900 by Suffolk, Va.

For 30 years after the Civil War, peanuts, roasted in the shell, were a treat sold by street vendors. Boiled peanuts were a delicacy associated with cotton-picking and cotton-ginning season. Neighborhood "peanut boilings" were a form of social intercourse in southern communities. Farmers in the Lower South planted peanuts for fall fattening of swine, a practice known in Georgia as "hogging off."

In the decade from 1889 to 1899, commercial production and consumption of peanuts increased over 300 percent. George Washington Carver's research in the 1890s revealed the peanut's high nutritional value as food as well as its over 300 other uses. Devastation to the cotton crop by the boll weevil after 1905 persuaded some farmers to change to peanuts. Increased mechanization between 1900 and 1910 reduced labor costs and increased production and consumption.

From 1899 to 1919, peanut production increased eightfold, and World War I established peanuts as a continuing factor in the southern economy. After World War II, production became highly mechanized. By the 1980s peanuts were the ninth most valuable farm crop in the United States, valued at over $1 billion. Today, seven states dominate production: Georgia produces almost one-half of the nation's peanut crop, followed by Alabama, North Carolina, Texas, Virginia, Oklahoma, and Florida. Four major varieties are produced: larger-kerneled Virginias, the medium-sized Runner in the Lower South, small Spanish peanuts in Texas and Oklahoma, and Valencias in New Mexico.

The United States makes greater use of peanuts for food than any other country, with annual consumption of nine pounds per person. Two-thirds goes into peanut butter, roasted and salted peanuts, and confectionary products. The remainder is exported or crushed for oil and animal feed. Boiled peanuts are still particularly identified with rural areas of the South, found for sale at roadside stands and eaten as a plain snack. The United States' production of peanuts today is only 10 percent of world production, but it accounts for more than one-third of world exports, principally to Canada, Europe, and Japan. Except for the period from 1942 to 1948, production has been controlled since 1934 by various regulations of the U.S. Department of Agriculture.

PERCIVAL PERRY
*Wake Forest University*

Frank Selman Arant, ed., *The Peanut, the Unpredictable Legume* (1981); F. Roy Johnson, *The Peanut Story* (1977).

## Pecans

Among the various images that summon to mind the South, pecans take first place in the category of edible nuts.

When European settlers first arrived in the New World, they found black walnuts, hickory nuts, chestnuts, chinquapins, and pecans growing wild in the South. All of these, except the chestnut (killed by a blight around 1920), continue to grow, but only the pecan is commercially important. The pecan is synonymous with the South because its natural habitat is the nine southern states from the Carolinas to Texas. Because of the high quality of the nut meat, the quantity of pecans produced annually, and the relative ease of propagating improved varieties, the pecan has become the "queen of nuts" in the United States. It is, moreover, the fifth most important nut tree in the world, and the southern states are the only substantial producers other than Mexico.

More than one-half of the total crop of pecans comes from wild and seedling trees, principally in Texas, Oklahoma, and Louisiana. The region from South Carolina to Louisiana is important for improved varieties, developed since 1890, with Georgia the chief producer. Seedlings are as flavorful as improved varieties, but the yield of the latter is twice as great. Production is shifting toward the Southwest (especially New Mexico) with concentration in larger orchards, increasing mechanization, and preservation by cold storage. Although the number of individual pecan farmers is decreasing, the number of trees bearing and being planted is increasing.

From approximately 1 million pounds in 1900, the pecan crop increased to an average of 10 million in the 1920s, to 20 million in the early 1930s, to 40 million by the late 1930s, and to 60 million around 1945. Since 1960 the average annual crop has been approximately 220 million pounds, valued at over $74 million. Great fluctuation in yields and price occur because of the tree's tendency to produce larger crops biennially. Since 1949 the federal government and growers' cooperative associations have attempted to stabilize prices.

Ground pecan shells are used as mulches for plants and as poultry litter; as filler in feeds and fertilizer; as abrasives in soap and polishes; and as filler in plastic wood, including artistic use in molded figures of birds and animals.

Pecans have a long association with southern life. Many Deep South residents plant pecan trees in the yard because the trees are both ornamental and productive. Pecans have contributed extensively to the culinary aspects of southern life. They are used in pralines, which appeared in Louisiana as early as 1762; in recipes for cakes, notably fruit cakes, for which Claxton, Ga., is famous; in the ubiquitous pecan pie; in cookies; in salad, meat, and bread recipes; and as roasted- and salted-nut treats for special occasions. They are also consumed directly from the shell around the family hearth in the evening, especially as a tradition of the Thanksgiving and Yuletide seasons.

PERCIVAL PERRY
*Wake Forest University*

USDA, *Agricultural Statistics* (annual); Jasper G. Woodroof, *Tree Nuts: Production, Processing, Products* (1967).

## Poe, Clarence Hamilton

(1881–1964) AGRICULTURAL JOURNALIST.

The life of North Carolina journalist Clarence Hamilton Poe affords insight into the evolution of southern farming from the 1890s into the 1960s. Beginning in 1897 as a "printer's devil" for the Raleigh-based *Progressive Farmer*, he achieved national prominence first as editor, then as owner—positions he held until his death. In the process he built the *Progressive Farmer* into the largest farm journal in the United States. Today, it continues to be one of the nation's most significant farm publications.

Using the *Progressive Farmer* as a podium, Poe championed a myth long dominant in southern history: agrarian life was morally and culturally superior to other types of existence. Poe believed that small, family-owned farms engendered unique cultural and character-building traits. Farm life developed strong, independent individuals with a respect for nature, a sense of community, a dedication to family, a clear understanding of life, a reverence for the earth, and a devotion to God. The farmer tilling the soil, with devoted wife at home rearing the children, created a society superior to that of northern cities, where a modern industrial system robbed labor of its dignity and where unrest and half-suppressed rebellion were constant undercurrents.

Poe feared, however, that backward southern farming methods would doom that agrarian lifestyle. Accordingly, he advocated such changes as improved educational facilities, the creation of agricultural cooperatives, and the diversification of farming. With these reforms, Poe envisioned idyllic communities "untouched by town influences" where farmers would own and operate grain elevators, livestock associations, and rural credit organizations. Community life would center around educational, religious, social, and intellectual activities. Successful farmers could purchase their own homes and fields and thereby end absentee landlordism. Finally, these communities would remain small, avoiding the problems associated with cities and towns.

Poe's advocacy of the preservation of a supposed superior southern agricultural life underscores one of the region's most persistent myths. Reality, however, was much different. Sharecropping and tenant farming dominated the South throughout the late 19th and early 20th centuries. Eventually, southern farming did change, but not because of Poe's influence. Rather, New Deal legislation favored large agricultural farm units, while World War II uprooted untold numbers of farmers. In the 1950s Poe reluctantly concluded that the family farm was a thing of the past—but he still believed in the superiority of rural life.

JOSEPH A. COTÉ
*University of Georgia Library*

Clarence Hamilton Poe, *How Farmers Co-Operate and Double Profits* (1915); Clarence Hamilton Poe Papers, North Carolina Department of Archives and History, Raleigh; *Progressive Farmer* (1899–1964).

## Poultry

A glance at cookbooks suggests that southerners have roasted, baked, fried, sautéed, grilled, and barbecued chickens for centuries. Chicken has been a key ingredient in such regional dishes as gumbo, jambalaya, and Brunswick stew. Cookbooks since the 19th century have also included recipes for wild duck, turkey, and goose, as well as such fowl as blackbird, lark, quail, grouse, guinea fowl, peafowl, pigeon, and other game. Given this fondness for eating poultry, it is not surprising that poultry has been a mainstay of southern agriculture since the beginning of European settlement. Southerners raised many types of poultry for household consumption and the market, but chickens were the most common.

Chickens were kept on practically every farm and often ran loose in the barnyard area. As a result, farmers virtually lived with their chicken flock. Chickens could be kept on a minimum of feed and were much more convenient to slaughter and prepare for eating than either pork or beef. Predators such as the fox and the hawk were a constant problem for the farmer's barnyard flock, thus requiring the farmer to keep both his dog and shotgun handy.

Since 1900 the per capita rate of consumption of chicken has increased markedly, outstripping the growth in demand for other meats such as beef and pork. During this period, and especially in recent decades, very important changes have occurred in the production of chickens, and these had an effect on both the economy and culture of the South. A few decades ago, the rural population of the South was largely self-sufficient in terms of supplying its chicken and egg needs. Farmers maintained small flocks of chickens for their

Farm woman, a vendor of chickens, in a farmer's market in Weatherford, Tex., 1939
(Russell Lee, Library of Congress [LC-USF33-012280-M1], Washington, D.C.)

own use. Often the demand by city dwellers for chickens and eggs was met by farmers who sold excess production to town merchants. This trade furnished butter-and-egg money for farm housewives. Women worked with county extension agents to improve and modernize their production and marketing of eggs and chickens, often setting up roadside stands or selling at special farmers' markets. Historians credit the profitability of women's egg and chicken sales with seeing many families through the Depression's hard times. Today, it is rare indeed to find farm families who produce chickens and eggs. In place of this production system have come the large-scale and highly specialized mass-production techniques involving the utilization of the latest technological advancements.

This modern era of poultry produc-tion dates from the 1930s; its methods had almost totally replaced the previous production techniques by the 1950s. The modern poultry farmer has one or more chicken houses growing 10,000 to 20,000 birds per house. Ordinarily each batch is grown under contract with large agribusiness firms during a period of 7 to 10 weeks. Market-ready chickens are taken to processing plants for slaughtering, dressing, and packing and are later transported by refrigerated truck to widely dispersed markets. The poultry industry is characterized by a vertical integration in which an agribusiness firm, either through direct ownership or contract, controls the entire production process. Such firms own processing plants, feed mills, and hatcheries, and they contract with farmers to raise the chickens. Because of these arrange-ments, the farmer has little voice in the industry. Some observers label this type of poultry farming a modern version of sharecropping. However, one advantage of this production system to the farmer is that it reduces the capital needed to start poultry farming.

Today, a large proportion of southern poultry is produced by farmers who derive only a part of their total income from this source. The chief wage earner may have a full-time industrial or commercial job while the family raises chickens as a supplementary source of income, or chicken farming may be ancillary to other agricultural pursuits. Labor needs of poultry farming are minimal because of the automation of the process. The management of two chicken houses of 10,000 to 20,000 chickens each can usually be accomplished during the evenings and on weekends by family members.

Several of the nation's main poultry-growing areas are located in the South. Northeast Georgia was one of the first areas to begin large-scale commercial chicken production, with Gainesville serving as a processing-plant center and location of feed mills and hatcheries. Both northeast Georgia and northwest Arkansas began to develop as poultry centers in the late 1930s and early 1940s. They were followed in the 1940s by centers in south-central Mississippi and central North Carolina, and in the 1950s by northern Alabama, around Cullman County. A trip through these areas today provides visible indications of the industry's continuing impact on the landscape, with the long, narrow chicken houses on farms and the specialized feed trucks and poultry-transport vehicles that operate between feed mills, farms, and processing plants.

The emergence of chicken production in these areas largely reflects changing conditions of traditional subsistence farming. Many of these regions were, from the beginning of settlement, poor farm areas. They were populated by low-income farm families who had lost a previous source of farm revenue from cotton in northeast Georgia, northern Alabama, and south-central Mississippi; tobacco in North Carolina; and fruit in northwest Arkansas. Any new source of farm income, such as chicken raising, was welcomed enthusiastically by these farmers. Local entrepreneurs and agricultural officials were largely instrumental in establishing this industry. J. D. Jewell, for instance, played an important role in establishing production in northeast Georgia. He owned a small feed store in Gainesville in the 1930s and encouraged neighboring farmers to grow chickens, affording him a market outlet for feed and other supplies. Because cash with which to buy baby chicks and feed was seriously limited among farmers, Jewell supplied his customers with credit until their chickens were marketed. However, when the chickens reached the proper age and size for marketing, the farmer had no way to get them to market. Jewell provided transportation to haul the live chickens to urban markets. Later his company became one of the major vertical integrators in northeast Georgia, and he became nationally recognized as an industry leader.

Southern poultry raisers dominate national chicken production, which together produced over half of the 8.5 million chickens raised in the nation in 2002. The five leading states are Arkansas, Georgia, Alabama, North Carolina, and Mississippi. Four of the five most profitable chicken companies began in the South: Tyson Foods in Springdale, Ark.; Gold Kist, a farm-cooperative business in Atlanta; Holly Farms in Wilkesboro, N.C.; and Perdue Farms, Inc., in Salisbury, Md. Tyson Foods acquired Holly Farms in 1989, acquired diversified food-production companies in the 1990s, and solidified its position as the world's largest poultry producer by merging with Hudson Foods in 1998. Critics have pointed to issues of pollution and inhumane treatment of poultry in this leading agribusiness. Chicken has become the fastest-growing part of the fast-food business, profiting such southern companies as Kentucky Fried Chicken, Church's Fried Chicken, Popeyes, and Bojangles'.

J. DENNIS LORD
*University of North Carolina at Charlotte*

Karen Davis, *Prisoned Chickens, Poisoned Eggs: An Inside Look at the Modern Poultry Industry* (1996); J. Fraser Hart, *Annals of the Association of American Geographers* (December 1980); Sam B. Hilliard, *Hog Meat and Hoecake: Food Supply in the Old South, 1840–1860* (1972); Lu Ann Jones, *Mama Learned Us to Work: Farm Women in the New South* (2002); Edward Karpoff, *Agricultural Situation* (March 1959); N. R. Kleinfield, *New York Times* (9 December 1984); J. Dennis Lord, "Regional Marketing Patterns and Locational Advantages in the United States Broiler Industry" (Ph.D. dissertation, University of Georgia, 1970), *Southeastern Geographer* (April 1971); Irene A. Moke, *Journal of Geography* (October 1967); Malden C. Nesheim, *Poultry Production* (1979).

## Progressive Farmer

The first issue of the agricultural periodical *Progressive Farmer* appeared on 10 February 1886. Colonel Leonidas L. Polk, a former Confederate officer and a farmer from Anson County, N.C., conceived the newspaper, which later became a monthly magazine, as a forum for promoting the goals of a better rural way of life, a more scientific agriculture, and an improved educational system for farm people. The *Progressive Farmer* became a successful North Carolina institution whose efforts led in the early 1890s to a reorganization of that state's department of agriculture and the founding of a new agricultural college, North Carolina State University. Polk, meanwhile, became president of the Farmers' Alliance and North Carolina's first agricultural commissioner.

Polk died in 1892, and Clarence Poe and four colleagues bought the *Progressive Farmer* in 1903 for $7,500. Poe was a self-educated farm boy who, as editor of the magazine and a leader in the country life movement, helped to transform southern rural life. Tait Butler, a veterinary medicine professor at Mississippi State University, also contributed to the shape of the *Progressive Farmer*. He began publishing a rural life newspaper called *Southern Farm Gazette* in 1895, sold it in 1898, and joined Poe's editorial team on the *Progressive Farmer* in 1908. Together they purchased the *Southern Farm Gazette* and made it the basis for

Farmer's son reading the Progressive Farmer in Carroll County, Ga., 1941
(Jack Delano, Library of Congress [LC-USF-34-440054D], Washington, D.C.)

a new western edition of the *Progressive Farmer*. The magazine's headquarters moved from Raleigh, N.C., to Birmingham, Ala., in 1911, and the staff was publishing five locally oriented, regional editions by 1928.

Tait Butler's son Eugene became an assistant editor in the Memphis office of the *Progressive Farmer* in 1917 and eventually replaced Clarence Poe as president of the Progressive Farmer Company in 1953. Monthly circulation of the magazine hit 1.4 million in 1959, although it had declined to 850,000 by 1986. The Progressive Farmer Network provides agricultural news to 50 radio stations. Under Butler, the magazine's "Country Living" section was expanded into a separate periodical, *Southern Living*. Time Inc. bought Southern Progress Corp., the parent company of the *Progressive Farmer*, in 1985.

CHARLES REAGAN WILSON
*University of Mississippi*

*Progressive Farmer* (1899–1964).

## Rice Culture

As the Carolina and Georgia rice cultures made adjustments to post–Civil War labor demands and farmers along the Mississippi River started growing rice using labor-intensive methods, a highly mechanized rice culture developed in the southwest Louisiana and Texas prairies. The completion of the transcontinental Southern Pacific Railroad in the early 1880s opened the area, and real estate promoters lured midwesterners to settle there. These new arrivals discovered that Cajuns grew rice, a grain similar to wheat, and they adapted wheat binders to the soggy rice fields. After several dry years in the early 1890s wilted "Providence" stands of rice (so called because farmers depended on providential rainfall), canal companies organized to furnish water while other farmers dug wells for irrigation. By the turn of the century, this highly mechanized rice culture eclipsed the declining East Coast and Mississippi River growing areas. In the early part of the 20th century, Arkansas prairie

farmers turned to rice cultivation and, from the beginning, utilized the latest machinery.

Prairie rice growers used binders, steam engines, tractors, threshers, and irrigation pumps. Unlike many southern crops, rice was capital- and machine-intensive rather than labor-intensive. Still, at harvest a team of workers shocked the freshly cut rice, and, after it dried, loaded the rice on wagons and hauled it to a threshing machine. Threshing rings thrived in rice areas of the South much as they did in the Midwest. The tenure system varied radically from that of other cash crops. In some cases, corporations purchased large tracts, sold off part, and rented other sections to tenants. A unique form of sharecropping emerged, and a cropper would pay a portion of his crop to the canal company for water, pay the landlord another portion for rent, and keep the remainder. Because the sharecropper furnished all the machinery, the arrangement did not resemble customary sharecropping arrangements in other parts of the South.

As in farm areas throughout the country, the boom-and-bust cycle of World War I stunted the rice-growing industry. During the 1920s the formerly expansive rice culture stabilized as farmers attempted to pay off loans for machinery bought during the war. By this time, tractors had become universal on the prairies, and this varied dramatically from other areas of the South that remained labor-intensive.

Rice prices declined, as did those of other commodities, during the early years of the Great Depression. When

Congress established the Agricultural Adjustment Administration (AAA) in 1933, rice was included as a basic commodity. Even before a rice program had been set up, prices climbed to a parity level. For the first two years, the rice section of the AAA fumbled with marketing agreements with millers, but in 1935 it set up a program that paralleled other commodity sections. In one important respect, the rice section proved innovative: it gave allotments to producers, not to landlords. It reasoned that because sharecroppers or tenants had such a large investment in machinery, they deserved allotments. Also, crop-rotation customs dictated that often a man farmed his land one year and sharecropped with a neighbor the next.

Throughout the 1930s the rice culture remained stable, and during World War II rice became a valuable food to feed the world. Rice farmers meanwhile turned to combines, making another technological jump and ending the need for shocking or hauling rice to threshers. Prosperity continued until the early 1950s, when the end of the Korean War caused a sharp decline in international demand. Rice allotments were cut drastically. The effects in the rice areas of the South paralleled those in the cotton culture 20 years earlier. The allotment system also was changed in parts of Louisiana and Arkansas, as state agricultural committees, without calling for a vote from growers, changed from producer to farm allotments, awarding allotments formerly held by sharecroppers to landlords. Because rice cultivation was highly mechanized by

the 1930s, rice farmers suffered much less from the forces of acreage reduction and human displacement than did those in other farm areas of the South.

Modern rice cultivation continues to take advantage of science and technology. Rice fields are laser-leveled and flooded to a three-inch level. Seeds are either drilled or broadcast by air. Increasingly, genetic engineering shapes the varieties planted, and pesticides guard rice from insects and weeds.

Rice cultivation in Arkansas continued to expand, and after 1972, the first year since 1956 that no quota was in effect, production increased drastically. With higher prices and no quotas, rice production spread quickly to new land in Arkansas, Missouri, and the Yazoo-Mississippi Delta. The expansive nature of the culture can be seen in the increased farm price that rose from $359 million in 1964 to $1.2 billion in 1973. By the turn of the 21st century, Arkansas produced more than twice as much rice as any other state, with California and Louisiana trailing. Rice was agribusiness from its origin in the prairies, and new opportunities only meant refinements in the culture—not the agonizing transformation that accompanied mechanization in other areas of the South. Today the rice culture celebrates its past with six festivals in Arkansas and two each in Louisiana and Texas.

PETE DANIEL
*Smithsonian Institution*
*Washington, D.C.*

Lawson P. Babineaux, "A History of the Rice Industry in Southwestern Louisiana" (M.A. thesis, University of Southwestern Louisiana, 1967); Peter A. Coclanis, *Agricultural History* (Spring 1995); Pete Daniel, *Breaking the Land: The Transformation of Cotton, Tobacco, and Rice Cultures since 1880* (1985); Henry C. Dethloff, *Arkansas Historical Quarterly* (1970); John N. Efferson, *The Production and Marketing of Rice* (1952); Rudolph Carrol Hammack, "The New Deal and Louisiana Agriculture" (Ph.D. dissertation, Tulane University, 1973); Seaman A. Knapp, *The Present Status of Rice Culture in the United States*, USDA Bulletin No. 22 (1899); Christopher M. Lee, *Louisiana History* (Spring 1996).

## Rural Electrification Administration

When the Rural Electrification Administration (REA) was created in 1935, less than 4 percent of the farms in the southern states had electricity. Without it, many of the comforts of modern life were unavailable, and for that reason the South enthusiastically welcomed the REA. In 1936, when Congress gave the REA statute authority, southern congressmen were among the agency's most ardent supporters. The Southern Policy Association, a group of southern congressmen eager to promote southern development, endorsed the REA bill and regarded electrification as an important step in that direction.

As the REA began operation, southern farmers quickly established electric cooperatives, and the percentage of farms with service slowly grew. By 1941 the national average had climbed to 30 percent, and, although the southern percentage was lower, the South moved steadily ahead. At the end of World War II, the REA started a massive construction program to finish the job, and by 1955 virtually 90 percent of the South's farmers had electrical service. Although the effects of electrification were evident nationwide, they had the most dramatic impact in the South, owing probably to the region's higher number of substandard homes when the REA started.

By providing running water and indoor toilets, the REA finally helped bring an end to the hookworm that had ravaged the South for over a century. Refrigeration had a similar beneficial effect on diets through the storage of perishable foods. In some small towns, cold-storage cooperatives were started. Incandescent lighting improved the quality of life in homes and schools, and radio became a regular feature in southern homes. Electrification stimulated diversification: the Bureau of Agriculture Economics reported an increase in dairy farming, and the South became a major poultry-producing region. Most important, however, was the greater comfort and sense of satisfaction that southerners felt as they began to enjoy the numerous conveniences provided through electricity. Electrification must be considered one of the most significant reasons for modernization of the rural South.

D. CLAYTON BROWN
*Texas Christian University*

Erma Angevine, ed., *People—Their Power: The Rural Electric Fact Book* (1980); Marquis William Childs, *The Farmer Takes a Hand: The Electric Power Revolution in Rural America* (1952); Louis J. Goodman, John N. Hawkins, and Ralph N. Love, eds., *Small Hydroelectric Projects for Rural Development: Planning and Management* (1981); Melissa Walker, *All We Knew Was to*

*Farm: Rural Women in the Upcountry South, 1919–1941* (2000).

## Rural Free Delivery

Although the free delivery of mail service was commonplace in the nation's cities and towns in 1900, American farmers were still going, usually once a week, to small fourth-class post offices for their mail. That year the farmers in 11 states of the old Confederacy and Kentucky had nearly 21,000 such post offices, over one-third of all those in the nation, to which the mail was carried from central post offices over more than 94,000 miles of star mail routes.

Slow and inefficient, this mail service offered little relief for the southern farmer's isolation, and in the 1890s, when Postmaster General John Wanamaker suggested delivering mail to farmers, southern members of Congress enthusiastically supported the proposal. In four successive years, Leonidas Livingston, Tom Watson, and Charles Moses, all Georgia congressmen, and North Carolina's Senator Marion Butler offered amendments to appropriation bills allocating money for a rural free-delivery experiment. Finally, in 1896 Postmaster General Wilson L. Wilson, acting upon Senator Butler's amendment, began a rural-delivery experiment in West Virginia with an appropriation of $40,000. During the next six years, southern members of Congress labored to keep the experiment alive, and in 1902, following the lead of Congressman Claude Swanson of Virginia, Congress made the rural free delivery of mail a permanent postal service.

In spite of the support southern congressional delegations had given, however, the South never received as much rural free-delivery mail service as did the midwestern states, largely because of postal regulations and politics. According to postal regulations, rural free-delivery routes were first established where the density and literacy of the population seemed likely to make the routes pay for themselves, and fewer such places existed in the South than in the Midwest. More importantly, the rural routes were first established when the Republicans controlled the government, and midwestern Republican congressmen found it much easier to secure mail routes for political reasons than did their Democratic counterparts from the South. By 1950, therefore, there was one rural mail route for every 1,278 rural inhabitants in the five midwestern states of Ohio, Illinois, Iowa, Kansas, and Indiana, and only one for every 2,038 people in the 11 former Confederate states and Kentucky.

Nevertheless, the rural free delivery of mail revolutionized communication in the South. Daily newspapers became commonplace in southern farm homes, more letters were written and received, more advertising filled the mails, and, more importantly, the rural South was brought into increasing contact with the North. Rural free delivery paved the way for the establishment of a modern parcel-post system, which was also supported by southern members of Congress and which helped to break the country storekeeper's monopoly on the southern farmer's trade.

Rural free delivery inspired a good roads movement throughout the South, led southerners to argue for government aid for building farm-to-market roads, and lured them away from their traditional stand on states' rights.

WAYNE FULLER
*University of Texas at El Paso*

Daniel J. Boorstin, *The Americans: The Democratic Experience* (1973); Wayne E. Fuller, *Journal of Southern History* (November 1959), *Mississippi Valley Historical Review* (June 1955), *Morality and the Mail in Nineteenth-century America* (2003), *R.F.D.: The Changing Face of Rural America* (1964).

## Sears, Roebuck Catalog

"Without that catalog," writes Harry Crews in his 1978 autobiography of a Bacon County, Ga., boyhood, "our childhood would have been radically different. The federal government ought to strike a medal for Sears, Roebuck Company for sending all those catalogs to farming families, for bringing all that color and all that mystery and all that beauty into the lives of country people."

A genuine piece of Americana, the "Farmer's Bible" or "Wish Book" had a special impact on the South. Predominantly rural for so much longer than their northern counterparts, southerners relied on the Sears catalog's images of urban life for light reading as well as for ordering merchandise. In many one-room schoolhouses, it served as a primer and reference book. The catalog might even be credited with standardizing material-culture terminology. When a southern farmer needed a new "slingblade" or "slam-bang," for example, he was forced to order it from Sears as a "weed cutter."

Company policy as well as copy

directly affected the region. By locating a major stove supplier in ore-rich Alabama in 1902, Sears became one of the first northern firms to recognize the South's industrial potential. In 1906 Sears's first mail-order branch was established in Dallas, and within the next 20 years both the Atlanta, Ga., and Memphis, Tenn., plants opened regional warehouses stocking items particularly suited to southern trade.

Well into the 19th century, country stores provided their rural customers with virtually all of their needs. Beginning in the last decades of the century, further extension of the railroads, good roads campaigns, the introduction of rural free delivery (1896), and, eventually, parcel post (1913) dramatically changed conditions that had kept southern farmers isolated and, whatever their dissatisfactions, loyal to the local merchant. Richard Sears's "Big Book" challenged the retail monopoly.

Sears by no means originated the mail-order business. Rooted in the colonial period (Benjamin Franklin's promotion of his Pennsylvania stoves was one of the original schemes), numerous mail-order firms existed by the end of the Civil War. Montgomery Ward, in operation since 1872 and distributing a wide variety of goods exclusively by mail, had even succeeded in getting his firm named the official supply house for the Grange. Yet by 1900, Sears had become the clear leader in the mail-order world and has conceded its edge to none of its competitors since.

Catalogs were designed for hours of fireside reading, with woodcuts and flamboyant descriptions to encourage cover-to-cover browsing. Rooted in the principle of "never omitting the obvious," the description of the "Long Range Wonder Double Barrel Breech Loading Hammerless Shotgun, the World's Wonder" totaled some 3,000 words. If there was not something among the stereoscopes and bicycles, buggies and mackintoshes, dry goods, furniture, and gramophones to catch the buyer's fancy, the final testimonials—glowing recommendations of satisfied customers—and, most convincingly, the famous money-back guarantee usually did.

Sears's successful tactics gave rise to an all-out campaign against the mail-order companies by local merchants. Shopkeepers lit bonfires in town squares and offered bounties for every new catalog turned in for fuel. Some merchants offered prizes and free admission to movies in trade for the books. Newspaper editors, dependent on the advertising revenues of local retailers, originated epithets ("Monkey Ward," "Rears and Soreback," "Shears and Sawbuck") and helped circulate accusations about cheap, damaged goods and "sewing machines" that turned out to be a needle and thread. No one had ever seen Richard Sears or Ward, so it was not hard to convince many southerners that both men were black—a rumor given added credibility by the later philanthropy of Sears president Julius Rosenwald in the cause of black education.

Ultimately, the automobile, urban growth, and the chain store did more than catalog buying to undermine the economic viability of small local retailers. As urbanization continued and its customers grew more sophisticated, Sears accommodated to the changing market. With the passage of the Pure Food and Drug Act in 1906, highly profitable, if suspect, patent medicines were dropped from the catalog. Gone were the superlatives "World's Largest," "cheapest," and "America's strongest," unless justified by fact. Catalog vocabulary was simplified ("lachrimal secretions" became tears, "nutrition" became food) and descriptions were streamlined. In 1976 Sears switched to the "Segmented People-oriented approach" to copy that "required the end of any pretension that the catalog is a work of literature."

Little in the 2003 catalog is reminiscent of the extravagant puffery of Richard Sears's "Wish Books"; and little about the diversified billion-dollar Sears corporation reflects its humble origins as a watch wholesaler. Yet some fundamentals remain: serviceable, affordable merchandise, a large rural clientele (accounting for more than 40 percent of current catalog sales), and loyal customers. In the words of former Georgia governor Eugene Talmadge, "God Almighty, Sears, Roebuck, and Eugene Talmadge" are names to count on.

ELIZABETH M. MAKOWSKI
*University of Mississippi*

Louis E. Asher and Edith Heal, *Send No Money* (1942); Lewis E. Atherton, *The Southern Country Store, 1800–1860* (1949); Thomas D. Clark, *Pills, Petticoats, and Plows: The Southern Country Store* (1944); Boris Emmet and John E. Jeuck, *Catalogues and Counters: A History of Sears, Roebuck and Company* (1950); Ted Ownby, *American Dreams in Mississippi: Consumers, Poverty,* and Culture, 1830–1998 (1999); Jack Salzman, ed., *Prospects*, vol. 7 (1982); Sears, Roebuck and Co., *Merchant to the Millions: A Brief History of the Origins and Development of Sears, Roebuck and Co.* (1959); *Time* (20 August 1984); Gordon L. Weil, *Sears, Roebuck U.S.A.* (1977).

## Soybeans

Soybean production in the United States increased from 13.9 million bushels in 1930 to 2.3 billion bushels in 1982. The acreage devoted to the crop increased from 1 million to 71 million acres in the same period. Introduced as a novelty as early as 1804, the soybean was first used in the United States primarily for forage, beginning about 1900. Although many people saw its potential as a source of oil, less than one-fourth of the planted acreage in the mid-1930s was harvested for beans, which were then pressed for the oil for industrial uses and for meal for livestock feeding. Then a group of German chemists developed refining processes that removed from the oil its unpalatable flavor and odor, making soybean oil usable in products for human consumption.

Since then, soybeans have had an impact on every part of the United States, but this impact has been particularly notable in the post–World War II South. As early as 1917, the U.S. Department of Agriculture (USDA) published bulletins urging southern farmers to consider replacing cotton with soybeans. Not until World War II, though, with its patriotic appeals, high prices, and exodus of labor from southern farms, did many farmers turn from cotton to soybeans. After the war, pro-duction declined when farmers found the new crop to be highly susceptible to damage from weather and insects. Shifts in cotton production, research, and government policies were among factors bringing soybeans back to prominence.

Cotton production shifted to the West and Southwest, where the land and climate were suited to mechanization and where irrigation reduced the chances of crop failure. Research led to the realization that many southern farmers could double-crop their land by planting in succession oats or winter wheat and then soybeans. While the development of the solvent extraction of the oil was particularly beneficial to southern farmers, new varieties of soybeans, which were less susceptible to weather and insect damage, were developed by the southern state agricultural experiment stations. The cultural significance of this was clear from the names given to the favorite strains raised in the South: the Davis, Lee, Bragg, Forrest, Pickett, Jackson, and Rebel. E. E. Hartwig, USDA soybean breeder at Stoneville, Miss., deliberately named his varieties after Confederate heroes.

The postwar accumulation of cotton surpluses led the federal government to cut back the acreage of cotton that farmers could grow with price supports, leading many southern farmers to turn their land from cotton to soybeans. In 1945 the nine southern and border states of Georgia, Alabama, North Carolina, South Carolina, Tennessee, Mississippi, Missouri, Arkansas, and Louisiana produced 6 million bales of cotton and 18 million bushels of soybeans. In 1982 these same states produced 4.6 million bales of cotton and 757 million bushels of soybeans. In 2004 soybean production still surpassed cotton production in these states but had declined to 571 million bushels. A quiet revolution brought about by a single new crop had changed the face of the South.

WAYNE D. RASMUSSEN
*U.S. Department of Agriculture*

Edward J. Dies, *Soybeans: Gold from the Soil* (1943); Harry D. Fornari, *Agricultural History* (January 1979); W. J. Morse and J. L. Carter, *Yearbook of Agriculture* (1937).

## Sugar Industry

Cane sugar is a key commodity in international trade and an important component of the modern diet. At one time or another, sugarcane was grown commercially in Alabama, Georgia, South Carolina, Texas, Louisiana, and Florida. During the 19th century, south Louisiana was the focal point of this dynamic industry; beginning in the mid-20th century, however, the center of innovative activities shifted to Florida.

Between 1880 and 1910, the Louisiana sugar industry experienced a scientific and technological revolution in methods, process apparatus, and scale of operation. The animal-powered mills and open evaporation kettles characteristic of the antebellum period were supplanted by large, technically designed, and scientifically controlled central factories. One commentator of the period, Mark Twain, described the modern sugar factory as "a wilderness of tubs and tanks and vats and filters, pumps, pipes, and machinery." This new industrial world, which emerged in rural Louisiana, was brought about in large

part by a variety of local institutions working in alliance with certain agencies of the federal government. They included the Louisiana Sugar Planters' Association (LSPA), the Louisiana Sugar Experiment Station, the Audubon Sugar School, Louisiana State University, and the U.S. Department of Agriculture (USDA). These institutions facilitated the introduction of a progressive chemical and engineering technology, derived in part from the European beet-sugar industry, into this traditional plantation culture of the Deep South.

Of these local organizations, the LSPA made the crucial contribution to this transformation in manufacturing. Established in 1877 and led by many of the wealthiest and most politically powerful sugar planters in Louisiana, the LSPA systematically developed connections with federal government officials, practical engineers, and academic scientists to gain its organizational objectives. The late 19th-century modernization of the Louisiana sugar industry took place within an international context. Louisiana sugar planters, confronted with competition for the European beet-sugar manufacturers, responded not only to an economic challenge, but also to a scientific and technological one. They met this foreign threat by creating local institutions for coordinating planters' activities, conducting research, and supplying the scientific and technical expertise necessary for the modernization of their industry.

The technologically dynamic nature of this industry was largely confined to the milling and processing end of the business until the late 19th and early

20th centuries. Field operations, while totally restructured in terms of labor relations after the Civil War, remained traditional in practice, with arrangements forged by a complex set of negotiations between planters and field hands. And while improvements in agricultural implements, including the steam plow and later the tractor, would be gradually introduced into Louisiana cane fields by the early 20th century, mechanical harvesters were not used on an extensive scale until the 1980s.

As a result of changes in national party policies concerning the sugar tariff and the concurrent emergence of sugar-producing areas in Hawaii, Puerto Rico, Cuba, and Java, the Louisiana sugar industry entered into a period of decline after 1900. Subsequently, a number of sugar planters and investors channeled their energies and capital into south Florida, where they attempted to apply the practices of the Louisiana industry to the completely different environment found in the Everglades. The economic feasibility of the Florida industry became a reality only after USDA scientists at Canal Point, Fla., and research scientists for the United States Sugar Corporation discovered new varieties of cane, established specific fertilizer requirements, and introduced cultivation techniques appropriate for the region's unique soil, drainage, and climatic conditions. By 1940 Florida's sugarcane industry surpassed Louisiana's not only in terms of yield, but also in quality of raw sugar produced.

The Florida and Louisiana sugar industries supply only a fraction of the sugar consumed in the United States today. However, they continue to have a significant impact upon their respective local and regional economies.

JOHN A. HEITMANN
*University of Dayton*

Louis Ferleger, *Agricultural History* (April 1998); John A. Heitmann, *Florida Historical Quarterly* (January 1998), *The Modernization of the Louisiana Sugar Industry, 1830–1910* (1987); John C. Rodrigue, *Reconstruction in the Cane Fields: From Slavery to Free Labor in Louisiana's Sugar Parishes, 1862–1880* (2001); J. Carlyle Sitterson, *Sugar Country: The Cane Sugar Industry in the South, 1753–1950* (1953); Wendy Woloson, *Refined Tastes: Sugar, Confectionery, and Consumers in Nineteenth-Century America* (2002).

## Tobacco Culture, Flue-Cured

Jamestown colonists raised the first commercial tobacco in the early 17th century, and the expansion and contraction of plantings varied with international demand and prices. Over the years, farmers developed different varieties that they cultivated throughout the country. After the Civil War, bright tobacco, so called because of its golden color produced by intense heat during curing, became a favorite of cigarette manufacturers. Flues running through the barn provided the heat, leading to the adoption of the name "flue-cured" for this type of tobacco. Growers of flue-cured tobacco changed the traditional work culture by harvesting only several ripe leaves each week instead of cutting the entire stalk. Expert "stringers" took bundles of leaves from "handers" and tied them to sticks that were hung on tier poles in barns. Increasing cigarette

North Carolina tobacco farmers, Chatham County, 1930s (Howard Odum Papers,
Southern Historical Collection, University of North Carolina at Chapel Hill)

demand set in motion a massive expansion of the flue-cured culture from its Virginia–North Carolina seedbed into eastern North and South Carolina and, by World War I, to Georgia. Imperialistic growers spread the secrets of flue-curing and cloned tobacco barns, packhouses, and auction warehouses as they conquered new territory.

The flue-cured culture was extremely labor-intensive. It was more than a clever saying that it took 13 months to cultivate, harvest, cure, and grade a crop for market. Because of the crop's intense labor requirements, most tobacco

farmers planted less than a dozen acres, the amount that a family could cultivate. The work routine began in the winter, when farmers cut wood to heat the curing barns. In January they cleared land for a plantbed and seeded it before breaking the land and running rows. In May they transplanted seedlings to the field, plowed, chopped, and, as the tobacco grew, picked off hornworms and broke off the flowery tops and suckers. When harvest season arrived in July, they "primed" three to four ripe leaves each week, and the process continued for five to six weeks. As primers walked through the fields, mules pulled narrow slides or trucks through the rows. "Truckers" drove the slides to the scaffold, where the crew set aside the sticks tied with green tobacco until the end of the day. At dusk, primers returned from the fields and hung the sticks in tin-roofed sweltering barns. Curing, a delicate temperature-sensitive process, took the better part of a week. The sticks of tobacco were then stored in a packhouse until "barning" ended. Each leaf was then graded and tied into "hands" for market. It was sometimes Christmas before all the tobacco had been graded and sold.

Tobacco farmers shared the slump in prices generated by the Great Depression, and the Agricultural Adjustment Administration (AAA) recognized tobacco as a basic commodity. When the markets opened in 1933, prices remained low, but over 90 percent of flue-cured growers voted for a marketing agreement that promised parity prices for the 1933 crop in exchange for acreage reduction the next year. The AAA stabilized flue-cured prices, and the number of tobacco farms increased during the 1930s and the 1940s.

In the 1950s acreage allotments were cut, and this forced many farmers, especially sharecroppers, out of farming. At the same time, remaining farmers cultivated their land more intensely, increasing production per acre from 922 pounds in 1939 to 2,200 pounds in 1964. Only in the 1960s did the flue-cured tobacco culture mechanize to any extent. In addition to tractors used for plowing and hauling sleds to the scaffold, a mechanical topper covered 20 acres

a day and not only removed the tops but at the same time sprayed chemicals to control suckers and hornworms. By the mid-1960s, farmers insisted on intracounty allotment leasing, allowing small-allotment holders to lease acreage to larger growers. In 1968 Congress extended loose-leaf marketing, which had been customary in Georgia, to all areas, ending the labor-intensive grading and tying tasks. By the 1970s farmers were using bulk barns, an innovation that ended handing and stringing tasks. Meanwhile, a mechanical tobacco harvester began cutting out primers. Some farmers preferred hand primers and often employed immigrant labor. Taking advantage of mechanization, chemicals, and changes in marketing rules, flue-cured tobacco farmers increased their units from 9.5 acres in 1972 to 30 acres by the end of the century. Still, as cigarette consumption decreased, tobacco farmers suffered constant reductions in allotments.

The forces set in motion in the 1950s, plus increasing mechanization and chemical use, disrupted the old tenure arrangements in the tobacco area and led to a massive displacement of farmers. Because the flue-cured culture mechanized so late, many ex-farmers found work in emerging factories, easing the transition from farming by preserving communities, churches, and schools. In 1982, largely because of the controversy over smoking and health, Congress changed the price-support program, instituting a no-net-cost-to-taxpayers scheme that shifted the cost to tobacco farmers. Also, nonfarm allotment holders such as corporations and educational institutions sold their allotments to active farmers. At the turn of the 21st century, the venerable warehouse system of sales collapsed and farmers sold their crop directly to manufacturers. Like other commodity cultures, tobacco farming became a large-scale and capital-intensive operation that bore little resemblance to the intense hand/mule culture that originated in the 19th century.

PETE DANIEL
*Smithsonian Institution*
*Washington, D.C.*

Anthony Badger, *Prosperity Road: The New Deal, Tobacco, and North Carolina* (1980); Pete Daniel, *Breaking the Land: The Transformation of Cotton, Tobacco, and Rice Culture since 1880* (1985); William R. Finger, ed., *The Tobacco Industry in Transition: Policies for the 1980s* (1981); J. Fraser Hart and Ennis L. Chestang, *Geographical Review* (October 1978); John Morgan, *Southern Folklore*, no. 3 (1998); Harold B. Rowe, *Tobacco under the AAA* (1935); Nannie May Tilley, *The Bright-Tobacco Industry, 1860–1929* (1948).

## Truck Farming

Truck farming emerged as a form of post–Civil War agriculture in the United States. This agricultural enterprise significantly influenced widespread and scattered regions of the South well into the 20th century. The growth and development of profitable urban markets throughout the United States attracted the attention of profit-hungry southern farmers during the last quarter of the 19th century. This new enterprise involved the sale of vegetables and annual fruit crops—as distinguished from orchard crops—in distant urban markets in fresh and marketable condition. Although the southern grower would produce a wide variety of truck produce, the primary crops were Irish and sweet potatoes, watermelons, strawberries, tomatoes, cabbages, and beans. Essential to the successful conduct of the industry was the fast and efficient delivery of the produce to market by refrigerated transport. During the formative stage following 1865, railroads were able to provide this vital service.

By 1900 truck farming engaged the energies of southerners in centers of production scattered throughout the Old Confederacy stretching from the Eastern Shore of Virginia to the Lower Rio Grande Valley of Texas. These ranged in size from single counties to groupings of adjacent counties. A listing of prominent trucking counties at this time included Norfolk and Northampton in Virginia, Seminole and Palm Beach in Florida, Copiah in Mississippi, and Cameron and Hidalgo in Texas. By the second half of the 20th century, however, producing areas in Texas and Florida clearly dominated southern output.

Contributing to truck farming's spread was the failure of southern cash crops, especially cotton, to maintain consistently acceptable returns. Local business interests and regional railroads, as well as farmers, turned to this new venture to gain higher returns in the agriculturally dependent region. In 1899 a Texan wrote that "thrifty and intelligent [Texas] farmers began to realize that success laid [*sic*] not in the direction of two bit corn and four cent cotton, but in the surer, more profitable and more pleasant lines of fruit and truck growing."

In those regions where southerners pursued truck farming energetically, a new form of agriculture with its own unique support activities developed. The cultivation of these crops required more intensive and careful effort than that needed for the traditional staple crops—cotton, sugar, and tobacco. Distinctive features of the industry included packing sheds where local produce was prepared for rail shipment, ice plants that provided refrigeration for freight cars carrying produce, box factories that manufactured shipping containers, and so-called hot spots adjacent to the packing sheds where producers and buyers met to transact their business. Producers from the very earliest also sought with varying degrees of success to gain market advantage through the collective efforts of growers' associations. Indeed, truck farming provided otherwise quiet and placid communities with a season of excitement and intense activity.

In those portions of the South with proper soil and climate conditions, in combination with transportation connections with urban markets, truck farming provided the southern farmer with an alternative to dependence on the region's traditional cash crops.

JAMES L. MCCORKLE JR.
*Northwestern State University of Louisiana*

Gilbert C. Fite, *Cotton Fields No More: Southern Agriculture, 1865–1980* (1984); James L. McCorkle Jr., *Agricultural History* (Winter 1992); Bruce McKinley and W. C. Funk, *An Economic Study of Truck Farming*

*in the Plant City Area, Hillsborough County, Florida* (1926); Wells A. Sherman, *Merchandising Fruits and Vegetables: A New Billion Dollar Industry* (1928).

## Viticulture

Commercial grape production is a vital part of the fruit industry of the South. The climate of the South offers the potential for growth of traditional and unique grape cultivars for the production of a range of grape products. Most of the grape acreage in the southern United States is planted to French American hybrid grape varieties (e.g., Chambourcin, Seyval); however, Concord and Niagara (*Vitis labruscana*) and muscadines (*Vitis rotundifolia*) are also grown commercially, and some *Vitis vinifera* (the standard European wine grape varieties) are successfully grown.

Muscadine grapes, the "grape of the Deep South," have thick skins, large seeds, and a unique, soft, musky-flavored pulp. They fruit in small clusters (10 to 20 berries), and as the fruit ripens, an abscission layer forms and causes mature fruits to drop. Cultivars vary in color from bronze to nearly black. Common names for the dark-fruited muscadines in the South include bullace, bull grape, and bullet grape. "Scuppernong" is often used to refer to all bronze-fruited varieties but is actually the name of a specific muscadine cultivar.

The history of the muscadine cultivar is unclear. In 1524 French navigator Giovanni de Verrazano recorded finding the muscadine grape in what is now North Carolina, and in 1584 Sir Walter Raleigh's colony is credited with discovering the scuppernong "mother vine" on Roanoke Island in 1584, yet others claim the discovery of muscadines occurred in the mid-18th century along the Scuppernong River. There is a muscadine vine on Roanoke Island that has been in continuous cultivation for 200 years and today has a trunk over two feet thick and covers half an acre.

Muscadine grapes have winter hardiness levels similar to *Vitis vinifera*, are more disease and insect resistant than the French American hybrids, *Vitis vinifera* or *Vitis labruscana*, and need approximately half the sprays of the other three types of grapes. They are usually considered adaptable in regions that can grow cotton and pecans. Muscadines and muscadine products are significant sources of several phytochemicals that have been associated with disease prevention in humans. They have a tremendous undeveloped market potential for the production of nutraceuticals.

The hardiest of the *Vitis vinifera* varieties, such as Riesling, Chardonnay, Cabernet Franc, and Cabernet Sauvignon, have been grown commercially in the Upper South. These varieties are the most cold-hardy and adaptable varieties. In the extreme southern areas, *vinifera* grapes are susceptible to Pierce's disease, which is spread by leafhoppers (also known as sharpshooters) and which kills the vines.

Concord grapes (*Vitis labruscana*), the dominant purple juice grape in the United States, can be grown only in the upper regions of the South. Farther south it will not ripen evenly and is therefore not economical for a once-over harvest. In order to address this limiting factor, researchers have developed a new high-quality, Concord-like juice grape variety, Sunbelt, which ripens evenly in the warmer regions and can be commercially harvested and handled just like the Concord.

The hybrid grapes in the South can be grouped into two categories, the French American hybrids and the American hybrids (e.g., Chardonel, Cayuga White). The French American hybrids are from crosses made by French hybridizers to develop grapes that would tolerate phylloxera root louse and resist fungal diseases. They fit somewhere between the *Vitis vinifera* and *Vitis labruscana* species in terms of susceptibility to winter injury and ability to adapt to the conditions in the South.

Cynthiana/Norton (*Vitis aestivalis*) is native to and adapted to most upper regions of the South. It is grown commercially in Arkansas, Tennessee, Virginia, North Carolina, and Georgia, as well as Missouri. Cynthiana is known for the production of wine with deep dark color and unique flavor. The major limiting factors to production of this species have been extremely low yields (around two tons an acre) and difficult propagation. Research has shown that yields in the range of four to six tons are possible when optimal cultural practices are used.

In recent years, there has been an increased interest in establishing local specialty markets for new grape products such as seed extracts and powders with nutraceutical potential. However, wine continues to be the major market for grapes in the South. Throughout the region, there has been an increase in small-scale wineries, many located on existing wine trails. Winery entrepreneurs often serve as business outlets for producers of jams, jellies, syrups, and other value-added grape products. The winery trails and events at the wineries are widely advertised in state tourism publications and flyers for interstate rest areas and tourism-trade businesses. A visit to wine country for winery tours and tastings is growing increasingly popular and has become the ultimate example of agritourism, bringing in a steady stream of year-round customers.

JUSTIN MORRIS
*University of Arkansas*

Leon Adams, *The Wines of America* (1990).

# Industry

The traditional wisdom that most antebellum southerners shied away from industrial investments and commercial ventures because they were by nature an "agricultural people" is more traditional than wise. If anything, these southerners were an "economic people" whose particular circumstances made it advantageous for them to become "agricultural." Some prominent figures in the Old South may have voiced their fears of industrialization and condemned its proponents as the advance agents of Yankee subversion in the region, but then, as now, the primary influences and motivations that shaped the development of southern commerce and industry were economic. Worries about cultural identity were secondary at best, and sadly enough, fundamental concerns about human welfare were generally of less consequence still.

For many years, historians held that slavery stunted the South's economy, particularly its commercial and industrial growth, by funneling the region's already scarce resources into the unpredictable and frequently unprofitable enterprise of cotton planting. At the same time, slavery not only discouraged in-migration by free workers but stigmatized manual labor as an activity unbefitting a white person, regardless of social status. The result was supposedly a society obsessed with land and slaves and lacking in the free labor, markets, capital liquidity, and human energy needed to stimulate industry and commerce.

This critique still has some validity, but in recent years economic historians have qualified it quite a bit by showing that cotton planting was a reasonably profitable endeavor in its own right, and that, contrary to long-standing perception, the South, in the aggregate at least, was one of the wealthiest places in the world by the middle of the 19th century. The key to this wealth was not cotton production, however, but slaves. A southerner who owned just 10 prime field hands was wealthier than all but 1 percent of the citizens of Boston in 1848. By 1860, with slave values at an estimated $900 per bondsman, a southerner who owned two slaves and nothing else was as well off as the average northerner.

**Antebellum Industrialization.** Scarlett O'Hara may have overstated the case just a mite when she declared "she'd never seen a factory or known anyone who had seen a factory," but the antebellum South was certainly capable of supporting considerably more industrial and commercial activity than it ever generated. In fact, annual returns from investments in southern manufacturing were often higher than the national average and sometimes twice as high as profits from cotton planting.

On the surface, such evidence might seem to suggest that southerners were either too naive to realize they were missing a good bet by not investing in a mill or a business or they simply succumbed to social pressures by pursuing wealth in cotton and slaves rather than in textiles, lumber, or general merchandise. Clearly fearful that any challenge to their social or political status might divide southern whites and undermine the institution of slavery, large slaveholders loved to hear orators lionize them as the noblest of southerners and their profession as the highest calling known to man.

Still, state and local policy makers rarely translated slave owners' anxieties into legislation that forbade or effectively stifled the expansion of industry and commerce. If there were few legal impediments to the growth of the nonagricultural sector in the antebellum South's economy, did most southern planters simply fail to recognize the potential profits they were forfeiting by clinging to agriculture? If not, why did they settle for returns so much lower than those they might have gained from investing in industry? The answer lies not in ignorance but in restrained investment behavior premised on the notion that the relatively dependable profits (in the neighborhood of 10 percent) offered by cotton production came at considerably less risk than the much higher profits possible in a still-uncertain manufacturing sector. Such behavior was certainly cautious but hardly irrational or abnormal, especially when the natural growth and rising value of their slaveholdings afforded an increasingly comfortable cushion of wealth.

Even if southern investors had been more venturesome, it is unlikely that the antebellum South ever would have been industrialized on a scale comparable to the North. Climate, topography, and the slave-labor system gave the region a comparative advantage in agriculture that shaped not only its economic destiny but its social and political development as well. In the antebellum era, most southern industry involved processing agricultural products and raw materials. Flour and corn milling accounted for much of this activity across the South, and the tobacco industry was crucial to the industrial economy of Virginia and the Carolinas. Cotton mills took advantage of the South's abundant cotton, waterpower, and cheap labor. Richmond's Tredegar Iron Works was the major heavy industry in a region whose entire industrial output was worth less than that of Pennsylvania in 1860.

As long as cotton prices were good, white southerners were in a position to overindulge their advantage in agriculture, but the end of the antebellum cotton boom and the slowing of the rate of growth in demand for cotton after the Civil War put the southern states well behind the vibrant northeastern and central states, which were experiencing an economic revolution in the late 19th century. With "King Cotton" ingloriously dethroned and technology, labor, capital, and resources all in their favor, the northern states attracted the overwhelming majority of investments in the dynamic industries and businesses needed to sustain rapid economic growth in that period. The South, on the other hand, had little to offer industries but abundant labor, certain raw materials (particularly cotton and wood), and a desire for industry that went well beyond fervent and bordered on fanatical.

**A New South.** The postbellum South's most prominent advocate of industrialization was Henry W. Grady, an Atlanta newspaperman who became famous as the grand prophet of the New South movement. Grady preached industrialism and economic independence and stressed sectional reconciliation in order to ensure a happy marriage between northern capital and southern labor and raw materials. Although Grady promised a "New" South, he also took great pains to assure southern planters that industrial development would not drain off the cheap, controllable labor that was essential to maintaining their agricultural system. Critics charged Grady with "selling out" to the planters as well as to the northern investors who hoped to perpetuate an exploitive colonial relationship with the South. Although Grady could not be exonerated on this count, if the South was going to attract industrial investment, he and his disciples actually had few options. In most southern states, agricultural interests remained influential enough to, if not block, then at least severely impede the industrial development effort if it posed a serious threat to their supply of cheap labor. As for facilitating further "colonization" of the South's economy, New South leaders may have had little choice given the region's similarities to other underdeveloped areas of the world that have achieved economic growth only by offering their labor and raw materials to absentee investors at bargain rates. As the economist Gavin Wright has shown, the problem was not that the South's economy was "colonial." The same might have been said of many of the western and midwestern states of that era as well. In contrast to these states, however, the South's postbellum colonization brought neither the investment in infrastructure and technology nor the significant in-migration of managerial or entrepreneurial personnel or skilled workers that might have allowed it to shed its laggard, labor-exploitive economy. Unscrupulous and short-sighted as many of its leaders might have been, the New South's economic destiny was no more in their hands than at the mercy of the external capital flows, as well as technological, labor, and market factors that defined national and international growth patterns in the late 19th century.

For example, the structure and administration of the South's railroad system helped to shape its economic development. With nearly all the region's railroad mileage controlled by northerners by the turn of the 20th century, highly discriminatory freight rates were the rule when shipping goods within the South. It was much cheaper, for example, to send Arkansas cotton to Massachusetts than to South Carolina. Also, as the railroads penetrated the countryside, small crossroads towns sprang up as self-contained mercantile, processing, and marketing centers. With such excellent connections outside the region, the products of these towns of approximately 10,000 people went directly to northern cities without passing through major southern cities (with the probable exception of the regional hub city of Atlanta). As a result, the configuration of the South's railroads played a major role in retarding urban growth in the region. Meanwhile, the country store and small-town merchant served as gatekeeper between the southern cotton field and the northern cotton market and became, like Faulkner's Will Varner, "the chief man of the country" by occupying the pivotal position in a capital-scarce economy where cotton often served as currency. Supplying not only credit but also everything from farm implements to face powder, such merchants became "the fountain head if not of law at least of advice and suggestion" to an unwitting constituency of local farmers who prized their independence but nonetheless came to men like Varner "not in the attitude of *What must I do* but *What do you think you would like for me to do if you was able to make me do it.*"

In the South of 1900, only 18 percent of the workforce was employed in pursuits unrelated to agriculture, and per capita income stood at 51 percent of the national average, exactly where it had been 20 years earlier. Industry remained largely confined to extracting raw materials and processing agricultural products. Absentee owners drew away much of the income from these activities, and wages were meager. In 1910 the manufacturing payroll for the entire state of Georgia was smaller than that for the city of Cincinnati. Moreover, much of the South's nonagricultural economy was devoted to commerce rather than manufacturing. Even in a relatively industrialized city like Memphis, the value of annual trade in 1900 was 10 times that of manufacturing.

The structure of the post-Reconstruction South's economy was directly related to its ultraconservative social and political climate. The region's commitment to low-wage, labor- and resource-exploitive industries required a parallel commitment to maintaining social and political stability and an austere, rigidly conservative government disinclined to regulate or tax too heavily or to see any side but management's in a labor-management dispute.

Southern racial attitudes and practices both shaped and were shaped by late 19th-century and early 20th-century economic development. Some southern industries like textiles relied on lily-white workforces, while an overwhelming majority of laborers in the lumber industry were black. In industries where both blacks and whites were employed, workers who performed the same tasks were generally paid the same, but the more desirable and remunerative jobs were reserved for whites. As whites and blacks increasingly encountered each other, both on an expanding rail network and in the region's new factories and bustling cities, a more formalized system of de jure racial segregation arose in the name of social order and economic stability. The commercial classes dominated policy making in southern cities, and their ties to the agricultural and processing activities of the countryside made them wary of any alterations of the status quo likely to disrupt an economy based on rigid control of labor, low taxes, and minimal government interference. Tensions were always present, but during the late 19th century and much of the first half of the 20th century, the urban South largely accommodated itself to the politics of the countryside.

The kingpin of this politics was a more evolved version of the aforementioned Will Varner, described by Ralph McGill as the "small-town rich man" who, "according to his geographic location," owned the gin, the cotton warehouse, the tobacco warehouse, or the turpentine works. He also owned the town's largest store, selling feeds, fertilizer, and other farm supplies. Often, he served as a director of the local bank. He controlled local credit and was on a first-name basis with his governor, his legislator, his senators, and his congressman. Paranoid about maintaining a large pool of cheap labor loyal only to him, he hated New Deal relief programs (except when he could manipulate them to feed and clothe his workers during the off-season) and union organizers with equal passion. Because he dominated the South's rurally skewed state political systems, the small-town rich man was a powerful agent of inertia, representing a large segment of the region's business and industrial capitalists.

**The Crusade for Economic Development.** Despite the region's social and political stagnation, the South's efforts to industrialize continued unabated as the 20th century unfolded. The almost religious fervor of the crusade for economic growth revealed itself in the "Atlanta Spirit," an urban booster ethos that rallied the leaders of southern cities to intense, competitive crusading for growth during the 1920s. Commercial and civic leaders, black spokesmen, and even the Ku Klux Klan joined the hunt for more smokestacks. Any industry was better than

Birmingham steel mill and workers' houses, 1930s
(Walker Evans, Library of Congress [LC-USZ62-34372], Washington, D.C.)

no industry to these zealots, but not so to the Vanderbilt Agrarians, a group of 12 conservative writers whose views were published in 1930 in *I'll Take My Stand*, a spirited critique of industrialism typified by John Crowe Ransom's assertion that "the dignity of personality is gone as soon as the man from the farm enters the factory door." The Agrarians offered a Depression-ridden South a stout defense of southern traditionalism but no real alternative to the impoverished, benighted society that dependence on agriculture had bequeathed to the region. Most southerners who knew about the Agrarians at all probably would have, for once, agreed with H. L. Mencken, who ridiculed them for "spinning lavender fancies under a fig tree."

The Depression era saw the campaign for industrial growth intensify and expand. The Atlanta Spirit spread from the cities to the small towns in response to a series of shocks, beginning with the boll weevil invasion of the 1920s. Plummeting cotton yields drove both landowners and sharecroppers from the land and posed a serious threat to the agriculturally oriented commerce and industry that was the mainstay of the southern economy. As Georgia's cotton belt played unhappy host to the boll weevil at its hungriest, the state amended its constitution to allow tax exemptions for new industries. Coming on the heels of the boll weevil, the Depression intensified the insect's impact, forcing both planter and sharecropper off the land. Ironically, the New Deal's Agricultural Adjustment Act, which paid farmers to produce less, further reinforced the trend toward farm consolidation and reduced farm labor requirements, leading to the displacement of one-third of the South's sharecroppers between 1933 and 1940 alone. The dwindling farm population posed a serious threat to the merchants, lawyers, bankers, and other professionals who comprised the small-town middle class because demand for goods and services was certain to shrink proportionally. Out-migration of uprooted farm labor might lead ultimately to a similar fate for many members of the small-town middle class if a means could not be found to provide alternative employment (and income) to a rapidly swelling surplus labor population. Industrialization seemed the most likely solution to the problem, especially since concerns over any potential shortage of agricultural labor had been greatly reduced.

In its zeal for payrolls, the small-town South prostrated itself at the feet of any and all industrialists who glanced its way. The enterprising employer who required no more than a building and a workforce could usually get the former for nothing and the latter for not much more. Subsidies for buildings were sometimes raised by public subscription or mandatory deductions from already meager employee paychecks. Tax exemptions, legal or not, were seldom difficult to secure, and local law enforcement officials stood ready to discourage any union organizers who might dare come to town. Not surprisingly, some companies exploited an already advantageous situation by hiring unpaid or barely paid trainees and then moving almost overnight to any industry-hungry community ready to up the ante. Out of this chaotic scramble for payrolls came more organized, state-sanctioned programs to attract industry, most notably Mississippi's "Balance Agriculture with Industry" program (1936–58), which used tax-free municipal bonds to finance plant construction, and Louisiana's organized tax-exemption plan for new industries. Both approaches spread across the South and ultimately much of the nation. Although designed to make southern communities more attractive to industry, subsidy programs only confirmed the existing pattern of industrial development based on competitive, labor-intensive industries because such operations, attracted to the South initially by their need to save on labor costs, were also the ones most likely to be swayed by an opportunity to save on construction and tax costs. Although the old agricultural system was yielding to mechanization and consolidation, the traditional pattern of industrial development remained fundamentally unchanged.

The concentration of southern manufacturing in small-town and rural locations helped to minimize the cultural and demographic impact of industrialization in the region. As Dixie's most industrialized state, North Carolina showed a population in 1900 that was still less than 10 percent urban. As technological advances slowed within the industry, southern textile expansion became less likely to spawn the rapid urbanization that had accompanied industrialization in the North. Moreover, first the automobile and then the proliferation of electric power allowed even greater dispersal of southern manufacturing facilities. Industrialists chose locations where they could draw on a large-scale surplus of underemployed agricultural workers eager to work for steady, if meager, wages. Such workers were also prepared to commute long distances in order to continue to work their farms. Because they were not forced to relocate in urban, industrial communities, they could maintain the cultural ties and lifestyles associated with life on the farm.

Worker-farmers sacrificed much of the independence and periodic leisure they had known when they were only farmers. Many of them took night-shift jobs so that they would be free to work their fields during the day, the result being that they actually held two jobs. Ironically, employers justified the substandard wages they paid such workers on the ground that these employees were supplementing their paychecks with their farm incomes and therefore needed less than their counterparts elsewhere in the country. The same was true for farm wives who were actively recruited for work in small "sewing" (apparel) plants. Not only did they live on a farm that supplied much of their food, but they also were working merely to supplement their husband's farm—or farm and industrial—income and should be willing to accept even lower wages than those paid farm-based male workers.

At the same time that she was being underpaid, the wage-earning farm wife was being overworked. She performed her eight-hour job at "the plant" while keeping up with her cooking, cleaning, and canning at home, just as she had when she was "only" a farm wife. Meanwhile, as the profitability of farming declined and government subsidies of the New Deal and post–New Deal era encouraged farmers to farm less or not at all, the former head of the household was often reduced to the status of a "go-getter" whose principal duty each day was to take his wife to work and later "go get 'er."

**The Effects of World War II.** Although much of the South's new industry continued to choose rural and small-town locations, World War II did more to alter the course and pace of southern economic development than any event since the Civil War. The war's greatest contribution consisted of a huge helping

Inside a Cherryville, N.C., textile mill, 1908
(Lewis Hine, Albin O. Kuhn Library and Gallery, University of Maryland, Baltimore County)

of federal money for a traditionally capital-starved region. More than $4 billion went into military facilities and perhaps as much as $5 billion into defense plants. The result was a 40 percent increase in the South's industrial capacity. Per capita income tripled during the 1940s, leaving southerners with enough disposable income, at long last, to make them attractive potential consumers for a number of market-oriented industries that had previously found the South's consuming capacity too puny to justify locating a production or distribution facility in the region. Automobile assembly and parts plants, for example, began to spring up in the Atlanta vicinity as executives realized the growing potential of the southeastern market.

With its rapidly mechanizing agricultural sector and its consumer markets expanded by World War II, the South became a region even more firmly committed to industry. The terrible memories of the 1930s spurred a renewed commitment to industrialization and a determination not to surrender wartime gains. All the southern states strengthened and extended their development programs, and more state and local leaders became involved. The governor became the state's supersalesman, and no gubernatorial aspirant dared to neglect economic development as a campaign pledge. Growth indicators suggested that this vigorous development effort was paying off, but the more rapid expansion of the post–World War II era was primarily the result of basic economic considerations related to costs, markets, and demographic shifts.

The neocolonial economy of the South had preserved lower labor and general operating costs even as the war-born boom stimulated consumer buying power. Meanwhile, the traditional pattern of out-migration gradually reversed itself in the 1950s, augmenting the South's historically high birthrate and enhancing the region's market attraction.

As the South was experiencing its long-awaited economic boom, the industrial North was beginning to show definite signs of decay. Mounting labor and tax costs, technological obsolescence, labor agitation, rising crime, and an increased government regulatory role were among the considerations that led industrialists to forego expansion or new investments in the North in favor of new plants in the South. As investment capital moved out, so did a number of residents, many of whom found new homes and jobs below the Mason-Dixon Line.

By 1960 the trends set in motion by World War II were readily apparent. Between 1940 and 1960, the South's population had shifted from 65 percent rural to 58 percent urban. In the latter year, only 10 percent of the population still worked in agriculture, while 21 percent worked in manufacturing. Average per capita income stood at 76 percent of the national average.

**The Sunbelt Era.** Although World War II marked the beginning of the South's economic takeoff, not until the end of the 1960s did the region begin to bask in the aura of prosperity surrounding the emergent "Sunbelt," a strip of states stretching across the nation's southern tier from the Carolinas to California. Between 1970 and 1976, the South enjoyed a net population gain of nearly 3 million. In contrast to the past, by the mid-1970s those moving into the region were significantly younger and better educated than the national average. The South's climate and relatively uncomplicated lifestyle were also pulling in retirees whose fixed incomes made lower living costs important. The South finally had its all-important nucleus of middle-class consumers. Industrial output and employment skyrocketed. Houston alone accounted for 79,000 new jobs in 1979. Much of Houston's growth was energy related, but the bulk of the region's expansion in the 1970s came in services such as retail trade, real estate, and banking. Overall, the southern economy had grown about 30 percent faster than the national average over the last quarter century by the mid-1970s, and dramatic increases in per capita incomes suggested that regional differentials might soon be a thing of the past in some parts of the South.

Paradoxically, however, these differentials remained the key selling point for those charged with attracting new industrial payrolls to the region. The South Carolina Department of Commerce was still bragging in 2006 that the state's manufacturing wages were "among the lowest in the country," one of the reasons being a union membership rate of 3.3 percent. North Carolina's unionization figures were equally anemic, and Georgia's and Virginia's were not much higher. Across the region, only Kentucky and Alabama showed union participation figures that exceeded one-half of the steadily shrinking national average of 12 percent. Workers who "talked union" were sometimes given a warning before they were fired, and sometimes they were not. On occasion, local developers even spurned prospective employers promising to hire large numbers of workers at generous salaries if their plants were likely to be unionized. The Spartanburg, S.C., Development Association wanted no part of a proposed Mazda assembly plant in 1984 because by employing "over 3,000 card-carrying, hymn-singing members of the UAW," it would have "a long-term chilling effect on Spartanburg's orderly industrial growth."

This rebuff of Mazda was one of the few rough spots in South Carolina's courtship of foreign employers, which had begun in the 1970s. Much of the industrial and commercial capital invested in the South had traditionally come from outside the region, and in the Sunbelt era an increasing amount came from outside the nation as well. Foreign investors moved in to take advantage of a devalued dollar, expanded markets, and all of the region's traditional enticements—cheap, nonunion labor; low taxes; cooperative government; and a generally lower cost of living. By the end of the decade, the South Carolina piedmont was spotted with plants from Germany, France, and Japan, to name but a few. Elsewhere, the Nissan truck plant at Smyrna, Tenn., attracted considerable attention as a prime example of the way in which Japanese management styles could be transferred to an American plant. After all, the "one-big-happy-family" approach favored by the Japanese bore a striking resemblance to the paternalism practiced in the cotton mills of the late 19th- and early 20th-century South. Developers cultivated this sense of kinship by promising Japanese industrialists a "cost-effective workforce" because "like Japan, South Carolina emphasizes a strong work ethic and pride in workmanship."

More than half of the foreign businesses drawn to the United States in the 1990s opened up shop in the South, and by 2002 one of eight manufacturing workers in the region was drawing payroll checks from companies headquartered in another country. Recruiting foreign industry clearly did little to diminish the traditional emphasis on cheap labor, however, and it may have actually intensified the "bidding war" for new payrolls, as southern states led the way in offering massive public subsidies to prospective employers. The $33 million that brought the Nissan plant to Tennessee in 1980 seemed paltry compared to the reported $253 million that Alabama bestowed on Mercedes to build a plant near Tuscaloosa in 1993. Alabama's $800 million in cumulative generosity to Mercedes, Hyundai, Honda, and Toyota over the last 14 years seemed absolutely extraordinary until its announcement in 2007 of an estimated $811 million payoff to a single employer, German steel giant ThyssenKrupp AG, for a new plant near Mobile. Running a distant second to Alabama, but apparently determined to catch up, Mississippi dumped a combined $660 million on Nissan and Toyota between 2000 and 2007.

Southern political and economic leaders were far more enthusiastic about investing in foreign corporations than in their own people. When, as part of a $295 million show of hospitality, Mississippi coughed up $80 million in 2000 just to train workers for Nissan's assembly plant near Canton, the cost per employee came out to more than four times the state's per pupil expenditures in K–12. Three years later, Alabama cut $266 million from its education budget before serving up $318 million in incentives to Hyundai and Honda. When Alabama opened the floodgates with its huge payoff to Mercedes in 1993, the state had ranked 41st overall in teachers' salaries. Fourteen years later, it ranked 47th. Mississippi, meanwhile, maintained a solid grasp on 50th. Across the region, it was hardly surprising that a 2007 assessment of the states' capacities to participate in a new, knowledge-based economy ranked eight southern states 40th or lower.

If the increasingly global mobility of industrial capital appeared to be a godsend to certain areas of the South, it seemed to be a curse for others. The $9.92 an hour earned by a sewing-machine operator in North Carolina hardly seemed extravagant—except to employers who knew that workers doing the same thing in Bangladesh were only taking home about 50 cents more for what could be a 70-hour workweek. Throw in the 1993 North American Free Trade Agreement, which opened up Mexico's enormous pool of cheap labor to foreign garment and textile operations, and it was easy enough to understand why North Carolina lost 35 percent of its manufacturing jobs between 1996 and 2006 and 10 other southern states suffered losses of 20 percent or more. Jobs in the textile and apparel industry were seldom terribly remunerative, but those who lost them often had little choice but to take pay cuts of 30 percent or more working as desk clerks and cashiers or in other such downscale service occupations.

The persistence of so much low-wage employment translated into a heavy regional concentration of the "working poor." In every southern state but Virginia, at least 40 percent of the families living below the poverty level in 2004 also had one or more members who worked full time for at least 10 months of the year. The best visual representation of the prevalence of the working poor came in the number of mobile homes dotting the southern landscape, especially in South and North Carolina, where they accounted for 19 and 17 percent, respectively, of each state's housing units in 2004.

Blacks were not only overrepresented among the working poor but also among the poor and unemployed in general. Kentucky was the only southern state in 2004 where the black poverty rate was less than twice that of whites, and in Mississippi and Alabama the ratio was more than three to one. In Georgia, meanwhile, blacks accounted for 25 percent of the workforce and 50 percent of the unemployed in 2000. For all of Atlanta's gleaming skyscrapers, at street level the reality was a median household income for blacks in Fulton County of only $29,000 in 1999 as compared to $68,000 earned by white households. Meanwhile, the strongly negative correlation between black population size and growth in manufacturing employment has long been established, leaving rural areas like the Mississippi Delta or the Alabama Black Belt with little immediate hope of alleviating severe black poverty and unemployment.

Those who were working actively to address this concern faced an added challenge as the 20th century became the 21st and the divisions between the South's "haves" and "have-nots" were no longer a mere matter of black and white. North Carolina's Hispanic population grew by nearly 400 percent during the 1990s, and five other states saw increases of over 200 percent. Researchers suggested that as many as two-thirds of these recent Hispanic immigrants might be in the country illegally. Amid a rising chorus of complaints that these newcomers were taking jobs that otherwise would have gone to blacks, data on Hispanic employment growth actually showed it concentrated in areas where black—and white—employment was also growing. In less dynamic areas, however, there was clearly head-to-head competition between blacks and Hispanics, especially in industries like poultry, meat, and catfish processing, where blacks once had held the overwhelming majority of the typically low-wage, arduous, and distasteful jobs. Experienced black workers saw themselves being undermined by the newcomers, who often seemed not just willing but eager to work long hours under substandard conditions at whatever wages the employer offered. In plants where union organizers had made some headway, Hispanics seemed generally unreceptive. Workplace tensions between the two groups sometimes erupted into confrontations and even violence. Suggesting that blacks saw Hispanics as a threat to their livelihood and prospects for advancement, a black worker at a North Carolina meat-processing plant predicted in 2000: "There's a day coming when the Mexicans are going to catch hell from the blacks the way the blacks caught it from the whites."

For all the rising tensions between Hispanics and blacks still struggling for economic stability, there was a definite perception of opportunity for many more upwardly mobile African Americans who began relocating to the South's large metropolitan areas like Atlanta and Dallas in the 1970s. What began as a trickle soon became a flood, as metro Atlanta claimed seven of the 10 fastest-growing counties for blacks by 2006. Clearly many of these black newcomers were established professionals looking not to "make good" but to "make better." South of Atlanta in Fayette County, Ga., nearly a third of all its black families actually showed annual incomes in excess of $100,000 in 2000. The Dallas–Forth Worth metropolitan area was also a magnet for higher-income black families; in the 1990s the number of its black households earning at least $100,000 more than tripled from 5,300 to 16,000.

**Economic Development and Southern Culture.** In 1973 country songwriter Bobby Braddock proudly reported his observations of "wooded parks and big skyscrapers where once stood red clay hills and cotton fields" and "sons and daughters of sharecroppers drinking scotch and making business deals." Not everyone shared Braddock's enthusiasm for a newly "risen" South. While some claimed that Sunbelt-era economic progress had left too many southerners still in the shade, others worried that its economic hotspots were in the process of losing their cultural souls. Many of those who were once critical of the South for its backwardness now complained that a strip-malled, suburbanized South was the next thing to no South at all. Marshall Frady moaned about a "cultural lobotomy" as fast-food restaurants, discount stores, and industrial parks smothered the landscape of the metropolitan South.

Frady's concern was, of course, not a new one. The Agrarians had already expressed the same fear by the end of the 1920s. In the face of the boosterism that enveloped the South after World War I, writers like Thomas Wolfe and William Faulkner decried the materialism of the booster ethos and expressed particular regret at the destruction of the South's wilderness areas. In *Tobacco Road*, Erskine Caldwell had the lowly Jeeter Lester doggedly refuse to abandon farming, even sharecropping, for work in a cotton mill. After World War II had accelerated the South's economic growth and spurred industrialization and the mechanization of agriculture, Flannery O'Connor wrote a short story about a "displaced person" who brings mechanical but impersonal, Yankee-like precision and skill to a rundown Georgia farm only to have his contribution rejected by the inhabitants, who allow him to be flattened by a runaway tractor.

The same concern had been reflected in country music, where examples of a fear and loathing of the alien, northernizing influences of the city and the factory and a preference for the idyllic agrarian lifestyle abounded. In the 1930s songs like "Cotton Mill Colic" and "Weave Room Blues" depicted the dreariness of industrial life, while in the 1960s "Detroit City" and "Streets of Baltimore" presented the northern city, for all its economic attraction, as a heartless and foreboding place. More recently, country star Alan Jackson told a story familiar to many small-town southerners when he sang about the "Little Man" who once "pumped your gas" and "cleaned your glass" until his little filling station could no longer compete with corporate-owned convenience stores because "he couldn't sell Slurpees" and he "wouldn't sell beer."

In many ways a tsunami of shopping centers and chain stores seemed to bring a chilling anonymity to the small-town South, where restaurants offering corn dogs and tacos sprang up to challenge those specializing in cornbread and turnip greens. Unknown and impersonal sales clerks and two pieces of identification to pay by check were other seemingly inevitable concomitants to progress. Many observers insisted that southerners had managed to some extent to humanize the technological and commercial advances that had bred anonymity and alienation elsewhere, but such contentions were sometimes more impressionistic than objective. To be sure, there were live bait stores that also rented videos, but it was sometimes difficult to identify what part, if any, of the region's response to economic modernization was clearly "southern" instead of the reaction of any traditional rural and small-town society to dramatic changes in its means of production and exchange.

Opinion surveys of better-educated, more affluent white southerners showed that economic progress was finally eroding the racism, traditionalism, and authoritarianism that constituted some of the darker elements of the South's longstanding value structure. Yet, as sociologist John Shelton Reed has shown, these primary beneficiaries of the region's economic progress were also those most likely to prize their identities as southerners and to express a preference for foods, friends, and an overall lifestyle that they identified as southern. Paradoxically, while economic progress appeared to be undermining certain traditional values, it was also kindling the cultural anxieties of those whose imminent baptism in the socioeconomic mainstream posed the threat of a rootless, anonymous existence. This fear of cultural anonymity made the marketing of southern identity a big business, not only for *Southern Living* magazine, whose circulation exceeded 2.7 million by 2005, but also for a host of websites hawking everything from T-shirts to fragrances designed to establish and convey one's "southernness."

Regardless of whether one was for it or against it, the notion that factories, skyscrapers, and interstate highways, not to mention television and the Internet, would "northernize" the South rested in no small part on the assumption that there were distinct value differences between industrial and agrarian societies and that, as industrialization proceeded, the presumably stronger, more modern industrial values were bound to triumph. For many years, liberal social scientists and journalists had seen agrarian traditionalism and economic progress as each other's archenemy, the former being the villain in the ongoing saga of southern backwardness and the latter cast in the role of oft-thwarted, would-be savior. In the widely accepted scenario, if southern traditionalism could be weakened sufficiently to allow economic modernization to gain a foothold, modernization's benevolent and progressive influences then would overwhelm the vestiges of racism and reactionary politics and transform Dixie into an enlightened liberal society like the industrial Northeast. Ironically, however, the South's economic emergence not only failed to follow this widely accepted model, it also practically turned it on its head. The "favorable business climate" so vital to the Sunbelt South's fabled economic success story was actually rooted in the historically conservative social and political atmosphere long condemned as the nemesis of southern progress. Cheap, intimidated labor, low taxes, and a cooperative rather than meddlesome government—all of these were both trademarks of the traditionalist, plantation South and keys to the Sunbelt South's appeal to business and industrial investors.

The South's belated economic emergence demonstrated that the "value gap" between agrarian and industrial-commercial societies had been greatly exaggerated. The experience of the Sunbelt South thus had profound implications for those who prescribed economic modernization as a panacea for the problems of underdeveloped nations, particularly those who continued to expect American investors to sponsor progressive reform and the overall democratization of these societies. Businessmen and industrialists fleeing northern locations were actually running away from labor activism, government supervision, and mounting tax and living costs. They were, therefore, generally opposed to any changes likely to introduce such conditions in their new southern locations. But what of the long-awaited middle class swelled by the in-migration of executives and managers? Would not this new "white-collar" class become a force for innovation and improvement in government and public services and facilities?

Nurtured by the more rapid commercial and industrial expansion of the post–World War II years, the South's business and professional middle class played an active, though ultimately limited, role in promoting social and political change in the region. Immediately after the war, young veterans returning to the South's business and professional ranks led a series of "GI revolts" that overthrew local political rings in urban areas and small towns across the South. These political uprisings represented the first wave of a long-awaited assault on a political structure built around an agricultural system rooted in the rural, small-town South and presided over by the small-town rich man.

Urban businessmen pushed for slum clearance, mass transit, and expanded public facilities and services. In cities like Atlanta, Dallas, and Charlotte, business leaders became the reluctant advocates of acquiescence once school integration had clearly become inevitable, and although their efforts seldom extended beyond what it took to satisfy court orders and stave off protests and demonstrations, the importance of their intervention was nonetheless underscored by the ugly scenes in Birmingham and New Orleans, where the business elite failed to act early or vigorously enough. Ironically, although it led to more liberal racial practices in the short run, the growth of the business and professional classes also hastened the emergence of a viable Republican political alternative in the traditionally Democratic South.

Middle-class expansion clearly did bring some major changes to the South in the post–World War II period, but in the main, business-inspired political reforms aimed to create conditions favorable to efficient operation and rapid expansion of industrial and commercial enterprises. Thus, government became more efficient and generally less corrupt but remained fiscally conservative and especially frugal in the social welfare arena. In Atlanta and elsewhere, business boosters patted themselves on the back for urban renewal, freeway, and mass-transit projects, but their enthusiasm for low-cost public housing was lukewarm at best. Tax structures remained quite favorable to business and industry. Regionwide in 2005, as a percentage of total revenue, state taxes on corporations generally ran from 38 to 80 percent of the national average, while the regressive sales tax accounted for more revenue in states like Mississippi and Louisiana than personal and corporate income taxes combined. The underutilization of tax potential left high-growth areas facing the dilemma of keeping taxes low enough to keep businessmen and industrialists happy without sacrificing the expanded services that a burgeoning population and revived economy seemed to demand. Meanwhile, areas that had lost industries after decades of neglecting schools and infrastructure in order to keep these same employers' tax bills light found themselves with neither the educated labor force nor the up-to-date facilities needed to attract replacements of any sort, suitable or otherwise.

In sum, the expansion of the business and commercial middle class fed many of the changes that marked the post–World War II years, but it failed to spark the extensive, self-sustaining social and political transformation many had predicted. This was due in no small part to the region's lack of a unified, upwardly mobile working class capable of forcing the middle class to support more far-reaching reforms in the interest of maintaining overall stability in southern society. The South's working class remained largely unorganized and hesitant about class-oriented political action. Persistent interregional wage differentials notwithstanding, significant improvement from one generation to the next had left many southern workers reluctant to challenge a system that they seemed to feel had rewarded them reasonably well. In the absence of pressure from below, the South's white middle class was left to use its influence to create and maintain the economic and living conditions it preferred. Many social scientists had predicted that a bona fide middle class would demand drastic improvement in education and other public services, but white-collar southerners generally embraced only such improvements as they deemed directly beneficial to them and theirs, opting otherwise to take advantage of the South's conservative tax climate and minimal service and social welfare commitments.

The story of the development of commerce and industry in the South suggests the difficulty of predicting the outcome of one society's economic development on the basis of another's. For many years, the Marxian perspective drew on the experience of Western Europe to identify certain supposedly inevitable social, cultural, and political concomitants of economic progress. American scholars extended this perspective by drawing on the industrial Northeast, which became, for them, the epitome of the modern, enlightened, liberal capitalist society.

Fascinated with the North's "success story," many observers underestimated the technological, demographic, and resource factors that accounted for the economic, social, and (supposedly) cultural differences that separated the South from the rest of the country. The South's apparent persistence as a distinctive region was so surprising only because so many scholars and other observers had assumed that economic modernization had certain universal results. In reality, the South's experience with economic transformation, though distinctive, was hardly remarkable. No society has ever modernized economically in precisely the same fashion as another because the same set of social, cultural, and economic circumstances is never in place in two truly distinct historical contexts.

As the 21st century unfolded, a contemporary South where skyscrapers, strip malls, and suburban mansions were juxtaposed with rural poverty, hardcore unemployment, and substandard housing bore little physical resemblance to the South where planters once presided over slaves in human bondage and sharecroppers in something that could approximate economic bondage. On the other hand, the symbolic resemblance between the two was sometimes difficult to ignore. After all, the leaders of both Souths had generally contented themselves with the kind of economic development that assured the comfort and satisfaction of their immediate cohort while leaving the more fundamental economic and human needs of a great many of their fellow southerners unmet.

JAMES C. COBB
*University of Georgia*

Fred Bateman and Thomas Weiss, *A Deplorable Scarcity: The Failure of Industrialization in the Slave Economy* (1981); Reinhard Bendix, *Comparative Studies in Society and History* (April 1967); Dwight B. Billings, *Planters and the Making of a New South: Class, Politics, and Development in North Carolina, 1865–1900* (1979); David L. Carlton and Peter A. Coclanis, *The South, the Nation, and the World: Perspectives on Southern Economic Development* (2003); James C. Cobb, *Industrialization and Southern Society, 1877–1984* (1984), *The Selling of the South: The Southern Crusade for Industrial Development, 1936–1990* (2nd ed., 1993), ed. with William Stueck, *Globalization and the American South* (2005); Pete Daniel, *Agricultural History* (July 1981), *Standing at the Crossroads: Southern Life in the Twentieth Century* (1986); Ronald D. Eller, *Miners, Millhands, and Mountaineers: The Modernization of the Appalachian South* (1982); Paul M. Gaston, *The New South Creed: A Study in Southern Mythmaking* (1970); David R. Goldfield, *Cotton Fields and Skyscrapers: Southern City and Region, 1607–1980* (1982); Emory Q. Hawk, *Economic History of the South* (1934); Broadus Mitchell and George S. Mitchell, *The Industrial Revolution in the New South* (1930); Wayne Mixon, *Southern Writers and the New South Movement, 1865–1913* (1980); Gerald D. Nash, *Journal of Southern History* (August 1966); William H. Nicholls, *Southern Tradition and Regional Progress* (1960); William N. Parker, *Southern Economic Journal* (April 1980); Robert S. Starobin, *Industrial Slavery in the Old South* (1970); Jonathan M. Wiener, *American Historical Review* (October 1979), *Social Origins of the New South: Alabama, 1860–1885* (1978); Gavin Wright, *Old South, New South: Revolutions in the Southern Economy since the Civil War* (1986).

## Antebellum Industry

The history of industry in the Old South has been obscured by the long shadow of the plantation. The roar of a blast furnace or the din of a cotton factory were more likely to jar the southern imagination than to capture it, given the South's traditional identification with the pastoral ideal. Much less specialized than their northern peers, southern factory owners often blended their careers with those of planter and politician. Planters who did not become businessmen themselves often invested capital in the industrial expansion, but industrial development in the South lagged far behind the North because it lacked both the capital and social commitment. Regardless of who financed or managed industry, however, established social and economic imperatives determined that slaves would turn the wheels of industry just as surely as they picked the cotton. In fact, slave labor was the most distinctive characteristic of southern industry.

Tobacco factories relied on slave labor almost exclusively. Tobacco products were manufactured in two distinct regions: the eastern district of Virginia and North Carolina and, by the 1850s, the western district of Kentucky and Missouri. Tobacco factories owned their skilled slaves, but they hired most of their bondsmen. The number of slaves employed by tobacco manufactories in the eastern district alone totaled 12,843 by 1860.

Hemp production represented another leading industry of the Old South. During the 18th century, Virginia hemp became a major staple from which osnaburg, linsey-woolsey, linen, rope, and sail were manufactured. Many Virginia planters, such as Robert Carter of Nomini Hall, erected small establishments for the commercial production of cloth. Even in these first small transitional shops between the homespun and the factory stages, slaves spun and wove the finished products. During the Revolutionary War, numerous slaves worked at Virginia's public ropewalk and similar establishments. By the turn of the 19th century, however, the center of the American hemp industry had shifted westward to Kentucky, where the fiber became a staple of major importance. In fact, without hemp, slavery might not have flourished in Kentucky. By the Civil War, nearly 200 Kentucky hemp factories utilized 5,000 bondsmen. By 1860 the industry had expanded into Missouri, where another 2,500 slave operatives toiled in hemp factories.

The Kanawha River Valley of western Virginia was the South's principal center for salt production. The constant demand for this vital food preservative led to a steadily increasing capital investment in its manufacture, and between 1810 and 1850 the Kanawha salt industry grew dramatically. As production in-

creased, the slave population grew apace to 3,140 in 1850. Because so few bondsmen resided in the district, the demand for labor always exceeded supply, so
they also relied on surplus hands from eastern Virginia and Kentucky to keep
their works in operation.

The South possessed an abundance of forest resources. Out of the Mississippi and Louisiana swamps, black bondsmen chopped, trimmed, and rafted
cypress to New Orleans and Natchez, where still other slaves operated the
steam-powered sawmills that could be found in most southern cities. These
mills became sizable operations, frequently employing more than 100 slaves.
Many slaves disappeared into southern swamps for months at a time to cut
wooden shingles and barrel staves. On the eve of the Civil War, most of the
16,000 men who labored in the region's lumbering operations were slaves.
Similarly, the naval stores industry relied on blacks almost entirely. The industry was centered in the Carolinas, an area that produced over 90 percent of
the nation's tar and turpentine in 1850. Large turpentiners, such as Daniel W.
Jordan of North Carolina, utilized slave workforces of 200 or more in 1850. By
1860 the southern turpentiners employed 15,000 bondsmen.

Southern fisheries yielded a very important protein supplement to the diet
of slaves and masters alike, and exports reached significant proportions. The
famous traveler and landscape architect Frederick Law Olmsted observed that
the fishing industry constituted a "source of considerable wealth." Like most industries, fisheries also employed "mainly negroes, slave and free." By 1861, up-
wards of 20,000 slaves operated fisheries in the region. Innumerable slaves not
only fished southern waters but also served as pilots, seamen, raftsmen, barge-
men, and roustabouts, and they could be found in a variety of other water-
related industries.

Although the South lagged far behind the North in internal improvements,
the region's turnpikes, bridges, canals, levees, railroads, city sewers, and water-
lines were all built by slave labor. Probably a total of 20,000 slaves toiled on the
southern railroads during the antebellum period. Blacks also frequently worked
in shipyards (Frederick Douglass being the most famous example) and labored
by the hundreds in southern brickyards and by the thousands in the small local
gristmills that ground flour throughout the region. Commercial mills, such as
the Gallego and Haxall mills (the world's largest) of Richmond, Va., operated
with a full complement of slave manpower. Throughout the South Carolina and
Georgia Tidewater, hundreds of slaves also toiled at the rice mills, while Louisiana and Texas sugar mills depended upon bonded labor exclusively.

Few nonagricultural occupations in the Old South utilized slaves so universally, and over such an extended period of time, as the manufacture of iron

and coal mining. For a half century prior to the American Revolution, Maryland and Virginia iron dominated the colonial export market. Even though the Chesapeake region lost its national preeminence after the Revolution, within the South it remained the most important single center for the production of iron. During the colonial era, at least 65 Maryland and Virginia ironworks, and about 80 during the antebellum period, were operated by thousands of slave laborers. Similarly, the eastern Virginia coalfield produced the major supply of coal for homes and industries along the Atlantic coast from the 1760s until the 1840s, when technological improvements shifted demand to the anthracite coal of Pennsylvania as the fuel of preference. Until the late 1850s, however, when the Alabama, Tennessee, and western Virginia bituminous fields began to attract the attention of serious investors, commercial coal mining in the South was confined almost exclusively to the Richmond Coal Basin, where at least 40 coal companies employed several thousand slave miners.

With the growth of southern industry, slave owners found themselves caught on the horns of a dilemma: which was the best form of labor, black slave or free white? More than simply a question of labor allocation, the ensuing debate reflected a mixture of economic, political, and social anxieties about the nature of southern society. Extensive industrialization threatened the planters with a relative loss of control over their slaves in the more fluid industrial setting, but planters could exert even less control over a free white industrial proletariat. In practice, however, the perennial labor shortage forced southern manufacturers to employ any kind of labor available, and frequently that meant a "mixed" labor force of whites, free blacks, and slaves. Whether slavery impeded the South's industrial development is a question that has vexed historians of the Old South ever since.

RONALD L. LEWIS
*West Virginia University*

Fred Bateman and Thomas Weiss, *A Deplorable Scarcity: The Failure of Industrialization in the Slave Economy* (1981); David S. Cecelski, *The Waterman's Song: Slavery and Freedom in Maritime North Carolina* (2001); James F. Hopkins, *A History of the Hemp Industry in Kentucky* (1951); Ronald L. Lewis, *Coal, Iron, and Slaves: Industrial Slavery in Maryland and Virginia, 1715–1865* (1979); Robert B. Outland III, *Tapping the Pines: The Naval Stores Industry in the American South* (2004); Joseph Clarke Robert, *The Tobacco Kingdom: Plantation, Market, and Factory in Virginia and North Carolina, 1800–1860* (1938); Robert S. Starobin, *Industrial Slavery in the Old South* (1970); Richard C. Wade, *Slavery in the Cities: The South, 1820–1860* (1964).

## Business, Black

West African slaves came from commercial economies and, when permitted, engaged in trade in the New World. The "Sunday markets" of the West Indies and South America were often dominated by Africans who filled them with produce from their garden plots. Such commercial activity, although less flourishing in North America, certainly existed, especially in colonial South Carolina. In fact, a subeconomy carried on by slaves and free blacks in 18th-century South Carolina became so vigorous that the master class legislated against what it feared could become a political as well as an economic underground.

This tightening of the slave system against communication and assembly, the essence of trading activity, intensified during the 19th century, while simultaneously the number of new Africans became proportionately smaller after the closing of the slave trade in 1807. The tendency, then, was for American slaves to become increasingly socialized and assimilated into a dependent and isolated plantation life, while free blacks were squeezed into the bleakest margins of the southern economy. Unlike Latin America, the American South never had a black majority who out of demographic necessity would come to occupy many of the more favorable niches in the economy.

There were, of course, exceptions. Free blacks in South Carolina, where blacks were a majority, established in Charleston a small elite dealing in goods and services for a white clientele. Skilled craftsmen, especially masons, along with barbers, fishermen, grocers, and caterers constituted this specialized business class not only in Charleston but also in New Orleans, Baltimore, Washington, D.C., and other southern cities. After emancipation, only the barbers retained a firm hold on these traditional black occupations. Black artisans, many of them ex-slaves, found themselves displaced by white workers and closed out of craft unions. Displacement and exclusion, however, did not dim the hopes of a rising class of black professionals and entrepreneurs who represented what Booker T. Washington called the "New Negro for a New Century," casting down their buckets in a New South.

Washington believed that business, above all else, could lift his people up from slavery. Beneath his rhetoric, Washington was no devotee of plantations and paternalism. He was bourgeois to the bone, a historical materialist on the right, who counseled that capitalism would neutralize racism and deliver from slavery all those who would attach themselves to its mighty engine. For black workers, this ineluctable force might not work its magic overnight, but in the meantime they were well-advised to invest their labor in the development of the New South, while the black middle class would "take advantage of the dis-

National Negro Business League Executive Committee, ca. 1910; Booker T. Washington, founder, is seated third from the left. (Library of Congress [LC-B2-2053-15], Washington, D.C.)

advantages" and build a duplicate black economy behind the walls of segregation.

Racial solidarity and black capitalism became watchwords in the face of an all-powerful Jim Crow. Benjamin J. Davis, a leading black businessman from Atlanta, reminded his colleagues in 1921 that "the white man does nothing with us that he can with a white man. He builds businesses for the employment of white boys and girls; we must build businesses for the employment of black boys and girls. We must have more producers of wealth." For the disciples of Washington, the black business movement amounted to middle-class millenarianism, with Washington presiding as the high priest and the conventions of the National Negro Business League (founded by Washington in 1900) serving as camp meetings of the faithful testifying to salvation through enterprise.

In retrospect, the business movement appears important mostly as myth and symbol, a bittersweet synthesis of two mainstays in American culture—capitalism and racism. But also there was substance. Black doctors, dentists, bankers, lawyers, journalists, and entrepreneurs, many of them educated in black institutions, took their places in black communities and served a black clientele. The highest statement of racial solidarity came from all-black southern towns, over

50 of which existed by 1910, each theoretically connected with the commercial life of the New South but otherwise separate—each symbolizing a kind of utopian apartheid. By all odds, the most famous was Mound Bayou, Miss.—"a town owned and operated by our people," exulted a black reporter in 1912, a town where "a black mayor with his black aldermen sit in the council chambers making laws," where "a black marshall carries the billy, a black postmaster passes out the mail, a black ticket agent sells the tickets and the white man's waiting room is in the rear."

Although important ideologically, the black towns could not compete economically or culturally with the "Negro Mainstreets" of southern cities, such as Beale Street in Memphis or "Sweet" Auburn Avenue in Atlanta. In these ethnic enclaves, not unlike those of European immigrants in northern cities, a vibrant combination of commercial and cultural life gave black business a larger meaning in the everyday lives of the people. Without Booker T. Washington's faith in American capitalism, these black southerners nonetheless affirmed what had come to be theirs in every community large enough to support a commercial district. Business institutions ranged from "mom and pop" stores and juke joints to modern retail stores, essential services, and, in the largest cities, newspapers, theaters, hotels, banks, and insurance companies.

The insurance firms deserve special mention because they formed the heart of black financial networks, the cultural beginnings of which can be traced to mutual benefit societies and the church. By the turn of the 20th century, the burial insurance offered by the semisacred benefit societies and fraternal lodges increasingly gave way to industrial and ordinary insurance offered by secular enterprises like North Carolina Mutual (1898) and Atlanta Life (1905). This process of modernization warmed the heart of Washington, and had he lived into the 1920s he would have joined in the celebration of Durham, N.C., as the "Capital of the Black Middle Class," the "Black Wall Street of America." By 1924 North Carolina Mutual had spawned in Durham a commercial bank, a savings and loan institution, a fire insurance company, and, along with a cotton mill and lesser enterprises, a national financial clearinghouse and chamber of commerce called the National Negro Finance Corporation (NNFC).

Symbolically, the failure of the NNFC in 1929 may have marked a turning point in the dream of black capitalism. The onset of the Great Depression, trenchant criticism from a new generation of leftist black academics, continuing black migration out of the South, and the impact of World War II and the civil rights movement on the accommodationist ideas of self-help all played a part in the replacement of the dream of Booker T. Washington with the dream of Martin Luther King Jr. The two were not necessarily mutually exclusive, however, and ambivalence on the liberating potential of black capitalism has continued to express itself. Ironically, integration in the South spelled doom for many black businesses whose customers chose to shop in white-owned stores, previously closed to them.

Future case studies may show that black business as culture and history has to be analyzed in subtle, creative ways outside the familiar models of protest and accommodation or neoclassical economics and Marxian theory. From the perspective of women's history, preliminary evidence would suggest that black women, having been less protected than white women by the Victorian cult of domesticity, may have faced fewer internal barriers to entrepreneurial activity. The best 20th-century example of a black woman who apparently felt no such cultural restraints was Madame C. J. Walker, who took her cosmetics industry North and garnered great fame and fortune. But in the long run, scholars may decide that the intimate association between black business and black culture, all within a poignant sense of community, went the way of Beale Street; and that it will be the creative music and the social memory that outlive the commercial meaning of these main streets.

WALTER B. WEARE
*University of Wisconsin–Milwaukee*

John H. Burrows, "The Necessity of Myth: A History of the National Negro Business League, 1900–1945" (Ph.D. dissertation, Auburn University, 1977); Louis R. Harlan, *Booker T. Washington: The Making of a Black Leader, 1856–1901* (1972), *Booker T. Washington: The Wizard of Tuskegee* (1983); Abram L. Harris, *The Negro as Capitalist: A Study of Banking and Business among American Negroes* (1936); Alexa B. Henderson, "A Twentieth-Century Black Enterprise: The Atlanta Life Insurance Company, 1905–1975" (Ph.D. dissertation, Georgia State University, 1975); Robert Kenzer, *Enterprising Southerners: Black Economic Success in North Carolina, 1865–1915* (1997); August Meier, *Negro Thought in America, 1880–1915* (1963); Howard N. Rabinowitz, *Race Relations in the Urban South, 1865–1890* (1978); Arnold Taylor, *Travail and Triumph: Black Life and Culture in the South since the Civil War* (1976); David M. Tucker, *Lieutenant Lee of Beale Street* (1971); Walter B. Weare, *Black Business in the New South: A Social History of the North Carolina Mutual Life Insurance Company* (1973).

# Civil Rights and Business

W. J. Cash argued eloquently in his classic *The Mind of the South* (1941) that the Old South did not die with the Civil War; indeed, he argued, that most tragic of American conflicts strengthened and confirmed Old South values. Extending his thesis into the late 19th and early 20th centuries, Cash argued that even the quest for economic progress of the New South prophets and the business progressives failed to dislodge the prevailing attitudes and values of the pre–Civil War southern mentality, which was characterized by individualism, intolerance, and a commitment to the maintenance of white supremacy. Cash hoped that his brave and original analysis of southern thought and behavior might inspire some introspection and change in his native region.

The convergence of World War II, the mechanization of agriculture, and the beginnings of significant southern industrialization, augmented by the onset of the Cold War (and perhaps by the impact of Cash's analysis), began to create a new pattern on the southern landscape, so much so that by 1958 the celebrated Arkansas editor Harry Ashmore could suggest that the time had come to start preparing an "epitaph for Dixie." Ashmore argued that in the interest of stability and economic progress, the South's businessmen and industrialists would lead the way toward their communities' acceptance of the adjustments the *Brown v. Board of Education* decision required; despite the apparent refutation of that argument in his own city, Ashmore's position proved prophetic.

The South's cities became the battlegrounds for most of the region's civil rights struggles, and the cities were dominated, as always, by small groups of economic or business elites. The degree to which these elites had accepted commercial and industrial values determined the nature of their cities' responses to the civil rights assault on traditional southern race relations. From the quintessential New South city of Atlanta, the city that was "too busy to hate," to the fine old southern community of St. Augustine, where violence and extremism abounded, the South's cities ranged across the spectrum from progressive to traditional. But in most of these cities, after the initial shock of disbelief and the occasional abdication of power to the extremists, the businessmen regained control of their communities and worked with varying degrees of enthusiasm to preserve their cities' progressive "images." Aided by representatives from the Little Rock Chamber of Commerce, who spoke widely across the region about the futility of resistance and the price of assuming such a stance, the South's business leaders spread the word throughout the populace that they did not want their communities to become "another Little Rock." In city after city— from Norfolk to Tampa, from Birmingham to Dallas—business leaders threw their influence behind desegregation efforts.

This is not to say that the businessmen became advocates of the civil rights cause or champions of racial equality. In fact, in most cases, again following the lead that Little Rock's business leaders suggested, southern businessmen worked to yield a minimum of change and to maintain control in their own hands. They did, however, defy the dominant ethic of resistance—often at considerable risk to their own economic and physical well-being—and become public advocates of the dreaded changes in southern race relations. They also used their influence to guarantee peaceful acceptance of the required modifications in their communities' traditional patterns of racial interactions. Responding to unremitting federal and activist pressures for change, the region's business leaders became reluctant advocates of the fundamental alterations of southern racial patterns that the *Brown* decision demanded. In doing so, they led the way toward acceptance of a new pattern of thought in the South.

For a brief period after World War II, southern business elites allowed themselves to believe they could maintain the traditional pattern of the South's race relations even as they pursued industrialization and progress. The *Brown* decision removed that chimera, and the subsequent civil rights movement made the South's business leaders realize they had to choose between the past and the future. In choosing, the leadership of the South's major cities consciously accepted a new ordering of their region's traditional priorities, placing economic imperatives above racial ones. At last, the "common resolve indomitably maintained" that the South should preserve white supremacy began to yield primacy in southern thought to the pursuit of economic advancement. It was a subtle but significant shift, and it heralded the arrival of a new era in southern life.

ELIZABETH JACOWAY
*University of Arkansas at Little Rock*

Harry S. Ashmore, *An Epitaph for Dixie* (1958); Wilbur J. Cash, *The Mind of the South* (1941); William Chafe, *Civilities and Civil Rights: Greensboro, North Carolina, and the Black Struggle for Freedom* (1980); David R. Colburn, *Racial Change and Community Crisis: St. Augustine, Florida, 1877–1980* (1985); Glenn T. Eskew, *But for Birmingham: The Local and National Movements in the Civil Rights Struggle* (1997); Elizabeth Jacoway and David R. Colburn, eds., *Southern Businessmen and Desegregation* (1982); Diane McWhorter, *Carry Me Home: Birmingham, Alabama, the Climactic Battle of the Civil Rights Revolution* (2001); J. Mills Thornton III, *Dividing Lines: Municipal Politics and the Struggle for Civil Rights in Montgomery, Birmingham, and Selma* (2002).

## "Colony," South as

From Jamestown to Fort Sumter, there was a three-way conflict over exactly who would control the output of southern labor, both white and black. The British Crown attempted, sporadically, to gain control of the southern surplus of goods for itself, or at least for its merchant friends; the commercial interests of the northern colonies, later states, wanted to control the surplus; and the southern planters thought it would be appropriate to keep it close to home. As long as the institution of slavery existed, the southern planters could explore strategies to maintain high prices partly through low labor costs. Once slavery and its political power were destroyed, it was hardly to be expected that a new system of high wages would replace it.

In this view, then, the colonial position of the South was first defined in the explicit establishment of the slave system. As in many "settler colonies," the planters of the South attempted to avoid the losses of unequal exchange with other areas and to keep the surplus of produced goods at home. In these efforts, the planters were extremely sensitive to the pitfalls of a colonial status, they advanced the cause of the American Revolution, and they subsequently propounded an ideology of southern nationalism. Their ultimate failure left the South in the late 19th and early 20th centuries in its most clearly colonial situation.

The treatment thus far of the South as a colony helps to reconcile conflicting views of the colonial status of the region. On the one hand, those historians who have tended to label the South as a colony have emphasized the striking sensitivity of southern leadership to symptoms of colonial status—low levels of urbanization, specialization in agriculture, and a poor system of transportation. On the other hand, those who have denied the colonial position of the South have pointed to the high levels of productivity and per capita income achieved in the mid-19th century. In the present approach to defining a colony, the relatively high per capita income of the South represented the remarkable success of the planter class in injecting itself between slave and market. The sensitivity of that class to symptoms of dependency underscored their awareness of the precarious role they were playing. Surely the most dramatic change in the distribution of the national income in the United States occurred between 1860 and 1880. The planters' success in the antebellum period represented a prodigious juggling act, and the Civil War seemed to expose their weakness.

It would be surprising if the southern worldview did not reflect the region's experience with colonial status. Indeed, some would argue that white southerners were far too engrossed in the colonial analogy. At least in part, this was the result of the white southerner's direct observation of slavery. The awareness of slave dependency gave a uniquely southern meaning first to the revolutionary protest and subsequently to a broad spectrum of political-economic initiatives. The assertion of the South's colonial status explained, even if it did not justify, the origin and persistence of slavery for many southerners. At the same time, the denunciation of the colonial status created a way for white southerners to prove that they, unlike the slaves around them, would not tolerate a condition of dependency. In the late 19th and early 20th centuries, these themes, only slightly modified, became stock components of southern politics. As a result, even those most closely allied to northern interests were likely to use the colonial analogy. And, of course, this analogy lies behind the entire history of the states' rights debate, both its serious content and its cliché rhetoric. The idea of economic and political dependency has been continually present in both the formal and popular thought of the South.

In the 20th century, the South experienced strong and surprisingly steady economic growth. This record has often been used to question the colonial designation. But the issue is not so much whether the South was dependent on the North circa 1900, which would be difficult to deny, but rather why its subsequent development was so different from a colonial area such as Latin America. Quite simply, some colonies are more favored than others. The South, because of location, political security, and political integration, was a logical first choice for capital seeking low wages. The process was anything but speedy. Nevertheless, it did occur, and the post–World War II economic development resulted in a substantial rise in southern wages. Indeed, the difference in development between the now-advanced southern United States and the Third World economies of Mexico or Argentina reveals the critical importance of geographic, political, and other noneconomic factors in the classical convergence of labor and capital to build a growing economy.

For years, the colonial analogy cited by southerners was sustained by an awareness of their differentness from other Americans and a sense of being abused. With the ongoing homogenization of the regions of the United States, there is the temptation to consider this matter closed. But southern writers who have considered the South's role in the nation have always insisted that the desirable alternative to overly specialized regional economies is not a characterless collection of interchangeable parts. For all of their reactionary leanings and racist psychology, intellectuals like George Fitzhugh in the 19th century and the Vanderbilt Agrarians in the 20th century understood that parity in income between the regions is not the same as self-determination for all of them in the national context. Although unequal wages between North and South may have long been the cause of the colonial condition, equal wages now still may not establish full southern economic independence. The degree of independence possible in the modern technocratic society remains in question. Recent scholarship on the "global South," moreover, positions the South as a postcolonial society linked to other places around the globe that suffered through similar histories.

JOSEPH PERSKY
*University of Illinois at Chicago*

David Bertelson, *The Lazy South* (1967); Clarence Danhof, in *Essays in Southern Economic Development*, ed. Melvin Greenhut and W. Tate Whitman (1964); Arghiri Emmanuel, *Unequal Exchange: A Study of the Imperialism of Trade* (1972); George Fitzhugh, *Sociology for the South* (1854); John McCardell, *The Idea of a Southern Nation: Southern Nationalists and Southern Nationalism, 1830–1860* (1979); Joseph Persky, *The Burden of Dependency: Colonial Themes in Southern Economic Thought* (1992).

## Expositions and World's Fairs

Beginning in the late 19th century, many cities in the American South hosted large expositions and fairs that were intended to promote the host cities by displaying the best of modern achievement. In part because the South had a more rural population, expositions set in southern cities were on a smaller scale than their northern counterparts. Yet, most of these southern expositions still managed to draw hundreds of thousands, if not millions, of visitors. For all of their popularity, however, southern fairs experienced a lull in the early 20th century. A half-century hiatus divides southern expositions into two distinct eras, the first spanning the decades following Reconstruction and the second occurring after the civil rights movement.

The first international fair hosted in the United States was Philadelphia's 1876 Centennial Exposition, and its economic success prompted other American cities to host large fairs. Prior to technological advancements in mass communication, these expositions operated as public relations campaigns, attracting tourists with sights that entertained and advertised local accomplishments. A disproportionately high number of fairs appeared in the South between 1881 and 1907, as city leaders worked to transform their civic and southern identity to jumpstart local economies and better compete in the Progressive Era.

The largest fair in America after 1876, Louisville's Southern Exposition opened on 1 August 1883. Over 770,000 people attended the fair, leading the exposition to remain open seasonally for the next four years in what is now the Old Louisville neighborhood. The exposition's main building covered approximately 13 acres and featured machinery exhibits. Additional displays included an art gallery, a lumber mill, a carriage house, and a working farm. As an incentive for fairgoers to stay into the night, Thomas Edison illuminated the fairgrounds with over 4,600 lights, the largest electric installation of the time.

After the Southern Exposition closed in 1887, real-estate developer William Slaughter built the Saint James Court development. Saint James Court, Belgravia Court, and Central Park remain popular Louisville landmarks in the vicinity of the former exposition.

Encouraged by the success of the Louisville fair, New Orleans city leaders planned the World Cotton Centennial for 1884. The planning and construction phases, however, were marked by scandal and setback when the fair's director, Edward Burke, absconded to Brazil with much of the fair treasury. Investors persevered, however, expecting to recoup losses in the fair's season. Construction continued as the chosen site, a tract of land stretching from St. Charles Avenue to the Mississippi, was transformed into a lush park featuring fountains, bridges, walks, tropical plants, and 5,000 electric lights. Despite local popularity, the fair did not recover the investors' losses. An attempt to repackage the fair as the North, Central, and South American Exposition a year later also proved financially unsuccessful. Fair buildings were publicly auctioned off, most going only for their worth in scrap materials.

In a span of just 14 years, the city of Atlanta held three large-scale expositions as civic boosters worked to promote the city as a national industrial center. Atlanta hosted its first fair, the International Cotton Exposition, in the fall of 1881. Oglethorpe Park, located west of downtown, was chosen for the fair's site. Organizers modeled the grounds after a cotton factory to promote Atlanta as a cotton center and to reuse the site after the fair's close. During the exposition's two-and-a-half-month season, 200,000 paying fairgoers visited. Afterwards, the main building was converted into the Exposition Cotton Mill, which operated from 1882 until 1971.

Atlanta's second fair occurred six years after the International Cotton Exposition. Located north of downtown at what is now Piedmont Park, the 1887 Piedmont Exposition was the smallest of the Atlanta fairs, running just 12 days in October 1887. The most notable highlight of the exposition was a visit by President Grover Cleveland. At the fair's close, the site was returned to the Gentleman's Driving Club, which changed its name to the Piedmont Driving Club shortly thereafter.

The tremendous cultural influence and economic success of Chicago's 1893 Columbian Exposition inspired Atlanta boosters to hold the city's last and largest fair. The 1895 Cotton States and International Exposition attracted 800,000 people to the grounds of the Piedmont Driving Club over its 14-week season. While President Cleveland visited and John Phillip Sousa composed

"King Cotton" for the event, the most remembered fairgoer was Booker T. Washington, who delivered his "Atlanta Compromise" speech on 18 September 1895. In addition to the famed orators, state buildings, Women's Building, fish exhibit, model jail, and touring liberty bell, the exposition held a 25,000-square-foot Negro Building containing portraits of famous African Americans alongside models of a slave mammy's cabin and a freeman's field. Afterwards, most buildings were torn down and materials sold for scrap.

On 1 May 1897 the gates of the Tennessee Centennial and International Exposition opened in Nashville. Prominent Nashvillians organized the fair, which started a year late, to celebrate Tennessee's 1796 entry into the Union. Designers constructed over a dozen neoclassical buildings, curvilinear roads, lush landscaping, and a man-made lake. Fine arts were housed in a replica of the Parthenon, which stood as the fair's centerpiece in homage to Nashville's nickname, the "Athens of the South." By closing day on 31 October, the fair had drawn approximately 1.8 million visitors, making it the largest 19th-century southern exposition. Afterwards, the city converted the fairgrounds into Centennial Park. The Parthenon still stands at the park's center.

The South Carolina Inter-State and West Indies Exposition opened just north of Charleston on 22 December 1901. Like many previous world's fairs, this exposition promoted its host city to help spur local economic development. The city of Charleston was severely damaged by a hurricane in 1885, and local businessmen hoped the exposition would increase trade through Charleston's harbor, developing it into a key port between the United States, the Caribbean, and Latin America. However, lack of federal support, inadequate funding, and no official foreign exhibits factored into the exposition's disappointing overall financial impact.

From 26 April to 1 December 1907, approximately 3 million visitors toured the grounds of the Jamestown Exposition near Norfolk, Va. Built to celebrate the 300th anniversary of Jamestown's founding, the fair fell short of expectations. Less than half the planned buildings were finished by opening day, and the historically significant yet remote location made travel undesirable for many potential fairgoers. While daily reenactments of the Battle of Hampton Roads and the San Francisco Earthquake attracted praise, the Negro Building was chastised by some African American leaders as exhibiting Jim Crow more than black accomplishment—all African American displays were confined to that building. Despite financial shortcomings and vocal criticism, the fair was influential in the construction of Naval Station Norfolk.

The number of expositions increased substantially after 1870. By 1915, up to six cities annually hosted some form of a world's fair. While world's fairs of varying sizes were held during the 20th century at many northern sites, southern cities hosted smaller exhibitions, including Knoxville's 1913 National Conservation Exposition, Yorktown's 1913 Yorktown Sesquicentennial, and Miami's 1931 Pan American Fair. A world's fair did not come to the southern United States until the late 1960s. By this point, fairs had gone out of vogue in mainstream America as new forms of entertainment arose. The three fairs held in San Antonio, Knoxville, and New Orleans did not reach financial expectations, prompting cities to consider other avenues of attracting international recognition.

The 1968 HemisFair, held in San Antonio, was the first and only officially designated world's fair to be held in Texas. Open 6 April through 6 October 1968, the HemisFair was held on the southeastern edge of San Antonio. The fair's theme, "The Confluence of Civilizations in the Americas," was displayed in the Tower of the Americas. While the HemisFair attracted over 6 million visitors, it never recovered the initial costs invested by donors. In April 1988 part of the fair site was rededicated as HemisFair Park.

With a population of only 180,000, Knoxville hosted the 1982 World's Fair. Over 11 million people visited the fair between 1 May and 31 October. The Sunsphere, a 266-foot tower topped with a five-story bronze globe, marks Knoxville's skyline from the fairgrounds between downtown and the University of Tennessee. Rides and refreshment stands, along with the U.S. Pavilion, Tennessee Amphitheater, and a 10-foot-tall Rubik's Cube, attracted enough visitors for the fair to be one of the most popular in U.S. history. However, the fair's profit of just $57 fell far short of the $5 million projected surplus.

Using the theme "The World of Rivers—Fresh Water as a Source of Life," New Orleans held the 1984 Louisiana World's Exposition along the Mississippi near the French Quarter. Twenty-six nations contributed pavilions and investors pumped $350 million into the fair's budget, which called for renovation of the fair site, an old railroad yard, and surrounding warehouses. While the timing of New Orleans' second exposition seemed appropriate (100 years after the city's World Cotton Centennial), the timing and placement of the fair were far from ideal. Two years and two states away from the last world's fair in Knoxville, the New Orleans exposition saw low attendance and was the only fair to declare bankruptcy during its six-month run.

Large expositions in the South sought not only to attract business but also to display the "New South" to a local, national, and international audience. Still, for all the flaunted leaps in mechanical and technological progress, exhibits tackling issues of race and gender were often relegated to separate pavilions if displayed at all. Southern fairs held in the post–civil rights movement chose to emphasize technology, ecology, and national identity over specific south-ernness. Nonetheless, all fairs held in southern cities contributed to American notions of economic progress, regional identity, and civic pride.

SARAH TOTON
*Emory University*

Kathryn Anne Bratcher, *Filson Newsmagazine*, vol. 4, no. 1 (2003); Bruce G. Harvey, "World's Fairs in a Southern Accent: Atlanta, Nashville, Charleston, 1895–1902" (Ph.D. dissertation, Vanderbilt University, 1998).

## Globalization

"Of all the Americans," James McBride Dabbs wrote, "the Southerner is the most at home in the world. Or at least in the South, which, because of its very at-homeness, he is apt to confuse with the world." One might see here a nascent ideology of globalism—southern hospitality as humanism—while recognizing also an insularity that was inward-looking rather than hospitable.

A historical perspective reveals a globalized South that preceded the south-ern identity, contributing to and then molded in part by the American Civil War, Reconstruction, and Jim Crow. In the 21st century, the American South is reemerging as a global player and is potentially a distinctive contributor to world culture.

As David Moltke-Hansen and others have shown, the concept of "the South" as a firm regional identity is relatively recent, emerging in about 1830. The South as an identity was created for political, economic, and cultural reasons as people spread from the older southeastern states westward to Arkansas and Alabama. Literary figures such as William Gilmore Simms forged the identity, and political dispute, then war, hardened it. It was preceded by a global time when the South was emerging as an economic force and was a culturally di-verse area attracting a variety of immigrants. At least 50 languages were spoken in Charleston alone in the 18th century. Charleston's per capita income in that century was the highest in the nation, perhaps in the world. Few thought of the South as a particular region of the emerging new nation. It is intriguing to imagine that Thomas Jefferson and John Adams, close friends whom we now imagine as southerner and northerner, might not have thought of those identi-ties at all in their day, the late 18th and early 19th centuries.

In its global connections, then, the 18th-century South had more in com-mon with the South of 2008 than with the late 19th- or 20th-century South. The intervening two centuries gave birth to the burden of southern history, with slavery and defeat forging a southern identity often oppositional to the

North and the nation. Now, in the 21st century, the South has reemerged as an economic force and again is attracting immigrants, particularly Asians and Hispanics. This global epoch provides an opportunity for southern identity to move from oppositional within the nation to integrative within the world.

Commentators such as Peter Applebome, writing as recently as the late 1990s, recognized changes in the South, but primarily within a national perspective—how the South was growing in national influence and how America was becoming "Dixiefied" even as Dixie was becoming Americanized, to use the phrase of John Egerton. But the South is, like the rest of the world, also part of the global economy and culture, and it has been accelerating toward greater globalization since the end of the 20th century.

What is globalization? More to the point, how is globalization emerging in the South?

Globalization is the integration of the world—economically, politically, and culturally. Globalization has local impacts in each of those areas. It creates diversity as people, goods, and ideas migrate from one place to another. Globalization is not just capitalism, booming when the economy booms, disappearing when it falters, as in recent times; it is also an attitude. Recent data suggest that southerners tend toward a global attitude, but "southernism" and "globalism" are not tangible things, absolute conditions, but tendencies. Southernism is defined culturally, historically, economically, psychologically, and geographically as a concern and identification with the South. Globalism is a concern and identity with the wider world. The two concerns and identities can clash but also overlap and interweave.

Data from the 2001 Southern Focus Poll, administered by the *Atlanta Journal-Constitution*, suggest that while some southerners see themselves as both different from nonsoutherners and connected to the world as a whole, a majority of those surveyed focus first on global ties. When asked whether they saw themselves primarily as different from nonsoutherners or linked to people around the world, nearly 50 percent of respondents answered "connected to people around the world." Less than a third of those surveyed viewed themselves initially in terms of their difference from nonsoutherners.

Aside from a poll, signs of globalization are everywhere in the South, though of course it is globalization with a southern accent. (This is true literally: children of immigrants from China, Germany, and elsewhere speak like their peers, many of whom have southern accents.) Diversity affects everyday life; teller machines at banks ask customers: "English or Spanish?" The majority of agricultural workers in North Carolina are now Hispanic.

Not only is the world coming to the South, but the South is also going to the world. The South has a long tradition of contributing globally. Even in its dark days, it led world missions, sent some of its children for education overseas, and traded its cotton on foreign markets, and now it is a leader in new global businesses.

Yet the South is a distinctive player within the American role of global leader. The South has a special connection to the Third World, for the South itself was and is in part a Third World nation. Studies show how the South as a plantation system displayed strong similarities to and differences from Russian and Prussian estate owners, Junkers of East Germany, and colonial plantation-based societies in the Caribbean, Latin America, and other places. James E. Crisp at North Carolina State University defines the South as a unique over-lap of a white majority and a plantation society. The South can be seen as the northernmost extension of the plantation system of South America and the Caribbean and the southernmost extension of a dominant northern European culture. Others compare the South with South Africa, and Alistair Sparks's *The Mind of South Africa* (1990) is explicitly modeled after W. J. Cash's *The Mind of the South* (1941). Others note parallels and connections among British, Dutch, and French colonial economies and societies and the antebellum South. Slavery or its equivalent ended almost simultaneously in all of these places around the 1860s, and often for similar reasons as in the South. The dramatic impact that Harriet Beecher Stowe's *Uncle Tom's Cabin* (1852) had on the slavery debate in the 1850s found a parallel in the impact of the book *Max Havelaar* by Multatuli (Eduard Douwes Dekker) in the Netherlands East Indies, later Indonesia, in the 1860s. The South is one example of a more general pattern of plantation-based society with a colonial background.

The South has, to be sure, many First World or "North" features: Bank of America is the nation's second-largest bank; Charlotte, its corporate home, ranks second after New York in banking assets; and the South represents the fourth-largest economy in the world. Southern products and services flow around the globe: Coca-Cola, cigarettes, CNN, Delta, SAS, Quintiles. Missionaries still provide enormous services. Southern Baptist missionaries, for example, have served as leaders in hospitals in many areas from Nigeria to Indonesia.

Are these, however, wholly "southern" enterprises? Yes, in that they originate in or are based in the American South. But the question remains whether the South conveys any distinctive ideas to the world. The South's cultural features, such as Protestantism and its general northern European heritage, connect it just as often with the global North as with a global version of itself.

Certain experiences and values define the South as potentially a mediating force between the United States and much of the world, especially other

"Souths," whether South Asia, South Africa, or South America. Blues and bluegrass, Cajun or New Orleans dishes, grits and cornbread are identified as southern, and the music conveys messages—spirituals with their deep themes of oppression and "we shall overcome." Lessons of life that the South can convey derive from its burden of history, including not only war, defeat, and the experience of being colonized, but also internal problems (the oppression of African Americans, women, poor whites, and Native Americans) and values (traditions of kinship, family, community, and the valuing of a sense of place). These experiences and qualities are distinctive yet also similar to those of other Souths, and they afford this South special roles in the traffic of international relations and cultural construction.

Michael O'Brien has argued that the South, as a part of the United States, can resonate with Europe in a special way—that is, as apart from unrelenting American triumphalism—and his point could apply throughout the world. One of the most famous fictional southerners, Scarlett O'Hara, has much in common, for example, with women in many societies throughout the world: she is part of a patriarchal order, one that is colonized and defeated; yet she struggles, fails, and prevails. Indonesian women's accounts of experiences that resemble southern women's during wartime suggest very similar attitudes. Perhaps this helps explain the appeal of *Gone with the Wind* globally. Scarlett is closer to women in much of the world than are, say, Gloria Steinem or Hillary Clinton. She is more like Megawati Sukarnoputri, whose name itself (Sukarnoputri, daughter of Indonesia's leader, Sukarno) bespeaks patriarchy combined with feminine power (Megawat).

The South makes a particular contribution to globalism by buttressing the value of place. Paradoxically, transcendent ethics that ignore place have fostered the destruction of the earth: they define mission and exploit place to achieve it. Alternative ethics value the earth, including the place we inhabit, and preserve and sustain it as an ultimate value in itself. The value of place, at least in principle, can be part of this position (as Thomas Berry shows in his 1999 book *The Great Work*). In this sense, the agrarian ethic of Jefferson and of Goethe is more communal and less destructive than the industrial ethic of Franklin. Southerners have long since claimed a special sense of place. Maybe the Vanderbilt Agrarians were right, but their views need refinement through global ecology.

Whatever the contribution of the South to the world, the key point is that a global South differs fundamentally from a regional South. The South as region is defined as oppositional to the nation, while the South as global is defined as integrated with the world. The South did not fight the world—it fought the rest of the nation. Hence it can be global without the resentment and emotional baggage that it brings when it reunites with the nation. And the South with its kinship to other Souths can be global with a difference—a tempered globalization, qualified and balanced by a sense of place.

JAMES L. PEACOCK
CARRIE MATTHEWS
*University of North Carolina at Chapel Hill*

Peter Applebome, *Dixie Rising: How the South Is Shaping American Values, Politics, and Culture* (1996); Thomas Berry, *The Great Work: Our Way into the Future* (1999); James C. Cobb and William Stueck, eds., *Globalization and the American South* (2005); Peter A. Coclanis, *The Shadow of a Dream: Economic Life and Death in the South Carolina Low Country, 1670–1920* (1989); James McBride Dabbs, *Who Speaks for the South?* (1964); John Egerton, *The Americanization of Dixie: The Southernization of America* (1974); David Goldfield, in *Which "Global Village"? Societies, Cultures, and Political Economic Systems in a Euro-Atlantic Perspective*, ed. Valeria Gennaro (2002); Lothar Hönighaussen, Marc Frey, and James Peacock, *Regionalism in the Age of Globalism*, vols. 1 and 2 (2005); David Moltke-Hansen and Michael O'Brien, eds., *Intellectual Life in Antebellum Charleston* (1986); Michael O'Brien, *Southern Cultures* 4, no. 4 (1998); James Peacock, *Virginia Quarterly Review* (Autumn 2002); James Peacock, Harry Watson, and Carrie Matthews, eds., *The American South in a Global World* (2005); Celeste Ray, *Highland Heritage: Scottish Americans in the American South* (2001).

## Industrialization, Resistance to

In the South before the Civil War, the prevailing philosophy held that a culture rooted in an agricultural economy and agrarian values was superior to any other. Although manufacturing, largely of the household variety, existed in the region on a level comparable to that of New England early in the 19th century, sectional differences soon began to emerge. Aided by the disruption of overseas commerce surrounding the War of 1812, the factory system began to expand in the North. By midcentury, northerners who 50 years before had harbored grave doubts about extensive industrialization viewed it as a positive good.

By and large, southerners underwent no such conversion. Here and there, a manufacturer such as William Gregg or an editor such as J. D. B. De Bow heralded the benefits of industrial progress. Yet economic factors seemed to offer no compelling reason to promote industrialization. If one might earn a high return on an investment in manufacturing, it was also possible to make good money in the more customary manner of investing in land and slaves. To many cautious and conservative southerners, the proper course was still the improvement of agriculture.

More important than narrow economic considerations in the antebellum South's resistance to industrialization were broad social concerns: the popular belief that a factory system might rely on the labor of black slaves and the accompanying fear that discipline would be diminished and the chance of rebellion enhanced; the suspicion that if white people were employed, their attachment to slavery might be weakened by adopting an industrial outlook; and the conviction that industrial labor robbed a person of humanity and rendered him or her a wage slave of little social worth.

In the good society that antebellum southerners believed was theirs, the planter was the beau ideal. Rare indeed was the plantation master who left the land to become an industrialist. Among the plain folk, or yeomen, there were many who believed with Thomas Jefferson that "those who labour in the earth are the chosen people of God . . . his peculiar deposit for substantial and genuine virtue."

The Civil War created a fundamental change in the attitude of many southerners. One of the region's most notable casualties was the agrarian ideal, severely wounded in the conflict. Union armies had hardly sealed the fate of the Old South before some southerners began proclaiming a "New South." For many of its leaders, a New South meant above all else an industrialized South with an economy modeled on that of the victorious North.

As the ranks of industrial promoters swelled—recruited largely by urban editors such as Henry W. Grady, Henry Watterson, and Richard H. Edmonds—those southerners who resisted industrialization increasingly found themselves a besieged garrison, heavily outnumbered. Still, they fought hard, from the end of the war to the end of the century. Whether opposing industrialization in general as contrary to the best in southern tradition or denouncing the form of regional industrialization as wantonly exploitative, the critics often upheld the ideal of the South as an Arcadian alternative to a materialistic national culture. Yet, despite the best efforts of an orator such as Charles C. Jones Jr., of editors such as Albert T. Bledsoe and D. H. Hill, of churchmen like Robert L. Dabney, J. C. C. Newton, and Benjamin M. Palmer, and of writers like Sidney Lanier, Mark Twain, George W. Cable, and Joel Chandler Harris, those who resisted industrialization were seldom able to effect action. Even the Populists of the 1890s, the strongest challengers of Gilded Age capitalism, could not reverse those policies of the New South establishment that encouraged reckless industrialism from which, the Populists argued, most southerners received little benefit.

As of 1900 the New South movement toward industrialization had failed to change the South's economic position relative to that of other parts of the nation. Notwithstanding a considerable increase in the number of factories, the South remained predominantly agricultural, with only a little more than 6 percent of its labor force working in manufacturing.

Undaunted, southern leaders early in the 20th century continued to pursue industry. Convinced that poverty, illiteracy, and disease were caused primarily by the region's agricultural economy, many southern Progressives believed that industrialization would deliver the region from those evils.

A few southerners were not so sure. Here and there, voices were raised in dissent. In the pages of *Uncle Remus's Magazine*, Joel Chandler Harris warned that the liabilities of industrialization might overbalance the assets. Historian William E. Dodd wondered what effect the educational philanthropy of northern industrialists would have upon the independence of southern academicians. Reverend Alexander J. McKelway, a leader in the movement to prohibit labor by children in southern factories, became disgusted with what he called the mercenary New South.

The objections of the skeptics notwithstanding, the industrial tide continued to roll in, cresting in the boosterism of the 1920s. During the "dollar decade," resistance came largely from bookish people whom practical people either ridiculed or ignored, although the work of some of those intellectuals would provide a telling critique of industrialism.

Many of the 12 men who contributed essays to *I'll Take My Stand: The South and the Agrarian Tradition* (1930) celebrated the yeoman ideal; all of them lamented the coming of an industrial society that massed individuals physically as it atomized them spiritually, reducing them to pawns of the marketplace. In more than 200 essays written throughout the 1930s, some of these Vanderbilt Agrarians continued to defend the South's agricultural society, charging that large-scale industrialization, by allowing too few people to own too much wealth and by creating a large, insecure proletariat, would rend the social fabric and encourage a politics dominated by either plutocrats or socialists. The Agrarians proposed that the pernicious influence of industrialism be contained by distributing land widely among the American people, by encouraging subsistence farming, and by establishing regional governments to ensure that the South remain free of northern domination.

Even more forceful in defending the agrarian ideal than the Vanderbilt intellectuals was the Georgia writer Erskine Caldwell. For Caldwell, who flirted with communism, upholding the ideal meant exposing the revolting reality of life on the land among the destitute, which he did in fiction (most notably, *Tobacco*

*Road* [1932]) and in nonfiction (especially *You Have Seen Their Faces* [1937]). The tenant-farming system, he argued, should be replaced by cooperative farming. Caldwell's most scathing denunciation of industrialization as it had developed in the South came in the novel *God's Little Acre* (1933), where he condemned not only predatory cotton-mill owners but also weak-kneed labor unions.

For a brief season in the 1930s, some of the proposals offered by Caldwell and the Agrarians received a hearing from public officials, but glimmerings of economic recovery rekindled the desire of southerners for more industry. Even before the Great Depression ended, the booster spirit of the 1920s had reappeared in full force.

Propelled by World War II, manufacturing accelerated throughout the South. The region was becoming more industrial than agricultural, with only one-third of its population still on the farm in 1945. After the war, the attempts of promoters to "sell" the advantages of the South to industrialists elsewhere reached unprecedented proportions. Public efforts to attract industry were many and varied: local governments financed plant construction, sometimes in violation of state constitutions; tax levies were either abnormally low or nonexistent; advertising expenditures far exceeded that of the rest of the nation; labor was kept cheap, docile, and unorganized; and state governments implemented "start-up" programs for new businesses. By 1960 southern cultural thought had come full circle. What distinguished the South from the rest of the nation was not the fervor of the region's resistance to industrialization but rather the intensity of its yearning for more of it. And the desire grew ever more ardent, as many southerners felt that, at long last, it was their turn to enjoy a fair share of American affluence.

Opposition either to the idea of further industrialization or to the form that it took in the South came largely from literary figures, a tradition that had emerged with Lanier and Harris, continued through the Agrarians, Caldwell, and William Faulkner, and found contemporary expression in writers such as Wendell Berry, Harry M. Caudill, Janisse Ray, and James Dickey. Opposition also came occasionally from scholars: a distinguished southern historian warned that, if the region's past were any guide, the South would fail to profit from mistakes made by the North during the course of its industrialization and would suffer many of the same problems. Organized opposition also came from those directly victimized by the excesses of industrialism: residents of Appalachia and other parts of the South suffering displacement by the strip mining of coal; miners suffering from black lung; and textile workers suffering from brown lung. Southerners generally became aware of a major cost of extensive industrialization: pollution. As industrial waste fouled the streams, coastline, and air of the South, state governments responded by creating agencies to control that refuse; each southern state had such a body by 1971. Moreover, chambers of commerce and development boards sometimes recruited industries more selectively. Occasionally, industrial projects were abandoned because it was feared that they would irreparably damage an area's ecology.

Critics of industrialization charged that all too often the regulators failed to enforce the inadequate restrictions that did exist, particularly against powerful offenders, and that a clean environment took second place to economic growth in the South's scale of values. Critics contended that the spillover from urban sprawl caused by industrialization was resulting in the overdevelopment of areas of great natural beauty such as the southern mountains. They questioned the promoters' claims that higher incomes and an unprecedented abundance of material goods meant perforce that life was better for most southerners. They pointed to data that suggested that the quality of life in the South had not been improved at all by industrialization and to other data that showed that for all the impressive gains the South had made, it remained, even in strictly economic terms, at the bottom of the nation, despite more than a hundred years of industrial promotion. Critics feared that if industrialization continued apace, the atomistic mass culture that characterized much of the rest of the country would overwhelm the organic folk culture that had long distinguished the South. Nevertheless, as the region entered the 21st century, those articulate southerners who resisted industrialization appeared to be the distinct minority.

WAYNE MIXON
*Augusta State University*

Fred Bateman and Thomas Weiss, *A Deplorable Scarcity: The Failure of Industrialization in the Slave Economy* (1981); James C. Cobb, *The Selling of the South: The Southern Crusade for Industrial Development, 1936–1990* (1993); Paul M. Gaston, *The New South Creed: A Study in Southern Mythmaking* (1970); Wayne Mixon, *Southern Writers and the New South Movement, 1865–1980* (1980), *The People's Writer: Erskine Caldwell and the South* (1995); Paul V. Murphy, *The Rebuke of History: The Southern Agrarians and American Conservative Thought* (2001); Norris W. Preyer, *Georgia Historical Quarterly* (Fall 1971); Twelve Southerners, *I'll Take My Stand: The South and the Agrarian Tradition* (1930); Mary Ann Wimsatt, *Mississippi Quarterly* (Fall 1980).

## Industrialization and Change

It is a persistent myth, running through popular and academic writing, that industry in the South is of recent origin. Some views attribute the birth of industrialism to the New South movement at the end of the 19th century, others to the notable rise of the Sunbelt South since World War II. Such truncated accounts of economic modernization ignore the deep roots and persistent patterns of southern industrial development. For at least 100 years, from the antebellum origins of the factory system to the collapse of the plantation system during the Great Depression, the shape and pace of industrial growth and social change in the region developed in relation to southern agriculture.

Slaveholding and the plantation system set limits on industrial and urban growth in the antebellum South. Antebellum cities developed as marketing and transportation centers for plantation products. Slaveholding inhibited the growth of domestic markets for manufactured goods, although some mass-produced items such as cheap clothing and farm implements were in demand. A limited number of antebellum industrial establishments developed in response to this market. Also, a significant number of factories, especially in the cotton textile industry beginning in the 1830s, were established to process plantation products. Many early factories were built by planters, some experimenting with the use of slave labor in manufacturing. In general, however, southern planters feared all-out industrialization, arguing that industry would compete with the labor needs of agriculture and threaten social control. Prior to the Civil War, most agricultural profits were reinvested in land and slaves.

Perhaps the most rapid phase of industrial expansion in the South occurred between 1860 and 1864. Southern planters sponsored a thoroughgoing, non-democratic, state-controlled form of industrialization through confiscation and government investment in order to build a war machine. Under the auspices of the Confederate States of America, the South rapidly built iron yards, shipyards, textile mills, coal and iron mines, machine shops, clothing and food-processing plants, and munitions factories. The South lost the war but acquired significant industrial experience.

The extent and rapidity of industrial expansion after the Civil War, especially in the piedmont states, led many observers to view the New South as an entirely new departure. Despite the claims of New South promotional literature, which stressed the demise of the planter class and the plantation system, recent studies show that planters remained economically and politically dominant in many southern states at the end of the 19th century. Former slaveholders retained their land and reasserted labor control through sharecropping and the debt peonage system that effectively bound tenants to the soil. A culture of paternalism persisted well into the 20th century, influencing industrial patterns. In the Deep South, where cotton growing remained profitable and white labor was relatively scarce, planters continued to oppose all but minimal industrial growth. In contrast, planter-industrialists in the Upper South—who were faced with declining agricultural returns and who drew on labor reserves of impoverished white farmers—accommodated industry to the postbellum agrarian social order.

Traditionally, the most important sector of southern industry was cotton textile manufacturing. Here the influence of plantation agriculture was greatest as the ethos of the cotton plantation was extended into rural mill villages. The South's forced labor system of plantation agriculture was transferred to the industrial-capitalist sector at first primarily through all-white wage labor in the textile mills, but this was done with great strain, requiring immense measures of social control. The old culture of paternalism and the new logic of capitalist industrialism were tensely interwoven. Despite industrial expansion, individual textile plants remained small and personal. Southern workers were far more dependent on mill-village services than were northern workers. Mechanization permitted heavy reliance on unskilled labor, including children, and isolation, paternalism, and racial exclusivity blunted occupational militancy. Low wages and long workdays enabled southern mill owners to compete with northern manufacturers and eventually to draw northern textile firms and capital into the region.

The textile industry set the pattern for southern industrial culture, though work relations outside the planter-dominated textile industry developed contrasting characteristics. This was most notably true in tobacco manufacturing and coal mining. As proclaimed for the whole of postbellum industry, the tobacco industry was built by "new men" in North Carolina after the Civil War. By 1900 the Dukes and their associates in Durham had transformed a small craft industry into the South's largest industrial enterprise, the American Tobacco Company. Outside the sphere of planter interests, tobacco manufacturers employed large numbers of black workers. Realizing greater profits than the textile industry, they paid significantly higher wages and accepted unionization. The coal industry in Alabama and the southern Appalachians also employed black workers and, faced with an extraordinarily militant workforce, was forced to accept unionization. Some of America's bloodiest labor struggles occurred in the mining communities of the southern highlands, where, unlike the textile villages, corporate paternalism and wage pressures did not accord with the mountain heritage of agricultural self-sufficiency and with underground worker autonomy.

By the era of the New Deal, the plantation system was giving way in southern cotton fields to crop subsidies, mechanization, and federal welfare payments just sufficient to keep an unemployed labor supply on the land. Southern agriculture became increasingly capital intensive. Institutionalized paternalism lingered in the textile industry; but consolidation, rationalization, and, more rarely, industrial conflict became the rule. The demise of the nonwage system in agriculture intensified the drive for further industrialization. Southern towns competed to lure industrial plants to their localities by offering tax incentives, subsidies, and nonunion labor to corporate employers.

Since 1950 the South's rate of economic expansion has been greater than the national average. New growth sectors include agribusiness, automobile manufacturing plants, defense industries, energy resources (oil and nuclear as well as coal, gas, and water), and "high-tech" research and development complexes such as North Carolina's Research Triangle Park (RTP). Educational and public services, along with race relations, have improved dramatically; but much industrial expansion is still dependent on a repressive, nonunion labor environment. (Research complexes such as RTP encourage highly paid managerial and research personnel to migrate south without their unionized blue-collar workforces.) Average industrial wages in the region remain substandard. North Carolina and South Carolina, in the heart of the textile industry, rank as the two most heavily industrialized states in the United States. At the same time, however, they rank near the bottom in wage and unionization levels. Both the accomplishments and the failures of southern industrialization are evident in such statistics. Most recently, globalization has disrupted traditional southern patterns, leading to the virtual collapse of the apparel and textile industries in the region, changes in the labor force because of transnational immigration, and new opportunities for major southern corporations.

DWIGHT B. BILLINGS
*University of Kentucky*

Dwight B. Billings, *Planters and the Making of a "New South"* (1979); David L. Carlton and Peter A. Coclanis, *The South, the Nation, and the World: Perspectives on Southern Economic Development* (2003); James C. Cobb, *The Selling of the South: The Southern Crusade for Industrial Development, 1936–1990* (1993); James C. Cobb and William Stueck, eds., *Globalization and the American South* (2005); Ronald D. Eller, *Miners, Millhands, and Mountaineers: The Modernization of the Appalachian South* (1982); Eugene D. Genovese, *The Political Economy of Slavery: Studies in Economy and Society of the Slave South* (1967); Jay Mandle, *The Roots of Black Poverty: The Southern Plantation Economy after the Civil War* (1978); Jonathan M. Wiener, *Social Origins of the New South: Alabama, 1860–1885* (1978); C. Vann Woodward, *Origins of the New South, 1877–1913* (1951).

## Industrialization in Appalachia

Although the southern mountain region has sometimes been said to be predominantly agricultural in its economy and rural in its culture, industrial development occurred there much as it did elsewhere in the United States and at the same times. During the antebellum period, extractive and manufacturing activities developed as decentralized, locally capitalized, and locally managed enterprises, serving a local or regional market. During the late 1860s, in Appalachia as elsewhere in the nation, these same activities became increasingly centralized through the emergence of large-scale enterprises serving a national or international market and developed with nonlocal capital by nonlocal entrepreneurs. The impact of these changes on all aspects of American life was substantial, not least because they completed the transformation, begun by the transportation revolution of the 1820s, of the mixed American landscape into the characteristic American cityscape of our own time.

As early as the 1840s, visitors to the southern mountains had noted the region's untapped resources in minerals, timber, and waterpower; its human resources of a hardworking, healthy population free of the taint of slavocracy and its ideology of leisure; the potential of its rivers to serve as arteries of commerce; and a landscape and climate conducive to the development of tourism. During the 1860s the list of apparent economic advantages of Appalachia came to include the availability of a rail system and the proximity of the region to major national markets. The list has remained intact, except that concrete roads and air transportation have been added. The persistence of these factors has made Appalachia seem an underdeveloped region of the nation even at times when economic development was most vigorous and the resources of the region—both natural and human—were being depleted most rapidly.

During the 1870s the first systematic cutting of the Appalachian hardwood forests was begun under the same impulse that spurred timbering in Wisconsin and Minnesota and then along the Pacific coast when the eastern forests were exhausted. During the 1880s the first systematic extraction of Appalachian coal, iron, and nonferrous metals was begun under the same impetus that promoted the growth of mining in Pennsylvania, Minnesota, and the Rocky Mountain states. Beginning in the late 1880s, a variety of manufacturing centers were established in Appalachia through the same drive that yielded the great industrial cities on the Great Lakes from Buffalo to Duluth. These manufacturing activities included steel production in Birmingham and Bessemer, Ala., and Middlesboro, Ky.; wood finishing and furniture production, most notably around Asheville, N.C.; glass production at several sites in West Virginia; and textile milling throughout the piedmont.

Lumber mill, Tappahannock, Va., 1941
(John Vachon, Library of Congress [LC-USF-34-62666-D], Washington, D.C.)

These developments in Appalachian timbering, mining, and manufacturing during the late 19th and early 20th centuries replicated the general pattern already evident in the American economy of a movement from small-unit production and local capitalization and control toward large-unit production and external capitalization and control. In these "new" industries, however, the conventional growth pattern, with its normal impact on society and culture, was compressed into a decade or less rather than spread over half a century or more. The social dislocations consequent to these developments in Appalachia, moreover, seem to have been more severe than the analogous dislocations felt in similar growth sites elsewhere in the nation.

Western timbering, for example, occurred largely on land acquired as part of the public domain. Much of the Appalachian timberland was owned, or at least claimed, by individuals who used portions of their holdings for agriculture. Many of these persons were displaced by the large timber companies, especially after the beginning of the 20th century, when large-scale forest preserves were established to ensure the profitability of future operations. Much of Pennsylvania coal mining, like most of western mining of all sorts, required deep-shaft mining and therefore yielded the establishment of permanent facilities for the industry and its workers and a more or less permanent workforce at a particular site. Most of the Appalachian coal mining around the turn of the century could be carried on as surface mining or by tunneling in short-term operations. When the mine played out, equipment, and often the buildings of a company town, were loaded on flat cars and moved to a new site. Appalachian coal mining thus tended to be a transient industry, worked by transients who followed the job from place to place, many of whom had themselves been displaced by timber- or coal-company land purchases. The emergence of large-scale timbering and coal mining displaced those persons who had engaged in the same industries on a small scale, either by squeezing them out of the market or by denying them access to the natural resources they had previously exploited for their own profit, frequently as a complement to farming or some other activity. With no other source of income, these persons were either forced into subsistence farming or entered the labor market as transients.

With the notable exception of such "model" town developments as Pullman, Ill., most of the Great Lakes manufacturing of the late 19th century occurred in or near already established population centers. By contrast, almost all large-scale manufacturing in Appalachia developed on new sites and required a skilled labor force of immigrants to the site, if not to the region. Although the real impact of massive immigration on the character of the Great Lakes cities cannot be denied, in Appalachia the development of manufacturing affected the rapid urbanization of a "rural" area previously dominated by small towns rather than cities, without displacing the system of social and political elites that dominated in courthouse and statehouse. At the same time, it brought to the region hundreds of thousands of new workers who were outsiders to the structure of local politics and society and who rapidly became either its victims, its rebels, or its exiles. That most of the manufacturing centers in Appalachia, as well as the short-lived timber towns and almost all the coal towns, were company owned and controlled exacerbated this situation by making impossible the local mediation of labor and social conflict that occurred in other urban areas during the Progressive Era.

Turn-of-the-century tendencies toward vertical consolidation within industries, exemplified by the establishment of the Standard Oil Company, were extended horizontally across industries in Appalachia, yielding a pattern in which single corporations routinely controlled several industries at once—land development, timber and coal operations, transportation and marketing, and frequently all services needed to support the several sectors of their economic activity as well as those needed by their workers. Finally, although industrial development elsewhere in the nation generally has enriched all strata of the local economies by generating markets for additional goods and services, industrial development in Appalachia has often enriched only the local elites and has left the local economies highly vulnerable to the vagaries of market conditions. Historian David L. Carlton concludes that, today, areas of Appalachia remain "economic basket cases," still dealing with problems left over from the earlier South.

HENRY D. SHAPIRO
*University of Cincinnati*

David L. Carlton, in *The American South in the Twentieth Century* (2005), ed. Craig S. Pascoe, Karen Trahan Leathem, and Andy Ambrose; Harry Caudill, *Night Comes to the Cumberlands: A Biography of a Depressed Area* (1962); Ronald D. Eller, *Miners, Millhands, and Mountaineers: The Modernization of the Appalachian South* (1982); John Gaventa, Barbara Ellen Smith, and Alex Willingham, eds., *Communities in Economic Crisis: Appalachia and the South* (1990); Helen Matthews Lewis, Linda Johnson, and Don Askins, eds., *Colonialism in Modern America: The Appalachian Case* (1978); Gordon B. McKinney, *Southern Mountain Republicans, 1865–1900: Politics and the Appalachian Community* (1978); Henry D. Shapiro, *Appalachia on Our Mind: The Southern Mountains and Mountaineers in the American Consciousness, 1870–1920* (1978); David E. Whisnant, *Modernizing the Mountaineers: People, Power, and Planning in Appalachia* (1979); John Alexander Williams, *West Virginia and the Captains of Industry* (1976).

## Industrialization in the Piedmont

Before 1830 the piedmont region had a small but relatively diverse manufacturing sector, including woolen mills, foundries, and nail and rifle plants. But such promising industry dwindled with the expansion of the slave economy and concentration on the lucrative cash crop cotton. By 1860 significant production was limited to a small number of cotton textile mills in towns such as Graniteville, S.C. The Civil War destroyed most of these modest gains, and manufacturing did not demonstrate any real momentum until the 1880s. But from that time through the 1980s, cotton textile expansion and piedmont industrialization became virtually synonymous. By the 1950s regional control of the textile industry was wrested from New England, with three-fourths of output produced in the piedmont states by the 1980s. Although northern competition was met successfully, that from foreign producers, first Japan and then Third World producers, led to the virtual demise of the textile industry in the piedmont.

One interesting difference between piedmont and New England textile development was the wholehearted community support that marked early southern efforts to establish local industry. Religious leaders as well as state and local officials joined farm populations in what has been termed a "crusade" in the 1880s to urge entrepreneurs to open mills. The collective hope was that heavy investment in cotton textiles would not only provide desperately needed jobs for local workers and effectively use the region's main crop, but it would also draw producers in related manufacturing and service industries to locate in the region. In turn, rapid urbanization would create demand for locally made goods as well as for meat, dairy, and other food items, leading to a healthier local agriculture that was less dependent on the fortunes of the cotton crop.

By the time investment in piedmont manufacturing began on a broad scale, machinery, power, and transport technologies were far more advanced than they had been at the inception of northern and midwestern industrialization earlier in the 19th century. Of particular importance was the critical impetus given piedmont progress by the widespread availability of cheap hydroelectric power after 1900. Investment by power companies in the region was stimulated initially by demand from cotton mills, but other labor-intensive light industry located there in part to benefit from its prevalence. Textile-finishing plants; wood, paper, and furniture factories; and knit goods, apparel, and later synthetic-fiber factories all became numerous.

Even the presence of excellent water and wood supplies, however, could not compensate for a relative regional scarcity of heavy mineral deposits such as coal and iron, which laid the foundation for investment in capital-intensive industry elsewhere. Although the chemical industry is strongly represented through artificial-textile production, the location of this component of the industry in the piedmont may be viewed as a function of the ease with which cotton mills and equipment could be converted for artificial-fiber manufacture. Its introduction into the piedmont was thus linked more to the presence of the older cotton manufacture than to the region's supply of skilled labor and natural resources. Traditionally, the region has not attracted heavy industry, although textile- and electrical-machinery producers have long clustered near cotton-mill centers. Nontextile manufacture tended to resemble cotton manufacturing in demanding a large supply of cheap unskilled labor and by having few economies of scale in production.

The social environment of the rural piedmont also contributed to the distinctive character of its industrialization experience. Because mills were constructed in rural places, housing had to be provided for workers and their families. In early New England textile towns, company-owned boardinghouses served an unmarried female workforce but disappeared with the advent of immigrant labor. The concentration of New England mills in a few locations contributed to the growth of large cities. Piedmont mill villages did not undergo such an evolution for the most part. The agrarian tradition so often noted by students of southern culture was reflected in mill dispersion over a wide geographical area. The relative isolation of mills strengthened a comprehensive paternalism on the part of owners that, in contrast to New England, persisted, assisting owners in effectively thwarting unionization efforts by keeping workers dependent and suspicious of outside organizers. In addition, a perennial threat facing white workers in this labor-surplus agricultural region was that black labor, heretofore excluded from cotton mills, would be hired to replace union sympathizers. Thus, mill villagers remained remarkably homogeneous in cultural and religious heritage, race, and ethnic origin. Although some have pointed to their transient lifestyle, they usually migrated only to another mill village that was similar to the last in social structure and economic opportunity. One outcome of textile dominance in piedmont industrialization was that alternatives to farm work for the large black population of the region were historically few.

By the time of piedmont industrial expansion, textile technology, particularly in spinning, allowed extensive use of child labor. This practice characterized piedmont mills long after it had been eliminated in New England. When states introduced age-and-hour legislation more widely after 1912, piedmont standards were distinguished by their inadequacy. The laws were rarely enforced, so the employment of entire families continued, entrenching the mill villages in the southern landscape and delaying the development of a skilled and literate nonfarm labor force—an essential resource for the attraction of high-wage, capital-intensive industry.

Although the very rapid rate of growth of piedmont cotton mills was a critical feature of its industrialization, it should not obscure the enduring rural character of the region. For example, although South Carolina was the preeminent southern textile state in 1900, fewer than 4 percent of its people were employed in a manufacturing industry of any kind. The piedmont's industrial pattern incorporated features of its rural heritage, and in this it contrasted with other regions where urbanization occurred relatively quickly as manufacturing expanded. Urban development in the piedmont, on the other hand, has been more typically expressed through the rise of small towns than the growth of large cities. Scholars sometimes emphasize a tension between the agricultural and manufacturing sectors because the progress of one could threaten the labor supply of the other. But the development of piedmont industry was accomplished by recruiting unemployed and underemployed white labor from local farms. The farm population increased for many decades at a rate more than sufficient to meet the demands of both farms and mills, so industrialization had a positive effect on the productivity of local farm labor.

As truck and automobile transportation became accessible in the 1920s, many piedmont workers commuted to factories from farms. Such retention of a predominantly agricultural character in the long run helps to explain the slow progress of the piedmont toward industrial diversification. The lack of skilled labor continued to dictate the type of manufacture located in the region. When considered with the related absence of essential large-scale economies, one can understand more fully the persistence of the region's low per capita income relative to other sections of the United States.

World wars, larger and more sophisticated markets for southern goods, and foreign competition more recently have lured more complex industry and have evoked a broader social and political awareness in the region. In small towns as well as in more urban areas, a middle class developed with ambitions and life-styles more American than regional. The peculiar industrialization experience of the piedmont had, nevertheless, a lasting impact on the cultural path of its society. The region's industrial structure was molded not only by circumstances of time, technology, and resource utilization but also by the character and social values of its populace.

The 1990s saw fundamental changes in the economic life of the piedmont. The textile industry, which once had sought out the piedmont for people who would work for cheap wages, moved out of the United States, resulting in closed factories, laid-off workers, and sometimes devastated communities. The North American Free Trade Agreement represented a victory for open markets but brought trouble for the South's old manufacturing belt. The Economic Policy Institute estimated that the nation lost over 3 million jobs from trade-related developments from 1994 to 2000. Eleven southern states lost 954,218 (31.3 percent) of these jobs. Many of the textile companies moved to Mexico but have since gone to nations in Southeast and East Asia.

At the same time, the piedmont attracted a major automobile employer with the coming of the BMW assembly plant in South Carolina. The capital-intensive automobile industry spurred growth in the area, with a complex system of suppliers arriving. Lower-paying jobs in the service economy, however, have more typically been the symbolic replacement for textile industry employees.

MARY J. OATES
*Regis College*

Fred Bateman and Thomas Weiss, *A Deplorable Scarcity: The Failure of Industrialization in the Slave Economy* (1981); Victor S. Clark, *History of Manufactures in the United States*, vols. 2 and 3 (1929); Alfred E. Eckes, in *Globalization and the American South*, ed. James C. Cobb and William Stueck (2005); Victor R. Fuchs, *Changes in the Location of Manufacturing in the United States since 1929* (1962); Patrick J. Hearden, *Independence and Empire: The New South's Cotton Mill Campaign, 1865–1901* (1982); Jeffrey Leitner, Michael Schulman, and Rhonda Zingraff, eds., *Hanging by a Thread: Social Change in Southern Textiles* (1991); William N. Parker, *Southern Economic Journal* (April 1980); Anthony M. Tang, *Economic Development in the Southern Piedmont, 1860–1950* (1958); George B. Tindall, *The Emergence of the New South, 1913–1945* (1967).

## Military and Economy

Since the Civil War, and especially since World War II, the South has become the most powerful base of support for the continued American military buildup that has resulted in the rise of the Military-Industrial Complex, a term coined by Malcolm Moss and popularized by Dwight D. Eisenhower. More accurately, the complex should be styled the Military-Industrial-Technological-Labor-Academic-Managerial-Political (MITLAMP) Complex. All sectors of modern technological society are involved in its functioning. Within the MITLAMP Complex are military and industrial beneficiaries, technical specialists, labor recipients of defense funds, academic elites, managerial elements, and political opportunists. These groups, especially in the South and in California, are reaping financial rewards and causing, particularly in the South, extraordinary cultural changes because of their continued support for the complex.

The origins of this regional military-economic relationship can be traced far back in southern history. Antebellum southern life and culture were conducive in many ways to an excessive spirit of militancy and extreme martial behavior. As the frontier moved westward in the 18th and early 19th centuries, southerners, like the frontiersmen of the Midwest, felt vulnerable to Indian uprisings. More importantly, as a slaveholding population, southern whites lived in constant fear of slave revolts, so the constabulary forces patrolled the rural roads nightly. Many southerners, weaned on the novels of Sir Walter Scott, were obsessed with a sense of honor. John Hope Franklin, W. J. Cash, and others have suggested this martial spirit of the South helped it face the consequences of secession with confidence, if not eagerness.

Following the Civil War, southern males were even more obsessed with proving their manhood and, above all, regaining their lost sense of honor. Combine this sentiment with the existence of poverty and extreme racism in the region and it is small wonder that southerners, white and black, have been attracted in large numbers to the military establishment, both in times of peace and war. The South has more enlistees serving in the armed forces than any other region, and no other section of the country has a greater percentage of personnel in the armed forces on a per capita basis. The report of the Secretary of Defense for Manpower, Reserve Affairs, and Logistics (1981) showed that in 1980, 35.7 percent of the enlistees in the professional armed forces were natives of the South, while southerners constituted 33.7 percent of the nation's population. A 2002 study led by the Institute for Southern Studies found that 42 percent of U.S. troops were born in the South.

The subsequent economic benefits for the region are obvious. Figures from the Cold War years are revealing. Southerners in the armed forces throughout the world fueled the southern economy with allotment checks deposited in local banks. Although military personnel served in many places during their careers, seldom did they escape service during the Cold War at some southern camp or station. This is especially true in the case of the army. Twenty-four of 46 major posts were located in the South in 1980. That same year, 48 percent of all service people were located in southern states and the District of Columbia. Moreover, colonies of military retirees lived along the Florida coastline and in San Antonio and El Paso, Tex.

The impact of military expenditures on the southern economy during the Cold War was immense. A total of 39.5 percent of all Department of Defense dollars ($50,091,677,000 of a total budget of $127,135,626,000) was spent in the South in fiscal year 1980. The one-party system, combined with the rule of seniority, enabled southerners to dominate the House and Senate Armed Services Committees and direct this heavy expenditure of defense funds to the South.

In addition, of the $10,696,556,000 allocated to the Department of Energy, $554,350,000 was expended in the South in conducting nuclear weapons activities for the Department of Defense. Further, National Aeronautics and Space Administration (NASA) funds, closely linked to defense needs, are primarily allocated to southern states and the District of Columbia. The total NASA budget in 1980 was $5,365,761,000; $2,169,012,000 of this was spent in the South. Finally, Veterans Administration expenditures in the South amounted to $8,635,108,000 of an agency total of $22,106,822,000. Thus, the entire amount of military money spent in southern states and the District of Columbia in 1980 was $61,449,911,000. If one employs a conservative multiplier effect in order to determine the number of real dollars spent in the South by the military in 1980, the amount equals $122,999,822,000.

The USS Charleston, *a World War II naval vessel (Ann Rayburn Paper Americana Collection, Archives and Special Collections, University of Mississippi Library, Oxford)*

Despite the end of the Cold War, the military's role in the South's economy has become even more significant than before. A 2002 study found that 56 percent of U.S. troops were stationed in the South, up from 48 percent in 1980. Of 49 American army bases in the United States in 2007, 21 were located in southern states. These bases benefited a few states in particular, especially Georgia, North Carolina, Texas, and Virginia, and they created a network of military towns that exerted a powerful influence locally and regionally. The Pentagon's plan to close 180 military installations was announced in May 2005, resulting in the closure of 62 bases in the South. The region, nonetheless, will gain a net total of 15,500 positions at over 50 military bases that will grow in size.

Cultural changes are wrought by such vast military presence and expenditures. In cities and towns where industries and military installations traditionally reflected racist views, employment and personnel policies have become more equitable. The white South has been forced to reconsider its racial attitudes as a consequence of the Supreme Court decisions and the civil rights legislation of the 1950s and 1960s enforcing equal employment opportunities for blacks in southern industries under contract to the federal government.

In addition, many northerners, including unskilled workers and skilled managers, technologists, engineers, and scientists, have moved South in search of the economic opportunities provided in the Sunbelt, further changing the character of life, especially in cities like Dallas and Houston. Thus, large military expenditures, producing social as well as economic results, must be considered important factors in the recent growth and development of the South.

ALVIN R. SUNSERI
*University of Northern Iowa*

W. J. Cash, *The Mind of the South* (1941); John Hope Franklin, *The Militant South* (1956); Geographical Distribution of Federal Funds in Summary, Fiscal Year 1980; Catherine Lutz, *Homefront: A Military City and the American Twentieth Century* (2002); "Missiles and Magnolias: The South at War," *Southern Exposure* (Spring 2002); Alvin R. Sunseri, in *War, Business, and American Society: Historical Perspectives on the Military-Industrial Complex*, ed. Benjamin Franklin Cooling (1977); U.S. Department of Commerce, *Statistical Abstract of the United States: 1981* (1982); U.S. Government Selected Manpower Statistics, Fiscal Year 1981.

## New South Myth

Defeated and frustrated, the postbellum South furnished fertile soil for the growth of myth—for grafting the imagined upon the real to produce a hybrid that itself became a force in history. Hardly had Union armies sealed the fate of the Old South in 1865 before some people began to speak of a New South. By the early 1870s, optimists were finding hope in defeat and envisioning a society that would be less sumptuous but more substantial than the antebellum plantation order to which they paid homage but whose flaws, they believed, had been exposed in the ordeal of war.

Advocates of a New South believed that economic regeneration was the region's most pressing need. To solicit the northern capital necessary to effect that regeneration, they encouraged reconciliation between the old enemies. They promised to treat black people fairly in their sphere, thereby seeking to soothe any northern consciences troubled by the abandonment of Reconstruction and promote a harmony between the races that would foster the social stability so highly prized by potential northern investors. Racial accommodation and sectional reconciliation would do much to guarantee the *sine qua non* of the New South program: the development of an industrial economy that would restore prosperity and prominence to the region.

During the 1880s, largely because of the ceaseless labors of publicists such as Henry W. Grady of the *Atlanta Constitution* and Richard H. Edmonds of the *Baltimore Manufacturers' Record*, the New South idea became increasingly popular. To such molders of opinion, the proponents of the industrial ethos were broad-minded and progressive, while its opponents, their numbers ever diminishing, were narrow and reactionary. In his celebrated "New South" address before an appreciative audience in New York in 1886, Grady proclaimed that southerners, having been converted to the Yankee way, were rejecting the ideal of leisure, replacing politics with business as their chief endeavor, and sharing the region's mounting prosperity generously with black people. Three years later, Edmonds wrote that the South's vast resources were already ensuring the recovery of the position the region had held in 1860 as the richest section of the country. For Edmonds, Grady, and others of like mind, the ideal had been transformed into the actual. By 1890 the myth of the New South as a land that was rich, just, and triumphant was perceived as reality by many southerners.

To a great degree the ascendancy of the myth was the result of wishful thinking. At the end of the 19th century, black southerners existed in circumstances little better than those of slavery; the prosperity vaunted by New South spokespersons was largely illusory; and the industrialization that had occurred—and it was never as great as claimed—was often controlled by northerners. Still the poor stepchild of the nation, the South was hardly triumphant, rich, or just.

Nevertheless, the New South myth survived not only the challenge of statistics but also the attacks mounted by the desperate agrarians who embraced Populism in the 1890s. With Populism dying, the intellectual temper of the next 30 years, like that of the 1880s, was characterized by a romantic, optimistic faith in progress. By the 1920s the business boosters were excelling their ideological forebears in touting the advance of southern industrialization.

That advance was indeed rapid. As numerous industries underwent significant expansion during the 1920s, the number of manufacturing workers in the South rose by almost 10 percent while the rest of the nation suffered a decline of the same proportion. Yet if the boosterism of the "dollar decade" had a sounder basis in reality than did the boomerism of the 1880s, there was ballyhoo in generous measure all the way from the Mason-Dixon Line to Florida's Gold Coast. The second-generation New South enthusiasts portrayed the region as a land basking in the rays of prosperity, even though the profits of southern industry often wound up outside the region and southern workers labored longer and earned less than did those in the North.

The bone-grinding poverty of the Great Depression, exposed in works by Erskine Caldwell and other southern writers, obscured the myth for a time. By the end of the 1930s, however, the booster spirit was again ascendant, lifted by hopes of recovery and by southern indignation over the region's being labeled the nation's primary economic problem. Moreover, the agrarian myth, which had earlier served as a counterpoise to the New South myth, lost much of its force as many of its adherents either abandoned farming as a commercial enterprise or, succumbing to hard times and New Deal policies, left the land altogether.

World War II ushered in a degree of industrialization long dreamed of by southern promoters. Between 1939 and 1972, the number of factories grew by more than 160 percent and the number of workers in them by more than 200 percent. Prosperity accompanied the expansion of industry, as per capita income in the South increased by 500 percent between 1955 and 1975—a rate 300 percent higher than that of the nation as a whole. The New South myth grew ever more compelling as the region's economic advance became ever more real. Yet just as important to strengthening the myth were the labors of the region's industrial promoters, who rivaled the boomers of the 1880s and the boosters of the 1920s in the quest for material progress. Intent upon maintaining what was called an "excellent business climate," chambers of commerce, development boards, and newspapers often urged local and state governments to offer industrialists a variety of inducements such as public financing of plant construction, "start-up" programs for new industries, tax reductions or exemptions, and courses in "union busting" at public universities to keep labor under control. Some promoters also encouraged the token integration of the races to help create a proper image elsewhere, which was but a minor variation on a major theme of the New South movement of a century before.

So striking was the region's economic advance and so successful was the selling of the South that by the late 1960s, pundits began referring to the latest New South as part of the Sunbelt, that region spanning the southern portion of the nation and growing rapidly in population, prosperity, and power. Underdogs for so long, southerners sometimes took what they considered well-deserved delight in the discomfiture of residents of the Frostbelt, who lamented the migration of workers to factories that had been relocated to the South. As had occurred a hundred years earlier, many southerners saw their region as just, triumphant, and rich—just in its treatment of black people, triumphant in its economic struggle with the North, and rich in material goods.

Yet again, the myth failed to reflect reality adequately. Despite changes in the law, blacks found that they were sometimes still the victims of segregation and inequality. Despite the hyperbole accompanying the Sunbelt phenomenon, the belief that the South would soon reduce the North to beggary betrayed an ignorance of the facts. Despite increasing prosperity, the South was hardly rich; as of 1981, average annual per capita income in the region lagged behind that of the rest of the country by almost $2,000. Nearly 20 years later, median hourly wages in the South were almost $1.50 less than those in the rest of the country, and only one state of the old Confederacy—Virginia—could boast annual per capita income that was above the national average.

For all the hope that the New South myth has inspired—no mean achievement in itself—it has countenanced complacency toward social ills, resignation to the abuse of the natural environment, and the rise of a mass culture that diminished the personalism in human relations long cherished in the southern folk culture. Unless the New South myth can be more tightly harnessed in order to serve the general welfare, the idea could remain a negative influence.

WAYNE MIXON
*Augusta State University*

Edward L. Ayers, *The Promise of the New South: Life after Reconstruction* (1992); Numan V. Bartley, *The New South, 1945–1980* (1995); Jared Bernstein and Lawrence Mishel, *Economic Policy Institute Issue Brief* (February 1999); James C. Cobb, *The Selling of the South: The Southern Crusade for Industrial Development, 1936–1990* (1993); Paul M. Gaston, *The New South Creed: A Study in Southern Mythmaking* (1970); Richard B. McKenzie, *Tax Review* (September 1982); Wayne Mixon, *Southern Writers and the New South Movement, 1865–1913* (1980); George B. Tindall, *The Emergence of the New South, 1913–1945* (1967), *The Ethnic Southerners* (1976), *Houston Review* (Spring 1979); U.S. Census Bureau, *Statistical Abstract of the United States* (2001); C. Vann Woodward, *Origins of the New South, 1877–1913* (1951).

## Sunbelt South

"Sunbelt South" and, more generally, the "American Sunbelt" were media creations designed to give coherence and meaning to the dramatic population growth and political upheavals that occurred in the South and Southwest after 1940. Coined by political analyst Kevin P. Phillips in his book *The Emerging Republican Majority* (1969), the concept of "Sun Belt" (or "Sunbelt") lay dormant and ill-defined until the mid-1970s, when a combination of census reports on migration, the growing Republican potential in the South and West, and the presidential candidacy of Georgian Jimmy Carter brought the lower tier of states to public attention. Although he did not use the term "Sunbelt," journalist Kirkpatrick Sale, in *Power Shift: The Rise of the Southern Rim and Its Challenge to the Eastern Establishment* (1975), alerted northern intellectuals to the emergence of the nation's "Southern Rim" as a new center of power. Soon the *New York Times*, the *Wall Street Journal*, *Fortune*, and other publications discovered the region. *Time*, prompted by Carter's nomination, devoted a special issue (27 September 1976) to the subject, titling it "The South Today." Yet definitions remained unclear. Nearly all observers included in the Sunbelt the area below the 37th parallel, along the northern borders of North Carolina, Tennessee, Arkansas, Oklahoma, New Mexico, and Arizona and the section of California below Fresno. Some added Virginia, Kentucky, southern Nevada, and northern California, while others cautiously included the slow-growing Mississippi Delta. All agreed, however, on the general concept of an expanding southern and southwestern region with a casual and inviting lifestyle, a favorable business climate, and conservative politics increasingly inclined to Republicanism.

For roughly five years, the press showered the nation with promotional reports of the "good life" in the Sunbelt that was seemingly unattainable elsewhere. By the early 1980s, however, the northern-based national media became less enchanted and focused reports on crime in Miami, the lack of services in Houston, and the high cost of living in Southern California. In 1982 *Newsweek* ran an article titled "Dark Side of the Sunbelt," and the *New York Times* began a follow-up on its glowing 1976 series under the headline: "Sun Belt Having Difficulty Living Up to Its Promise." As a media creation, the concept of the Sunbelt faced severe revising.

If the Sunbelt South was partly a mythic image, it did reflect real demographic and economic trends. Between 1940 and 1980, the number of Americans living below the 37th parallel increased by 112 percent, whereas the combined populations of the Northeast and Midwest rose by only 42 percent. Southern California, Florida, and Texas each gained over 7.5 million new residents. By 1980 the Los Angeles–Long Beach, Dallas–Fort Worth, Houston, and Atlanta metropolitan areas each had grown to over 2 million people, and 18 Sunbelt metropolises (including 11 from the former Confederate states) had joined the nation's 50 most populous metro regions. This growth was especially strong during World War II, the 1960s, and the early 1970s.

Most commentators attributed this increase to economic development fostered by federal and state aid to business and to changing American lifestyles. Beginning with World War II, the federal government poured enormous sums into the South and West for the construction and maintenance of military installations and the production of modern weaponry. From Miami to Mobile to Monterrey, these defense bases and plants lured wartime migrants who came and stayed. Cold War and Vietnam expenditures, protected by powerful congressional leaders such as L. Mendel Rivers (S.C.), John Stennis (Miss.), Edward Hebert (La.), and John Tower (Tex.), guaranteed millions of Sunbelt jobs. Nondefense spending, shared more equally with the other states, also boosted Sunbelt growth through funding for items ranging from construction projects to transfer payments. State governments scrambled for these federal dollars but also for new industries and their private payrolls. Beginning with Mississippi's plan to "Balance Agriculture with Industry" (1936), southern and southwestern government and civil officials attracted branch plants and encouraged new operations with promises of low costs for land, buildings, equipment, labor, and taxes, plus expanding markets. Packaged as, in the Texas vernacular, a "good bidness climate," these appeals emphasized tax concessions and weak labor unions—by-products of southern prejudice and right-to-work laws. "Business Loves the Sunbelt (and Vice Versa)," proclaimed a 1977 *Fortune* article.

A warm and inviting climate encouraged this mutual attraction and convinced many businessmen to move South. Winter high temperatures often above 60 degrees and 250 to 350 days of sunshine annually made for an informal, outdoor-oriented lifestyle, equally appealing to retirees in Fort Lauderdale, top executives in Atlanta, and oil-field workers in western Oklahoma. Postwar affluence gave many northerners the wherewithal to relocate, and many moved to improve their quality of life.

This mighty demographic shift has triggered significant economic and political realignments. Economic power drifted south and west, where Miami, New Orleans, Houston, and Los Angeles are now international trade centers, and Atlanta and Dallas service substantial regional markets. The Sunbelt is becoming dominant in energy development, technical innovation, tourism, and many categories of agribusiness. In national politics, the region has flexed its new muscles for decades. The 1970 census was the first to give the South and West a majority in the electoral college, but every elected president since 1964 has come from the southern rim (counting George H. W. Bush as an adopted Texan). In 1964, 1980, 1988, and 2000, voters chose among or between Sunbelt candidates. In 1940 only 121 congressmen came from below the 37th parallel, but the 1980 census awarded the region 145 seats, a gain of 12 since 1970. Drawing support from newcomers and old-line Democrats upset over civil rights and federal spending priorities, Republicans won many of the seats. Some were conservative ideologues, but most were pragmatic business types. Republicans swept west to east, from coastal areas to the inland and into the suburbs to win national and statewide offices barred to them a generation earlier. Blacks and Hispanics, encouraged by the civil rights movement and federal support, integrated the Democratic Party and won local races. In the cities, once entrenched commercial elites began to share power with young business promoters, suburbanites, and neighborhood and minority groups. The degree of sharing has varied, from almost none in Dallas–Fort Worth to an almost total power shift in Atlanta, where a black majority now rules.

The probusiness, laissez-faire attitude of the region has allowed problems, especially those related to density, to multiply unchecked; but so far crime, poor schools and services, and low wages have not destroyed the Sunbelt's appeal. Eventually, Sunbelt governments will have to expand their activities, but their constituents are in no hurry. As one observer claimed of archetypical Houston, it has a 19th-century outlook with 20th-century technology. In the meantime, migrants continue to stamp their approval on the region, for although lessening economic advantages and higher relocation costs have slowed Sunbelt growth, the march is still southward.

RICHARD BERNARD
*Marquette University*

Carl Abbott, *The New Urban America: Growth and Politics in Sunbelt Cities* (1981); Richard M. Bernard and Bradley R. Rice, eds., *Sunbelt Cities: Politics and Growth since World War II* (1983); James C. Cobb, *The Selling of the South: The Southern Crusade for Industrial Development, 1936–1990* (1993); Raymond A. Mohl, ed., *Searching for the Sunbelt: Historical Perspectives on a Region* (1990); David C. Perry and Alfred J. Watkins, eds., *The Rise of the Sunbelt Cities* (1977); Kevin P. Phillips, *The Emerging Republican Majority* (1969); Kirkpatrick Sale, *Power Shift: The Rise of the Southern Rim and Its Challenge to the Eastern Establishment* (1975); Bruce J. Shulman, *From Cotton Belt to Sunbelt: Federal Policy, Economic Development, and the Transformation of the South, 1938–1980* (1991); Bernard L. Weinstein and Robert E. Firestone, *Regional Growth and Decline in the United States: The Rise of the Sunbelt and the Decline of the Northeast* (1978).

## Airline Industry

In the 1920s there were no clear distinctions between aircraft manufacturers and aircraft dealers, nor between aircraft dealers and aircraft operators. Furthermore, the market as a whole had yet to determine whether aviation had any business potential beyond, perhaps, rapid mail service. One company, the Huff Daland Company, launched a branch that designed, manufactured, and eventually operated crop-dusting services aimed at southern plantation owners. The Huff Daland Dusters branch would later establish business links to Mexico and Peru from its base in Monroe, La. When legal troubles erupted, Huff Daland Dusters was dissolved. The international operations were placed under new management and eventually became Pan American Airlines, while the Louisiana-centered crop-dusting business soon added passenger service and became Delta Air Services. Delta, under the leadership of C. E. Woolman, exemplified the paternalistic southern model of entrepreneurship for decades, and it would be the only airline owned and operated principally by southerners.

In the South, as elsewhere in the nation, the institution of airmail service between major cities created a frenzy among the many small aircraft operators, each hoping for a lucrative government contract. To counter accusations of favoritism, Congress reorganized the airmail contract system. Among many other provisions, the Air Mail Act of 1934 effectively banned aircraft manufacturers from operating their own mail or passenger services. One major beneficiary of this reorganization was the newly christened Delta Air Corporation, while Pan American retained its monopoly over international airmail.

Delta moved its headquarters to a new facility in Atlanta in 1941, thanks in part to a significant subsidy from that city's government. Expansion into nonsouthern routes began the same year, with the acquisition of a particularly lucrative Cincinnati connection. By the end of World War II, the newly renamed Delta Air Lines, Inc., had become a major national airline with connections to Chicago and Miami emanating from its Atlanta operation, and by 1949 Delta it established direct service to San Francisco and Los Angeles. In the 1950s a merger with Chicago & Southern gave Delta more thorough coverage of midwestern markets, while a new Civil Aeronautics Board ruling allowed the company to establish direct service between Atlanta and New York. These moves sparked renewed competition between Delta and larger national lines (most notably Eastern Air Lines), while the emergence of smaller "feeder" airlines such as Piedmont Aviation also complicated the picture of air travel.

By 1960 Delta offered jet service between Atlanta and the nation's other major cities, as well as connections to Cuba, Jamaica, and Venezuela. In 1964 Delta began direct service from Atlanta to London and Paris. In 1972, over the opposition of Eastern Air Lines and National Airways, Delta took over the struggling Northeast Airlines, acquiring access to Boston, Montreal, and

Bermuda while receiving permission to eliminate smaller and unprofitable destinations throughout New England.

In the 1980s airline deregulation led both to a wave of mergers and to the development of a new route system, the hub-and-spoke system. Modeling their plans on Delta's long-standing Atlanta operations, airlines placed more and more of their departures at hub airports in order to save on maintenance and infrastructure costs. Atlanta's William B. Hartsfield International Airport became one of the world's largest hubs, and, with the bankruptcy and dissolution of Eastern Air Services in 1989, Delta came to control nearly three-fourths of the passenger gates there. The hub system also served other southern cities well. U.S. Airways merged with Piedmont Airlines in 1987, significantly broadening its operations in Charlotte in an attempt to rival Delta's southern coverage, while the world's largest airfreight carrier, Federal Express (now FedEx), also transformed the Memphis airport into a massive cargo hub.

Delta Air Lines became such a huge presence in Atlanta and throughout the South that it passed into the realm of popular culture. Delta's giant neon sign was as much a part of the downtown Atlanta skyline as the Peachtree Plaza Hotel. When suburbanites transplanted from northern cities complained about any dimension of southern life, Atlanta residents were quick to quote Delta's well-known slogan: "Delta is ready when you are."

STEPHEN WALLACE TAYLOR
*Macon State College*

W. David Lewis and Wesley Phillips Newton, *Delta: The History of an Airline* (1979); Barbara Sturken Peterson and James Glab, *Rapid Descent: Deregulation and the Shakeout in the Airlines* (1994).

## Atlanta as Commercial Center

Atlanta's role as the commercial center of the Southeast began in the late 1830s when the Georgia legislature decided to build a railroad from the Chattahoochee River northwesterly to Chattanooga, Tenn. Atlanta grew around the terminus of this Western & Atlantic line. By the mid-1840s two private lines had arrived, and Atlanta had connections to Augusta and Savannah. Eventually, 15 rail lines would converge on the "Gate City" as it far surpassed its state rivals.

During the Civil War, Atlanta served as a major manufacturing and supply point for Confederate forces until General William Sherman's troops destroyed it in 1864. Atlanta's location, railroads, and spirit guaranteed its phoenixlike revival from the ashes of war. In 1869 the city became the state capital, and in 1871 the chamber of commerce was formed. Boosters organized international trade expositions in 1881, 1887, and 1895. The Cotton States and International Exposition of 1895 drew 800,000 visitors to the ambitious city of 75,000. Atlanta had become the principal distribution center for the country-store economy of the South.

The city's population passed the 100,000 threshold shortly after the turn of the 20th century. In the 1920s the chamber of commerce sponsored the "Forward Atlanta" movement, which attracted nearly 800 new businesses with over 20,000 employees. This was also the takeoff decade for Coca-Cola, Atlanta's most famous business. Although the city had some important factories, manufacturing always lagged behind the trade and services sectors in a diversified employment picture.

As World War II began, Atlanta fell behind New Orleans and ranked close to Memphis and Birmingham in size. By 1980, however, metropolitan Atlanta had 2 million residents, far outstripping these regional competitors. The prewar base had been built on railroads, distribution, and state government. In the postwar era, Atlanta built on that foundation and became the preeminent southeastern center for air transportation, trucking, corporate offices, and federal government activities. The local power structure believed that a moderate approach to race relations would be good for the business climate, and Atlanta forged its image as the "City Too Busy to Hate." In the 1960s boosters launched another "Forward Atlanta" campaign. This one brought urban renewal, a gleaming skyline, and the Southeast's first major-league sports team: baseball's Atlanta Braves. Georgia could not match the phenomenal population growth of Florida, but none of the Florida cities could challenge Atlanta's commercial dominance of the eastern third of the Sunbelt. As the executive secretary of the chamber of commerce noted in 1976, "We found out that while Atlanta was trying to be a regional city, it had become one of a handful of national cities."

In the 1990s Atlanta became an international city. The Coca-Cola Corporation has long been engaged in international commerce, CNN beams news programming around the world, and the United Parcel Service delivers packages across the globe. All of these Atlanta-based businesses rely on Hartsfield-Jackson Atlanta International Airport, the largest air hub in the world, and Delta Airlines, the city's largest employer. Atlanta hosted the 1996 Summer Olympics, the preparations for which helped modernize the city and project a new international image.

BRADLEY R. RICE
*Clayton Junior College*

Franklin Garrett, *Atlanta and Environs: A Chronicle of Its People and Events* (1969); Truman A. Hartshorn, *Metropolis in Georgia: Atlanta's Rise as a Major Transaction Center* (1976).

## Automobile Industry

In the past 30 years, the South has experienced a tremendous growth in the automotive industry. While many observers claim the southern automobile industry started in the early 1980s, it actually began in the early days of automobile manufacturing and remained a small part of the region's industrial base until the 1980s. In 1900 the G. H. Waters & Sons Buggy & Carriage Factory in New Bern, N.C., built a horseless carriage. In 1902 a Richmond, Va., machine manufacturer built a prototype called the Coffee. A Jacksonville, Fla., repair-shop owner built a few automobiles in 1905 that he called the Hutto. These southern attempts never went further than a couple of vehicles produced.

As prices began to fall in the 1910s, an increasing number of southerners were able to purchase automobiles. In 1914 Ford opened a factory in Atlanta where workers assembled parts to make Model Ts. Ford also opened assembly plants in Charlotte, Dallas, Houston, Atlanta, Louisville, and Memphis. General Motors (GM) opened an assembly plant in Atlanta. Ford later opened assembly plants in Norfolk, Va., (1925) and Louisville, Ky., (1955). Ford sold its original Atlanta plant during World War II and opened a new factory in Hapeville, Ga. (1946). In 1948 GM opened an assembly plant in Doraville, Ga.

During the 1910s, demand for automobiles continued to grow and constantly outpaced the supply. All across the country, hundreds of new companies were started to meet the demand. In the South, over 150 new automobile manufacturing companies were organized. Most southern companies never went further than a prototype and a promise to become successful. Some of the short-lived companies were the Great Southern in Birmingham, the Grove Park in North Carolina, the Billy Four in Atlanta, and the Texmobile in Texas.

There were a few companies that had some success in producing more than a handful of automobiles. Hanson in Atlanta, Anderson in Rock Hill, S.C., Dixie Flyer in Louisville, Ky., Marathon in Nashville, Kline Kar in Richmond, and Piedmont in Lynchburg, Va., each produced a few thousand automobiles before succumbing by the early 1920s to economies of scale and the emergence of the "Big Three" in Detroit. By

the mid-1920s all southern efforts to compete in the automobile industry had failed.

Although the Big Three did not open any automobile assembly plants in the South before the 1980s, they did open truck plants. Ford converted its Louisville assembly plant to trucks in 1969, and GM opened a truck plant in Shreveport, La. In the late 1960s, GM tried to open a factory in the South to take advantage of lower labor costs, but the United Auto Workers blocked their efforts. Eventually, in 1981, GM purchased and converted a parts manufacturing facility in Bowling Green, Ky., and built Corvettes. A few years later, GM chose a site near Spring Hill, Tenn., for its new concept automobile: the Saturn.

Foreign automobile manufacturers led the movement of the industry to the South. They were drawn to the region because of the growing consumer market, the perceived quality of life, low energy and land costs, inexpensive labor, good transportation networks, a pleasant climate, "right-to-work" state legislation, more available open space, and state and local governments willing to offer greater incentives.

In 1980 Nissan Motors and Honda both announced that they would build factories in the United States. Nissan selected Smyrna, Tenn., as the location for their factory. Toyota opened its Georgetown, Ky., factory in 1988, moved its U.S. corporate headquarters to Elizabethtown, Ky., in 2006, and announced in 2007 plans to build a factory in Blue Springs, Miss. In 1992 BMW selected a site along I-85 in Greer, S.C., for its first assembly plant outside of Germany. Nissan chose Canton, Miss., for its new assembly plant in 2000 because of the large incentives from the state. Toyota chose San Antonio in 2003 for its Tundra pickup truck plant.

Alabama has been particularly successful in attracting assembly plants. In 1993 Mercedes-Benz selected the town of Vance for an assembly plant. Much of Alabama's success lay in the amount of incentives offered. When Honda announced in 1999 the selection of Lincoln, Ala., for an assembly plant and Hyundai selected Montgomery a few years later, it became apparent that incentives worked. In 2007 Isuzu Motors announced that it was locating a factory in Pinson, Ala.

New automobile assembly facilities attracted supplier companies. By 2005 over 1 million workers were involved in manufacturing motor vehicle parts, plastics, tires, instruments, hose, automobile batteries, hardware, bodies, and light bulbs. In addition to automobile-parts manufacturers, other industries and services needed to handle the demand of new residents and increased spending power also grew.

Southern states have created agencies to coordinate campaigns to lure automobile manufacturing and parts plants. The campaigns have been successful because of incentives offered by state and local governments. The incentive package is usually a mix of benefits from tax abatements (38 percent), infrastructure (44 percent), and employee training and recruitment (18 percent). States like Ala-

bama have extended these incentives to parts manufacturers as well, approving over $255 million in incentives to lure companies like Goodyear and Thyssen-Krupp.

The average annual wage of an automobile worker in 2007 was almost $80,000. These jobs are secured by state incentive packages that amount to over $87,000 per job created. In 2007 the state of Georgia offered over $409 million—about $163,000 per assembly job—for Kia Motors to open a factory in West Point, Ga.

Southern states have spent huge amounts to provide training programs to create a well-trained labor pool. Two examples are Mississippi's Workforce Investment Network and Alabama's Industrial Development Training program. In addition to providing state-funded training for the workforce, some southern states have created high-tech automobile research programs like the University of Alabama's Institute for Manufacturing Excellence, the University Transportation Center for Alabama, and Mississippi State University's Center for Advanced Vehicular Systems.

Today, the South has 28 percent of all automotive-parts manufacturers and 31 percent of the nation's assembly capacity. Over the last 30 years, a network of automobile manufacturing plants and parts suppliers referred to as the Southern Auto Corridor has emerged—following the path of I-65 and I-75 from the Midwest into the South. There are other pathways, like I-20 and I-55, where numerous companies have established operations. Also, the proliferation of automobile-related industries along I-85 from Virginia to Georgia represents another corridor; one section near Spartanburg, S.C., is called the "Autobahn."

CRAIG S. PASCOE
*Georgia College and State University*

Karsten Hülsemann, in *The Second Wave: Southern Industrialization from the 1940s to the 1970s*, ed. Philip Scranton (2001); Choong Soon Kim, *Japanese Industry in the American South* (1995); Beverly Rae Kimes and Henry Austin Clark Jr., *Standard Catalog of American Cars, 1805–1942* (1996); Andrew Mair, Richard Florida, and Martin Kenney, *Economic Geography* (October 1988); Craig Steven Pascoe, "Manufacturing a New South: The Business Biography of John Gary Anderson" (Ph.D. dissertation, University of Tennessee, Knoxville, 1998); Joe Sherman, *In the Rings of Saturn* (1993).

## Banking

During the colonial period, banking and financial intermediaries, except for general fire and life insurance companies, were almost nonexistent. By 1781 the situation was beginning to change with the establishment by Robert Morris of the Bank of North America and the later creation of the First Bank of the United States.

Under Alexander Hamilton's guidance, Congress chartered the First Bank of the United States (1791–1811) to provide a uniform currency and enhance the stability of the economy. Although the First Bank was not completely successful in achieving these objectives, it did provide financial services to the South through its branches in Baltimore, Charleston, New Orleans, Norfolk, Savannah, and Washington, D.C. In 1811, with political opposition growing, Congress refused to renew the bank's charter. The financial difficulties that resulted from the War of 1812 convinced Congress, however, to create another central bank, the Second Bank of the United States (1816–36). Under the leadership of Nicholas Biddle, the Second Bank operated more consciously as a central bank in its attempts to provide for economic stability and as a way of controlling state banks. However, the Second Bank also encountered opposition, especially from President Andrew Jackson, who convinced Congress not to renew the bank's charter.

Centralized banking was a highly important, if short-lived, development for the growing American economy. Another state-supported form of banking developed thereafter. With the demise of the Bank of North America in 1784, both New York and Massachusetts incorporated banks, thereby setting a precedent that other states followed.

In the South, the development of banking largely paralleled the financial development of the North. Southern states chartered a large number of private commercial banks and a smaller number of state banks. However, there were differences. Savings banks did not become important in the South because the region did not possess the large middle class that provided the necessary funds for such banks in the East. In the South, "property banks" were unique in that their purpose was to attract foreign capital for agriculture and internal improvements, using real estate as collateral for notes. The liquidity of southern banks was low and bank runs were disastrous, causing southern state legislatures to be the mainstay of these banks.

The 1830s was a critical decade for southern banking. President Jackson's attack on the Second Bank in the early 1830s reduced its influence over other financial institutions, leading to a rapid expansion of banks throughout the nation. However, the southern agricultural depression from 1837 to 1843 retarded this growth and even forced many southern banks to close.

In the aftermath of these financial failures, most states adopted regulations, especially stricter reserve requirements, to promote sounder banking practices. The most famous such action was Louisiana's Bank Act of 1842, which provided for a specie-backed currency. By providing specie reserves as a percentage of bank notes issued and thereby limiting the amount of notes, Louisiana successfully stabilized its banking system. Several other southern states during the 1840s and 1850s adopted the free-banking system outlined in the Free Banking Act of New York. In some cases, like Louisiana, the free-banking system worked well.

The turbulence of the 1830s and the political hostility toward banks in the 1840s were replaced by cautious expansion of southern banking in the 1850s. Reflecting the growth of the southern economy, a period of sustained prosperity appeared imminent, until the outbreak of the Civil War. In 1861 many southern banks began to suspend the convertibility of their notes into gold. In the same year, southern banks sub- scribed heavily to the first Confederate loan, thereby losing much of their specie. During the Civil War, the specie that the Confederate States of America (CSA) was able to obtain came largely from Britain and the Continent. With limited ability to tax and to borrow, the CSA used the printing presses to pay for the war effort.

Between January 1861 and January 1864, the South's money supply increased over 11 times. Bank notes and deposits increased less than threefold, because southern commercial banks drastically raised their reserve ratios in anticipation of mass withdrawals triggered by the approach of Union troops. Although this behavior moderated the increase of the money supply somewhat and provided some protection for individual banks, many southern banks did not survive the Civil War. And the aftermath of the war was even worse.

The major feature of the years 1865 to 1913 was the South's financial underdevelopment; banking services were severely limited relative to other regions. The South, in fact, was the last region to be integrated into a national capital market. Most economic historians attribute this situation to the banking structure that resulted from the National Banking Acts of the Civil War years. This legislation limited national banks in the South by restricting agricultural loans and imposing relatively large capital requirements. Its tax on state bank notes, moreover, hindered the development of state banks. The result was that many banks operated in a noncompetitive market, thereby limiting the amount of bank credit available and raising interest rates. Because of local bank monopolies, country stores began channeling credit to borrowers, with serious long-term ramifications for the structure of southern agriculture.

After 1880 interest-rate differentials declined as institutional changes, such as the spread of commercial paper and a reduction of the money power of local banks, took place. Local monopoly power of southern banks declined, in part because of the 1900 Gold Standard Act, which formally put the nation on a gold standard and reduced minimum capital requirements for national banks, thereby making it easier for small banks to become national banks.

The next major change in the nation's banking system was the establishment of the Federal Reserve System (FRS) in 1913. The FRS was designed to prevent financial panics by acting as a lender of last resort—or, in other words, by operating as a central bank. However, the original legislation also attempted to diffuse power geographically by establishing 12 regional or district banks, which were to play a role in formation of monetary policy. Federal Reserve Banks in the South were located in Atlanta, Dallas, and Richmond. The framers of the legislation hoped that the regional banks would be more aware of and concerned with the problems of banks within their region than would one central bank in New York City or Washington, D.C.

The establishment of the Federal Reserve System did not solve southern banking problems, as witnessed by the difficult experiences of southern banks in the 1920s. Indeed, the Roaring Twen-

ties saw the South experience a disproportionate number of bank failures when measured either by the number of bank closings or by deposits. The high rate of bank failure was probably caused by the long agricultural depression beginning in the early 1920s, the large number of small state banks, lax supervision, and incompetent management.

The Depression of the 1930s was extremely traumatic for the southern banking industry, as it was for the nation's banking industry generally. From 1929 to 1934, assets of southern banks fell from $7 billion to $4.7 billion, a decline of about 33 percent, compared with 21 percent in the rest of the country. Southern assets reached the 1929 levels only a decade later.

Although after World War II the South's banking structure grew to more closely resemble the national system, in 1945 a larger percentage of southern banks were small, nonmember state banks. They were also nonpar, not paying the full value of checks but deducting a service charge from the face value of each check. More importantly, southern banks still held large net deposits in banks outside the region. After 1945 the substantial economic growth that the South experienced caused rapid expansion in southern banking as well.

During the 1950s southern states experienced a reduction in the number of banks and a rapid expansion of branch banks. This was due to the increased urbanization of the South and the concurrent growth of suburbs. In the 1960s and 1970s bank expansion was fostered in some states like Georgia, Texas, and Virginia through the device of bank holding companies. Major financial centers developed in Atlanta, Dallas, Houston, and Miami, while North Carolina National Bank Corporation and Wachovia Corporation became important regional banks.

During the 1960s the major southern banks rapidly expanded by following the national trend of increased utilization of liability management techniques. Rather than just manage assets within a given liability structure, southern banks began to aggressively pursue additional deposits in order to obtain a target asset growth. The period of rapid and often reckless expansion ended abruptly in 1974 when the real estate market collapsed. Because so much construction was going on in the South, southern banks were more affected by this collapse than were northern banks. Banks such as North Carolina National, Atlanta's Citizen and Southern, and Florida's Flagship Banks wrote off millions of dollars of bad loans. Since then, cautious growth on the long-term pattern of Wachovia has been the dominant trend. Although such stringent credit practices curtail asset growth, they do provide banks with the increased ability of surviving economic difficulties.

Not all modern southern bankers are cautious, however. Bert Lance was forced to resign as President Jimmy Carter's budget director because of repercussions from his loose, small-town Georgia credit practices. Tennessee banking magnate Jake Butcher, a Democratic candidate for governor in 1978 and the driving force behind the 1982 Knoxville World's Fair, used to claim that he rose from southern rural poverty to financial and political power the honest way—by borrowing. In 1983, however, his financial empire began to unravel when the Tennessee Banking Commission shut down Butcher's flagship, the United American Bank of Knoxville, a $760 million institution. This fourth-largest U.S. commercial bank failure since the 1930s resulted from what the commission cited as "large and unusual loan losses," many of them to Democratic politicians and the bank's directors.

Looking back, American banking in general underwent some highly significant changes after 1945. These changes affected not only the larger investment banks on Wall Street but also smaller regional banks, including the southern banks that typically had not been subjected to national events and trends.

Essentially, three major developments took place. First, technology began to have an impact on the banking industry. While bankers used the idea of "small, homey, and personal" in their sales pitches for depositors, the truth of the matter was that small depositors were costly. In order to minimize such costs, banks generally began to use technology. Today, the American people have become accustomed to automatic teller machines (ATMs) and online banking. The ATMs actually promoted bank branching, while online banking helped reduce personnel and other ancillary costs. Other important technological innovations included smart cards and the possibilities of "e-money."

A second development that has affected American banking generally, and especially southern banking, is consolidation. In today's global economy, in which international markets impact each other daily, the idea of local, small-town banks is becoming obsolete. In reality, it is becoming harder and harder for such banks to survive. Today, banks are consolidating into regional-sized systems such as Regions Banking in the South. Another interesting advance here is the intrusion of such large investment houses as Wachovia into the banking business, along with insurance companies like State Farm, which now offers its customers the familiarities of banking along with its other services.

The last major development changing the face of American banking is government regulation. This is not a new development. In fact, regulation goes back into the 1830s and 1840s, when free banking was first introduced. Today, however, the regulation occurring is far-reaching and very intrusive into banking operations. The Federal Reserve is actually benefiting as it assumes more and more authority and influence in the American banking system. As early as 1956, the Bank Holding Company Act had been passed to prohibit interstate acquisition of banks unless the state approved them. A few years later in 1961, Congress put into effect the Interest Rate Adjustment Act, which extended Regulation Q to the thrift industry. More regulations came in the 1970s and 1980s, but it was the 1980 Depository Institutions Deregulation and Monetary Control Act that really changed things. Through this act, the Fed was given authority over reserve requirements for all banking

institutions. In 1982 Congress allowed money-market accounts and interstate mergers with banks under the terms of the Garn–St. Germain Act. Other regulatory laws were passed, including the 1983 International Lending Supervisory Act and the 1989 Financial Institutions Reform, Recovery, and Enforcement Act (which restructured the FDIC). In 1991 Congress passed the Federal Deposit Insurance Corporation Improvement Act.

While all this legislation sounded very important, it was not until 1999 that President Bill Clinton signed one of the most comprehensive banking laws in American history with the Financial Services Modernization Act. This law alone removed restrictions on banks affiliating with securities firms, provided for state regulation of insurance, and hosted a large number of other reforms that had the federal government watching the banking industry under a microscope.

These regulatory laws affected all areas and regions of American banking. Today, American banking may be highly regulated, but the Fed is also one of the most powerful financial institutions in American, and perhaps world, history. Banking, in short, has come a long way from its meager beginnings in the colonial era.

MICHAEL V. NAMORATO
*University of Mississippi*

Mansel Blackford and Austin Kerr, *Business Enterprise in American History* (1990); Lance E. Davis, *Journal of Economic History* (September 1965); Thomas P. Gavan, *Banking and the Credit System in Georgia, 1810–1860* (1978); George D. Green, *Finance and*

Economic Development in the Old South: Louisiana Banking, 1804–1861 (1972); Bray Hammond, *Banks and Politics in America: From the Revolution to the Civil War* (1957); Emory Q. Hawk, *Economic History of the South* (1934); Calvin B. Hoover and B. U. Ratchford, *Economic Resources and Policies of the South* (1951); John A. James, *Journal of Interdisciplinary History* (Winter 1981); George Macesich, *Commercial Banking and Regional Development in the United States, 1950–1960* (1965); Fritz Redlich, *The Molding of American History* (January 1977); Larry Schweikart, *Banking in the American South from the Age of Jackson to Reconstruction* (1988); Herbert Stein, *The Fiscal Revolution in America* (1990); Richard Sylla, *Journal of Economic History* (December 1969); Elmus Wicker, *Journal of Economic History* (September 1980).

## Bulldozer Revolution

Historian C. Vann Woodward has suggested that the most apt "symbol of innovation" in the modern South is the bulldozer. "The roar and groan and dust of it greet one on the outskirts of every Southern city," he wrote in a 1958 essay titled "The Search for Southern Identity." The mule had been the popular symbol of the South's traditional agricultural economy, but the giant earthmoving machine in the post–World War II period had become central to the industrial revolution in the region. The bulldozer symbolized the revolution "in its favorite area of operation, the area where city meets country; in its relentless speed; in its supreme disregard for obstacles, its heedless methods; in what it demolishes and in what it moves."

The bulldozer made possible the rapid and concentrated urbanization of the South in the 1940s and 1950s, and it facilitated the clearing of land for suburban development in the same period. Southerners and others traveling through the region became familiar with the giant machine on the landscape. It was essential to the transforming work of the Tennessee Valley Authority, the Corps of Engineers, and the construction crews building interstate highways. The bulldozer swept away sharecroppers' shacks to make way for Sunbelt shopping malls.

Robert G. LeTourneau was perhaps the most notable bulldozer businessman in the South. Born in Vermont and raised in Minnesota, LeTourneau spent his young adulthood in California, working as an automobile repairman. A natural inventor, he developed tools for sale to contractors and opened a small factory in Stockton, Calif., in 1935 and another one later in Peoria, Ill. His southern operations were at Toccoa, Ga., Longview, Tex., and Vicksburg, Miss. In the latter case, the Warren County Chamber of Commerce purchased much of the land LeTourneau needed in order to encourage him to come to the site eight miles south of Vicksburg. LeTourneau's factories made much of the earthmoving equipment used by the armed services during World War II. By 1952 the Mississippi plant alone produced 22 types of heavy machinery used in 44 states and many foreign nations.

LeTourneau sold his earthmoving business in 1953 for $31 million to Westinghouse Air Brake Company. He retained, however, his factories in the South and converted them to the production of offshore oil rigs and missile-loading transport machinery. LeTourneau reentered the bulldozer business in 1958. Though not a native southerner, LeTourneau came to live in the South and "adopted" it as his home. He was an evangelical who found the region a congenial place with many like-minded Christians. Known as "God's business-man," he once described the "three planks" of his life: "speed, the welding torch, and the Bible." This southern earthmover provided financial support for the Billy Graham revivals in the early 1950s, and Graham helped dedicate and bless LeTourneau's work.

CHARLES REAGAN WILSON
*University of Mississippi*

James C. Cobb, *The Selling of the South: The Southern Crusade for Industrialized Development, 1936–1990* (1993); Longview, Tex., *News-Journal* (1 January 1953); Vicksburg, Miss., *Evening Post* (26 November 1942); *Wall Street Journal* (28 January 1957); C. Vann Woodward, *The Burden of Southern History* (1960).

## Casino Gambling

Casino-style gambling houses have long been part of the South's social fabric, but only since the early 1990s have such establishments carved a legitimatized footing in the region's soil. Southern antebellum gaming dens were most common in the Mississippi River cities of Memphis, Vicksburg, and New Orleans, where they tempted a transient crowd of riverboat travelers. More elite and permanent clubs, most notably in New Orleans, catered to wealthier gamblers, while the more common and rougher variety typically operated along the waterfront. These riverside working-class "gambling hells" often earned reputations for violent crime, cheating card sharps, and all manner of elicit vice. Yet, all gambling houses of the period faced an uncertain relationship with legal authorities and weathered periodic reform initiatives launched by citizens opposed to their operation.

During the late 19th and early 20th centuries, more substantial elicit casinos prospered in the same communities that had been only somewhat hospitable before the Civil War. Fueled further by the invention of the slot machine in 1895, these establishments increasingly came to resemble modern casinos. Gaming "resorts" in Biloxi, Miss., Hot Springs, Ark., and just outside the city limits of New Orleans became the destination of choice for vice-seeking tourists and locals alike. Operation of these casinos remained outside the law, requiring governmental complicity, corruption, and bribes in exchange for the ability to function openly. During the first half of the 20th century, southern gambling houses navigated these legal obstacles with relative ease, but by the late 1960s most fell on hard times. In 1967 the city government of Hot Springs shut down its once famous gambling establishments for good. Growing competition from legitimate casinos in Las Vegas and Atlantic City forced many of the South's other illegitimate operations to slip back into the shadows.

The modern era of casino gambling in the South began in 1989, when Mississippi's state legislature approved the first in a series of bills authorizing local-option dockside "riverboat" gambling

*Mississippi riverboat casino in the port of Greenville, Miss. (Courtesy James G. Thomas Jr., photographer)*

in counties bordering the Gulf Coast and the Mississippi River. Plagued by the chronic poverty of its citizens and significant state budgetary shortfalls, Mississippi followed an increasing national trend toward the adoption of casino-style gambling for the purpose of generating desperately needed revenue. Passage of gambling legislation opened a public debate that brought religious, state, and community leaders into conflict. Opponents of gambling in the Bible Belt argued that moral decay, gambling addiction, and the spread of governmental corruption would accompany the new casinos. Boosters promised a panacea for the state's economic ills and job growth in counties dogged by high unemployment. By the mid-1990s, the new casinos around Tunica and Biloxi had indeed produced a dramatic increase in both state and local revenue and had generated many jobs. Unfortunately, they also brought some of the negative aspects that detractors had warned about, most conspicuously crime. Moreover, contrary to promises made by progambling forces, the advent of gambling in Mississippi has yet to significantly ameliorate the low wage

levels of the state's sizable minority population.

Critics of legalized gambling received more ammunition when neighboring Louisiana sought to adopt competing "riverboat" casinos. While Mississippi avoided government corruption scandals, Louisiana did not. Federal authorities ultimately would convict Louisiana governor Edwin Edwards on charges of bribery and racketeering for his role in awarding state casino licenses to a host of shady characters. Further, most Louisiana casinos have failed to live up to the economic success of their Mississippi counterparts. While casino gambling as an economic solution for southern state governments has had mixed success, their impact on the region's culture is profound. The legalization of these establishments reflects a seemingly widespread acceptance of an activity once considered a criminal vice into a legitimate industry. The presence of casinos in the South also highlights the paradoxical relationship between Bible Belt evangelical Christian values and Sunbelt economic pragmatism.

JOHN NYSTROM
*University of Georgia*

Tyler Bridges, *Bad Bet on the Bayou: The Rise of Gambling in Louisiana and the Fall of Governor Edwin Edwards* (2001); Dee Brown, *The American Spa: Hot Springs, Arkansas* (1982); Henry Chafetz, *Play the Devil: A History of Gambling in the United States from 1492 to 1955* (1960); Ann Fabian, *Card Sharps, Dream Books, and Bucket Shops: Gambling in Nineteenth-Century America* (1990); Ben C. Toledano, *National Review* (7 April 1997).

## Chain and Specialty Stores

After the Civil War, the rural South witnessed the development of country or general stores. Mail-order houses such as Sears, Roebuck and Co. caused socioeconomic rumblings, but the real merchandising revolution was the advent of specialty stores and their spread as chains under common ownership. These new stores, which sold one product (such as shoes) rather than a variety of products, grew in number during the early 20th century, and by the 1920s they held a sufficiently large share of the market to feed the growing cult of consumerism through the promise of standardized goods and lower prices made possible by economies of scale. But if there was the prospect of a better standard of living, there was also the threat—or so it seemed to some—of the destruction of local proprietorship and community involvement in states held by absentee owners from the North. The issue of regional versus national culture was expressed in populist rhetoric in the context of an urban-industrial progressive spirit.

By the 1930s, in the face of the Great Depression, numerous attempts were made across the nation to regulate chain stores by means of municipal and state taxation and fair-trade laws. Many of these measures originated in the South, and some of the most significant Supreme Court cases concerning chain-store regulation involved southern states (*Stewart Dry Goods v. Lewis* [Kentucky]; *Liggett v. Lee* [Florida]; *A&P v. Grosjean* [Louisiana]). Among the more prominent antichain figures were southerners such as Congressman Wright Patman of Texas, who sought national chain-store regulation, and W. K. "Old Man" Henderson, who broadcast nationwide tirades against the chains over radio station KWKH in Shreveport.

Even in the face of such opposition, chain stores prospered as the South's urban areas joined in the creation of innovative merchandising. Clarence Saunders of Memphis pioneered many self-service techniques in his Piggly Wiggly stores, and the Florida-based Winn-Dixie stores became leaders in the food field. The growth of national and regional chains within the South reflected its increasing urbanization and transformation from a region characterized by Franklin D. Roosevelt as the "nation's no. 1 economic problem" to a part of the developing Sunbelt. As it changed from exploited to exploiter, the South altered its characteristic forms of marketing. In a nation where merchandising is a key to culture, the results have been startling.

CARL RYANT
*University of Louisville*

Thomas D. Clark, *Pills, Petticoats, and Plows: The Southern Country Store* (1944); Godfrey M. Lebhar, *Chain Stores in America, 1859–1959* (3rd ed., 1963); Ted Ownby, *American Dreams in Mississippi: Consumers, Poverty, and Culture, 1830–1998* (1999); Carl Ryant, *Journal of Southern History* (May 1973).

## Coal Mining

Although coal was discovered in Virginia in the early 1700s, southern coal mining remained a small-scale enterprise until the late 19th century because of the lack of transportation. Following

Bank Boss, Turkey Knob Mine, Macdonald, W.Va., and a great fall of slate that blocked entry, 1908 (Lewis Wickes Hines, Library of Congress, [LOT 7477, no. 0147 (P&P)], Washington, D.C.)

the Civil War, the increased demand for coal as a fuel for the Industrial Revolution, the development of the steam-driven plow (which tunneled out the Appalachian Mountains), and the appearance of railroads in the mountains promoted the emergence of coal as a significant southern product.

The rise of the coal industry consumed farmland and farm life, as well as mountain culture, as the industrial transformation tied the previously rural, isolated regions to the international economy. In 1890 McDowell County, W.Va., produced 245,000 tons of coal a year; two decades later it was producing 13 million tons annually. In 1910 Harlan County, Ky., did not produce a single ton of coal; by 1926 the county yielded over 13 million tons of coal annually. By 1940 southern coalfields produced

over 40 percent of the coal mined in the United States, and that proportion grew to more than 50 percent by 1960. West Virginia and Kentucky in that year accounted for 80 percent of southern coal production.

To house, feed, and shelter a workforce in the isolated coalfields, coal companies established company towns in which the company built and retained control over every aspect of community life, including houses, stores, churches, and schools. Miners in the northern coalfields struggled to unionize for higher wages, but southern miners sought to unionize for social, political, and economic reasons. To preserve their feudalistic controls and capitalistic profits, the coal companies fought back tenaciously. The result was bitter and bloody labor-management conflicts; the "Armed March on Logan," the Mingo County Strike of the 1920s, and the Harlan County strikes of the 1930s are extreme but powerful examples of how far each side would go in pursuit of its objectives.

The southern coalfields were unionized in the 1930s, a combined accomplishment of John L. Lewis (the legendary chief of the United Mine Workers of America), President Franklin Roosevelt and his New Deal, and, most importantly, a massive uprising of miners. The union, however, failed as a counterbalance to the power of the coal companies as it became bogged down in internal corruption and autocracy. The coal companies established cultural and political hegemonies over the states of West Virginia and Kentucky and continued to exercise considerable political clout in other southern coal-producing states.

Mining tragedies, labor-management strife, various disasters (such as the flood resulting from a broken slag dam that killed 125 people in February 1972 at Buffalo Creek, W.Va.), and strip mining (which, in 1970, accounted for about 35 percent of southern coal mining) have been the coal industry's legacy to southern culture. For example, on 23 September 2001, gas explosions in the Blue Creek No. 5 mine in Brookwood, Ala., located between Birmingham and Tuscaloosa, killed 13 coal miners. Mine No. 5 was the nation's deepest vertical shaft at the time, and the No. 5 mine explosion was the worst mining accident in the United States since 1984, when 27 workers were killed in a mine near Orangeville, Utah. Since then, a number of fatalities have occurred at the mines in Brookwood, including one in 1995 involving falling materials, one electrocution in 1995, an asphyxiation in 1996, and two falling deaths in 1999 and 2001. Another major mine disaster occurred in a Sago, W.Va., mine on 2 January 2006. The disaster received nationwide media coverage, and because of the frantic, round-the-clock nature of the reporting, wrong information was circulated. The most staggering mistake occurred when it was reported that rescuers had found 12 of the 13 miners alive, when in reality 12 had died and only 1 had survived. The Sago community and the nation were grief stricken and outraged.

By their control of the land, the coal companies have prevented the economic diversification of the coal regions. Underdeveloped and bound to a single industry, the economies of the southern coalfield regions fluctuate with the boom-and-bust cycle of the coal industry. A protracted and disastrous bust began in the 1920s with the rise of competing fuels, mainly oil and gas, and an overabundance of coal mines. In the late 1940s, the southern coal industry mechanized, mainly in the form of the Continuous Miner, a machine that did the work of many miners. Automation may have saved the southern coal industry, but it prompted massive unemployment and poverty throughout the coal regions and resulted in thousands of miners migrating to the midwestern urban-industrial areas in search of employment.

The energy crisis and oil embargo of the 1970s produced another boom in the industry as the nation, especially under President Jimmy Carter's administration, turned to coal as the means of achieving national energy security. The 111-day coal strike in 1977–78, a worldwide oil glut, and Reaganomics, which wiped out federal energy programs, led the nation away from coal and produced another bust in the southern coalfields.

In the 1960s oil companies began purchasing the southern coal companies. Occidental bought Island Creek, Continental Oil took over Consolidation Coal, and other mergers followed. The impact of these business ventures remains to be seen, but with more capital and a greater emphasis on technology, especially strip mining, the oil companies' takeover of the southern coal industry does not promise a bright future for the land or the people.

DAVID A. CORBIN
*Arlington, Virginia*

Appalachian Land Owner Task Force, *Who Owns Appalachia? Landownership and Its Impact* (1983); David A. Corbin, *Life, Work, and Rebellion in the Coal Fields: Southern West Virginia Coal Miners, 1880–1922* (1981); Ronald D. Eller, *Miners, Millhands, and Mountaineers: The Modernization of the Appalachian South* (1982); Roger Fagge, *Power, Culture, and Conflict in the Coalfields of West Virginia and South Wales, 1900–1922* (1996); William Graebner, *Coal-Mining Safety in the Progressive Period* (1976).

## Coca-Cola

William Allen White once called it the "sublimated essence of all that America stands for," and an anonymous but no less fervent admirer called it the "holy water of the American South." The "it," as the latest in a long line of slogans proclaims, is, of course, Coca-Cola.

John S. Pemberton, known as "Doc" like most pharmacists of his era, concocted Coca-Cola in 1886 primarily as a hangover cure. It has subsequently been many things to many people; to Robert Winship Woodruff, its high priest for nearly 60 years, the drink is a "religion as well as a business." Pemberton first made Coke, its nickname from early on, in Atlanta, and leaders of the Coca-Cola company have bestrode that city ever since. Pemberton was pleased soon after his invention to sell the rights to it for $1,750 to another Atlanta pharmacist, Asa Candler. Candler was even more pleased to sell the Coca-Cola Company for $25 million in 1919. It was, at the time, the biggest financial deal in the history of the American South. (Candler sold only part of his bounty; earlier, in 1899, thinking that consumption of the drink would be limited largely to soda fountains, he had disposed of practically all of the bottling rights to it for exactly one dollar. The drink had first been bottled back in 1894 by Joseph Biedenharn in Vicksburg, Miss.) The prime mover in the 1919 transaction was the banker Ernest Woodruff. His son, Robert (1889–1985), took over the company in 1923. "Asa Candler put us on our feet," one Coca-Cola executive would say years afterward, "and Bob Woodruff gave us wings."

Dwight D. Eisenhower once speculated that his good friend Bob Woodruff might be the richest man in the United States. Atlanta's Emory University, on whose predecessor campus Woodruff had spent less than a year as an undergraduate before being invited to leave, over the ensuing years would be endowed by Woodruff and his family with some $150 million of Coca-Cola largess.

Until World War II, when the Coca-Cola Company construed it to be its patriotic duty to get Coke to every thirsty American serviceman and servicewoman abroad, the drink was chiefly marketed in the United States. Soon it was universal. Asa Candler briefly flirted with the idea of Coca-Cola cigars and Coca-Cola chewing gum at the turn of the century, but until the 1950s the company was strictly a one-product enterprise. Then it began to diversify. Orange juice, other soft drinks, eventually even wines, and most recently films (Columbia Pictures) were merchandised around the world. The placid liquid that Doc Pemberton had first mixed in a backyard, three-legged iron pot (stirring it with an oar) had become the foundation of a multibillion-dollar industry.

In 1985 Coca-Cola chairman Roberto Guizueta announced that, for the first time in 99 years, the drink's taste formula would be changed, leading to much hoopla and criticism from some for yet another change in a southern tradition. The company relented in the face of public pressure and continued marketing "classic" Coke. However, despite (or perhaps because of) the overwhelming public demand for a return to the "classic" Coke taste, Coca-Cola currently comes in a variety of flavors, such as Cherry Coke, Diet Coke, Coca-Cola Zero, Vanilla Coke, and Coca-Cola with Lime. As of 2006 the Coca-Cola Company operates in over 200 countries and produces over 400 brands. It is undoubtedly the most ubiquitous consumer product in the world.

E. J. KAHN JR.
New Yorker *Magazine*

Frederick Allen, *Secret Formula: How Brilliant Marketing and Relentless Salesmanship Made Coca-Cola the Best-Known Product in the World* (1994); Bob Hall, *Southern Exposure* (Fall 1976); Constance L. Hayes, *The Real Thing: Truth and Power at the Coca-Cola Company* (2004); E. J. Kahn Jr., *The Big Drink: The Story of Coca-Cola* (1951); Kathryn W. Kemp, *God's Capitalist: Asa Candler of Coca-Cola* (2002).

### De Bow's Review

Established in New Orleans in 1846 by James Dunwoody Brownson De Bow, *De Bow's Review* was the preeminent southern antebellum journal of business, economics, and public opinion. Modeled on Freeman Hunt's *Merchant's Magazine of New York*, the *Commercial Review*, as it was often called, was initially devoted to "the diversities and ramifications of commercial action." Always a partisan of the South, De Bow increasingly advocated southern nationalism and the defense of slavery after 1850, and he opened the journal's pages to supporters of secession, including Edmund Ruffin and George Fitzhugh.

Despite the *Review*'s importance, De Bow always had difficulty keeping the journal in print. Southerners refused to subscribe in sufficient numbers, and De Bow was forced to suspend publication in 1847 and 1849. Circulation never exceeded 5,000. Slow to realize the possibility of revenue from advertising, De Bow on the eve of the Civil War found the advertisements of northern firms to be his best source of income. He was also forced, after repeated failures with southern printers, to have the *Review* printed in the North, a fact that he kept hidden from his readers. De Bow managed to keep the publication alive during the Civil War until April 1862, when financial problems, scarcities of printing supplies, and the fall of New Orleans forced suspension. One issue was published in 1864; the journal then lay dormant until war's end. De Bow resumed publication of the *Review* in January 1866, devoting its pages to the restoration of national unity and the development of the nation's wealth and resources. Some of the familiar contributors returned, such as George Fitzhugh, but De Bow was unable to restore the magazine to its prewar eminence. De Bow's death in February 1867 brought a quick end to his journal. Sold in March 1868, the *Review* soon ceased publication.

Influential beyond its limited circulation, *De Bow's Review* reflected both southern opinion and the somewhat idiosyncratic views of its editor. Always advocating southern interests, *De Bow's* contributors ardently defended slavery, argued the superiority of southern civilization, promoted the improvement of southern agriculture, and after 1850 championed southern nationalism. De Bow, however, also firmly believed in promoting southern commercial, mercantile, and industrial interests. His frank advocacy of the urgent need to achieve commercial and industrial independence for the looming contest with the North set De Bow apart from the

reigning planter ethos and probably limited the *Review*'s appeal to the planter elite. De Bow astutely recognized the economic and industrial weaknesses of the South, yet his untiring campaign to build a solid commercial and industrial economy failed. Not wholly typical of antebellum southern thinking, then, *De Bow's Review* still provides a superb window into the southern mind during the 15 years before secession and civil war.

DANIEL J. WILSON
*Muhlenberg College*

*De Bow's Review*, vols. 1–34 (1846–64), *After the War Series*, vols. 1–8 (1866–70), New Series, *After the War Series*, vol. 1 (1879–80); Michael O'Brien, *Conjectures of Order: Intellectual Life and the American South, 1810–1860*, 2 vols. (2004); Paul F. Paskoff and Daniel J. Wilson, *The Cause of the South: Selections from De Bow's Review, 1846–1867* (1982); Ottis Clark Skipper, *J. D. B. De Bow: Magazinist of the Old South* (1958); Diffee William Standard, "*De Bow's Review, 1846–1880: A Magazine of Southern Opinion*" (Ph.D. dissertation, University of North Carolina at Chapel Hill, 1970).

## Delta Airlines

Beginning in 1924 as Huff Daland Dusters and specializing primarily in crop spraying in the southern United States and Latin America, Delta adopted its enduring name in 1928 from the Mississippi Delta region. Guided by Collett Everman "C. E." Woolman, a former county agricultural agent who ultimately became its patriarch and longtime chief executive, the airline began passenger operations in 1929 from its Monroe, La., base on a route eventually extending from Fort Worth to Atlanta. Forced to abandon this service in 1930 when it failed to win an essential federal government airmail contract, Delta survived precariously on meager earnings from crop dusting and fixed-base activities.

In 1934 congressional probing of irregularities in the awarding of previous airmail contracts led to cancellation of most existing contracts and fresh opportunities for Delta, which in June of that year won an airmail route from Fort Worth to Charleston via Atlanta and other cities. Resuming airline operations, the company became a vigorous regional carrier. Increasing capital requirements, partly connected with the acquisition of Douglas DC-2 and DC-3 aircraft, led in 1941 to a transfer of Delta's headquarters to Atlanta.

Delta Airlines stewardess with portable Coca-Cola coolers, ca. 1945 (Coca-Cola Company Archives, Atlanta, Ga.)

Delta's intensive use of a restricted fleet in World War II produced earnings that, coupled with a Chicago-to-Miami route award granted by the Civil Aeronautics Board in 1945, laid the basis for postwar expansion. Inflation, mounting costs, and other industrywide problems produced spotty earnings in the late 1940s; but thereafter Delta enjoyed steady profits, enlarging its system by absorbing another regional carrier, Chicago and Southern, in a 1953 merger and winning a route the following year from Atlanta to Washington, D.C., and New York.

Delta was a pioneer of the jet age, the first airline to inaugurate DC-8, DC-9, and Convair 880 service. It also won new routes to such key destinations as Los Angeles, and in 1971 it absorbed Northeast Airlines in another merger. Woolman's ability to project the company as a southern-style extended family promoted loyalty among Delta's mainly nonunion employees. After his death in 1966, a management team trained under his tutelage continued to emphasize this "family feeling" and retained his conservative financial policies. Such strategies, coupled with rigorous fleet standardization and new routes to such places as London, England, made Delta the most consistently profitable firm in the airline industry, a position it continued to hold in the 1970s and early 1980s despite rising fuel costs, periodic recessions, and the onset of federal deregulation.

Delta dramatically expanded its operation with the 1991 purchase of Pan Am's European routes, which gave Delta the nation's most extensive overseas connections. The 1990s also saw major expansion into Latin America and the

Caribbean, but the airline also struggled with debt during the decade, leading it to file for bankruptcy in September 2005. Delta emerged from bankruptcy in April 2007. As of that time, the airline had routes to over 332 destinations in 57 countries, making it one of the South's leading global enterprises.

W. DAVID LEWIS
WESLEY P. NEWTON
*Auburn University*

W. David Lewis and Wesley P. Newton, *Delta: The History of an Airline* (1979).

## Duke, James B.

(1856–1925) BUSINESSMAN AND PHILANTHROPIST.

The youngest of three children of Washington Duke and Artelia Roney Duke, James Buchanan Duke was born in Orange (now Durham) County, N.C., on 23 December 1856. Although his mother died in 1858 and his father was later drafted into Confederate service, "Buck" Duke, as he was known in the family, spent most of his childhood on his father's modest farm about three miles from the new village of Durham. He received some schooling at an academy in Durham and, after a brief stay at New Garden School (later Guilford College), attended the Eastman Business College in Poughkeepsie, N.Y.

Washington Duke began the home manufacture of brightleaf smoking tobacco after the Civil War, and James B. Duke grew up with a firsthand knowledge of every phase of the tobacco business. In 1874 Washington Duke sold his farm and moved his family into Durham to launch a more ambitious

James B. Duke, North Carolina businessman, ca. 1900 (Duke University Archives, Durham, N.C.)

manufacturing operation. Displaying a rare talent for business and an appetite for hard work, James B. Duke became a full partner in W. Duke Sons and Company when it was incorporated in 1878. Though the company prospered, it was overshadowed by the older, larger W. T. Blackwell Company, which produced the famed Bull Durham brand of tobacco. After bringing in hand rollers from New York to produce the newfangled cigarette, the Dukes, inspired largely by James B. Duke, gambled in the mid-1880s on a machine-made cigarette and entered into an important, secret contract for the machine invented by James A. Bonsack of Virginia.

The gamble paid off handsomely, for by 1890 W. Duke Sons and Company was the leading manufacturer of cigarettes in the nation, and James B. Duke, who moved permanently to New York in 1884 to manage the branch factory there, had played a key role in organizing the leading cigarette manufacturers into a combination or "trust," the American Tobacco Company. Within a decade the company, with Duke as its president, controlled the major portion of the nation's entire tobacco industry (save for cigars) and, with operations in Britain, Japan, and elsewhere in the world, became a pioneer multinational corporation.

Even before the U.S. Supreme Court called for the dissolution of the American Tobacco Company in 1911, James B. Duke, along with his older brother Benjamin N. Duke and others, had invested heavily in textile manufacturing in Durham and elsewhere in North Carolina. Partly as a result of that activity, the Dukes became interested in the new electric-power industry and specifically in hydroelectric power. In 1905 they launched the Southern Power Company with headquarters in Charlotte, N.C., and, under the leadership of James B. Duke and William S. Lee, a brilliant engineer with whom Duke worked closely, the business eventually grew into the giant Duke Power Company, serving the piedmont regions of North and South Carolina.

Starting in the late 19th century, Washington Duke and his family began regularly to give substantial support to various philanthropic causes, especially, but not exclusively, Methodist-related ones. The Dukes were instrumental in bringing the Methodist-sponsored Trinity College to Durham in 1892, and Benjamin N. Duke became the family's main link with the college as well as its chief patron. In December 1924 James B. Duke, after several years of careful planning, established the Duke Endowment as a perpetual trust for certain philanthropic purposes in the Carolinas. Systematizing on a perpetual basis a long-standing pattern of family giving, James B. Duke specified that a prime beneficiary of the endowment was to be a new university organized around Trinity College, which, at the suggestion of Trinity's president William P. Few, was to be named Duke University. Annual support from the endowment went also to nonprofit hospitals for both races in the Carolinas, three other colleges (Davidson, Furman, and Johnson C. Smith), child-care institutions in the Carolinas for blacks and whites, and rural Methodist churches and retired Methodist preachers in North Carolina.

After a first marriage that ended in a much-publicized divorce in 1906, James B. Duke in 1907 married a Georgia-born widow, Mrs. Walker P. Inman (née Nanaline Holt), and in 1912 a daughter, Doris Duke, was born to the couple. James B. Duke died in his mansion on New York's Fifth Avenue on 10 October 1925 and is buried alongside Washington and Benjamin N. Duke in the Memorial Chapel on the campus of Duke University.

ROBERT F. DURDEN
*Duke University*

Robert F. Durden, *Bold Entrepreneur: A Life of James B. Duke* (2003), *The Dukes of Durham, 1865–1929* (1975); John K. Winkler, *Tobacco Tycoon: The Story of James B. Duke* (1942).

## Flagler, Henry

(1830–1913) ENTREPRENEUR.
Henry Morrison Flagler led the development of the east coast of Florida from 1885, when he launched his business ventures in Florida, until his death in 1913. Born in western New York State in 1830, Flagler moved to Ohio as a young man to seek his fortune. With the help of relatives, he became a successful grain dealer. He married his first wife, Mary Harkness, in 1853. From this marriage came his only children, Jenny Louise and Harry. During the Civil War, Flagler invested his life savings in a salt-manufacturing business that failed. After the war, he joined John D. Rockefeller as a founding partner in Standard Oil Company. Flagler was instrumental in developing the railroad rebate system and other competitive practices that helped Standard dominate the oil industry. By the 1880s he was a very wealthy man.

Flagler first went to Florida for the benefit of his wife's precarious health. After Mary's death, Flagler married Ida Alice Shourds and returned to Florida for a winter excursion. In 1885 he commenced a major building and improvement program in the old resort town of St. Augustine that was designed to make it the "winter Newport" for America's wealthy elite. The centerpiece of his work was the Hotel Ponce de Leon, designed by architects Thomas Hastings and John Carrere. Artists such as Louis C. Tiffany contributed to the elaborate structure.

To ensure convenient travel from the North to his hotels, Flagler bought and consolidated short-line railroads to create the Florida East Coast Railway. Subsequently, he extended his rail line along the Atlantic coast all the way to Key West. To encourage his railroad construction, the state of Florida gave Flagler large tracts of land, making Flagler one of the largest landowners and land developers in the state.

Warmer weather in south Florida drew Flagler to Palm Beach, where he built two huge luxury hotels: the Royal Poinciana and the Breakers. By the mid-1890s his railroad and hotel chain reached Miami. Flagler then embarked on the daunting task of building his railroad over miles of open water and small islands to Key West, a feat that was accomplished by 1912.

During his lifetime, Flagler was widely hailed as a great benefactor of Florida. Flagler himself spoke of his business enterprises as a kind of philanthropy, and he seems not to have been overly concerned with the immediate profitability of his businesses. In addition, he contributed to the financial support of churches, hospitals, and other civic institutions. However, he was also criticized by populist leaders as the personification of "big corporate interests" with too much power in the state. For example, when his second wife, Alice, went insane, Flagler lobbied the state legislature to change the divorce law to make insanity grounds for divorce. The influence he evidently exerted on the legislature made the "Flagler Divorce Law" a political issue.

After divorcing Alice, Flagler married Mary Lily Kenan and built a palatial home, Whitehall, for her in Palm Beach. His health had declined with old age, and on 20 May 1913 he died in Whitehall. His body was entombed with his first wife Mary and his daughter Jenny Louise in Memorial Presbyterian Church in St. Augustine.

The bulk of Flagler's estate passed to his third wife, Mary Lily, who soon married Robert W. Bingham of Kentucky. When Mary Lily died in 1917, the Flagler fortune passed to her brother, two sisters, and a niece.

Today, Flagler's influence in Florida is evidenced in the cities that he founded or promoted: St. Augustine, Ormond Beach, Palm Beach, Miami, and Key West. The Florida East Coast Railway continues to do business as an independent corporation. His magnificent Hotel Ponce de Leon became Flagler College in 1968. Flagler's home, Whitehall, is the Henry Morrison Flagler Museum. The Breakers Hotel, rebuilt in the 1920s, remains as the sole survivor of Flagler's hotel chain.

THOMAS GRAHAM
*Flagler College*

Edward N. Akin, *Flagler: Rockefeller Partner and Florida Baron* (1988).

## Foreign Industry

Foreign industry, or commercial enterprises owned by residents outside of the United States, has been part of the American and southern economy from the beginning of American history. Food, tobacco, and forest-products industries were among the first sectors of foreign investments, followed by textiles and numerous other industries. Much of the early railroad and canal construction in the United States was also done or financed by foreign investors. However, the major influx of foreign industry occurred during the 20th century and became particularly significant for the South as late as the 1960s and 1970s. For example, only 10 percent of the foreign industry in South Carolina existing in 1983 was established before 1970. Much of the increase in foreign investments in the South during the 1970s was attributed to increased awareness of foreign investors about the South in both cultural and economic terms—an awareness caused in large part by the worldwide media coverage of the presidential campaign and subsequent presidency of Jimmy Carter.

While the South is not the dominant region of foreign investment in the United States, it does have a disproportionately high percentage of foreign industry, based on comparative population and industrialization. Since 1970 it has been the fastest-growing region in terms of attracting foreign investment. In several southern states, such as South Carolina, foreign investment accounts for more than 25 percent of all new manufacturing investments. In addition, southern employment in foreign industry is at levels generally four to five times higher than the national average.

The Dutch, English, Germans, French, Canadians, and Japanese are the primary investors in the South. In addition, more than a dozen other nations have invested in the region. The textile industry brought many early foreign investors to the South, but today foreign backing is pervasive in rubber and plastics, petrochemicals, electronics, automobile manufacturing, chemicals and pharmaceuticals, metal working, machinery, scientific equipment, and stone, clay, glass, and cement. Still other foreign investments have occurred in retailing, commercial real estate, agriculture, and banking. In short, as the South's economy has diversified, so too has its foreign industry. In fact, much of the South's diversification occurred as a result of foreign investment.

No two states have equal amounts or varieties of foreign industry, making generalizations difficult. In value terms, South Carolina is the leader, but in employment, North Carolina is the leader. Georgia has the most Japanese investments and South Carolina the most German ones. Foreign industry in Florida is concentrated in banking and real estate; in Louisiana it is in petrochemicals, in South Carolina it is in chemicals and tires, and in Georgia it is in sales offices and warehousing/distribution. In the Mississippi Delta, a large tract of land is owned by the Queen of England.

Major similarities in all of these include the motivations of the investors and the high degree of state promotional activity and investment incentives. Overall, the major investor attractions of the South appear to be labor, land, and lifestyle considerations. Labor is still relatively abundant, inexpensive, and nonunionized, and the labor force has an excellent track record of high productivity, low absenteeism, and stability of employment. Land is also comparatively abundant, inexpensive, and generally well connected through

transportation to other areas of the nation and the world. The lifestyle of the South is perhaps the most similar of all American regions to that of Europe and Japan—more traditional, family oriented, and hospitable, with numerous recreational opportunities.

Virtually all the southern states have become active and aggressive in state investment-promotion activities and incentives. Numerous trade and investment missions are conducted to promote the states to foreign business interests, and packages of free worker training, site selection, tax credits, and industrial revenue bonds are also offered to potential investors. Numerous southern governors have played active roles in these promotional activities, underscoring the states' interest in and commitment to foreign investment in the minds of potential foreign investors. German and Japanese investment in the 1990s and 2000s symbolized the new importance of foreign industry in the South. In 1992 the German automaker BMW selected Greer, S.C., as the location for its first assembly plant outside Germany. Nissan and Toyota have opened plants in Mississippi, and Alabama has attracted assembly plants from Mercedes-Benz, Honda, Hyundai, and Isuzu.

Foreign industry has had an increasing impact on the South, both economically and socially. The development of new industries, the expansion and modernization of existing industries, the upgrading of worker skills and wages, and the broadening of tax bases are only a few of the direct economic impacts. In turn, income generated directly by foreign investments creates additional income for suppliers, retailers, and other parts of the community. Foreign industry also has brought foreign people to the South—largely management and technical employees and their families—resulting in an internationalization of the communities in which they locate.

JEFFREY S. ARPAN
*University of South Carolina*

Jeffrey S. Arpan and David Ricks, *Directory of Foreign Manufacturers in the United States* (1993); Jeffrey S. Arpan, Edmond Flowers, and David Ricks, *Journal of International Business Studies* (Summer 1981); David L. Carlton and Peter Coclanis, *The South, the Nation, the World* (2003); Rosabeth Moss Kanter, *World Class: Thriving Locally in the Global Economy* (1995); Choong Soon Kim, *Japanese Industry in the American South* (1995); Marko Maunula, in *Globalization and the American South*, ed. James C. Cobb and William Stueck (2005); Cedric Suzman, ed., *The Costs and Benefits of Foreign Direct Investments from a State Perspective* (1982); U.S. Department of Commerce, *Foreign Direct Investment in the United States*, vols. 1–9 (1976); Mira Wilkins, ed., *Foreign Investment in the United States* (1977), *Foreign Enterprise in Florida: The Impact of Non–United States Direct Investment* (1979), *New Foreign Enterprise in Florida* (1980).

## Furniture Industry

Most of the fine furniture used in the South during the colonial period was imported from England. As towns and cities grew in size and wealth, however, skilled craftsmen from England, Scotland, Ireland, Germany, and France and from northern cities in America made their way in increasing numbers into lucrative southern markets such as Williamsburg, Charleston, New Bern, and Savannah. Some of the early craftsmen were itinerants, some were employed on large plantations, and some established shops in the larger towns and cities. The common folk made most of their own furniture or used the products of local carpenters.

Woods used by early southern furniture makers were largely walnut, cherry, and pine. Mahogany became increasingly popular after 1750, but pine, oak, and poplar continued to be used for framing and as the base for mahogany veneers. Maple and birch were not used extensively until 1800.

Although a few small factories had been established in Nashville, Tenn., and Danville, Va., somewhat earlier, the South's entrance into modern furniture manufacturing occurred in 1888 when local businessmen built a factory in High Point, N.C. The abundance and low cost of both wood and labor gave High Point a cost advantage over northern competition, and the industry spread from there into nearby centers in North Carolina and Virginia. As worker skills improved, so did the quality of High Point furniture. The industry grew rapidly after World War I, and following World War II North Carolina moved ahead of New York to become the leading furniture-manufacturing state. By that time, High Point and southwestern Virginia had established reputations for producing furniture of high quality, with cheaper grades coming from newer centers to the south and west. Besides

North Carolina and Virginia, important centers of furniture manufacturing are found in Tennessee, Texas, Arkansas, Georgia, and Mississippi. The American Furniture Hall of Fame in High Point chronicles industry history.

The southern furniture industry began, and remains, a largely craft-oriented, family-owned business. During recent years, a number of small companies have been purchased by larger competitors, and other corporate structures have shown increasing interest in the high return on capital investments that has characterized the southern furniture industry. Surging imports from new global producers such as China, and the arrival of immigrants such as skilled woodworkers from Mexico, are transforming the furniture industry in the South. Still, furniture manufacturing remains the fifth most decentralized American industry, with many family-owned and privately held companies. Whatever ownership structure may develop in the future, however, the South's abundant wood supplies and high-quality labor should continue to provide the competitive edges needed for substantial growth.

SIDNEY R. JUMPER
*University of Tennessee*

Bill Bamburger and Cathy N. Davidson, *Closing: The Life and Death of an American Factory* (1998); Paul H. Burroughs, *Southern Antiques* (1931); B. F. Lemert, *Economic Geography* (April 1934); *New York Times* (25 October 1984); Lonn Taylor and David B. Warren, *Texas Furniture: The Cabinetmakers and Their Work, 1840–1880* (1975); Meenu Tewari, in *The American South in a Global World*, ed. James Peacock, Harry L. Watson, and Carrie Matthews (2005); U.S. Bureau of the Census, Census of Manufacturers: 1958 (1961).

## Grady, Henry W.

(1850–1889) NEWSPAPER EDITOR.

Born on 24 May 1850 in Athens, Ga., to William Sammons and Ann Gartrell Grady, Henry Woodfin Grady enjoyed a comfortable upbringing. Wise financial management by his father, a successful merchant who died in 1864 from wounds received serving in the Confederate army, enabled Henry to enroll at the University of Georgia in 1866. Following graduation in 1868, he attended the University of Virginia for a year, excelling in oratory and displaying journalistic talent as a contributor to the *Atlanta Constitution*. Returning to Georgia in 1869, Grady located in Rome, edited various newspapers there, and married Julia King, his childhood sweetheart, in 1871. The next year, he purchased an interest in the *Atlanta Daily Herald* and moved to that bustling city to join the *Herald*'s editorial staff. When the *Herald* ceased publication in 1876, Grady, while serving as special correspondent to a number of papers outside of Georgia, joined the staff of the *Constitution*, the newspaper with which he would be associated until his death on 23 December 1889.

Part owner and managing editor after 1880, Grady helped build the *Constitution* into the region's most popular newspaper as he himself emerged as the leading spokesman of the New South movement—the attempt to revive the region largely through industrialization. For economic progress to occur, he said, the South must cultivate the goodwill of northern investors. Reconciliation between the sections depended, he believed, upon the social stability that would result from an amicable resolution of the race issue in the South. Given northern restraint and trust, white southerners would respect the civil and political rights conferred upon black southerners during Reconstruction but would maintain white supremacy and segregation—an arrangement, he argued, that merely reflected the instinct of both races.

Not only in the pages of the *Constitution* but also before audiences from Boston to Dallas, Grady spread the gospel of southern progress. In his celebrated "New South" address of 1886, he assured New York's New England Society that southerners, while cherishing the memory of the Old South and the Confederacy, had accepted the verdict of war and bore the North no ill will. Working hard to rebuild, the South, he contended, treated blacks equitably, desired intersectional harmony, and wished to promote further economic development.

Grady's vision of a South characterized by "sunshine everywhere and all the time" gave hope to many of his contemporaries, yet at his death it remained still a vision.

WAYNE MIXON
*Mercer University*

Paul M. Gaston, *The New South Creed: A Study in Southern Mythmaking* (1970); Mills Lane, *The New South: Writings and Speeches of Henry Grady* (1971); Raymond B. Nixon, *Henry W. Grady: Spokesman of the New South* (1943).

## Gregg, William

(1800–1867) BUSINESSMAN.
William Gregg was born on 2 February 1800 in Monongalia County, Va., and died 13 September 1867 in Graniteville, S.C. His outspoken advocacy of manufacturing and his entrepreneurship of the Graniteville Manufacturing Company (1846–67) fixed his reputation as the "father" of the southern textile industry, an image enhanced by Broadus Mitchell's laudatory biography (1928). Initially, Gregg amassed a fortune as a jeweler and silversmith in Columbia (1824) and Charleston (1838). Introduced to cotton manufacturing at his uncle's small mill (circa 1810) near Madison, Ga., Gregg in 1837 purchased stock in the Vaucluse Mill (1833) in the Horse Creek Valley of Edgefield District, S.C.

In 1844 he retired as a merchant and devoted his energies and financial resources to industrialization. After touring New England mills, Gregg authored a series of newspaper articles, later published as *Essays on Domestic Industry* (1845), admonishing southerners to build more textile factories. By the late 1840s most South Carolina newspaper editors supported Gregg's crusade. In 1846 Gregg launched his own mill at Graniteville in the Horse Creek Valley. For the next 20 years, he planned and directed every detail of the large-scale (initially 9,245 spindles and 500 looms), two-story granite factory and its surrounding village. Although only

one of several pioneer southern entrepreneurs, Gregg was the region's best-
known industrial publicist. In a cultural
context, his ideas and policies at Graniteville played a major role in creating
the stereotypical image of the rural,
paternalistic southern mill village. Anti-
urban in his writings, Gregg refused to
invest in the nearby Augusta mills being
erected during the 1840s. He advocated
the model of an isolated, self-contained
community. His company controlled
the lives of the rural poor white families who moved into his picturesque
wooden cottages. Such control over
white operatives was possible in the
South, Gregg suggested, because of the
presence of potential black workers. His
rhetoric punctuated the central tenet
of the South's cotton-mill ideology:
social as well as economic dividends
flowed from industrialization. Mill
villages would "uplift" the poor whites.
Although his social ideas persisted and
his mill paid reasonable dividends, the
antebellum South, in general, failed to
adopt Gregg's industrial philosophy.

JOHN S. LUPOLD
*Columbus College*

Ernest M. Lander Jr., *The Textile Indus-
try in Antebellum South Carolina* (1969);
Thomas P. Martin, *Journal of Southern
History* (August 1945); Broadus Mitchell,
*William Gregg: Factory Master of the Old
South* (1928); Tom E. Terrill, *Journal of
Economic History* (March 1976).

## Insurance

The persistence of deep-rooted facets
of southern socioeconomic life and
culture—limited financial assets,
African-bred burial practices, rural

lifestyles long retained by urban dwellers, insecurities derived in the painful
adjustment from plantation paternalism to semifreedom—go far to explain
the seeming paradox of the region's
high personal-security consciousness
linked with its below-average insurance
coverage. In 1982, for example, southern states accounted for 9 of the top 17
states in the number of life insurance
policies in force, but only 5 states were
above the national average in per family
life insurance in force. No southern-
headquartered insurer ranked among
the top 30 in terms of assets, and in
the early 21st century there are few
southern-based insurance companies
remaining at all.

In the antebellum period, limited
southern commercial expansion failed
to lure scarce capital into the casualty
business. The region also failed to share
in the northern surge of life insurance
activities induced by the extensive
breakdown of rural-bred kinship ties.
High mortality rates for poor white
southern males discouraged sales, although plantation owners paid high
premiums to northern insurers on the
lives of their skilled slaves, especially
those hired out for railroad construction and industrial work. As early as the
1790s, free southern blacks organized
mutual benefit societies to fulfill their
obligations to the deceased in the "sweet
sorrow" of passage to the nether world,
as well as to assure their own avoidance
of a pauper's burial or, worse, disposal
of their body to a medical school.

In the postbellum era, southern
white mortality rates improved, enhancing the market for large northern-based

insurers, whereas black death rates rose dramatically, especially in the urban South. Black churches and lodges established a plethora of benevolent, often secret and ritualistic self-help societies. Over time, poor business practices and occasional embezzlement led to rising contempt for "coffin clubs." Between 1890 and 1910, as discriminatory hiring practices eroded employment opportunities for black males and denied them the franchise in state after state, black-owned and black-managed health and life insurance companies were organized, primarily to provide sickness and burial insurance coverage to all family members. The small weekly premiums were paid primarily by black women, who had an employment rate more than double that of white women.

Joining altruism with capitalistic incentives and motivated by black pride, such black entrepreneurs as Alonzo Herndon and John Merrick—both barbers with white clienteles—created well-managed companies that provided employment opportunities for college-educated black youth faced with restricted regional opportunities. (Thus, Walter White agonized over the decision to give up his job with Standard Life of Atlanta in 1917 in order to accept an administrative post in New York City with the National Association for the Advancement of Colored People.) Over the years, successful black insurance companies, often associated with funeral homes and banks to which they channeled premium income, emerged as one of the most significant sources of wealth and high status in the southern black community.

Although they viewed the southern black population as their legitimate preserve, black insurers faced vigorous competition from white-owned regional stock companies offering the same coverage, usually at similar rates. Both white- and black-managed insurance enterprises in many instances achieved excellent records for solidity and financial reliability, provided mortgages for home buyers, and generated funds that flowed into regional utilities and state and municipal bonds. The failure rate for smaller and weaker insurers, however, was considerable, and when so dynamic and hitherto successful an enterprise as black-owned Standard Life collapsed in the mid-1920s, even a stalwart exponent of racial self-help like policyholder W. E. B. Du Bois was plunged into despair. Convinced that white-managed firms were safer institutions and that holding one of their contracts conveyed a measure of prestige, blacks in large numbers continued to favor white insurers. Successful white-owned enterprises provided a powerful vehicle for wealth accumulation in the region, and they afforded extensive employment to a legion of high school–educated home service agents. Increasingly, large home-office operations stimulated the growth of Richmond, Nashville, Jacksonville, Atlanta, and Dallas as regional financial centers.

The burgeoning southern economy of the post–World War II period, with its expanding white middle class, led many larger insurers to phase out home service to the lower-income groups. A proliferation of small concerns, primarily white owned, were organized to serve the still-large traditional market. A number of region-based, white-owned firms attempted to cultivate the biracial market, with its wide income disparities. They relied for a time on "sociological underwriting" to justify rate differentials between black and white policyholders.

With the passage of civil rights legislation in the mid-1960s, the top management of white-owned insurers began to take steps to integrate their sales and home-office staffs. The pace of compliance varied widely as many insurers experienced difficulty in overcoming the opposition of white employees and decentralized sales staffs. The conventional belief was that black agents could not possibly sell white prospects, and widespread apprehension appeared regarding the ramifications of integrated staffs at social functions and company conventions. Nonetheless, a Wharton study in 1970 found that some southern white-owned insurers exhibited a greater willingness than those elsewhere to actively pursue nondiscriminatory hiring practices. By the early 1980s black-owned insurers found themselves outbid for black sales and technical specialists. Complaints of a "black brain drain" were voiced, and stress was placed on the necessity for cooperative training programs and shared infrastructure in order to compete effectively.

During the 1970s a major merger-and-acquisition movement took place among white-owned insurers in the region, altering the structure of the industry. In the acquisition of Nashville-based National Life and Accident Insurance Company by American General Life Insurance Company of Houston, Tex., competition was considerably reduced. In 1979 Nationale-Nederlanden NV, the Netherlands' largest insurance company, acquired the Life Insurance Company of Georgia (organized in 1891 with negligible funds) for $360 million. Also representing the centralization of once regional firms into corporate entities, the Jackson National Life Insurance Company, a subsidiary of Prudential, acquired in 1991 the Insurance Company of Georgia. The declining role of small and medium-sized regional insurers and the probable impact of this change upon the socioeconomic and cultural life of the South deserves broader study.

JACK BLICKSILVER
*Georgia State University*

Charles S. Johnson, *The Negro in American Civilization* (1930); Robert Kenzer, *Enterprising Southerners: Black Economic Success in North Carolina, 1865–1915* (1997); Hugh K. Rickenbaker Jr., *Generations: The Centennial History of the Life Insurance Company of Georgia* (1991); Armand J. Thieblot Jr. and Linda P. Fletcher, *Negro Employment in Finance: A Study of Racial Policies in Banking and Insurance*, vol. 2, *Studies in Negro Employment* (1970); Walter B. Weare, *Black Business in the New South: A Social History of the North Carolina Mutual Life Insurance Company* (1973); Viviana A. Rotman Zelizer, *Morals and Markets: The Development of Life Insurance in the United States* (1979).

## Liquor Industry

The distillation of southern liquor dates from the early colonial period. Efforts to reproduce European wines and beers generally failed, but colonists quickly learned to distill local fruits and grains. They made corn whiskey in Jamestown, for example, while Georgians distilled peach brandy. By the late 1600s cheaply imported rum had further confirmed colonial preferences for hard liquor, and Scots-Irish immigration in the mid-1700s widely popularized whiskey making, particularly on the frontiers. Rye and barley distilling consequently flourished in Maryland and parts of Virginia, where even George Washington made some rye liquor.

Whiskey production soared after the Revolution (which had disrupted the rum trade) as new western harvests increased grain supplies. Farmers routinely distilled surpluses, as whiskey kept better and brought higher prices than grains. By 1810 good water and abundant corn centered American distilling in Kentucky, where 2,000 stills annually produced over 2 million gallons of liquor. Some of these early Kentucky ventures became companies of considerable reputation (e.g., the James Beam Distilling Company), and important enterprises also grew in Tennessee, Virginia, Maryland, and North Carolina. By midcentury, liquor was one of the South's most important products and had a firm place in sectional heritage. Southern producers, however, competed among themselves and with northern distillers, and by 1850 overproduction and falling prices increasingly forced them to view their operations in a national perspective.

Commercial whiskeys were chiefly corn blended with varied amounts of rye and other grains. Bourbon, aged in charred oak barrels, was the most distinctive. First distilled in Kentucky as early as 1789, production centered in Bourbon County until the 1840s and then spread regionally. Bourbon won national acclaim, while other blends, such as Tennessee whiskey, were also popular. Rye remained important in Maryland. The industry standardized most blends by the turn of the 20th century, a process formalized in federal regulations by the 1930s.

By 1900 large distilling concerns, such as the Kentucky Distilleries and Warehouse Company, were created as smaller producers merged in the face of competition and temperance agitation. National prohibition accelerated this trend as investors, anticipating repeal, acquired many southern distilleries. Thus, with exceptions such as Jack Daniel's and Jim Beam, many brand names steeped in southern tradition are now products of a few national beverage corporations.

Moonshining, never exclusively southern, also secured an important place in sectional history. As early as 1794, the Whiskey Rebellion, although centered in western Pennsylvania, engendered considerable sympathy in the South, where many distillers ignored federal excises on their product. Over time, Kentucky probably was the largest single source of illegal whiskey, although Georgia, the Carolinas, Virginia, and sections of other states also boasted significant production, and moonshiners often enjoyed considerable local prestige. Moonshine was essentially corn liquor, and it was frequently of higher proof than legal whiskeys.

Production peaked in the 1950s but then dropped off as quality fell, law enforcement cracked down, and drinking preferences shifted away from distilled beverages.

Despite the prominence of southern distilling, beer and wine did maintain a regional presence. Early attempts to establish European grapes, including efforts by Washington and Jefferson, failed as commercial ventures, but some small southern vineyards survived, generally using local vines. The most important of these was the Catawba grape, native to North Carolina, which became the basis of a viticulture that spread beyond the South. Commercial brewing—never a significant part of the antebellum South—expanded with growing southern urban populations around the turn of the 20th century. Northern capital helped establish such regional companies as Lone Star Brewing (San Antonio) as early as 1883; and as the century advanced, Anheuser-Busch, Carling, Schaefer, and other national concerns opened brewing and distribution facilities in many southern cities (Richmond, for instance, saw the nation's first sales of canned beer in the early 1930s). The border South was the center of regional beer production, notably in St. Louis and Louisville. New Orleans's Dixie Brewing Corporation utilized regional imagery in marketing. Compared to distilling—legal and illegal—however, brewing and viticulture remain lesser aspects of southern tradition.

MARK EDWARD LENDER
*Kean College of New Jersey*

Stanley Baron, *Brewed in America: A History of Beer and Ale in the United States* (1962); Gerald Carson, *The Social History of Bourbon: An Unhurried Account of Our Star-Spangled American Drink* (1963); Charles K. Cowdery, *Bourbon, Straight: The Uncut and Unfiltered Story of American Whiskey* (2004); William L. Downard, *Dictionary of the History of the American Brewing and Distilling Industries* (1980); Peter Krass, *Blood and Whiskey: The Life and Times of Jack Daniel* (2004); Mark Edward Lender and James Kirby Martin, *Drinking in America: A History* (1982); Jim Murray, *Classic Bourbon, Tennessee, and Rye Whiskey* (1998); Gary Regan and Mardee Haidin Regan, *The Book of Bourbon and Other Fine American Whiskeys* (1995).

## Mobile Home Industry

Mobile homes are more popular in the South than elsewhere in the United States, and sociologists have struggled to understand the reasons behind this phenomenon. Some argue that southerners are simply driven by the low cost of these dwellings, while others look to cultural factors such as individual autonomy and the potential for mobility. The mobile home industry, too, has its own culture, driven by many of the same factors.

In the early years of the 20th century, "homes on wheels" were designed for recreation, an affordable way of taking the comforts of home along for the ride. Trailer camps served as an alternative to expensive hotels and were particularly well suited to western travel, where scenery was the main attraction. But as early as 1920, some individuals began using these trailers as semipermanent accommodations. Trailer camps in

Detroit and Los Angeles became not recreation centers but de facto slums that housed transient workers.

In an effort to combat a growing image problem, trailer builders developed trade associations. Manufacturers in the western states joined the Trailer Coach Association, while the manufacturers in the East and Midwest launched the Trailer Coach Manufacturers Association (TCMA) in Detroit. Both groups promoted the use of trailers primarily as recreational vehicles, and while conformity was optional, both groups soon promulgated construction standards to improve safety and durability.

World War II brought the need for massive numbers of workers for defense industries, and housing for these workers was scarce. The Tennessee Valley Authority commissioned several home designs, including both trailers and "demountable" homes. The former made no pretense of permanence, while the latter attempted to mimic the design of site-built housing in a dwelling that could be set up and ready for occupancy within four hours of its arrival at the site. Industrialists such as Henry J. Kaiser and Henry Ford also commissioned mobile or temporary home designs and even set aside land for the establishment of trailer camps to accommodate their wartime employees.

A split soon emerged between those advocating trailers as recreational vehicles and those who saw them as affordable housing. This split was reflected in the renaming of the TCMA, which became the Mobile Home Manufacturers Association in 1953. This new term, "mobile home," reflected the fact that many owners saw their trailers as something other than a recreational vehicle. By the end of the 1950s, the question of whether or not a mobile home was a vehicle had been resolved in the market. Aerodynamic styling and metal trim gave way to pitched roofs, casement windows, and faux wood siding, as buyers emphasized "home" rather than "mobile."

In 1952 the first planned mobile home subdivision, Trailer Estates, was established in Bradenton, Fla. A rental fee covered the cost of maintaining the roads, landscaping, and other features, allowing white-collar employees and retirees the luxury of an affordable vacation home. But away from resort areas, the image of the trailer park—often with the homes themselves rented out—remained a powerful signifier of poverty, which mobile home dwellers and manufacturers alike found difficult to combat. Throughout the South, wherever zoning allowed it, many owners placed mobile homes parallel to the road, like a conventional home, and frequently added carports, patios, and other amenities to emphasize the permanence of the site.

Unlike the automobile industry, mobile home construction never became centralized in a single location, nor did the industry ever develop a "Big Three" that dominated the market. Because of the cost of transporting the product, mobile home manufacturing is most profitable when it is centered within a day's drive of the customer. This, along with the inexpensive and low-tech nature of the business, allowed small southern firms to compete effectively. In 1970 Horton Homes of Eatonton,

Ga., launched what eventually would be promoted as the largest single facility for the manufacturing of mobile and modular homes in the nation.

In the 1970s new building codes for mobile homes recognized the fact that they were no longer vehicles in any real sense. The new codes specified no particular construction techniques but based conformity on test performance. With greater quality assurance, federal loans could also be used for mobile home purchase, bringing financing into line with site-built homes. In keeping with these changes, the Mobile Home Manufacturers Association was reorganized as the Manufactured Housing Institute in 1975, further blurring any distinctions between mobile homes and prefabricated modular housing.

STEPHEN WALLACE TAYLOR
*Macon State College*

Robert Mills French and Jeffrey K. Hadden, *Social Problems* (Autumn 1968); Richard C. Fuller and Richard R. Myers, *American Sociological Review* (June 1941); Allan D. Wallis, *Wheel Estate: The Rise and Decline of Mobile Homes* (1991).

## Music Industry

The development of commercial popular music in the South has paralleled trends in other industries. The region has served as a source of musical raw materials—styles, performers, and creative talents—for the nation as a whole. Until World War II, however, nonsoutherners controlled most of the institutions vital to marketing popular music, including publishing houses, recording companies, and theater chains. Professional musicians in the South pursued

the American goal of material advancement, but profits tended to flow toward New York, Chicago, or Hollywood, the three major music centers of the United States before World War II. Of course, there were exceptions to this generalization, chiefly in the form of southern publishers who were beginning to tap a market for spiritual music by the mid-19th century. Between the Civil War and World War I, minstrelsy and ragtime music offered opportunities for both black and white southern musicians.

Northern executives also held sway in the pop market, the mainstream of American commercial music centering on Broadway shows, New York's "Tin Pan Alley" music-publishing district, and, later, Hollywood film musicals. This pattern continued as the music industry turned to country music (then called "hillbilly") and jazz in the 1920s. Both genres were southern based, but their markets were not strictly regional. In that decade the phenomenal growth of commercial radio frightened many recording executives, who saw radio as a competing source of popular entertainment. Northern record companies, eager to reach new markets, had ready access to the southern-born jazz musicians of both races who had left their native region for the thriving jazz centers of Chicago and New York. Record firms also sent white hillbilly singers north, or sent agents to Atlanta, New Orleans, Memphis, Charlotte, and other southern cities to record dozens of local musicians in the hillbilly and jazz fields. These musicians frequently received only flat fees (as opposed to long-term royalties) for their work. Northern businessmen and their southern allies (typi-cally retailers in some other line who carried recordings as an adjunct prod-uct) often secured control of musical copyrights or stole them outright from relatively unsophisticated performers.

Some southerners were more in-dustry savvy, and they began to sell their own songbooks. A handful moved north and set up publishing houses. The most successful southern entrepreneurs in music-related endeavors prior to World War II were those who organized radio stations, in many cases compan-ion operations to insurance companies, newspapers, or retail stores. Stations like Nashville's wsm originated programs for network broadcast and served as proving grounds for pop singers and big bands.

The modern southern music indus-try took shape during the two decades after 1940. Prosperity revived popular music markets that had been blighted by a decade of economic depression. Urbanization and interregional mi-gration advanced the nationalization of country music, rhythm and.blues, and rock and roll, all styles with solid southern foundations. The formation of the performance-rights society Broad-cast Music, Incorporated (bmi) in 1940 paved the way for a decentralization of music institutions. Set up by radio networks to rival the older, exclusive, and pop-oriented American Society of Composers, Authors, and Publishers (ascap), bmi allowed songwriters and publishers in all fields to join, and it monitored local as well as network programming. By collecting and dis-tributing performance royalties on a

wide range of music, it assisted fledgling publishing operations that sprang up across the South and Midwest, includ-ing firms that soon captured significant shares of the pop, country, and rhythm-and-blues markets. After 1945 record manufacturers and recording studios complemented broadcasting and pub-lishing in emerging music centers like Nashville, Atlanta, and Dallas. Southern music entrepreneurs extended a long tradition of urban boosterism through shrewd promotion and publicity, formed national trade organizations like the Country Music Association, and enhanced urban growth by investing in banking, real estate, and other ventures. Southern businessmen now sit on the boards of most national music organiza-tions.

Today, southern musicians and their business allies operate in a commercial world more complex than ever before. New media, including cable television, satellite radio, and the Internet, together with changing business structures, have brought both challenges and op-portunities. On the one hand, consoli-dation in the recording industry and advances in multitrack recording have driven up both recording costs and sales expectations, making it difficult for newly emerging talent to find sus-tained record-label support. Similarly, consolidation in radio broadcasting, the fragmentation of the radio market into stations aiming at specific demographic groups, and the reliance on consultants to program entire chains of stations has tightened stations' playlists, thus limit-ing exposure for both rising talent and older, established stars seeking continued airplay. On the other hand, the development of relatively inexpensive digital recording equipment has allowed artists to make their own records, while the Internet provides a platform for record sales.

In the processes of commercialization and nationalization, southern music entrepreneurs have helped to transform the social settings that originally spawned folk-derived styles like country music and jazz and to dilute these music forms to the point that they have lost many of their qualities as southern-based idioms. To be sure, southern executives, after the fashion of their northern counterparts, have helped to perpetuate images of the region as a land of folksy and sometimes backwards characters, such as the unlettered white hillbilly or the exotic, sensual black. More often, southern businessmen have prompted the adoption of the cowboy or western image, a nonsouthern image more palatable to a national audience.

Some scholars believe that in country music, at least, such images have helped to dilute the music to the point that western attire and stock allusions to rural life have become clichés, mere symbols unconnected to an authentic culture underlying southern-based popular music. Others insist that country music maintains genuine connections to regional culture and also reflects the adoption of southern sounds, musical styles, and images on a national basis. However one strikes the balance between these opposing views, all of these images have furthered the purposes of southern entrepreneurs

and musicians, who continue to assert their own interests within the now-international world of commercial music.

JOHN W. RUMBLE
*Country Music Foundation*
*Nashville, Tennessee*

Bill C. Malone, *Southern Music/American Music* (2003); John W. Rumble, "Fred Rose and the Development of the Nashville Music Industry, 1942–1954" (Ph.D. dissertation, Vanderbilt University, 1980); D. K. Wilgus, *Journal of American Folklore* (April–June 1970).

## Naval Stores

The naval stores industry, whose principal products were tar, pitch, and turpentine, derives its name from the use of these products for waterproofing the rigging and hulls of early wooden sailing vessels. Based on the exploitation of the pine woods for resinous juices, the industry is one of the oldest industries in the South. It was developed at Jamestown in 1608, but it is associated especially with North Carolina because of the highly resinous longleaf pine (*Pinus palustris*), whose natural habitat is the approximately 100-mile-wide coastal plain that spans the southern coastline from Virginia to Texas.

Until 1835 the people of North Carolina were often referred to, somewhat derisively, as "tar, pitch, and turpentine folk." At the time of the American Revolution, North Carolina produced in value three-fifths of all the naval stores exported from the continental colonies. The naval-stores industry continued throughout the antebellum period, and its uniqueness ultimately bequeathed to the state and its people the nickname "Tar Heels."

Tar was produced by a process of dry distillation in an earthen kiln of pieces of dead longleaf pine. Lengths of dead wood, called lightwood, omnipresent in the forest, were gathered, split into short pieces, placed in a kiln, covered with earth, and subjected to a slow fire that forced out the resinous matter. The tar was dipped from a pit outside of the kiln and poured into barrels. Pitch was obtained by boiling tar to a thicker consistency.

After 1820 production of tar declined, and by 1835 the production of turpentine and its derivatives, spirits of turpentine and rosin, became the main focus of the industry. This developed from improved processes of distilling and from new uses for spirits of turpentine and rosin. Spirits of turpentine was used as a paint thinner and preserver of wood, but after 1835 it was used also as a solvent in the burgeoning rubber industry, particularly as an illuminant. Camphene lamps were the chief form of light in homes and businesses after the decline of whale oil and prior to the development of kerosene. Camphene (spirits of turpentine mixed with alcohol) provided a bright light and was relatively inexpensive, but it was highly flammable. Rosin, a residue from distilling, found new uses in the manufacture of soap, lamp black, and ink and in sizing paper for printing.

With the development of the second phase of the industry, planters entered the business on a large scale, employing slave labor. Once trained in turpentine operations, blacks preferred turpentining to other forms of farm labor because it was based on the task system and they were somewhat more independent in their work. One man could attend a "crop" of 10,000 boxes spread over 50 to 100 acres of land. The industry required a number of specialized workers: "boxers" cut holes in the base of the tree as a container for the resin; "chippers" periodically reopened the wound in the tree above the box to increase the flow of resin; "dippers" removed the resin from the boxes every 10 days; distillers refined the product at a nearby distillery into spirits of turpentine and rosin; and coopers made barrels for the products.

With the development of this phase of the industry, North Carolina's economy boomed. Until the Civil War, the state remained the preeminent naval-stores producer, with production of all forms of naval-stores products valued in 1860 at approximately $12 million.

A turpentine orchard was exhausted in 5 to 10 years of cultivation, and the industry was necessarily migratory. In the post–Civil War period, it spread rapidly southward into South Carolina and the Gulf states. The exploitation of the longleaf pine forest of the Deep South between 1870 and 1920 was one means by which southerners recouped their capital after the war. Factors in Savannah, Jacksonville, Pensacola, and Mobile obtained control of large tracts of pineland and controlled the trade. They leased timber to operators, advanced the capital in the form of goods and tools, and subsequently marketed the products. Savannah became the leading naval-stores port from 1880 to 1920 and continued to set the world price of naval stores until 1950.

In the surge southward, North Carolina procedures were followed, and skilled turpentine workers were sought from the Carolinas. Sometimes entire communities of people, plus their household goods, cattle, cats, dogs, chickens, and other property, were transported by train to Georgia, Alabama, or Mississippi. A new community was born in the piney woods of the Deep South, complete with dwellings, distillery, commissary, and a combination church-school. The overseer was operations supervisor, enforcer of law and order, director of the commissary and distillery, and physician. It was a primitive, isolated, lonely, harsh, and unique way of life. In approximately two generations, from 1870 to 1930, most of the original stands of longleaf pine, covering 130 million acres, were consumed.

The industry underwent little change until the 20th century, when the imminent exhaustion of the timber supply prompted the use of clay and metal cups to receive the resin and avoid the premature destruction of the trees. Producers were reluctant to change methods until forced to do so in 1908 by the factors. The federal government attempted to improve techniques and quality by establishing a Naval Stores Experiment Station at Olustee, Fla., in 1932, and by providing a cost-sharing subsidy to producers after 1936.

In the post–World War II period, the development of the sulphate process for making paper led to the production of turpentine and rosin as by-products, and the old man-and-axe turpentine industry fell prey to the more efficient competition of modern chemistry and chainsaw technology. Instead of weekly trips to the woods to chip the trees, the operator removed the entire tree, transported it to the mill, and mechanically and chemically separated it into its component products for subsequent use. Between 1967 and 1972, the federal government liquidated its stocks of naval stores and ceased its subsidy, and in 1973 it closed the Olustee Station. Like the village blacksmith, the trail-driving cowboy, and the one-horse shay, the "turpentine man" had had his day.

PERCIVAL PERRY
*Wake Forest University*

Charles C. Crittenden, *The Commerce of North Carolina, 1763–1789* (1936); Thomas Gamble, ed., *Naval Stores: History, Production, Distribution, and Consumption* (1920); Robert B. Outland III, *Tapping the Pines: The Naval Stores Industry in the American South* (2004); Percival Perry, "Naval Stores" (Ph.D. dissertation, Duke University, 1947), *Journal of Southern History* (November 1968).

## Nuclear Industry

During the 1950s and early 1960s, the development of nuclear energy for peaceful purposes was widely regarded as a glamorous technological breakthrough that could offer dramatic benefits in industry, agriculture, medicine, and the generation of electrical power. The southern states acted with particular enthusiasm to promote the use of nuclear energy as a part of their effort to encourage economic growth. They also played a leading role in increasing the authority of state governments to safeguard public health and safety from radiation hazards, a reflection of their determination to protect traditional state responsibilities from federal infringement.

When Congress passed the Atomic Energy Act of 1954, it ended exclusive government control over nuclear technology and opened it to commercial enterprise for civilian applications. The South moved promptly to investigate the opportunities the measure presented. Responding to the appeals of Florida governor LeRoy Collins, who argued that "nuclear energy for the South can mean economic emancipation," the Southern Governors' Conference sponsored a series of studies and meetings on the advantages that the technology could provide for the region. In February 1957, after concluding that exploitation of atomic energy promised substantial economic benefits, the governors created the Regional Advisory Council on Nuclear Energy. The council embarked on an ambitious program to foster the growth of atomic technology in the South, not only through construction of nuclear power reactors but also through expansion in the use of radioactive isotopes and increased private investment in atomic energy–related industries.

At the same time, the advisory council and other southern spokespersons were lobbying to extend to the states regulatory authority over atomic energy,

which had been largely delegated to the U.S. Atomic Energy Commission (AEC) by the 1954 act. Many state leaders protested federal "usurpation" of the states' traditionally dominant role in public health and safety. The South played an important part in persuading Congress in 1959 to amend the 1954 act to explicitly acknowledge state authority to regulate radiation hazards arising from certain atomic-energy operations, not including those from power reactors. Under the amendment, a state with demonstrated technical competence could sign an agreement with the AEC to assume specified functions. Kentucky became the first state to enter such an agreement in February 1962.

In the early period of peaceful atomic development, the promotional and regulatory activities of the South were not unique. Other states also acted to obtain economic benefits by encouraging atomic growth and state participation in regulating against the hazards of atomic energy. Yet southern efforts were exceptional in degree, if not in manner and motivation. As a region, the South established broader programs more promptly than other sections and most individual states. The South's economic status relative to other parts of the country made atomic technology especially appealing and gave southerners greater incentive to move quickly. Southern leaders heeded LeRoy Collins's 1955 warning that unless they took immediate measures, "nuclear energy for industrial use will gravitate to the existing industrial areas, mostly in the North." The South's particular sensitivity on the matter of states' rights, especially at a time when the growing civil rights struggle made the issue increasingly controversial, intensified its commitment to preventing exclusive federal authority over nuclear regulation. Sooner and in greater numbers than states in other sections, southern states signed agreements with the AEC to undertake the regulatory responsibilities permitted them. In these respects, the response of the South to the opening of atomic technology to private enterprise was distinctive.

In the late 1960s and early 1970s, southern utilities played a leading role in triggering a boom in the construction of nuclear power reactors. In 1966 the Tennessee Valley Authority provided a major impetus to the growth of the nuclear power industry when it announced plans to build two plants of unprecedented size at Browns Ferry, Ala. The impact of the decision to place nuclear plants in an area of plentiful and inexpensive coal was summarized by the title of an article in *Fortune* magazine: "An Atomic Bomb in the Land of Coal." Other southern utilities followed suit. The nuclear industry suffered a major slump in the late 1970s that was greatly exacerbated by the accident at Three Mile Island in Pennsylvania in 1979. Nevertheless, many plants already under construction were completed and began operating in the 1980s. Of the 95 power reactors in the United States that were licensed to operate at the end of 2002, 41 were located in the South.

J. SAMUEL WALKER
*United States Nuclear Regulatory Commission*

Redding S. Sugg Jr., ed., *Nuclear Energy in the South* (1957); J. Samuel Walker, *Prologue* (Fall 1981), *Three Mile Island: A Nuclear Crisis in Historical Perspective* (2004).

## Oil Industry

Within a year after E. L. Drake brought in the nation's first oil well outside Titusville, Penn., the South entered the petroleum picture. In the spring of 1860, a well in Wirt County, Va., (about 12 miles southeast of Parkersburg) began producing 37 to 50 barrels per day. After the creation of West Virginia, all of the oil activity was in the new state. As important as oil was in West Virginia (well into the 20th century), significant numbers of West Virginia and Pennsylvania oil-field workers migrated to the nascent Texas industry. The 1894 discovery in Corsicana signaled the beginning of commercial production in Texas, but the strike at Spindletop, near Beaumont, on 10 January 1901 immediately made the South a major force in the industry. The Texas Gulf Coast fields in the next few years produced quantities of oil that transformed the national, as well as the regional, economy. This new industry attracted much northern capital, mainly from Pennsylvania, and it created thousands of jobs to which farm boys flocked, thus beginning to shift the balance from a rural to an industrial economy. Once farmers went into the oil field, they usually stayed, following the booms from one new field to another.

Although Spindletop caught the national spotlight, other southern states quickly contributed significant quantities of oil. Louisiana's first important field, just outside Jennings, opened in

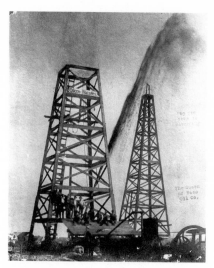

Workers at a Queen of Waco Oil Company derrick, Wortham, Tex., ca. 1925 (Seley Collection, Baylor University, Waco, Tex.)

September 1901, to be followed by the Caddo field in 1906 and the Haynesville field in 1921. Since World War II, southern Louisiana has continued prolific production. Arkansas had two banner fields in the early 1920s—El Dorado (where H. L. Hunt entered the business) and Smackover. Oil wrought tremendous changes in the lives of farm folk in Texas, Louisiana, and Arkansas, but it had much more impact on the Indians of Oklahoma. Even before statehood in 1907, Oklahoma had experienced several notable strikes at Bartlesville (1897), Red Fork (1901), Cleveland (1904), and Glenn Pool (1905). The last occurred on Creek land south of Tulsa, making the Creeks wealthy and Tulsa the "Oil Capital of the World." The Burbank field (1920) tapped the Osage pool, and members of that tribe experienced far more affluence than most could pru-

dently manage. Developing that field was E. W. Marland, who in 1935 became governor of Oklahoma. That oilmen were influential in politics was also attested to when Ross Sterling, onetime president of Humble Oil, was elected governor of Texas in 1930.

Along with oil fields, refineries have been important in the urbanization and industrialization of the South. The region's first sizable refinery, the Standard Oil (now Exxon) plant in Baton Rouge, opened in 1909. From the 1920s onward, the Texas Gulf Coast has boasted such giants as the Magnolia (now Mobil) in Beaumont, the Gulf and Texaco in Port Arthur, and the Humble (now Exxon) in Baytown. Offshore drilling symbolizes today's technological sophistication, but the South's first wells in water were in the Goose Creek, Tex., field in 1908. Subsequent drilling in the Red River between Texas and Oklahoma helped develop the techniques that now enable behemoth rigs to drill in the deep Gulf waters off Texas and Louisiana.

WALTER RUNDELL JR.
*University of Maryland*

William R. Childs, *The Texas Railroad Commission: Understanding Regulation in America to the Mid-Twentieth Century* (2005); Kenny A. Franks, *The Oklahoma Petroleum Industry* (1980); Carl C. Rister, *Oil! Titan of the Southwest* (1949); Walter Rundell Jr., *Early Texas Oil: A Photographic History, 1866–1936* (1977).

## Radio Industry

Radio communication designed for reception by the general public is known as broadcasting. The origins of southern broadcasting are indistinct. Clearly, southerners engaged in wireless telegraphy and telephony before the advent of formal broadcasting. As early as 1892, Nathan B. Stubblefield, a melon farmer, transmitted speech successfully from a small shack near his farmhouse in Murray, Ky., but he hardly intended to reach the general public. Nevertheless, a historical marker on the outskirts of Murray announces to all that the site is "The Birthplace of Radio."

Beginning in 1912, federal regulation required every wireless-transmitter operator to secure a license from the Department of Commerce's Radio Service Section. The Radio Act of 1912 made amateur operators aware that a significant number of them were scattered across the country. Under the law, "call letters" were assigned to each licensee, and a list of the radio stations so licensed was published. Radio clubs sprang into existence for the exchange of information, and the contact between them tended to reinforce the enthusiasm of their members. From such organizations came many of the early broadcasters of the 1920s.

The first licenses issued in the South under the specific classification of broadcasting were granted in February 1922 to two utility companies, one in Alabama and the second in Arkansas. Montgomery Light & Water Power Company of Montgomery, Ala., received the call letters WGH, and the Pine Bluff Company, a division of Arkansas Light and Power, was given WOK. As with many early stations, though, the realities of broadcasting quickly overcame the glowing visions of the initial moments on the air. The result was that both soon vanished from the roster of operational stations.

Within a month the pace had quickened. During March 1922 nine more southern stations were licensed, including two destined to be mainstays among the region's broadcasters—WWL in New Orleans, licensed to Loyola University, and WSB, operated by the *Atlanta Journal*. But the southern states were slower to develop substantial radio facilities than the nation as a whole. Indeed, a continuing complaint of Dixie politicians during the mid-1920s was the supposed discrimination being suffered by a South saddled with inadequate radio service.

The 1928 *Annual Report* of the Federal Radio Commission, created by Congress in 1927 to bring some order out of the chaos of broadcasting's first decade, revealed that the 11 former Confederate states (excluding the border states of Missouri, Kentucky, and Maryland) could boast only 77 operating stations, slightly more than the state of Illinois alone and just 11.6 percent of the nation's total. Further, per capita incomes that trailed badly behind national figures prevented the number of "radio families" in the South from approaching the totals for the United States as a whole. While the South's share of American families was 28.9 percent in 1930, its percentage of radio families was a scant 11.9 percent. Northern radio families at the same time exceeded 76 percent.

Despite the relatively slow overall

development, some individual broadcasters made their impact felt. One of the most flamboyant and controversial was William Kennon Henderson, whose unvarying formula—"Hello, world, doggone you! This is KWKH in Shreveport, Lou-EE-siana, and it's W. K. Henderson talkin' to you"—introduced him to a daily radio audience that stretched across the bulk of the United States. He continually exceeded his authorized power and usurped frequencies not assigned to him. A New Orleans newspaper referred to Henderson as the "Bolshevik of radio" but admitted that "nearly every home in the South where there's a radio set has listened to him."

In 1929 Henderson embarked upon his most famous crusade: he declared war on the nation's retail chain stores. He castigated them on the air as "dirty, low down, daylight burglars" and as "damnable thieves from Wall Street." Moreover, Henderson established a nationwide organization, ostensibly to assist him in the chain-store struggle. Naming it the "Merchant Minute Men," he bragged that it numbered 35,000 independent merchants in 4,000 towns throughout the country by 1931. The deepening depression, however, mired Henderson in debt, and increasing pressure from creditors forced him to acquiesce in the sale of the station to new owners in 1933.

From its earliest days, southern broadcasting developed a close association with country music. With the coming of radio, southern folksingers found an important new outlet for their talents. Probably the first station to feature country music was WSB in Atlanta.

Within a few months after going on the air in 1922, WSB was presenting several folk performers, including the Reverend Andrew Jenkins, a blind gospel singer, and Fiddlin' John Carson. With WSB leading the way, radio stations all over the South and the Midwest began offering country musicians and singers.

No discussion of southern country music and its relation to radio would be complete without recognizing the impact of Nashville's *Grand Ole Opry*. The vehicle by which it gained attention was WSM, a station owned by the National Life and Accident Insurance Company. In November 1925, just a month after WSM first went on the air, it broadcast a program initially known as the *WSM Barn Dance*. A year later the country music show acquired the new name of *Grand Ole Opry* (to contrast it with the *Grand Opera* concerts being broadcast by the networks). Agents of National Life often took advantage of the connection by introducing themselves to potential clients as being from the *Grand Ole Opry* Insurance Company. By World War II the program had become the most important country music show on the air, especially after 1939, when the National Broadcasting Company began carrying a 30-minute segment on the network every Saturday night.

Stations such as Memphis's WDIA and Nashville's WLAC were key institutions in the spread of black music in the 1940s and 1950s. WDIA popularized the blues of the Mississippi Delta and Beale Street. WLAC was typical of other stations in broadcasting news and popular music during the daytime but switching to blues, gospel, and rhythm and blues at night. The station's 50,000-watt signal reached 20 states, and its format made celebrities of disc jockeys such as William T. "Hoss" Allen and John R. (Richbourg).

The immediate postwar years saw a broadcasting explosion. In October 1945 there were some 900 commercial AM stations in the United States, but soon that number increased dramatically. By June 1948 over 2,000 AM broadcasters were on the air, joined by about 1,000 FM licensees and 109 television stations, the latter representing the wave of the future. Translated into community terms, the number of towns and cities with stations grew from 566 on V-J Day in August 1945 to 1,063 in early 1947. The growth was greatest in the smaller hamlets, which lacked radio facilities before the war. In Louisiana, for example, there were just 13 operating stations in 7 cities in 1941, but 10 years later there were 45 stations and local service had finally come to the rural areas of the state. Although the best-known programs deserted radio for the new medium of television, radio was still regarded as a successful business opportunity. The number of AM and FM licensees continued to grow to the point that virtually every American town of respectable size now has its own station or stations. As for the larger cities, to cite just three southern examples, Atlanta today has a choice of 13 AM and 11 FM stations, the Houston area has 25 AM and 32 FM stations, and New Orleans has 11 AM and 13 FM stations.

Outstanding among stations based in the larger metropolitan areas are those broadcasting on clear-channel frequencies with 50,000 watts of power, making them regional or even inter-regional rather than just local operations. Among this group are such long-time southern broadcasting leaders as WSB (Atlanta), WHAS (Louisville), WWL (New Orleans), WOAI (San Antonio), WSM (Nashville), and WRVA (Richmond). All date from the 1920s and thus can cite close to a century of broadcast experience.

C. JOSEPH PUSATERI
*University of San Diego*

Louis Cantor, *Wheelin' on Beale: How WDIA-Memphis Became the Nation's First All-Black Radio Station and Created the Sound That Changed America* (1992); John H. De Witt Jr., *Tennessee Historical Quarterly* (Summer 1971); Robert Gordon, *It Came from Memphis* (1995); C. Joseph Pusateri, *Enterprise in Radio: WWL and the Business of Broadcasting in America* (1980); Christopher H. Sterling and Michael C. Keith, *Sounds of Change: A History of FM Broadcasting in America* (2008); Barnwell R. Turnipseed, "The Development of Broadcasting in Georgia" (M.A. thesis, University of Georgia, 1950); Wesley H. Wallace, "The Development of Broadcasting in North Carolina, 1922–1948" (Ph.D. dissertation, Duke University, 1962).

## Railroad Industry

Even though the South possessed many navigable rivers and had basically an agricultural rather than an industrial economy, it was active in the promotion of railroads in the early 19th century. Baltimore businessmen obtained a charter for the Baltimore & Ohio in 1827, and Charleston interests built a 136-mile railroad to Hamburg, S.C., between 1830 and 1833. In 1860 the 15 slave states had more than 10,000 miles of railway, or about a third of the national total. Virginia, Georgia, and Tennessee led the South in rail mileage. On the eve of the Civil War, southern railroads lagged well behind northern lines in the quality of original construction, equipment, the number of employees, traffic volume, and maintenance facilities. Long before Appomattox, the southern lines were suffering from a growing deterioration of service because of general neglect, poor track repair, lack of equipment, and the war itself. By early 1865 Confederate railways were in a crippled condition.

In the late 1860s and early 1870s, the South suffered from railroad carpetbaggers, men more interested in personal profit than in building new railroads. The greatest corruption was in North Carolina, South Carolina, Georgia, and Alabama. After the panic of 1873, nearly half of the southern lines faced the sequence of default, receivership, and foreclosure. Southern rail mileage expanded with the appearance of the New South, however, and by 1900 the former slave states possessed a network of about 60,000 miles, nearly a third of the national total. In the last years of the 19th century, many southern lines were merged into larger systems, consolidations generally dominated by northern businessmen and money.

By the turn of the century, the major lines serving the South included the Baltimore & Ohio, Chesapeake & Ohio, Norfolk & Western, Southern, Atlantic Coast Line, Seaboard Air Line, Louisville & Nashville, Mobile & Ohio, Illinois Central, Southern Pacific, and Missouri Pacific. In both World War I and World War II, the contributions to victory made by southern railroads were unique because so many of the military installations were located in the South. By the 1920s southern railroads, like those of the entire nation, were being hurt by the growing competition from highways, airlines, pipelines, and improved river and canal barge service. During World War II southern railroads prospered even more than northern or western lines. This prosperity continued after the war as southern rail freight expanded with the economic surge toward the Sunbelt. The Staggers Rail Act of 1980 deregulated railroads, leading to the abandonment of many less-profitable routes, an improvement in rail physical plants, and a generally sound financial footing. One of the most important railways in the South today is the Norfolk Southern, which formed from mergers in 1990. It is a Class 1 railway covering 21,500 route miles in 9 southern states and 13 other eastern states. Another major line, CSX, also serves much of the South. Coal is the most important freight hauled today. The National Railroad Passenger Corporation (Amtrak) provides limited passenger service to the South.

JOHN F. STOVER
*Purdue University*

Robert C. Black III, *The Railroads of the Confederacy* (1952); Rudolph L. Daniels, *Trains across the Continent: North American Railroad History* (2000); George W. Hilton, *American Narrow Gauge Railroads* (1990); Scott Nelson, *Iron Confederacies: Southern*

Railways, Klan Violence, and Reconstruction (1999); U. B. Phillips, *A History of Transportation in the Eastern Cotton Belt to 1860* (1908); John F. Stover, *The Life and Decline of the American Railroad* (1970).

## Research Triangle Park

Research Triangle Park (RTP) is a planned industrial research park in piedmont North Carolina that includes more than 5,000 acres near three research universities: Duke University, North Carolina State University, and the University of North Carolina at Chapel Hill. Governor Luther Hodges initiated the program in 1955 with the appointment of the Governor's Research Triangle Committee, which was made up of corporate and university leaders. With private funding, the Governor's Committee was incorporated in 1956, and sociologist George Lee Simpson Jr. from the UNC–Chapel Hill faculty was appointed as director. The plan was to promote the region for industrial research, and faculty members were employed initially to promote the idea. The objectives were to improve the state's low per capita income by attracting industrial laboratories and high-technology industry to North Carolina; to diversify the industrial base from the traditional tobacco, textiles, and furniture industries; to reverse out-migration of North Carolina youth trained in science and engineering; and to help the universities attract and retain science and engineering faculty members by expanded consulting opportunities.

In 1957 private venture capital, with public stock offerings, was invested in 4,000 acres of scrub pinelands as "Pinelands, Inc.," but by the fall of 1958 the committee recognized the advantages of nonprofit ownership of the research park. With the theme of "an investment in North Carolina," banker Archie K. Davis raised $1.5 million in gifts from corporations and citizens of North Carolina to purchase Pinelands. In December the committee became the Research Triangle Foundation, Inc., and the Research Triangle Institute was established. RTP is now the largest research park in the world, with over 130 research facilities in 2007, employing 39,000 people for 157 organizations. The park contains industrial laboratories and trade associations, federal and state government laboratories, nonprofit research institutes, and university-related research activities. Areas of concentration include environmental sciences, pharmaceuticals and agricultural chemicals, microelectronics, and computer technology.

Educational support activities in RTP include the North Carolina Board of Science and Technology, the Triangle Universities Computation Center, and the Triangle Universities Center for Advanced Studies, Inc. (TUCASI), which holds 120 acres in the park for joint activities of the three universities. On the campus of TUCASI are the National Humanities Center and the Microelectronics Center of North Carolina (now MCNC).

Although RTP was developed without state appropriations, the state provided leadership, cooperation, and the support of its educational base. The success of RTP is a notable example of effective cooperation among state government, higher education, and the corporate community.

WILLIAM F. LITTLE
*University of North Carolina at Chapel Hill*

Victor J. Danilov, *Industrial Research* (May 1971); W. B. Hamilton, *South Atlantic Quarterly* (Spring 1966); Luther H. Hodges, *Businessman in the Statehouse* (1962); A. N. Link, *A Generosity of Spirit: The Early History of the Research Triangle Park* (1995); Ruth Walker, *Christian Science Monitor* (15 June 1982); Louis Round Wilson, *Louis Round Wilson's Historical Sketches* (1976).

## Savannah River Site

When it was built in the early 1950s, the Savannah River Site was hailed as an engineering marvel on par with the construction of the Panama Canal. Containing five nuclear reactors, a number of other large-scale nuclear and chemical facilities, high-tech research centers, multiple waste treatment sites, and a host of other support buildings, the entire site is spread over 310 square miles of mostly wooded land owned by the U.S. government on the western border of South Carolina, approximately 30 miles southeast of Augusta, Ga. Construction began on the site in 1950 when the Atomic Energy Commission contracted with E. I. duPont de Nemours and Company to build and run a major facility that could produce the key materials for America's nuclear weapons on an industrial scale, particularly tritium and plutonium-239. As the U.S. government responded to the growing challenges of the Cold War and the arms race with the Soviet Union, this new plant formed a crucial part of America's nuclear defense network, as well as ongoing national research programs in nuclear, chemical, and environmental processes. Perhaps not quite as famous as sites in Oak Ridge, Tenn., or Los Alamos, N.M.—though it plays an important role in the 2002 film *The Sum of All Fears*—the Savannah River Site was in many ways the nucleus of America's atomic age, and it continues to manage the legacies of that era while promoting new forms of scientific research and technological innovation.

Among the numerous variables that helped determine the site's location was the fact that the larger region of the Central Savannah River Area had a long history of industrial development dating back as far as the 1830s and 1840s, when local entrepreneurs brought some of the first textile and flour mills to the South. Yet it was inevitable that the site's impact on the surrounding area would be greater than any other industrial force preceding it. During construction, the towns of Ellenton and Dunbarton, as well as a number of smaller hamlets, were completely evacuated and dismantled; many of Ellenton's original buildings were pulled off of their foundations and moved to what is now New Ellenton, just outside the site's northern boundary. The site also brought significant change to nearby Aiken, S.C., where scientists, professionals, and other skilled workers relocated from all over the country, mixing with the long-established, southern white and African American residents as well as the wealthy, mostly northern socialites who regularly spent their winters there. As a social critic wrote at the time, "It [was] as if Scarlett O'Hara had come home from the ball, wriggled out of her satin gown, and put on a space suit."

The Savannah River Site is still managed and run through agreements between the Department of Energy and different subcontractors. And while none of the site's original reactors still operate as they once did, the mission of the Savannah River Site has evolved as global politics have shifted. In addition to continuing to support the stabilization of existing nuclear weapons, one of the site's main operations now involves waste management, particularly with the Defense Waste Processing Facility, which converts radioactive waste from America's defense program into glass for long-term storage. Other parts of the site, including the Savannah River National Laboratory and the Savannah River Ecology Lab, conduct experimental research for a wide range of applications, such as fuel production, nonproliferation, and environmental cleanup and management. Although the Cold War may technically be over, the Savannah River Site remains a vital component of America's national security program and a center for scientific and technological advancement whose influence extends far beyond the region that surrounds it.

MICHAEL P. BIBLER
*University of Manchester*

Dorothy Kilgallin, *Good Housekeeping* (May 1953); Daniel Lang, *New Yorker* (7 July 1951); Mary Beth Reed, Mark Swanson, Steve Gaither, J. W. Joseph, and William Henry, *Savannah River Site at 50: Proceedings of the South Carolina Historical Association* (1994).

## Southern Growth Policies Board

The Southern Growth Policies Board was established through an interstate compact in December 1971 by nine southern governors who saw that the region was undergoing rapid growth in its population and economy. Terry Sanford, former governor of North Carolina and president of Duke University, proposed the idea for a regional planning agency in a speech to a reform group, the L. Q. C. Lamar Society. Sanford suggested that interstate planning and cooperation would be the keys to helping the South "win the awesome race with time to save the cities and preserve the countryside. Now is the time, and the South can lead the way."

The member states now include Alabama, Arkansas, Georgia, Kentucky, Louisiana, Mississippi, Missouri, North Carolina, Oklahoma, South Carolina, Tennessee, and Virginia, as well as the Commonwealth of Puerto Rico. Texas, Maryland, Delaware, and the Virgin Islands are also eligible to join.

The agreement specifies that the board shall consist of five members from each participating state—the governor, a state senator, a state representative appointed by their respective presiding officers, and two leading citizens appointed by the governor. A governor serves as chairman of the board for a one-year term. The work of the staff is reviewed quarterly by an executive committee of approximately 15 board members, and the staff is headed by an executive director.

Article III of the Interstate Agreement directs the board to prepare and maintain a "Statement of Regional Objectives," including recommended approaches to regional problems. The statement may also identify projects deemed to be of regional significance. It is amended or revised at least once every six years.

The first "Statement of Regional Objectives" was prepared in 1974 by a distinguished panel of civic leaders appointed by the governors. The mission of this panel, known as the Commission on the Future of the South, was to recommend policies to foster continued economic growth while at the same time mitigating adverse sociological and environmental effects. The commissioners concluded that a policy of "no growth" for the South was neither feasible nor desirable and suggested that the staff consider policies to influence the distribution of growth in the region.

Within this framework, the board strengthened its research and information capabilities, emphasizing region-wide economic development activities. The board also developed a significant role in representing the interests of the southern states in Washington in the so-called Sunbelt-Frostbelt conflict. As the board became more deeply involved in federal issues, a second office was staffed in Washington in 1977 to monitor federal actions that could result in negative consequences for the region.

In 1980 the second Commission on the Future of the South framed a new report to guide the board's program activities. Their recommendations focused on four areas of regional development: the economy, cities, children, and energy. Utilizing this basic planning document, the board began to assess and redefine its mission.

In 1982 the board relinquished its Washington office, maintaining a reduced presence in a new office to be supported by the Southern Governors' Association. At its 10th Anniversary Conference, the board rededicated itself to regional economic development—specifically, "to provide an early alert system for our states as to intermediate-range policy options of regional importance which will maximize opportunities for and minimize impediments to economic growth and development."

The board today represents a unique vehicle for regional coordination and public-private cooperation. The availability of opportunities in the region, the positive attitudes regarding future growth potential, and the healthy confluence of business and government interests provide a strong framework for future progress. The organization sponsors annual conferences, community forums, innovator awards, and publications in such areas as technology, globalization, the workforce, and community development. The board's annual report on the future of the South anchors its ongoing work.

WILLIAM WINTER
DAVID CREWS
*Jackson, Mississippi*

James C. Cobb, *The Selling of the South: The Southern Crusade for Industrial Development, 1936–1980* (1982); *New York Times* (9 January 1977); Southern Growth Policies Board, *Annual Report* (1977).

## Stevens, J. P., and Company

J. P. Stevens and Company traces its beginnings to a Massachusetts woolen mill founded in 1813 by Nathaniel Stevens. In 1899 John P. Stevens, Nathaniel's grandson, established the New York commission house from which the present firm takes its name. Stevens came to serve as selling agent for a number of southern cotton textile firms, eight of which merged with the Stevens family interests in 1946 to form the modern corporation. In succeeding years, Stevens transferred its woolen operations to the South, in part to counter unionization efforts. It also expanded its holdings of southern mills, becoming the second-largest publicly held American textile corporation.

In 1963 the Textile Workers' Union of America (TWUA) launched a campaign to organize Stevens's southern plants. Company management, notably board chairman James D. Finley, a native Georgian, responded aggressively, being found guilty repeatedly of illegal harassment of organizers and prounion workers. The TWUA was unable to win a representation election at any Stevens mill until workers at the firm's Roanoke Rapids, N.C., plants gave the union a small majority in August 1974. Despite its victory, however, the union was unable to negotiate a contract. Complaining of company delay tactics, the newly created Amalgamated Clothing and Textile Workers' Union (ACTWU) launched a boycott in June 1976 against Stevens products. The boycott proved ineffective, but it successfully focused national attention on Stevens as a symbol of southern antiunion obduracy.

Numerous church groups endorsed the boycott, and demonstrators besieged stockholders' meetings; the Roanoke Rapids saga became the basis for a critically acclaimed motion picture, *Norma Rae* (1978).

More telling than the boycott was the ACTWU's innovative "corporate campaign," which mobilized the investment power of unions and their sympathizers to press Stevens's lenders and "outside" directors to sever their links to the company. Pressure of this sort, along with growing internal problems, began to sap the company's strength, while the retirement of Finley in January 1980 permitted it to take a more flexible stance. In October 1980 Stevens and the ACTWU reached an accord, the company agreeing to contracts at unionized mills and the union to calling off its anti-Stevens campaign. JPS Textile Group, Inc., was established in 1989 from assets of J. P. Stevens and Company. West Point Pepperell acquired the company in 1993 to form West Point Stevens. All outstanding legal disputes between the company and the union were settled in October 1983.

DAVID L. CARLTON
*Vanderbilt University*

Mimi Conway, *Rise Gonna Rise: A Portrait of Southern Textile Workers* (1979); Lloyd C. Ferguson, *From Family Firm to Corporate Giant: J. P. Stevens and Company, 1813–1963* (1970); Jim Overton and others, *Southern Exposure* (Spring 1978).

## Textile Industry

Small-scale textile mills could be found in the South as far back as the American Revolution, and the textile industry gained a firm foothold in the piedmont area of Virginia, North Carolina, South Carolina, and Georgia during the antebellum era. By 1850 more than 200 textile mills operated in the South. Leaders of the industry included William Gregg and Daniel Pratt, both of South Carolina. The textile mill made its greatest impact on the region in the 100 years after the Civil War. Developing rapidly after 1880, the industry soon rivaled the enormous New England textile center in plants, equipment, and personnel. The number of spindles in operation more than doubled in the 1890s, and the amount of capital invested in the southern textile industry rose from $22.8 million in 1880 to $132.4 million in 1900. As recently as the 1980s, it was the region's major industrial employer.

The pattern of mill expansion in the South differed in important ways from that which marked the older textile region chiefly because of distinctive physical and labor conditions of the area. Hydroelectric power, developed extensively because of the geographic advantages of the piedmont, enabled mill entrepreneurs to locate their factories in rural areas where labor was relatively more plentiful. Textile technology required comparatively large numbers of unskilled workers. Cheap labor was to be found in the Southeast; this, more than any other single factor, stimulated indigenous textile expansion and, in time, lured northern capital to the region.

Although the pool of surplus white farm labor in the piedmont has varied over time with changing agricultural and industrial conditions, it has gener-

ally been large. Unlike other southern industries, textile-mill jobs were long reserved for these white workers. The virtual certainty of widespread social protest long discouraged mill managers from employing black operatives. Not until the 1980s were black workers welcomed in the mills, where they quickly accounted for approximately one-fourth of southern textile employees.

Remote mill sites encouraged the construction of owner-controlled mill villages to house workers and their families. The pattern developed in the antebellum era, from the factory and mill village built by William Gregg at Graniteville, S.C. Mill villages traditionally contained housing for workers as well as schools, general stores, churches, and sometimes medical centers and recreational areas, all owned and operated by the manufacturing company. Although mill housing was worker owned after the 1950s, this strong community orientation continued to distinguish the industry in the South. The Southeast was a region with good transportation facilities and few large cities. Its rate of urbanization throughout the 20th century was slower than that of other industrial centers, a fact related to its established dependence on the textile industry. The organizational structure adopted by the industry in the South was dictated by unique qualities in the factors of production in the region. In turn, the textile industry powerfully influenced the culture and socioeconomic position of the modern South. Competition from developing nations had affected southern textile mills from the 1970s, as they used the same low-cost strategy that southern mills had once used to lure northern textile mills to the South. The 1990s witnessed the rapid decline of the textile industry in the piedmont, leaving many communities without economic resources and workers without jobs or skills for new industry.

MARY J. OATES
*Regis College*

Mildred Gwin Andrews, *The Men and the Mills: A History of the Southern Textile Industry* (1987); Jack Blicksilver, *Cotton Manufacturing in the Southeast: An Historical Analysis* (1959); Glenn Gilman, *Human Relations in the Industrial Southeast: A Study of the Textile Industry* (1956); Jacquelyn Dowd Hall, James Leloudis, Robert Korstad, Mary Murphy, Lu Ann Jones, and Christopher B. Daly, *Like a Family: The Making of a Southern Cotton Mill World* (1987); Jeffrey Leiter, Michael D. Schulman, and Rhonda Zingraff, eds., *Hanging by a Thread: Social Change in Southern Textiles* (1991); Toby Miller, *Journal of Business and Economic History* (Winter 1999); Broadus Mitchell, *The Rise of Cotton Mills in the South* (1921).

## Timber Industry

Beginning with a concentration on naval stores (turpentine and pitch), the southern timber industry has come to include a diversity of products related primarily to southern yellow pine but including cypress and other hardwoods as well. The 17th- and 18th-century timber industry was located in the Carolinas and characterized by small, low-capital establishments with low annual production. Sawmills and distilleries for turpentine were located in the woods. Those industries used slave labor organized on a task system. The small, less-

developed but still important business of searching for live oak timbers used in shipbuilding often involved migrant crews who searched the coastal islands for appropriate timber.

By the middle of the 19th century, the entire industry was shifting its location and broadening its scope. During the years immediately after the Civil War, naval stores and sawmill operations moved into Georgia, Florida, and the Gulf Coast South. In the 1880s Georgia led the South in naval stores and timber production, and in the 20th century Florida and the Gulf Coast states dominated. That shift was accompanied by the increasing use of southern pine not only for naval stores but also for other timber products, including crossties, building materials, and, increasingly, pulpwood for paper manufacturing.

Changing labor patterns accompanied expansion. Slave labor gave way to free labor at the end of the Civil War. Many of the early postwar laborers were migrants from the Carolinas who followed the timber industry into other states. Later timber workers included both contract migrant workers and seasonal workers who retained ties to the agricultural economies of the Southeast. In some areas of the timber belt, labor came from the often harsh convict-lease system. Lumber camps and lumber towns similar to textile towns appeared throughout the South—particularly the Gulf Coast South—as the industry expanded. Regardless of the source of the labor, the laborers were a colorful transient population. Not as radical as their Pacific Northwest counterparts, south-

Three boys posing in swamp as if felling a giant cypress, place and date unknown
(Courtesy of the Center for the Study of Southern Culture Collection)

ern timber workers nevertheless participated in the activities of the Knights of
Labor and the International Workers of
the World.

In the 20th century, small-scale
industries gave way to large concerns
owning substantial tracts of land
throughout the South. Although originally exploitive and unscientific, southern timber industries have built on the

turpentine and conservation experiments of Charles Holmes Herty to provide an important example of scientifically inspired diversity of products and management of renewable resources. Led by trade associations such as the Southern Pine Association, timber operators have standardized the product and often controlled the price. A diverse product line, large-scale operations, and the control of land continue to make the timber industry an important part of the southern economic landscape. For many southern laborers and cities, such operations are crucial to survival, with the expansion of a paper mill or the closing of a wood-processing plant the basis of major economic rearrangements in local areas throughout the region.

THOMAS F. ARMSTRONG
*Louisiana State University
at Alexandria*

Thomas D. Clark, *The Greening of the South: The Recovery of Land and Forest* (1984), *Mississippi Quarterly* (Spring 1972); James Defebaugh, *History of the Lumber Industry of America* (1906); Percival Perry, "The Naval Stores Industry in the Ante-Bellum South" (Ph.D. dissertation, Duke University, 1947); Robert B. Outland III, *Tapping the Pines: The Naval Stores Industry in the American South* (2004).

## Tobacco Industry

Tobacco was once the fifth most important cash crop in the United States. It has been an important element of southern agriculture since the days of Sir Walter Raleigh, though it has experienced considerable decline in recent years. North Carolina and Kentucky are the principal tobacco-producing states in the country, but Virginia, South Carolina, Georgia, Tennessee, and Florida all contain areas where tobacco is and has long been grown. All five major tobacco-producing regions of the United States are in the South: the Burley, Old, New Bright, Border, and Georgia-Florida Belts. In the 1960s tobacco meant $1 billion annually for farmers in North Carolina and about half that amount for their counterparts in Kentucky. In North Carolina alone, production dropped from 1 billion, 200 million pounds in 1970 to approximately 550 million pounds in the year 2000.

Towns in tobacco regions are traditionally dotted with large warehouses, some as big as a football field, where the crop was sold at auction. Anywhere from 2 to 12 such structures were concentrated in a single town, giving it a distinctive character. As tobacco continues to decline, more and more of it is produced under contract with tobacco companies, bypassing the auctioneer and warehouseman, thus rendering a rising number of warehouses obsolete. In the past, a typical tobacco town of 40,000 people had, for example, 3 million square feet of floor space under the roofs of structures designed only for selling tobacco, a process that lasts for only three and a half months.

The processing of tobacco (redrying, cleaning, and stemming) is carried on in the same towns where the sales warehouses are located; thus, the processing has traditionally taken place within the borders of producing regions. This too may change as demand and econo-

Scene at Kentucky tobacco auction, ca. 1960
(Photographic Archives, University of Louisville
[Kentucky])

mies evolve. Tobacco products such as cigarettes, pipe and chewing tobacco, and snuff are manufactured in large cities—near but not necessarily in the areas where the crop is grown. Notable among tobacco-manufacturing centers are Richmond, Va., and Durham and Winston-Salem, N.C., and Louisville, Ky. Partially processed tobacco and tobacco products are important American agricultural exports. The two outstanding tobacco ports of the United States are Norfolk, Va., and Wilmington, N.C.

Tobacco was the last important cash crop in the United States to be mechanized. Within the past 45 years, that process replaced thousands of workers in all the flue-cured tobacco producing areas. The shift to machinery freed a large labor force from agriculture. Unlike the mechanization of other cash crops, tobacco mechanization did not

result in massive out-migration of recently emancipated farm workers; they remained at home and became a powerful force in attracting many new factories into the old tobacco districts. In fact, the "eastern" or "New Bright Belt" of North Carolina shifted from a predominantly rural economy to a mixed economy in a single generation.

One of the oldest agricultural products of the United States and an indigenous crop, tobacco was for many years the cornerstone of the agricultural economy of no less than five southern states. As a revenue source, tobacco remains a crop of national significance. When additional money is needed, tobacco products are always on the list for a tax increase. In spite of a warning by the surgeon general of the United States that tobacco was dangerous to one's health, which was printed on every cigarette package, the industry continued to thrive. Not until lawsuits, heavy fines, and public support for smoke-free zones in restaurants and public buildings hit the industry did it begin to wane. A $206 billion settlement between tobacco companies and 46 states that had sued over public health issues dramatized the decline. Congress passed a national tobacco quota buyout in 2004, which ended federal tobacco price-support and supply-control programs and provided compensation to tobacco growers for the end of the system. Today, titles such as "Turmoil in Tobacco Land" and "Remaking Tobacco-Dependent Communities" are common for written works and conferences that address tobacco issues and regional concerns.

Tobacco has been so important as

Trucking on U.S. Route 29 in Georgia, 1943
(John Vachon, Library of Congress [LC-USW-3-21955-D], Washington, D.C.)

an extremely high-value crop that it is difficult to find adequate substitutes. For example, a 1997 University of Kentucky study indicates that to yield the income from five acres of tobacco, a farmer would have to plant 100 acres of corn and 50 acres of hay or double-cropped wheat and soy beans.

ENNIS L. CHESTANG
*East Carolina University*

W. W. Garner, E. G. Moss, and others, *U.S. Department of Agriculture, Yearbook of Agriculture* (1922); Fraser Hart and Ennis L. Chestang, *Geographical Review* (October 1978), *Geographical Review* (October 1996); *North Carolina Geographer*, vol. 10 (2002 special issue).

## Trucking Industry

Although trucking emerged first in the Northeast and Midwest during the 1910s, its appearance in the South was not too far behind. By the late 1920s and early 1930s, the business had expanded enough to challenge railway control over southern transportation. Rail executives pressured legislators in Texas,

Louisiana, Kentucky, and Tennessee to enact restrictive motor carrier laws. Ad hoc trucking associations, which had emerged in part through encouragement from insurance and truck-manufacturing firms, failed to block these laws. In 1932 the state of Texas won two important Supreme Court cases that authorized restrictive controls over trucks. Ironically for the southerners, those court cases laid the foundation for national regulation of trucking.

The business was recognized as an industry under the New Deal's National Recovery Administration (NRA), and the American Trucking Association (ATA) became the industry's leading trade association. The ATA-NRA coalition attempted to establish minimum-wage scales, but the southern two-wage system (one white, one black) held back progress. (Ironically, the two-wage system was supported by black businessmen in North Carolina.) In 1935 the national movement to regulate trucking through the Interstate Commerce Commission succeeded. For the next four or five decades, trucking flourished and the South as a region led the way. By the 1970s every southern state except Arkansas, Mississippi, and South Carolina received over $1 billion in salaries (Texas truckers earned over $5 billion).

Meanwhile, a movement to deregulate the industry moved forward; economists and policy makers argued that regulation raised costs and stymied innovation in the industry. (Airlines, railways, and telecommunications were other industries targeted.) In the 1980s Congress deregulated economic controls over interstate trucking (safety issues were still subject to government oversight). The political clout of truckers, however, stymied deregulation in about one-half of the states; most southern states, with Florida being the exception, blocked deregulation. By the mid-1990s, however, Congress overcame the usual states' rights claims and preempted all state economic regulations over trucking.

It is not yet clear whether deregulation is the final policy statement on trucking. While deregulation has increased competition and lowered costs, it has also brought instability in service, as many trucking firms have gone out of business and service to small communities has been curtailed. By the beginning of the 21st century, trucking in the South remained an important industry, although in comparison to the smaller Midwest region, the industry contributed less to the overall economy in terms of economic impact and taxes paid.

WILLIAM R. CHILDS
*Ohio State University*

William R. Childs, *Trucking and the Public Interest: The Emergence of Federal Regulation, 1914–1940* (1985); Milton S. Heath, *Southern Economics Journal* (August 1934); Motor Vehicle Manufacturers Association of the United States, Inc., *Motor Truck Facts* (1974).

## Wal-Mart

In 2002, for the first time, a service provider topped the *Fortune* 500 list of the world's largest corporations, edging out the traditional winners from the manufacturing and resource-extraction sectors. Arkansas-based discount retailer Wal-Mart Stores, Inc., passed Exxon-Mobil to become the biggest company on earth. Since 2002 it has held the number one position on the ranking for five out of six years. This development is a turning point in economic history and a useful synecdoche for the impact of southern-style business culture on globalization.

While northern observers often marveled that the "backward" Ozarks could produce such a revolutionary model, Wal-Mart's innovations built upon parallel developments in its home region, from evangelical revival to the country music boom and the continued flow of federal revenue into the former Confederacy. Just as the factories of Detroit and Chicago shaped the nation during its industrial heyday, Wal-Mart stores, supply chains, and policy priorities decisively influenced the post-1973 political economy.

The Wal-Mart retail empire got its start in the weeks after V-J Day in August 1945, when Samuel M. Walton bought the first in what was to become the nation's largest chain of Ben Franklin five-and-dime franchises. In 1962 Walton adopted the discount retailing model—low prices, edge-of-town sites, and rapid stock turnover—after researching its success in the Northeast. Opting to open stores in small county seats that larger chains eschewed, Walton ironically erected the largest retail chain on earth on the home turf of the antichain movement of the 1920s and 1930s. Shares in Wal-Mart Stores, Inc., were sold on the New York Stock Exchange beginning in 1972. Remarkable steady expansion exploded into exponential growth in the 1980s, and in 1985 *Forbes* magazine named Walton the world's richest man. Surviving Walton family members are today collectively worth more than $90 billion and own approximately 40 percent of Wal-Mart Stores, Inc. The company's international headquarters remain in Bentonville, Ark.

With more employees than any other private-sector entity, a satellite system rivaled only by the Pentagon's, and sales receipts that on a single day topped the gross domestic products of 36 sovereign nations, the Arkansas corporation has become, in the words of *Fortune* reporter Jerry Useem, "a lot like America: a sole superpower with a down-home twang." As the South's influence grew in national culture, the comparison seemed like more than a metaphor to many. In any given week, the equivalent of more than one-third of the American population visits a Wal-Mart, the majority in rural and suburban markets. "If you want to reach the Christian population on Sunday, you do it from the

church pulpit. If you want to reach them on Saturday, you do it in Wal-Mart," explained Christian Coalition executive director Ralph Reed in 1995. Pollster John Zogby declared the "weekly Wal-Mart voter" a key demographic in national electoral politics, pointing out that over three-quarters of this group had voted for George W. Bush in the landmark 2004 presidential election. As the leading retailer of music, food, and toys, the company's cultural impact reaches far beyond its original home territory and mirrors the broader diffusion of southern consumer tastes.

Its tireless drive for efficient operations placed Wal-Mart at the forefront of late 20th-century economic transformations. Reflecting the feminine face of low-wage service work, in 2004 a federal judge certified the largest class-action civil rights lawsuit in history, *Dukes v. Wal-Mart Stores, Inc.*, which alleges systematic sex discrimination in Wal-Mart's wages, salaries, and promotion practices. The company's early innovations in bar-code scanning, satellite communication, automated distribution centers, and container shipping all set the industry standards, taking "just-in-time" inventory stocking to an unprecedented pace and allowing it to produce annual cost reductions among its suppliers. This unflagging commitment to "roll back" prices may well contribute to keeping domestic inflation in check, though critics offset this effect against the public subsidies the company absorbs and the pressure it creates for offshoring by American manufacturers. From its widely touted "Bring It Home to the USA" product promotion of the mid-1980s, Wal-Mart has shifted to an almost purely import-driven model, with Chinese imports alone accounting for 70 percent of its products in U.S. stores by 2007. Indeed, Wal-Mart has become one of the 21st century's chief vehicles for linking the U.S. South to the global South.

BETHANY E. MORETON
*University of Georgia*

Charles Fishman, *The Wal-Mart Effect: How the World's Most Powerful Company Really Works—and How It's Transforming the American Economy* (2006); Nelson Lichtenstein, ed., *Wal-Mart: The Face of Twenty-First-Century Capitalism* (2006); Bethany E. Moreton, *The Soul of the Service Economy: Wal-Mart and the Making of Christian Free Enterprise, 1929–1994* (2006); Bob Ortega, *In Sam We Trust: The Untold Story of Sam Walton and How Wal-Mart Is Devouring America* (1998); Sandra Vance and Roy Scott, *Wal-Mart: A History of Sam Walton's Retail Phenomenon* (1994).

## Walton, Sam M.

(1918–1992) BUSINESSMAN.
*U.S. News & World Report* magazine in 1986 proclaimed Sam Moore Walton of Bentonville in northeastern Arkansas the wealthiest man in the United States. He had, at that point, made $4.3 billion from his 900 Wal-Mart discount stores that operated in 22 states, mainly in the South and Southwest.

Walton began his retail career by working for J. C. Penney. In 1945 he and his brother J. L. raised $25,000 to open a variety store in Newport, Ark., and later bought a five-and-dime store on the town square. By 1962 the Waltons operated 15 dime stores, and the number had

Sam Walton, founder of Wal-Mart Stores, Inc., 1980s (Wal-Mart, Bentonville, Ark.)

grown to 30 by 1970, when the business went public. Walton especially targeted small towns for his stores, which have been vital economic forces in many southern states. Walton, through Wal-Mart and a new business, Sam's Wholesale Club, created more employment in Mississippi in the 1980s than any other person. Walton's eldest son, S. Robson Walton, is chairman of the board of Wal-Mart Stores, Inc. The Walton family fortune was valued at over $90 billion in 2004.

Despite his success, Walton remained an almost stereotypical traditional southerner in many ways. He continued to live in a modest house on a shady street in his small hometown in Arkansas; he drove a 1979 Ford pickup truck, hunted quail, and had his hair cut at a traditional, three-chair, no-waiting barbershop. He encouraged a family feeling among his Wal-Mart employees, and his store openings have been southern theater—combining the emotionalism of revivalism, fiddling contests, and school pep rallies.

CHARLES REAGAN WILSON
*University of Mississippi*

*Forbes* (28 October 1985); John Huey and Sam Walton, *Sam Walton: Made in America* (1993); Bob Ortega, *In Sam We Trust: The Untold Story of Sam Walton and Wal-Mart, the World's Most Powerful Retailer* (2000); Robert Slater, *The Wal-Mart Decade: How a New Generation of Leaders Turned Sam Walton's Legacy into the World's Number One Company* (2003); *U.S. News & World Report* (21 July 1986).

# INDEX OF CONTRIBUTORS

Page numbers in boldface refer to articles.

Apalachee, 166

Appalachia, 101, 160, 251; industrialization in, **256–59**

Appalachian Mountains, 19, 90, 103, 127, 148, 164, 254, 287

Applebome, Peter, 245

Apples, **141–42**

Aquaculture, **143–44**

*Arator*, 13

Arizona, 37, 105

Arkansas: rice in, 14, 61, 105, 192, 193; black farmers in, 32; poultry in, 37, 189, 190; rural education in, 42; soybeans in, 60, 198; grange in, 68; mechanization in, 87; farmer organizations in, 97, 99–100, 137; apples in, 142; aquaculture in, 143, 144; peaches in, 182; grapes in, 205; furniture industry in, 299; oil industry in, 314; radio industry in, 315

Arnett, Alex M., 113

Asheville, N.C., 256

Ashmore, Harry, 236

Associated Milk Producers of Texas, 37

Atlanta, Ga., 84, 190, 196, 211, 221, 225, 236, 270, 271, 289, 302; "Atlanta Spirit," 213, 214; automobile industry in, 217, 276; African Americans in, 221, 222, 233, 234, 271; expositions in, 241, 274; Delta Air Lines in, 273, 274, 292; as commercial center, **274–75**; banks in, 280, 281; music in, 307, 308, 316, 317

Atlanta Automobile Show, 84

*Atlanta Constitution*, 245, 266, 299–300

*Atlanta Daily Herald*, 299

*Atlanta Journal*, 84, 315

Atlanta Life, 234

Atlantic City, N.J., 284

Atlantic Coastal Highway, 85

Atomic Energy Act, 312

Atomic Energy Commission, U.S., 312, 313, 320

Audubon Sugar School, 199

Augusta, Ga., 64, 181, 274, 301, 320

Augusta County, Va., 73

Automobiles, 56, 84, 216, 262; manufacturing of, 217, 220, 255, **275–78**

Autry, Gene, 23

Axtell, James, 49

Bacon County, Ga., 196

*Balcony Stories* (King), 16

Baldwin, Calvin B., 159

Baldwin, Joseph Glover, 112

Baltimore, Md., 140, 232, 278, 317

*Baltimore Manufacturers' Record*, 266

Bank Act (Louisiana), 279

Bankhead Cotton Control Act, 94

Bankhead Highway Association, 84

Bankhead-Jones Farm Tenancy Act, 96, 124, 158–59

Bank Holding Company Act, 282

Bank of America, 246

Bank of North America, 278

Banks, 26, 67, **278–82**

Banneker, Benjamin, 39

Barbados, 150

*Barren Ground* (Glasgow), 24

Bartlesville, Okla., 314

Bartram, William, 10

Baton Rouge, La., 314

Baytown, Tex., 314

Beaumont, Tex., 314

Bentonville, Ark., 331, 332

Berckmans, P. J. A., 181

Bermuda, 274

Berry, Thomas, 247

Berry, Wendell, 251

Bessemer, Ala., 256

Beverley, Robert, 76, 166

Biddle, Nicholas, 278

Biedenharn, Joseph, 289

Biloxi, Miss., 284, 285

Birmingham, Ala., 97, 191, 225, 236, 256, 275, 276

Black Belt, 97, 103, 119, 128, 145, 221

*Black Boy* (Wright), 78

Blackwell, W. T., Company, 293

Blake, "Blind," 23

Federal Farm Board, 138
Federal Radio Commission, 315
Federal Reserve System, 280, 282
Felknor, Jessie, 75
Fence/stock laws, **159–60**
Fertilizers, 129, **161–62**
Few, William P., 294
Fields, Mamie Garvin, 51
Financial Institutions Reform, Recovery,
    and Enforcement Act, 282
Financial Services Modernization Act, 282
Finley, James D., 323
First Bank of the United States, 278
Fisheries, 230
Fish farming, 143–44
Fitzgerald, Deborah, 18
Fitzhugh, George, 13, 239, 290, 291
Flagler, Henry, **295–96**
Florida: cotton in, 10, 105; black farmers
    in, 32; pasture crops in, 35; fruits and
    vegetables in, 36, 90; citrus in, 37, 149,
    150–51; Indian reservations in, 92; soil
    in, 126; aquaculture in, 143, 144; cattle
    in, 146; fertilizer industry in, 161, 162;
    pork in, 166; migrant labor in, 179, 180;
    peanuts in, 185; sugar in, 199, 200; truck
    farming in, 203; population growth, 275;
    foreign industry in, 297; timber in, 325
Florida East Coast Railway, 295, 296
Folk culture, 106–10
Folklore, 110
Food and markets, women's roles in, **72–75**
Forage crops, **162–64**, 198
*Forbes* magazine, 168, 331
Ford, Henry, 306
Ford automobiles, 276
Foreign industry, 219–20, 259, **296–98**
Fort Lauderdale, Fla., 271
*Fortune* magazine, 269, 313, 330, 331
Frady, Marshall, 222
France, 219, 298
Franklin, Benjamin, 196
Franklin, John Hope, 263
Free Banking Act (New York), 279

Freedmen's Bureau, 134
Fulton County, Ga., 221
Furniture industry, **298–99**
Future Farmers of America, 43
Future Farmers of Virginia, 43

Gainesville, Ga., 189
Garden patches, **75–78**
Garn–St. Germain Act, 282
Garvey, Marcus, 165
Garvey Movement, **165–66**
Gaskin, Stephen, 153
Gender divisions, 11, 12, 89
Genealogy, 109–10, 116
General Education Board, 19, 178
General Motors (GM), 276
George, James Z., 40
Georgetown, Ky., 276
Georgia: cotton in, 9, 103, 105; black
    farmers in, 32; poultry in, 37, 189, 190;
    peanuts in, 37, 185; rural education in,
    42; soybeans in, 60, 198; rice in, 61, 192,
    230; corn in, 62; roads in, 83; mecha-
    nization in, 87; part-time farmers in,
    101; plantations in, 102, 105; soil in, 126;
    Native Americans in, 134; antebellum
    agricultural societies in, 140; apples in,
    142; boll weevil in, 145, 172, 214; com-
    munal farms in, 152; fence/stock laws in,
    160; peaches in, 182, 183; pecans in, 185;
    sugar in, 199; tobacco in, 201, 202, 327;
    grapes in, 205; manufacturing in, 212;
    unionization in, 219; black workforce in,
    221; army bases in, 265; automobile in-
    dustry in, 277; banking in, 280; foreign
    industry in, 297; furniture industry in,
    298; liquor industry in, 304; railroads
    in, 318; textile industry in, 324; timber
    in, 325
Georgia, University of, 299
Georgia Horticultural Society, 181
Germany, 219, 298
Glasgow, Ellen, 24, 113
Glenn Pool, Okla., 314

Hughes, Everett C., 56
*Human Geography of the South, The*
(Vance), 113
Humble (Exxon), 314
Hunt, Freeman, 290
Hurston, Zora Neale, 24, 172
Hyundai, 220, 277, 297

Idaho, 143
Illinois, 195
*I'll Take My Stand*, 24, 33, 214, 250
Immigration, 82, 180
Income: per capita, 17, 212, 217, 218, 244,
262, 268, 269, 315, 319; farm, 19, 37, 66,
96; women's, 74–75; African American,
221, 222
Indentured servants, 6
Indiana, 195
Indian Territory, 91
Indigo, 8, 45, 61, 80, 102
Industrialization, 18, 119, 131, 211, 213, 215,
216, 217, 224, 267, 268, 300, 301, 314;
antebellum, 209–11, **229–31**, 253; resis-
tance to, **248–52**; and change, **252–55**; in
Appalachia, **256–59**; in the piedmont,
**259–62**
*In Old Virginia* (Page), 16
Insecticide Act, 176
Insects and insecticides, 25, 88, 105, 145,
**172–77**, 193. *See also* Boll weevil
Institute for Southern Studies, 264
Insurance, **301–3**
Insurance Company of Georgia, 303
Interest Rate Adjustment Act, 282
International Harvester Company, 35, 87
International Lending Supervisory Act,
282
International Workers of the World, 326
Internet, 54, 223, 308, 309
Interstate Commerce Commission, 329
*In the Tennessee Mountains* (Craddock), 16
Iowa, 168, 177, 195
Iowa State College, 178
Iron, 230–31, 260
Isuzu Motors, 277, 297

J. R. Watkins Company, 52
Jackson, Alan, 223
Jackson, Andrew, 103, 278, 279
Jackson Highway Association, 84
Jackson National Life Insurance Company,
303
Jacksonville, Fla., 275, 302, 310
Jamaica, 273
Jamestown, Va., 6, 134, 200, 237, 242, 304,
309
Japan, 144, 178, 219, 259, 294, 297
Java, 200
Jay, John, 8
Jefferson, Thomas, 8, 36, 102, 137, 244, 249,
305
Jeffreys, George W., 64
Jenkins, Reverend Andrew, 316
Jennings, La., 313
Jewell, J. D., 189
Jitney Jungle, 52, 53
Jones, Charles C., Jr., 249
Jordan, Daniel W., 230
Jordon, Clarence, 152
JPS Textile Group, Inc., 323

Kaiser, Henry J., 306
Kakata, Liberia, 44
Kanawha River Valley, 229
Kansas, 91, 195
Kelley, Robin D. G., 97
Kelly, Oliver H., 68
Kendrick, Benjamin B., 113
Kentucky: early settlers in, 8; crops in,
10, 103; black farmers in, 32; corn in,
62; revivalism in, 108; soil in, 127, 128;
communal farms in, 152; mules in, 171;
unionization in, 219; poverty rates in,
221; tobacco in, 229, 327; coal mining in,
287; liquor industry in, 304; nuclear in-
dustry in, 312; trucking industry in, 329
Kentucky, University of, 329
Kentucky Distilleries and Warehouse
Company, 304
Kerr-Smith Tobacco Control Act, 94
Key West, Fla., 295, 296

Muscadine grapes, 204–5
Muscle Shoals, Ala., 161
Music, 12, 16–17, 22–24, 27, 65, 222–23; industry, **307–9**, 316

Nashoba, 152
Nashville, Tenn., 22, 242, 276, 298, 302, 308, 316, 317
Natchez, Miss., 9, 103, 128, 230
National Aeronautics and Space Administration (NASA), 264
National Airways, 273
National Association for Stock Car Auto Racing (NASCAR), 27
National Association for the Advancement of Colored People, 302
National Banking Acts, 279
National Broadcast Company, 316
National Christmas Tree Association, 148
Nationale-Nederlanden NV, 303
National Farmers' Alliance and Laborers Union, 69
National Fertilizer Research Center, 161
National Future Farmers of America Organization (NFFAO), 43, 44
National Humanities Center, 319
National Life and Accident Insurance Company, 303, 316
National Negro Business League, 233
National Negro Finance Corporation, 234
National Railroad Passenger Corporation (Amtrak), 318
National Recovery Administration, 329
National Research Council, 132
National Vocational Education Act, 43
Native Americans, 3, 10, 49, 75, **88–91**, 125–26, 129, 130, 133–34, 173, 181
Naval stores, 4, 80, 230, **309–11**, 325
Naval Stores Experiment Station, 311
*Negro World*, 165
Neighborhoods, 110, 115
Nemours, E. I duPont de, and Company, 320
Neoplantations, 36, 81, 105
Netherlands, 303

*Neuer Hagerstauner Calender Stadt und Land* (Gruber), 39
Nevada, 37
New Bern, N.C., 275, 298
New Deal, 21, 23, 26, 65, **92–96**, 104, 114, 119, 123–24, 136, 156, 158, 171, 179, 187, 216, 288; farmer organizations, **97–100**, 138
New Farmers of America, 43
New Farmers of Virginia, 43
New Hanover County, N.C., 184
New Mexico, 185
New Orleans, La., 39, 117, 225, 230, 232, 241, 243, 271, 275, 278, 284, 290, 291, 305, 307, 315, 316, 317
Newport, Ark., 332
New South, 211–13, 236, 243, 250, 252, 253, 299–300; myth, **266–69**
*Newsweek*, 270
Newton, J. C. C., 249
New York, 142, 278, 279
New York, N.Y., 267, 273, 292, 302, 307
*New York Herald*, 84
*New York Times*, 78, 269, 270
Nissan, 219, 220, 276, 277, 297
Nixon, Herman C., 113
Nixon, Nicholas N., 184
Norfolk, Va., 184, 236, 242, 276, 278, 328
Norfolk County, Va., 203
Norfolk Southern, 318
*Norma Rae*, 323
North American Free Trade Agreement, 220, 262
North American Lumber and Timber Company, 178
Northampton County, Va., 203
North and South Bee Line Highway Association, 84
North Carolina, 72, 73; early settlers in, 8; crops in, 10; black farmers in, 32; hog farming in, 38, 166, 168; agricultural education in, 39, 40; soybeans in, 60, 198; Populists in, 71; gardens in, 76; roads in, 83, 84; mechanization in, 87; Indian reservations in, 92;

homes in, 221; slavery in, 232; industrialization in, 255; textile industry in, 261, 324; automobile industry in, 262; foreign industry in, 296, 297; turpentine in, 310; railroads in, 318; timber in, 325
Southdown, 37
*Southern Agriculturalist, Horticulturist, and Register of Rural Affairs*, 39
*Southern Cultivator*, 64, 173
*Southerner and World Affairs, The* (Hero), 79
*Southern Farm Gazette*, 190
Southern Farmers' Alliance, 17, 135. *See also* Farmers' Alliance
*Southern Good Roads*, 85
Southern Governors' Conference, 312
Southern Growth Policies Board, **321–22**
Southern Heritage Apple Orchard, 142
Southern identity, 223, 244, 245–47
*Southern Living* magazine, 192, 223
Southern Pacific Railroad, 192
Southern Pine Association, 327
*Southern Planter*, 170, 173
Southern Policy Association, 194
Southern Power Company, 294
Southern Progress Corp., 192
Southern Railway, 83
*Southern Regions of the United States* (Odum), 113
Southern Sustainable Agriculture Working Group, 132
Southern Tenant Farmers Union (STFU), 22, 97, 98–100, 123, 180
*Southern Worker*, 97
Southland, 37
*South Looks at Its Past, The* (Kendrick and Arnett), 113
South Union, Ky., 152
Soviet Union, 320
Soybeans, 27, 35, 60, 65, **198–99**
Spain, 184
Sparks, Alistair, 246
Spartanburg, S.C., 23, 219, 278
Spartanburg County, S.C., 182
Spencer, Samuel, 83

Spindletop, Tex., 313
Springdale, Ark., 190
Spring Hill, Tenn., 276
Spruill, Julia Cherry, 76
Staggers Rail Act, 318
Standard Life, 302
Standard Oil Company, 258, 295, 314
State Farm Insurance Company, 282
Steinbeck, John, 179
Stennis, John, 270
Sterling, Ross, 314
Stevens, J. P., and Company, **323**
Stevens, John P., 323
*Stewart Dry Goods v. Lewis*, 286
Stockton, Calif., 283
Stoneville, Miss., 198
Stowe, Harriet Beecher, 246
Stribling, Thomas, 113
Stubblefield, Nathan B., 315
Suffolk, Va., 184
Sugar, sugarcane, 10–11, 14, 34, 60, 86, 93, 103, 105, 179, **199–200**
Sukarnoputri, Megawati, 247
Summertown, Tenn., 153
Sunbelt, 36–37, 218–19, 253, 265, 268, **269–72**, 286, 318, 322
Supreme Court, U.S., 41, 94, 95, 265, 286, 294, 328
Sustainable agriculture, **130–33**
Sustainable Agriculture Research and Education, 132
Swanson, Claude, 195

Tallapoosa County, Ala., 97
Talmadge, Eugene, 197
Tampa, Fla., 236
Task system, 7, 48, 156, 310, 325
Tate, Allen, 24
Taylor, John, 13, 64
Teed, Cyrus R., 152
Telephone, 58
Television, 317
Tenancy, 14–16, 17, 18, 19, 22, 55, 64, 65, 66, 77, 96, **120–24**, 137, 159. *See also* Sharecropping

Tenneco, 37

Tennessee: early settlers in, 8; crops in, 10; and Civil War, 14; Farmer's Union, 18; black farmers in, 32; soybeans in, 60, 198; rice in, 61; roads in, 83; mules in, 171; grapes in, 205; automobile industry in, 220; coal mining in, 231; furniture industry in, 299; liquor industry in, 304; railroads in, 318; tobacco in, 327; trucking industry in, 329

Tennessee Valley Authority, 114, 161–62, 283, 306, 313

Texaco, 314

Texas: cotton in, 9, 62, 87, 103, 105, 128, 145, 157, 169; black farmers in, 32; cattle and sheep in, 36, 146; agricultural education in, 40; rice in, 61, 86, 192, 193; corn in, 62; wheat in, 62; grange in, 68; exports from, 82; mechanization in, 87, 88; soil in, 128; agricultural cooperatives in, 137, 138; aquaculture in, 143; boll weevil in, 144, 145, 169, 175, 178; citrus in, 150; dairy farms in, 158; fence/stock laws in, 160; home extension services in, 169; mules in, 171; migrant labor in, 180; peaches in, 182; peanuts in, 185; pecans in, 185; sugar in, 199, 230; truck farming in, 203; army bases in, 265; automobile industry in, 276; banking in, 280; furniture industry in, 299; oil industry in, 313, 314; trucking industry in, 329, 330

Texas A&M University, 40, 41

Textile industry, 216, 220, 253, 254, 255, 259–60, 261, 296, 300, **323–25**

Textile Workers' Union of America (TWUA), 323

*Their Eyes Were Watching God* (Hurston), 24

Thompson, William Tappan, 112

ThyssenKrupp AG, 220

Tidewater, 5–6, 102, 230

Tiffany, Louis C., 295

Timber industry, 4, 19, 256, 257, 258, 311, **325–27**

Time Inc., 192

*Time* magazine, 269

Tobacco, 4, 5–6, 8, 10, 14, 19, 33, 46, 60, 61, 102, 103, 119, **200–203**, 210, 254, 293–94; prices, 21, 47, 138; and diversification, 63, 64; as export, 80, 81; and New Deal, 93, 94, 96; and fertilizer, 161; industry, 229, **327–29**

*Tobacco Road* (Caldwell), 222, 250

Toccoa, Ga., 283

Tower, John, 270

Town Creek Indian Mound, 126

Townsend, Tyler, 175

Toyota, 220, 276, 297

Trailer Coach Association, 306

Trailer Coach Manufacturers Association, 306

Tredegar Iron Works, 210

Trinity College, 294

Tropicana, 37

Truck farming, **203–4**

Trucking industry, **329–30**

True, Alfred C., 41

Truman, Harry S., 43

Tugwell, Rexford, 95, 96

Tull, Jethro, 39

Tulsa, Okla., 314

Tunica, Miss., 285

Turner, Ike, 27

Turpentine, 230, 309, 310, 311, 325, 327

Tuscaloosa, Ala., 220

Tuskegee Institute, 43, 170

Twain, Mark, 199, 249

Twin Oaks, 152–53

Tyson Foods, 190

*Uncle Remus's Magazine*, 250

*Uncle Tom's Cabin* (Stowe), 246

*Uncle Tom's Children* (Wright), 24

Unions and unionization, 219, 221, 254, 255, 261, 271, 287–88, 323

United American Bank of Knoxville, 281

United Auto Workers, 276

United Farm Workers, 180

United Mine Workers of America, 288

United Nations, 131, 153

LUTHERAN THEOLOGICAL SOUTHERN SEMINARY

3  5898  00155  5875

For Reference

Not to be taken

from this library